Elizabeth Harrower

Susan Wyndham is a writer and journalist who has been New York correspondent for *The Australian* newspaper and literary editor of the *Sydney Morning Herald*. Her most recent book, co-edited with Brigitta Olubas, is *Hazzard and Harrower: The letters*. In 2024 she was awarded a National Library of Australia Fellowship to research the life of Elizabeth Harrower.

'*Elizabeth Harrower: The woman in the watch tower* is the first (and perhaps final) word on one of Australia's most brilliant and bedevilling writers. Like Harrower's, Wyndham's prose is meticulously observed, emotionally attuned and full of grace, insight and vision. It's a fantastic achievement.'

DOMINIC AMERENA

'This is an extraordinary biography of one of the finest, and most important, Australian writers, Elizabeth Harrower. In a braiding so skilled you can't see it, Susan Wyndham takes us from Harrower's life into her work and her friendships, and then back into her work and life. This is a deceptively simple, beautifully detailed, psychologically acute portrait worthy of its subject.'

ANNA FUNDER

'This is a wonderful book. It gives us the complexities of Harrower's life and of her fascinating character – so naïve and at the same time so intelligent, her prickly diffidence coupled with a kind of gormless passion. And it sets her compellingly into the decades when modern Australian literature was coming into being. An indispensable contribution to Australian writing.'

BRIGITTA OLUBAS

Also by Susan Wyndham

An Eloquent Sufficiency: 50 writers talk about life and literature over lunch (editor)
Life in His Hands: The true story of a neurosurgeon and a pianist
My Mother, My Father: On losing a parent (contributing editor)
Hazzard and Harrower: The letters (co-edited with Brigitta Olubas)

Elizabeth Harrower

the woman in the watch tower

SUSAN WYNDHAM

NEWSOUTH

UNSW Press acknowledges the Bedegal people, the Traditional Owners of the unceded territory on which the Randwick and Kensington campuses of UNSW are situated, and recognises the continuing connection to Country and culture. We pay our respects to Bedegal Elders past and present.

A NewSouth book

Published by
NewSouth Publishing
University of New South Wales Press Ltd
University of New South Wales
Sydney NSW 2052
AUSTRALIA
https://unsw.press/

Our authorised representative in the EU for product safety is Mare Nostrum Group B.V., Mauritskade 21D, 1091 GC Amsterdam, The Netherlands (gpsr@mare-nostrum.co.uk).

© Susan Wyndham 2025
First published 2025

10 9 8 7 6 5 4 3 2 1

This book is copyright. Apart from any fair dealing for the purpose of private study, research, criticism or review, as permitted under the Copyright Act, no part of this book may be reproduced by any process without written permission. Inquiries should be addressed to the publisher.

A catalogue record for this book is available from the National Library of Australia

ISBN   9781761170195 (paperback)
       9781761179204 (ebook)
       9781761178429 (ePDF)

Cover design Debra Billson
Cover image Elizabeth Harrower, 1961. Photograph © Jill Crossley, State Library of NSW, ON 651/Folders 1–5
Picture section Photo credits listed on p. 282
Internal design Josephine Pajor-Markus

All reasonable efforts were taken to obtain permission to use copyright material reproduced in this book, but in some cases copyright could not be traced. The author welcomes information in this regard.

Contents

Introduction	1
PART ONE: 1928 to 1971	
Betty	11
A shady character	25
The Old Country	41
Elizabeth Harrower	49
Homecoming	70
New connections	81
The Watch Tower	97
Allies and impediments	113
Orphan Betty	127
PART TWO: 1972 to 2020	
La vie bohème	149
Whitlamania	169
Stanley Avenue	197
Slowly spreading circles	215
In the world of life and death	241
Retirement	252
Renaissance	261
Reckoning	270
Acknowledgements	281
Select bibliography	283
Editions of Elizabeth Harrower's works	289
Notes	292
Index	317

For my mother Shirley Wyndham (1929–2011) and the women of her generation, with love, gratitude and respect.

Introduction

'Her eye is always on the sparrow – the essential detail
that exposes character and motive ...'
ST BARNARD, CRITIC, 1963

When Patrick White won his Nobel Prize in 1973, he avoided formal ceremonies and celebrated by cooking for an intimate group at his Centennial Park home in Sydney. Among the eight people at his table, drinking champagne and eating food he'd sweated over in the kitchen, were the artist Sidney Nolan, who had accepted White's medal in Stockholm, the Swedish Ambassador and his wife, and the writer Elizabeth Harrower.

White's chief booster on the Nobel committee, Artur Lundkvist, had also dined with Harrower at Centennial Park in 1970 and took home a copy of her novel *The Watch Tower*. He named her in an article for the Swedish press as White's most important successor among Australian novelists, with her own style of razor-sharp psychological writing.

So why is she not better known?

Elizabeth Harrower was at the centre of Australian literary life in the middle of the twentieth century: talented, hard-working and highly regarded, but mostly invisible, or glimpsed on the edges of more famous lives. Patrick White himself left her out of his 1981 memoir, *Flaws in the Glass*, an absence that was preferable to the caricatures and settled scores he handed out to some friends. Yet she left her imprint on a circle of friends that included writers such as White, Christina Stead, Kylie Tennant, Judah Waten, Shirley Hazzard and Cynthia Nolan.

Harrower was often described as an underestimated, neglected author, even before she stopped writing in the 1970s. Neither word is quite accurate. Critics gave serious and expectant attention to the four novels that came in quick succession in the 1950s and '60s. *The Watch Tower*, her fourth, raised her in some eyes to the status of White and Stead. And then, silence.

Fervent champions of her intense domestic dramas were quick to laud her as one of Australia's most important writers, but gradually became frustrated as her novels fell out of print and no more followed. The reasons for her disappearance were many – complex questions of timing, character and luck. In an age before the publicity machine, in a book industry dominated by men, Harrower did not seek attention for herself. She tolerated interviews, thought self-promotion was vulgar, and believed books should tell their own story. She was, even with close friends, a very private person who kept her life in locked compartments. Such a secretive subject is either forgotten or, at some point, becomes an obsession for the curious biographer.

Fortunately, Elizabeth Harrower lived another lifetime beyond her writing years. Before she died in 2020 at the age of ninety-two, she enjoyed a flash of fame that reintroduced her novels as vibrant documents of their time and timeless dissections of the human heart.

*

None of Harrower's novels was on the reading list for Australian fiction courses at the University of Sydney when I was a literature student in the late 1970s. Leonie Kramer, who was Professor of Australian Literature, rated Harrower's writing highly enough to include her in both an Oxford anthology and a history of Australian literature she edited. But Harrower disliked Kramer's conservative politics and literary taste, and she was not retiring in her views. In 1976, my first year as an undergraduate, Harrower wrote to Shirley Hazzard, who was planning a trip to Sydney:

> The only person that neither Patrick nor I would urge you to meet is Professor Leonie Kramer, Aust. Lit., Sydney University. She has all the bone-deep dislike of art of the dedicated right-winger, is positively damaging to (living) Australian writers ... Patrick and Christina Stead call her Goneril.

A decade earlier, the writer Joan London happened upon *The Watch Tower* as a university student in Perth, where there were no Australian literature courses. She read the novel as if gripped by a thriller, and thought: 'I didn't know there was writing like this, in Australia, now, by a woman.'

I failed to discover this rare author for myself as a young woman. Still tilted towards English literature, I wrote my honours essay on the novelist Ivy Compton-Burnett, not knowing what an apt choice she was for a future biographer of Elizabeth Harrower, and by the 1980s I was dazzled by a new writer from Melbourne, Helen Garner.

The name Elizabeth Harrower first struck me in November 1996 on a press release announcing she was the recipient of that year's Patrick White Award. Her benefactor, who died in 1991, had invested his Nobel money to fund an annual prize for an Australian writer of achievement but inadequate recognition. As literary editor of the *Sydney Morning Herald*, I had the serendipitous job of interviewing the winner, and after some swift research I spoke to Harrower by phone at her Mosman home. She had a pleasant, dignified, unpretentious voice, with a tinge of British accent, and an about-time tone of wistful amusement at White's posthumous nudge. He had tried for years to 'rescue me from myself', she said, and when I asked naively if she would write again, she replied, 'I think I would feel very fed up with myself if I didn't.'

I regret not going to her house that day with the photographer, who posed her with coffee cup and creased brow glancing over her shoulder through a window towards Balmoral Beach. I have often regretted that, swimming in the constant sea of new books, I didn't follow up with a visit and a longer interview, and that I still didn't read her novels, which had become hard – but not impossible – to find.

Elizabeth Harrower retreated from public view again until 2012, when Text Publishing in Melbourne began to reissue her novels, *The Watch Tower*, *The Long Prospect*, *Down in the City* and *The Catherine Wheel*. Reviews bloomed with a spring freshness, and Harrower gave interviews as if she had emerged from cold storage. No, she hadn't read her novels since she wrote them; no, she couldn't remember them. In 2014 there was more excitement when Text released *In Certain Circles*, a novel she had withdrawn from publication in 1971.

At last I read her books, reminding myself to breathe, wondering if her characters could extricate themselves from her finely spun web of psychological torment. I seized my chance to interview Elizabeth Harrower again, this time at her apartment overlooking Sydney Harbour. She was friendly, talkative and evasive, pleased to be rediscovered but detached from her novels and the person who wrote them. She said of *In Certain Circles*, 'Someone asked me what it was about, so I looked up the blurb and it said it is "an intense psychological drama", and I said, "That sounds like me".'

I had afternoon coffee with Elizabeth many times over the following years. We liked each other and had plenty to chat about, including our Scottish forebears, parts of Sydney and London we both knew, and of course books and writers. One year she followed my travels to Scotland enthusiastically by email and, as far as I could tell, she gratefully read the fat biography I gave her of Clement Attlee, who had been prime minister when she first went to Britain. I valued her company as a woman of my mother's age, and we commiserated as daughters who wished we had done more for our selfless mothers. We were both childless and only children of divorced parents.

Questions bubbled up in my mind from the depths of her past. How did this good-humoured woman write such disturbing novels? And why did she stop? They were questions she didn't want to answer, or couldn't after all this time. Later I realised they were the wrong questions. While I wanted to know about her childhood, her parents, her writing, her love affairs, she veered into talking about friends past and present. I should have taken the clue that her stories about Patrick, Christina and Judah were not just sentimental memories but the scaffolding of her adult life. She was a kind and porous friend, sometimes more concerned about the lives of others than was good for her. Her wide circles of friends were her family.

I interviewed Elizabeth again, for the last time, shortly before her ninetieth birthday in February 2018 and found her fully engaged in the present. She was worried about workers losing their jobs as Australian factories were closing. She had been watching on television a Melbourne production of her favourite operas, *The Ring Cycle*, and a tournament starring her favourite tennis player, the 'spontaneous' Spaniard Rafael Nadal. Cool Swiss Roger Federer was also impressive, she agreed – 'but is he too perfect?'

In that long conversation she explained the quality that made her a writer:

> I always took an inordinate interest in everybody. People like me are dangerous, we really are. I'm sometimes with people and either I think, go away, or protect yourself, or don't tell me things, because if they're telling me lies, or whatever they're telling me, I can hear it. I'm not a good person to be around for this reason.

She showed me a paragraph clipped from a recent newspaper review of Helen Garner's book *True Stories*, and said: 'Apparently Helen Garner in one of her stories quotes Nadine Gordimer, who claims that writers have "powers of observation heightened beyond the normal" and are made by "the tension between standing apart and being fully involved". The bit I think is absolutely true is powers of observation beyond the normal.'

Elizabeth was watching me as I watched her and, I learnt years later from a friend of hers, she thought I wanted to write her memoirs. I wouldn't have dared ask but perhaps she was anticipating interest in her biography.

*

I last saw Elizabeth a few months before she died in July 2020. Later that year, as she had instructed, her papers at the National Library of Australia were opened to the public and revealed her extensive correspondence with publishers, writers and other friends, as well as her manuscripts and assorted treasures. Although she had culled the collection, she had left enough to form an impressionistic self-portrait, and because she always wrote reams of letters, fragments of her life were scattered through the papers of others who had left them at the National Library and elsewhere. Her neatly spaced typing and graceful signature with its rounded E became instantly recognisable. Her clear voice was unmistakable.

Shirley Hazzard was another writer I had interviewed and come to know, and a few weeks after her death in 2016 I was invited to look through some of her papers at her New York apartment. Professor Brigitta Olubas, working on a biography of Hazzard, had found a stash of letters from Elizabeth Harrower in the basement. I knew as I read them that there was enough material for a biography of Harrower and that I was hooked. Brigitta invited me to work with her on an edited collection of the Hazzard and Harrower letters, which was published in 2024, and from that springboard I dived more deeply into the collections of the National Library.

Elizabeth Harrower emerged like a mosaic or a puzzle, revealing different pieces of herself to different people, and unwittingly caught – with all her strengths and foibles – in letters between other people, as well as in newspaper reports, book reviews, photographs and documents. Living relatives, friends and acquaintances remembered her in their particular ways. A fascinating picture filled out – not complete but alive – of this mysterious, sensitive, tenacious, contradictory woman. She deserves to be understood and valued. But she lives on most of all in her own remarkable books, and I hope this biography will lead readers to them.

PART ONE

1928 to 1971

Betty

As an adult Elizabeth Harrower summed up her early life in a sentence: 'I was a divorced child.' Those words, direct but opaque, held all the disruption that shaped her character and powered her fiction. She would not talk about her father, who seemed to have vanished into oblivion. She rarely mentioned that she had a stepfather. She dismissed questions about the past with a sweep of her hand, a glance at the sky, and a change of subject. If pushed, she said there were no happy marriages when she was growing up.

In her fiction, Harrower was far more forthcoming about her private life, especially the worst experiences. Having taken a scalpel to them there, she was able to bury the remains. Her childish feelings of unloved abandonment are examined most closely in her second novel, *The Long Prospect*, published in 1958, the year she turned thirty. This was the story she was aching to tell when she began writing in London and misery was still heavy in her bones, but postponed until she had finished another novel for 'practice'. *The Long Prospect* opens, as most of her novels do, with a cinematic vista of its urban setting. Twelve-year-old Emily lives with her grandmother, Lilian, in the most western suburb of an Australian industrial city called Ballowra. The camera soars over the ironically named Greenhills and its 'hundreds of corrugated iron rooftops, and smoke from acres of steelworks' before tightening focus like a trap on the domestic tensions within the walls of Lilian's boarding house. Fictional Ballowra is recognisable as a stand-in for Newcastle, where Betty Harrower spent her first twelve years. Emily's pubescent suffering and Lilian's caustic narcissism can't be read as autobiographical in every detail but they chart the topography of the author's rugged emotional life. 'I think the emotional truth is there in all of the books, but none of the facts. It's like putting real electricity into a dream palace,' she said in 1980. Many of the facts are there, too, despite Harrower's denials.

As well as disguising Newcastle in her fiction, Harrower avoided public association with the city that left her in turmoil and tears. She sometimes misled interviewers by saying she was born in Sydney, 'because I don't like Newcastle'. Even the latest editions of her books repeat the lie. But the proof is in the four-line birth notice published in the *Newcastle Morning Herald and Miners' Advocate* on Saturday, February 11, 1928: 'HARROWER – At Nurse Johnston's Private Hospital, on February 8, to Mr. and Mrs. Frank Harrower, of 31 Church-street, Mayfield – a daughter (Betty).'

Betty's birth came just nine months after her young parents had married on May 14, 1927 at the Presbyterian Manse in Newcastle. Francis Sharp Hastings Harrower, or Frank, was twenty years old and Margaret Burns Hughes, known as Daisy (from the French flower name, 'marguerite'), was seventeen on their wedding day. They had grown up in and around Newcastle as children of workers with Broken Hill Propietary (BHP), the mining and steel company that was the roaring engine of Newcastle's economy. As a child Betty lived in Newcastle, mostly with her maternal grandparents, absorbing her Scottish heritage so naturally that she became homesick for a place she didn't know.

Frank gave his parents' address as home when he married Margaret Hughes, as Scottish a lass as he could choose with her creamy skin and dark auburn hair. Frank, too, had a strong Scottish connection – coincidentally, his father had emigrated from the same coal-mining region as Margaret's family in Fife. Following the birth of their daughter at Nurse Johnston's Private Hospital – a lying-in hospital for new mothers and babies at 56 Maitland Road – they brought her home to a rented cottage a few doors from Frank's parents. Catherine and David Harrower still lived at 37 Church Street, Mayfield, the Federation brick house where Frank was raised, close to the Newcastle steelworks, which pumped smoke into the sky and dropped black coal dust on the furniture.

For decades the Harrower and Hughes families inhabited a large quadrangle of blocks around the main commercial centre of Maitland Road, not far from the Waratah train station and the Presbyterian church in Hanbury Street. They were all Presbyterian, but the Hughes family had no interest in religion and the Harrowers made a choice of convenience.

Betty

The Harrower house sat between St Columban's Catholic Church and St Andrew's Anglican Church. The family attended St Andrew's, claiming Church of England as their religion, and Frank's sister Adell – the only daughter among the six children – played the church organ at services. In a family of practical Scots, their mother Catherine encouraged – even pushed – her daughter into the arts. Adell was an accomplished pianist who gained honours in her music exams and a gold medal for her solo in the Steel Works Eisteddfod. She played and sang at private parties, and in 1927 qualified as a piano teacher. This was the first show of creativity in the family that would produce Elizabeth Harrower. But the pressures of study, performance and housework tipped Adell into a nervous breakdown and she retreated into marriage and motherhood.

Margaret 'Daisy' Hughes had been born in the Scottish mining town of Kelty, before making the voyage to Australia in 1920 at the age of eleven with her parents Robert and Helen Hughes and younger brothers, Robert and James. Robert senior found employment at the BHP Steelworks, known locally as The Works, and by the men as 'The Slaughter House', 'The Grinding Machine' or 'The Bloody Hell Pit'. From there he moved to the slightly less hellish BHP-owned Commonwealth Steel Products, manufacturer of wheels and steel castings for the railways.

Robert and Helen Hughes were a poor match: he was an alcoholic with a flaring temper that threatened violence, and she was a strong-willed matriarch with an eye on other opportunities. He had been a teetotaller for two years before they married, but two weeks after the wedding he came home drunk and abusive, and the pattern continued. On several Sundays she had to bail him out of the police station, and there were times when he went to work drunk. Fortunately, Helen was a trained nurse with an entrepreneurial bent. Knowing her husband was unreliable, she brought in extra income by running a series of small private hospitals and boarding houses in Mayfield and nearby suburbs. As Robert earned more, he drank more, and in 1930 he gave Helen just £3 a week to run the house and pay rent of more than £2 on her hospital premises in Hanbury Street. Profits were slim and he made trouble by answering the phone in a belligerent voice and turning on lights in the house late at night.

Betty Harrower's childhood was buffeted by domestic conflict. The two families didn't get on, the Harrowers disapproved of the drunken uproar in the Hughes household, and the Hughes family thought Margaret had married beneath her. Betty's parents were gentler people than her grandparents but no better suited to each other, and their marriage frayed as Frank's work took him away from Newcastle. Unlike most of his brothers, who followed their father into working for BHP at the steelworks or in the mines, Frank joined the railways. In 1935, when Betty was seven, he was transferred to a small railway siding at Tamban, in forest north of Kempsey, with no home for a family. Margaret insisted on staying with Betty at her parents' house in Mayfield. In the next two years Frank was moved around the back blocks of north-east New South Wales to Gurranang, north of Grafton, and then further north to the town of Casino. He pleaded with 'Daisy' to join him, but she remained in Newcastle.

Betty's upbringing was secured, more than some, by a circle of grandparents, aunts and uncles, and parents who cared for her, even if absent, distracted, drunk or inept. Her mother's mother, Helen Hughes, nicknamed 'Mummum', taught her to sing traditional Scottish songs, and all her life Elizabeth could break into Robbie Burns's 'My Heart's in the Highlands'. Her Harrower grandparents and aunt Adell put on small family parties for her birthdays, trying to create some fun under the shadow of the Great Depression. In photographs Betty looks like Milly-Molly-Mandy from the children's book published in the year she was born – a tall, long-legged girl with a serious pale face, rabbity front teeth, and short brown hair with a fringe. She liked dressing up, though she looked self-conscious in her costumes. For one birthday she had a cake adorned with a figure of Mickey Mouse and wore an improvised nurse's uniform with a white pointed cap. In more fanciful outfits, she was a fairy with wings and a wand, and a shy Spanish dancer under a dark mantilla, a fan spread under her chin. A later photo shows her strumming a banjo and dressed in a worn school tunic, tie and blazer, her skinny legs ending in tartan slippers.

The Harrower and Hughes men still had work, even as factory output slowed in the early 1930s. Unemployment rose above 30 per cent for

Newcastle's male workforce by 1933. BHP flogged their workers harder than ever, with the threat of others at the gate to take their jobs and no trade union strength before the war years. Vera Deacon, a lifelong Newcastle resident and writer, was two years older than Betty Harrower and went to the same primary school. In the depths of the Depression, Vera's family moved to the estuary islands in the Hunter River and to a dirt-floored shelter in the Mayfield West Unemployment Camp. Vera's unemployed father, who had tended the coke ovens at the steelworks until he was badly burned, fed his family with fish and oysters caught in the river. Deacon remembered her mother managing to buy some pale green georgette to make a dress so she could dance around the school maypole 'with the best of suburbia's daughters'. Betty could have been dancing around the same maypole at Mayfield West Public School, a stern two-storey brick building close to the camps. There's no account of the two writers meeting then or later. But Betty knew the children of the dole families as well as the middle-class children of industry managers who lived in Victorian mansions and villas at the top of the hill, looking down on the steelworks and catching any breezes from across the Hunter. Mayfield East Public School was closer to the Hughes and Harrower homes, but as the steelworks expanded the suburb grew quickly, and the overflow of pupils necessitated a second primary school and a long daily walk for Betty to the edge of her known world.

Elizabeth Harrower could still picture those walks as she approached her ninetieth birthday: 'When I was small, pottering along, you would see children with bare feet, which they wouldn't have chosen, and tattered pants, boys, and then in the hills outside Newcastle people living in tents and shooting rabbits – I don't know if they were shooting them to eat or sell the skins. Fires to cook the rabbit, presumably, and men hanging around hotels, no work, except the men who did have work and they would be black from working in steel, no showers, on bicycles going home at all sorts of hours.'

She used to brood about the 'tragic, dirty, patched, poor little deprived children' at school, knowing that for all her misery she was not deprived in the way they were. She was a well-fed suburban child who liked roaming through the bush and down the slopes to the river flats where men fished and children played under fallout from the steelworks on the opposite shore. Even more, she loved the beaches and ocean baths that fringed Newcastle, and she became a strong swimmer. There were occasional holidays in the country, where she most remembered the fresh air.

*

Betty chose to be exceptional, a self-image Elizabeth Harrower accentuated in the young women in her fiction. She thought of herself as cheerful and friendly, but also as a proud, sensitive misfit in her family and social milieu, deserving of better. Her mother told her she was intense, to her surprise. Like many only children, she was solitary and self-sufficient, a quiet observer of adult misbehaviour, and a constant reader of books, newspapers, labels, anything printed with words. She picked up new vocabulary from the many visitors to her Hughes grandmother's house and, raised among relatives with Scottish burred voices, she was sent to elocution lessons to avoid picking up an Australian accent. Stories and songs from the Old Country swirled around her like magic spells and Betty learnt a Halloween rhyme about 'three wee witches' that she would recite decades later.

Margaret Harrower read aloud British childhood favourites, cold with snow and lost children. Betty knew *Alice's Adventures in Wonderland* by heart before she could read, and corrected her mother's mistakes and omissions. AA Milne's *Winnie-the-Pooh*, JM Barrie's *Peter and Wendy*, and *Grimm's Fairy Tales* gave her all the light and dark of fiction. At primary school she was naturally bright and at the age of six she won a decorated coathanger for a composition, which she would remember as her only writing prize until much, much later. At seven or eight she sent a story to a children's newspaper and took encouragement from the advice, 'Keep trying'. Looking back, she described herself as 'A Word Child', a reference to Iris Murdoch's novel of that name about a delinquent boy redeemed, for a time, by education.

The adult Harrower would write a short story titled 'Alice' ('Alice in Australia' for one draft), which made a sad fairytale from her mother's life, mixed with family lore and glimpses of her own psyche. Alice is old-fashioned, feminine, with red-gold sausage curls – a good girl, obedient, kind, pretty and clever. She looks after her brothers and strives to please her Scottish-born mother, an 'irrational, raucous, bony, quick-tempered, and noisy' woman who resembles the traditional witch. Against a background of Depression poverty, Alice meets an ordinary boy called Eric and 'woke up married'. When Eric's work takes him into the country, Alice stays with her mother 'in the hideous place with the smoky skies', even while bleeding from the lashes of her harsh tongue. Rather than blame her mother, she turns against her rough, awkward husband and her spoilt brothers. When Eric sleeps with another woman, and then another, divorce follows. Alice's mother has already found another man for her, an older man who is 'demanding, critical, sarcastic, powerful, brutal' but might make more money. Now she has 'two who could never be pleased, two who believed that anything could be bought'.

Notably, there is no child, no Betty figure, in the Alice story, only a nameless girl who is a helpful neighbour in Alice's later years. Dominated by her mother and 'the man', idolising them despite their tyranny, Alice finds the girl's presence 'no more pleasing to her than the chirp of a small canary'. The story ends with a vision of the girl, dressed as a bride, floating in to see Alice. Wishing there was someone she could tell about her experience, Alice is transformed by the realisation that she doesn't need a confidant: 'But *I* know. *I* know.' Whether this is the end of her life or a new self-possessed beginning, the phantom bride signifies the happy marriage that twice eluded Alice – and Margaret. It is the harsh lesson about romantic love that Harrower carried into adulthood. Such endings are common in her fiction, unresolved yet offering a glimmer of hope and escape from a suffocating existence. The words also foreshadow Harrower's frequent comment that she wrote because she 'knew things' other people needed to know – things she did not often specify or explain beyond the pages of her books.

She was gathering material from childhood, feeling and seeing sharply, long before she knew she would be a writer. Newcastle boarding houses filled up during the Depression years, charging up to one pound 10 shillings, half a man's wage, for basic bed and board. Her grandmother's residentials housed all kinds of working men, and some women, who would give Harrower the cast and drama for *The Long Prospect*. Every time Betty walked down Church Street to the T-intersection with Maitland Road, she faced Vaisey's Store, the largest business among Mayfield's shops, banks, hotels and the art deco cinema where she went to movie matinees. Advertised as a 'universal provider', Vaisey's family-owned store sold groceries, hardware, footwear, drapery, all kinds of domestic goods. The name VAISEYS is still visible on the parapet of the 1916 building, although the business is long gone. Harrower surely remembered the name when she created the sisters Laura and Clare Vaizey in *The Watch Tower* – a novel set in Sydney but also in the landscapes of the author's psychic history.

The grandmothers would, each in her different way, live on in Harrower's imagination. Helen Hughes, especially, provided ingredients for Emily's insensitive grandmother in *The Long Prospect*, as well as for the mother in 'Alice'. Harrower wrote a piece in the 1970s, which she called a story but which reads as revealing memoir. 'The Retrospective Grandmother' is a middle-aged woman's reconsideration of her blunt judgements as a child. The storyteller is both Harrower and her alter ego, further blurring the distinction between Emily and Betty, and weaving cross-references that run throughout her writing. In her memory of childhood, the girl's two grandmothers could not have been more different. Irish-Scottish 'Helen of Troy' was wild, funny, generous, and a bully: 'She could out-shout and out-pose Bette Davis.' Contemptuous of men and yet slavish to them, she had a string of husbands and fancy men. The only man she idolised was her spoilt and demanding younger son. Slipped into these recollections is a paragraph that also summarises Emily's tragedy at the heart of *The Long Prospect*:

> Once, while living with her, someone loved me – a stranger, for no reason except that I was myself, and I loved him. My grandmother sent him away, in an unusual, even unique, excess of common sense or propriety. It was dreadful. I was put on a train to another city, to return to my mother, and I said in my head, and possibly, though I can't be certain, out loud to her: I'll never forgive you.

The other grandmother, 'Colonial Grandma', was formal, pious and dull, 'the baddy' according to the child's mother, who blamed her mother-in-law for making her life miserable. Not the obvious stuff of fiction, Grandma made addictive jellies, arranged piano lessons until the child could play 'The Blue Bells of Scotland', took her down the hill to church, and to a skin specialist for her adolescent spots. (The treatment, not named in the story, was x-rays, which scarred Betty's skin.) She encouraged her granddaughter to get an education, advice dismissed by a girl who was 'restless, wary, conscious of myself as one who always had good marks in class without effort'. The adult Harrower reassessed Colonial Grandma's wise lessons: 'Health! Ethics! Culture! Education!' She thought again about the propaganda spread by Helen of Troy and saw 'her erratic pronouncements, open-handedness, wrong-headedness, violence'. Neither of them understood her but they had taken her in and shared her 'unconditioned childhood', and at last she appreciated the gifts of 'that gratuitous care and carelessness'. The more forgiving adult could see that she, too, had been Trouble.

*

Betty was eight or nine years old when she realised her unsteady home life was collapsing around her. Feeling unloved, unheard, and powerless to hold her family together, she lay down on the road near her home and hoped a car would drive over her. She must have changed her mind, or perhaps traffic was sparse, but this was the melodramatic gesture of a child screaming silently for attention.

Harrower more coolly summarised the reasons for her parents' break-up for an academic researcher in the 1980s: 'Youth, hard times, separations and families at odds with each other caused them after a few years to divorce.'

Frank Harrower filed for divorce in 1936, on the standard grounds that his wife had withdrawn from cohabitation and refused him conjugal rights for the past year. Margaret Harrower responded with her own petition for divorce, claiming that Frank had committed adultery over the previous Christmas and New Year while living without his family.

Elvy Shaw, the other woman, had been an untrained nurse at Morriset Mental Hospital, and was staying with her father at Tamban Loop when she met Frank. But the lawyers could not find her, even after accusing her of adultery in a legal notice published in the Sydney *Sun*. As the proceedings dragged out, Frank was ordered to pay Margaret alimony of one pound ten shillings a week and another ten shillings maintenance for Betty. He sent a typed letter to 'Dear Daisy' from his home in Gurranang on September 30, 1936, enclosing £4 but saying he could not afford to keep doing so and asking her to reach a decision about their future. 'For my part,' he wrote, 'I am both anxious and willing that this present unsatisfactory state of affairs should end and that we should re-start our lives together again.'

This letter, or subsequent pleas, must have had some effect, for in February 1938, when Betty turned ten, she and Margaret caught the train to join Frank in Casino. They lasted just two weeks in the summer heat, and Margaret refused to leave Newcastle again. Or, truthfully, she refused to leave for Frank.

In April 1939 Frank was settled in Murrurundi, and wrote to 'Daisy' at her mother's address, Paramount Court, 196 Maitland Road, Mayfield:

> I know that you feel reluctant to leave Newcastle but unfortunately I have to live where my work is. Also we have our little girl Betty to consider. It is not fair to her for us to be apart like this. I love you both and I want you both with me. I am sure that we can all be very happy.

But Margaret was already moving on. Betty, now aged eleven, continued to live with her Hughes grandmother while Margaret was more often in Sydney, training as an obstetric nurse at the Royal Hospital for Women in Paddington. 'Daisy' rebuffed Frank: 'I do not intend to go to Murrurundi, and Betty will be quite alright with me, as you know.'

Betty was not all right. Surrounded by floundering adults, she was desperately unhappy. There were rumblings of war abroad, and Betty the peacemaker, unable to save her own family, talked with other children at primary school about what they could do to help. 'I thought we could go across and talk to Hitler and explain to him that this wasn't a good idea.'

Familiar with the films of Shirley Temple, she may have heard the child star's famous denouncement of the invasion of Abyssinia when they were both seven years old: 'Why doesn't somebody tell Mussolini to stop?'

In 1939 Hitler ordered the invasion of Poland, then Britain and France declared war on Germany, and Frank Harrower again sought a divorce on the grounds of desertion. The judge, Sir Thomas Rainsford Bavin, a former premier of New South Wales, found in Frank's favour and ordered Margaret to return to his home. Margaret made the journey to Murrurundi with Betty, but hearing that Frank had again been unfaithful, she refused to stay. He denied any infidelity and told the court his wife was leaving because she found the community too small for the private hospital she wished to open.

It would be another two years before the case was finally settled.

*

In 1940, Betty's grandmother Helen Hughes also filed for divorce, blaming Robert for habitual drunkenness and leaving her without any means of support. The police had often been called to the house. She had thrown him out for months at a time. During one violent argument, their son James, a promising young boxer, saw his father about to strike his mother and punched him on the nose. Robert sometimes went to watch James fight as 'Billy Ridley', and went home drunk wanting to re-enact the fights with his son. This was the household where Betty lived for much of her childhood, with her mother and without her after Margaret began working in Sydney.

The couple had not lived together since Easter 1939, after Helen returned to chaos from a trip to Sydney with James and her daughter-in-law, leaving her daughter, Margaret, to keep house for her husband and Betty to cower from his verbal and physical violence.

All three adult children gave evidence of their father's drunken misbehaviour. Even when he was sober, the household was in a state of 'armed neutrality', said Robert Reid Hughes, Betty's 'Uncle Rob', now a member of the Australian Imperial Forces. Margaret Harrower, in the midst of her own divorce, said that her father, when he was drunk, had pulled down the red light outside her mother's hospital. She had seen him feed his dinner to the dog and then complain he hadn't eaten.

Robert, in turn, accused his wife of 'associating improperly' with her boarders — one named Andrew Fotheringham, another man of seventy whom she'd invited up for a cup of tea, and the butter man. 'He was always making these allegations and making my life a hell,' she said. In court Helen was shown an anonymous letter she had allegedly written to Mr Fotheringham's wife:

> Well, Mary, your time has come. I was speaking to some friends of mine who were speaking to Andy, and my word he is fond of his friend ... By all accounts he has much need to. When you thought you were clever, you left him with nothing but a few rags ... He was a poor, nervis wreck.

Helen denied writing the letter but her handwriting and misspelling of 'nervis' gave her away. Justice Street, who would become Chief Justice of the NSW Supreme Court in 1950, dismissed the case because he was unconvinced that Mr Hughes left his wife without support. He judged the anonymous letter as proof that Mrs Hughes was not above resorting to 'the assassin's dagger' in her own interests and was not entirely blameless in her marital quarrels. Two months later Helen was arrested at home and committed to trial for perjury, admitting that she had written the letter and regretted lying, but had been 'halfway mad the way the barrister was putting questions to me and the way my husband was sneering at me'. With a police officer and the local Presbyterian minister as character witnesses, she was fined £10 and given a two-year good behaviour bond. Robert was by then renting a small house in Mayfield and Helen had left their old house for a flat. Nurse Hughes, as neighbours called her, sought her divorce again in December 1942 on the grounds of desertion, and within months the marriage was formally ended.

World war and family wars invaded Betty's life on every front. Both were all over the newspapers, which reported the latest aggression in the divorce courts alongside escalating tensions in Europe. Humiliation piled on top of sorrow for Betty, and she felt the derision of some classmates towards a divorced child, an oddity in those days. Whether or not she had been the victim of physical violence, which her fiction does not suggest, she was emotionally harmed by the arguments, drunken fights and estrangements that clamoured through her childhood. She retreated further into reading and writing, a serious girl with plaits tied in droopy bows, and always a book or a pencil in her hand. As well as long diaries and little stories, she wrote letters, as she would do all her life, sending news to her scattered parents, relatives and friends. 'I just always kept writing something and if I had eventually school friends, if anything happened in their lives I would write to them – if they went into hospital with appendicitis or if they won the lottery, all kinds of things.'

One of her few friends from Mayfield days was Barbara Johnson, a girl whose family were neighbours in the block of flats in Maitland Road where Betty lived with Helen Hughes when she was eleven or twelve. With Barbara's brother Ken they joined a drama group, and the girls would sit on the front steps of the flats musing about their life ahead. 'Barb' and 'Bet' became lifelong friends and correspondents. During the war, Betty also wrote to soldiers who threw their names and addresses on to country railway tracks from trains carrying them north, hoping for a human connection, as she did while her family dispersed and dissolved. Sometimes they wrote back.

As a child, amid family tensions, Betty liked her mother's two brothers, especially the elder 'Uncle Rob'. The three siblings 'were brought up to be very fond of each other and praise each other', Elizabeth remembered. 'My mother had a beautiful singing voice, the boys praised it. One of the boys was good at art, Uncle Rob was musical, and they were kind to me when I was little.'

Robert was sixteen years older than his niece, their birthdays two days apart. He would get down on the floor to play board games with her, brought her Easter eggs, played the mouth organ, and taught her to whistle. An ironworker like his father, he had served nine years with the Australian Army Medical Corps before enlisting with the Australian Field Ambulance in 1941. His service ended with his death in 1945 at the infamous Sandakan prisoner of war camp in Borneo. He was thirty-three years old and left an unblemished record and a widow with one child. His mother, Helen Hughes, would never get over the loss of her heroic son.

Betty's father had done a stint in the merchant navy as a young man but did not serve in the Second World War, so he was not at risk when Japanese submarines torpedoed two ships from Newcastle. As a railwayman he was an essential worker like the Newcastle men who churned out steel for shells, helmets and other military equipment.

Hard times battered three generations of the Harrower and Hughes families. The survivors went on and, as a counterbalance to all the grief, there were weddings and children. Frank Harrower's sister Adell married Charles McIntosh, and her daughters, Verity and Thurza, were born in 1942 and 1947.

Betty the child was hypersensitive to other people's misfortunes, as well as her own. As a writer Elizabeth Harrower would examine the way human nature was shaped by 'luck' – a word she often used. Looking back in 2017, she said:

> These thoughts were always in the back of my mind, the consciousness of how terrible things can be in the world and how vulnerable people are. People often think how well they've done and how lucky they are, and they don't fully realise how much of your luck comes from where and when you're born. It's beyond your control, just where you're dumped down and who your parents might be. So you just turn up and if you're quite bright and you can look after yourself or you're frail … You probably can see from the books it's very easy for me to worry about people and pity people and wish I could fix things for them. I would say it's a handicap probably but it's part of the nature you're stuck with … I have certainly known happy people but luck enters into it as well. If things have gone well for people they're very reluctant often to put any of that down to sheer good luck.

A shady character

At the end of 1939, Betty was one of six pupils from Mayfield West Public who passed the entrance exams for Newcastle Girls' High. If she had been there three years later, she might have been taught by the left-wing activist writer Dymphna Cusack, whose prize-winning 1943 play, *Morning Sacrifice*, was set in the staffroom of a girls' high school.

But in the New Year her mother moved Betty to Sydney as a boarder at Manly Grammar School for Girls on the northern beaches, still a long way from Margaret's nursing work at St Luke's Hospital in Potts Point. Founded by Miss Stella Strachan, with an emphasis on English, history and drama, the school occupied a gracious house on Ashburner Street, which ran between the harbour and surf beaches. The steamer company that carried passengers from Circular Quay to Manly had coined the famous slogan for the holiday suburb, 'Seven miles from Sydney and a thousand miles from care.' Not so for Betty, who hated boarding school. Frank paid the school fees of £22 a quarter, but Margaret asked him for a total of £100 a year to cover other costs such as books, amusements, pocket money, travel and clothes. He baulked at the extra expense, which he argued was a stretch on his salary of £7 a week as assistant station manager.

Their divorce was finalised in 1941. Late that year Manly Grammar had its premises overlooking the ocean beach commandeered by the military and, like many schools, moved its pupils to the safety of Katoomba in the Blue Mountains, but without Betty. Harrower remembered that she had been 'best in English, but suspected of planning an escape. Was found to have one shilling and threepence in my handbag. Was removed.' Living with her mother in Sydney, she shuffled restlessly from school to school and found no special teacher to nurture her.

Frank, now in Wallarobba, sent his final child maintenance cheque for three pounds, six shillings and sixpence on February 5, 1944, three days before his daughter turned sixteen. Her formal education ended. He kept one photograph of them together: Frank dapper in a suit, spotted tie and panama hat, his hands lightly holding Betty's shoulders; she, as high as his waist, looks out from under her hat and daintily holds the skirt of her short dress with Peter Pan collar. Behind blank faces, their feelings are unreadable.

*

Margaret Harrower's move to Sydney with Betty seemed like a fresh start, free from a domineering mother, demanding men, and drudgery. By 1940 she was employed as Sister Hughes, an obstetric nurse with St Luke's Hospital at Potts Point, which adjoined the more raffish Kings Cross in the eastern suburbs. However, she had another reason to be in Sydney: a man named Richard Kempley.

In 1941, while Betty was still at Manly Grammar School for Girls, Margaret Burns Hughes – having reverted to her maiden name after the divorce – gave her address as care of R. Kempley, No. 4 Flat, Alta Vista, Raglan Street, Manly. In fact, she and Betty began living with Kempley that year and she left nursing.

Helen Hughes had quite likely introduced the couple, as the mother in the story 'Alice' found a second husband for her daughter. Kempley was much older than Margaret (he was forty-nine, she was thirty-two in 1941), made more money than Frank did, and turned out to be 'demanding, critical, sarcastic, powerful, brutal', all characteristics of the man in Harrower's fable. He might have seemed a good catch to a mother and daughter desperate for financial ease and attracted by a veneer of swaggering glamour. They either didn't do their research, or chose to ignore their findings, because the newspapers of the times were littered with his exploits. Although Betty didn't know it then, living with Kempley was the unwanted gift she needed as a writer, a source for every villain she could imagine. Shards of his history are scattered through her fiction.

Richard Herbert Kempley gave Margaret a connection back to Britain, and they would make many trips to the Old Country. Born in 1892 in Suffolk, he was the son of John and Ellen Kempley, and brother to John, three years younger. Richard attended naval school in Greenwich and went to sea as a teenager. He was short and wiry, just five feet six, with dark hair, dark eyes, dark complexion, and KK (or perhaps a faded RK) tattooed on his left wrist. At eighteen he was an unmarried administrative writer with the Royal Navy, giving his home address as Grays Thurrock, Essex, with his mother and his father, who was a naval pensioner and customs watcher, and expected his sons to follow his career.

By the time he was twenty, in 1913, Kempley had disembarked in Australia with an English wife, Jessie (née Hawkins), and was living in the Sydney suburb of Bondi Junction. His new life began with passing the intermediate examination with the Incorporated Institute of Accountants and a move to the western limits of the city as auditor to Lidcombe Council and, as 'Brother RH Kempley', to the Masonic Lodge in Parramatta. In 1919 he and Albert Irving Martin formed a partnership as public accountants in Castlereagh Street, Sydney, but after a year Kempley went solo again. Among his clients were Waugoola Shire Council on the south-west slopes of New South Wales and the Pambula Butter Factory on the state's far south coast. Kempley's widowed father followed him out to Sydney with his brother, John, who had served in the Royal Navy through the First World War. Richard's wife Jessie stayed with their two sons, Richard and Jack, until his impetuous behaviour made family life impossible and in November 1919, Mrs Kempley and Masters RJW and JH Kempley, aged seven and one, sailed for Britain on the SS *Euripides*. The restless Kempley, claiming health or business reasons for his departure, also spent the next two years away in England and the United States.

Back in Sydney, in 1925 he attracted the attention of the tabloid newspaper *Truth*, which described him as 'a bright, keen, dark-eyed young man of only 33'. A photo showed a slight man in jacket, tie and fedora with a cigarette hanging from his mouth, as if he'd come from the racetrack or pub. He had recently lost his job as manager of the Liberty Confectionery College in Sydney and been charged with attempting to steal £50 by false pretences from his employer, Victoria Flora Cohen, 'a well-built, superior-looking woman of prepossessing appearance'. Acquitted of that charge, he was back in Central Police Court two weeks later for robbing Mrs Cohen of five pounds, twelve shillings and sixpence. Although the amount was small, the tabloid reported 'a dramatic case extending over three days, illuminated by legal fireworks and punctuated by tense and exciting moments'. Liberty College was itself a dubious Pitt Street business that made sweets and taught the methods by correspondence course. While working there, Kempley had started what he called 'a mail order stunt' on the side, using company letterhead, contacts and money for printing to set up the Commonwealth and Dominion Confectionery College, a direct competitor.

Mrs Cohen accused him of leaving her company with her recipes and formulas and Kempley bad-mouthed his former employer in another scandal rag, *Smith's Weekly*. Most of the fireworks in court came from the prosecutor, who called him 'a crook, thief and cheap take-down' and 'one of the biggest rascals that ever lived'. *Truth* delighted in pronouncing that his admissions 'could not be classed as other than the gravest reflections on his moral character, or lack of it'. He was convicted and fined £50. A judge who dismissed his appeal said: 'He is of shady character and his actions are as shady as can be. He is living with a woman in Darlinghurst, or he has committed bigamy. I cannot believe him.' That woman left the scene, unnamed. Keeping track of Kempley's wives and mistresses became as hard as counting his business ventures.

Kempley boasted during the Liberty Confectionery case of having made £3000 a year as licensee of the Golden Fleece Hotel in Crown Street, Surry Hills. He had bought a six-year lease on the corner hotel for almost £2000 in 1922, and built the run-down pub into a profitable business. The licensing board closed the hotel and thirteen others in Surry Hills in 1923 in an effort to reduce drunkenness in a poor, crime-infested neighbourhood oversupplied with public bars. Kempley received compensation but was out of pocket once he paid off his mortgage. Perhaps this was why he was working for Mrs Cohen at £5 a week and trying get-rich-quick lurks. But hotels and booze would remain his favourite money makers. A country newspaper in Candelo on the New South Wales south coast reported his hotel misadventure with interest under the headline 'Richard's Luck'. As licensee of the Candelo Hotel after his return from America, he had hosted conferences of district and national horseracing clubs and the Candelo Football Club. He seemed a jolly citizen when he played district cricket for Candelo and ran the publican's booth at the annual Candelo Show and Picnic Races. But after two years he sold up and was gone.

Never beaten, after his confectionery bungle Kempley turned up in Newcastle as a motor car dealer, RH Kempley and Co., selling British cars. He drove a Morris Minor in local road trials and did surprisingly well against American Dodges and Chevrolets. But reckless Kempley was in Scone Police Court in 1932 for drunk driving after causing a head-on crash with another car and going to hospital with a bleeding face. He swore he hadn't been drinking, despite a doctor's evidence that he was swaying and his remarks 'were on the silly side'. Kempley got off with a fine after pleading that as a commercial traveller he couldn't work if he couldn't drive. He and his brother had been arrested a few months earlier in Muswellbrook for keeping two illegal stills and three thousand gallons of spirit, including a thousand litres of rum, after raids on two Newcastle houses. Police were hopeful that the discovery of these stills would stop the marketing of 'moonshine', which had taken off around Newcastle as the Depression bit. Kempley and a lorry driver were fined for conveying illicit spirits and operating 'a bootleg joint', which a Customs officer described as 'the largest found in Australia since the inception of the Commonwealth'.

Kempley's name was linked with several mysterious fires in properties he owned around Newcastle, one of them a timber cottage that housed the illicit still. He seems to have dodged any charges. Olive Beatrice Kempley was living with Richard in a house at Carey Bay, south of Newcastle, when it was destroyed by fire in 1933. She saw flames rising from the house while she was out rowing on the lake with friends. Olive had been one of three partners in Kempley's motor garage in Hunter Street, Newcastle, in 1930, but she too disappeared from his life.

The Depression hurt the Newcastle motor trade, and as well as running his side hustle in liquor, Kempley was in and out of court, owing and chasing debts. He was briefly a resident of Boggo Road Gaol in Brisbane when a claim of £63 pounds against him was heard at Newcastle District Court.

After his company went into receivership in 1936, his address was Maitland Road, Mayfield, making him a neighbour of Helen Hughes – and Margaret and Betty. When Frank Harrower filed for divorce in 1936, it was because his wife refused to leave her mother's home at 196 Maitland Road, Mayfield, to live with him in the country. Richard's brother John had also become a neighbour in 1935 when he took over the licence of the Mayfield Wine Saloon at 173 Maitland Road.

Despite her contempt for her husband's drunkenness, Helen kept an open house with refreshments on the table, a salon that would have attracted the likes of the Kempleys. If Harrower's account in 'The Retrospective Grandmother' can be trusted, Helen had at least three or four husbands, whom she labelled the poor fish, the old woman, the dummy and the gigolo. She ended her long life as Helen Wilson. Certainly she had no trouble finding unsuitable male companions for herself, so why not one for her struggling daughter and fatherless granddaughter?

With her divorce from Frank Harrower underway, it's possible Margaret was identified as Kempley's wife as early as 1936 when the women's pages of the local newspaper reported the presence of Mrs RH Kempley, draped in 'a graceful lace cape with a brown georgette frock', at the Artists' Ball at the Palais Royale in Newcastle.

There's also a question of whether Richard Kempley and Margaret Hughes ever legally married. The New South Wales records have no marriage certificate for them. Margaret's death certificate says she married her second husband in Sydney when she was thirty-one, which would have been in early 1941, as soon as her divorce was decree absolute. But those details were given by Elizabeth Harrower, who also mistakenly put Margaret's age at nineteen rather than seventeen when she first married. The couple possibly wed elsewhere, but knowing Kempley's messy history with women, it is imaginable that he remained married to Jessie, the mother of his sons in England, while Margaret had to accept the tenuous position of de facto wife. Nevertheless, she was always known as Mrs Kempley.

Betty's schoolfriend, Barbara Johnson, believed that 'Uncle Dick' was kind to Betty and Margaret, and that he – or at least his wealth – was their salvation. Coming from a poor family herself, she might have imagined with some envy that money solved all problems. Barbara's daughter, Toni Eyles, knew only what she'd heard from her late mother:

'When Mum talked about Uncle Dick it was that he came on the scene and that fixed everything because he had lots of money and was very rich and whipped the mum off to Sydney, and Bet didn't want to go. She and Mum were very upset that she had to go to Sydney. I don't remember Mum saying anything nasty about him, only that it gave Bet a new life and she was suddenly a rich girl.'

*

For Betty Harrower, her mother's second 'marriage' was a leap from the frying pan of a broken family into the fire of an alcoholic stepfather. She did not accept Kempley as a father figure and her distrust gradually curdled into loathing. She was forced to call him 'Uncle Dick' but she would later refer to him as 'my stepfather, I suppose' and 'that man'. Her adolescent years passed by in Sydney, moving to different houses around the northern harbourside suburbs from Manly to nearby Balgowlah and Cammeray, and from school to unremarkable school. As a divorced child she always felt different, bullied for her lack of a father, and unable to find close friends as she moved around. High school was a brief blur in her adult memory: 'I was always good at English and writing compositions, even not bad at adding up and doing problems. But you have to stay in one place and one school, one teacher. You can be lucky, all the people you read about or hear loved their teachers.'

Betty loved to swim at the beaches that lined the Manly peninsula, and at school she was an agile tennis player with a long reach across the court, but not part of the social groups that kept up their matches. There were trips back to Newcastle, sometimes when Margaret and Kempley were travelling, as he especially liked to do. Betty took her first aeroplane flight with them, and had a Christmas in Hobart. Throwing snowballs on Mount Wellington in midsummer was exotic fun, a sign that she was made for cold climates.

Margaret had left her brief nursing career to slip on the persona of the successful businessman's wife. He did not want more children and she did not need to repeat the tests of motherhood. Her pleasures were buying clothes, decorating their houses and wearing the jewellery Kempley brought home. She dressed up to sit in the passenger seat of his latest fancy car. In exchange she sacrificed herself and her daughter to the demands of an infamous racketeer and domestic tyrant. Betty, the girl who read everything, saw everything, felt everything, was mortified by his crimes and crude personality. She loved her gentle mother but even as a teenager she was exasperated by her blinkered passivity.

Alcohol flowed through Richard Kempley's life like blood. He was back in practice as an accountant based in Pitt Street, Sydney, as the war began until 1943, when the offices of his firm, Kempley Wilde Castor, were taken over by the Australian Military Forces as office space for the RAAF. Some of Kempley's business may have been respectable, as he travelled to country towns offering his services, but his illegal deals still attracted more attention.

In 1944 he was tried in the Central Criminal Court for black market liquor sales, along with publicans at the Macquarie, Sussex and Criterion hotels in Sydney for selling large amounts of Scotch and Australian whisky for tens of thousands of dollars. With Aston Wilde, his accountancy partner, he had taken over a second firm that kept the books of fifty or sixty hotels. Wilde gave evidence that Kempley had invested in the city hotels at inflated prices and offered his managers 3 per cent commission on all underground liquor sales. Wilde did the rounds of country pubs buying up liquor, which was resold for exorbitant prices, mostly to American servicemen, at makeshift bars in the cellars of the Sydney hotels. Profit from those sales was ten times that of bar sales. 'They would probably take £1000 a week from the Yank trade,' Wilde told the court.

Kempley had a high-profile barrister in Garfield Barwick KC to launch his defence. That year, Barwick would famously argue, but lose, the claim that William Dobell's Archibald Prize–winning portrait of artist Joshua Smith was a distorted caricature. Barwick would later be Chief Justice of the High Court, and had risen to prominence for challenging the *National Security Act 1939*, which centralised power in the Australian Government during the war. Kempley and his cronies pleaded not guilty to the charges of conspiring to defeat national security regulations, which in October 1943 had fixed liquor prices to counteract wartime shortages. They boldly, but unsuccessfully, sought an order for contempt of court against the Minister for Customs and Associated Newspapers for his statement about the extent of black-marketing in New South Wales and an attempt to round up racketeers. The jury found the four men guilty and sentenced Kempley to serve the maximum three years in prison, along with David Blank, licensee of the Macquarie Hotel. The others had two-year sentences. The judge blamed their crime on greed and cupidity, and condemned their anxiety to make easy money as a grave social evil. The High Court of Australia unanimously refused an application for leave to appeal and, strangely, after months of relentless coverage, there was no further mention of the men's fate in the press.

Imagination has to fill in the three years that Kempley might have passed in prison. With his ability to sidestep the law and reinvent himself, there would be no surprise to find that his sentence was shortened. His name came up in 1951 when he was overseas and the Royal Commission on Liquor Laws in New South Wales was looking into irregular trade by hotels, some with a link to Kings Cross crime boss Abe Saffron. David Blank, now a company director living in the wealthy eastern suburb of Darling Point, fervently denied that his hotel investments had any ongoing association with his former partner, Kempley. Other witnesses distanced themselves from both Kempley and Blank.

Kempley came out older and wearier into a world exhausted by war. Margaret Kempley had kept vigil for her husband and her younger brother, Robert – Betty's 'Uncle Rob' – from her home in White Street, Balgowlah, near a picturesque northern bay of Sydney Harbour, far removed from the pubs and courthouses Kempley frequented. In October 1945 she sought news of 'Staff/Sgt R. Hughes', in a newspaper notice that said he was 'last heard of in Borneo'. In fact, he had been dead for six months.

John Kempley, the 'dearly loved father' of Richard and John, also died that year, in November, aged eighty-seven. Both sons and their wives invited relatives and friends to a service held in the private chapel of Walter Carter funeral directors in Bondi Junction, an establishment where many respectable citizens, and some less so, were farewelled. Whether Kempley was sitting in the front pew or locked in a cell is anyone's call.

1928 to 1971

*

Sydney was ready to declare its peacetime freedom, and so was Betty Harrower. In 1943, her haphazard high school education petered out against the disruption of war and Kempley's shameful trials. Through the war years her sleep was haunted by nightmares about Japanese invasion, and fears that 'everybody was going to kill you'. Trams were full of soldiers, food was rationed, and she queued with crowds at newsreel theatres to see the latest footage of air raids, marching troops, and the ruins of Allied victory.

At sixteen she was an intelligent girl but her ambitions were limited by opportunity and family expectations. She told her friend Barbara she wanted to be a writer, but she had no model for how to make the vision a reality, and her only outlets were letters and diaries where she kept her secret thoughts. She considered following her mother and grandmother into nursing and reported to a hospital in her uniform to begin training, but she felt queasy when she heard what she would have to do. Inner life for Betty meant thoughts and feelings, not bodily functions. A senior nurse took her aside, gave her a glass of water, and kindly advised that the job would not suit her. Believing she had important work to do, without knowing what it was, she took vocational tests with useless results: one counsellor suggested she should be a tennis player, and another said she could do anything. She yearned for one person who could appreciate her unique brilliance. No one stepped forward.

And so, like many young women of her time, she went to business college to learn shorthand and typing, which set her up for office work and experiences she used in her fiction. With another girl from college she searched the classified ads and went to work at a box factory, clumsily putting cardboard boxes together. Manual work was not her strength. There were short-lived clerical jobs in offices and factories run by men she remembered as courteous rough-diamonds.

At nineteen she had the initiative to place her own ad, and she was hired by McGinley and Carpenter, a women's clothing manufacturer on the second floor of 449A Pitt Street at the Haymarket end of the city. She sat at her desk next to the accountant, doing office tasks and calculating quantities of fabric for the two women designers. Through a doorway was the workroom where she saw rows of 'harried women with ratty hair and missing teeth' hunched over sewing machines. The manager would dart into the office to warn when union reps were coming. Divisions between bosses and workers, rich and poor, were as clear as they had been in Newcastle. Her later recollections edited out the clothes themselves, the wedding dresses and ballgowns, which featured in magazines and adorned society women at events such as the Black and White Ball. Tall and slender, Betty was an ideal clotheshorse to model the company's garments for the dressmakers and for buyers from the city department stores, David Jones, Farmers and Mark Foy's.

She got on well with her co-workers, Marion Plackett and Claire Oatley, young women who designed, made patterns, cut and constructed dresses with whale-boning and other intricate details. Mary Partridge, co-owner of the business, trusted Betty to babysit her small daughter at her home in Bellevue Hill. Margie Clarke, who was born in 1944, remembered 'Auntie Betty' as 'always sweet and kind and softly spoken; she always looked nice, dressed nicely'. Margie's mother – known at work by her maiden name, Miss Maclean – was 'like a mother to Elizabeth, kind and full of empathy. She was her anchor in life, as she was for Marion. Elizabeth was short of friends and she had a crush on my mother.' At the age of twenty-two, Betty wailed into her diary that she was 'mad as a hatter' if Miss Maclean left her alone in the office, and knew she had grown 'too fond of her for my own good'. Miss Maclean's, or Mrs Partridge's, husband had taken a job managing a finance company on a 'huge salary' and Betty worried she might give up work. Intense attachment and fear of abandonment would pattern the whole life of this lonely only child.

Betty's working days were a stunted version of her unformed dreams. Her small wage enabled her to sit in coffee lounges, launch a lifetime taste for coffee, and observe all of Sydney society in a city waking up from war restrictions. After years of blackouts, the lights came back on one night, the neon signs flashed dazzling colours, and she was in love with the glamour of the place. Catching the ferry to Circular Quay, and a train to Central Station, she looked up at the Tintara Wine sign and a neon wine glass endlessly emptying and refilling. A witty advertising slogan imprinted itself: 'Wine, the height of a grape's ambition.' She was coming into her own as a good-looking young woman dressed in the tailored knee-length skirts, baggy trousers, fitted jackets and sweaters of the 1940s, her shoulder-length dark hair carefully waved and pinned off her forehead in the style of Katharine Hepburn. At the beach she cut a Betty Grable figure in a polka-dot swimsuit and white-framed sunglasses.

Behind the vulnerable girl was a watchful writer in waiting. Harrower looked back at this period in short stories she wrote in the 1950s. 'The City at Night' pairs office workers Janie, her sixteen-year-old alter ego in her first high heels, and the more sophisticated seventeen-year-old Leonie as they edge towards friendship over grilled chops and caramel sundaes at a city restaurant. Lonely Janie came from the country at thirteen and lives at Manly; Leonie is an outsider as a postwar immigrant from Lithuania. They begin to confide and laugh: 'The strange silent world of adolescence had exploded, the eggshell walls had collapsed, proclaiming, *You are not alone.*' Whole histories and personalities are sketched in one conversation, and Sydney seduces with scents of frangipani blossoms and fresh-ground coffee.

Office politics, snobbery and prejudice darken 'Summertime' in the person of the comically dangerous supervisor, Miss Frazer. The office and factory of JW Baker's wholesale fashion house, where forty women bend over sewing machines and ironing boards, resemble Harrower's descriptions of her workplace. The story could be a continuation of 'The City at Night', but the main character is Claire Edwards, seen leaning on a filing cabinet in the opening scene, and her friend is Annette, an Estonian-born girl who has left Baker's to work for a Double Bay furrier while awaiting the inevitability of marriage. Harrower hints at the checkmate to come in the older woman's manipulative power game. Hearing news of Annette from Claire, Miss Frazer 'felt slighted by the girl's self-sufficiency'. Under pretence of concern, she wheedles and pries, casually asks Claire whether Annette is a naturalised Australian, and uses scraps of personal information to destroy their friendship.

Betty stayed at McGinley and Carpenter's clothing factory for almost four years and at work and home endured what she called 'a dull, tedious, horrible period' while waiting for her real life to begin. The nearby

City of Sydney Public Library became her haven and, she remembered, 'I spent all my life there'. The lending library was in the former concert hall of the Queen Victoria Building, a grand Romanesque-style pile of sandstone and stained-glass near Sydney Town Hall that was originally a marketplace and still houses shops along its galleried floors. Harrower associated her visits with the smell of hops or oats, thinking there was a brewery in the basement, and she would also have breathed the fermented air rising from Penfolds' vast wine cellars. (In her 1978 novel *Tirra Lirra by the River*, Jessica Anderson wrote of prewar Sydney: 'the smell of the downstairs hall of the city library. Was it malt? Or vinegar?') Upstairs she began to work her way through the thousands of books on the shelves, hungrily reading classics, contemporary fiction, and non-fiction about literature, history, politics, philosophy and psychology. She read English, French and especially Russian novelists in translation – the masters of morality and the human spirit, Tolstoy, Dostoevski and Chekhov. She did not read a single book by an Australian author. No one guided her reading except the books themselves, and one great writer led to another. 'I was so full, I just leapt on it. So when I went out into the world I was somehow prepared because I'd read this diverse body of literature.' Theatre was her other great love, though tickets had to be bought, and when the English companies started touring after the war, a highlight was seeing Laurence Olivier and Vivien Leigh perform with the Old Vic Theatre Company.

When her friend Barbara Johnson visited from Newcastle, they 'talked and talked, then heard *La Bohème* right through'. With her mother she came away singing from popular films such as *If You Feel Like Singing, Sing* with Judy Garland and *Flamingo Road* with Joan Crawford. She cried all night after seeing the melodramatic *Flamingo Road* again on her own when her mother was in hospital for an operation. 'I was so miserable and sure something awful would happen to Mum,' she wrote in her diary. However, 'Mum got through the operation better than I did.'

*

While her mind was expanding like a new universe, Betty had to return each night to her intellectually arid home. Margaret was pleased to see her daughter going out and bringing home books, but her own life was spent in service to her husband. Kempley was by necessity mostly retired and seeking a more private existence. For a man who had lived so brazenly in the public eye, he managed to withdraw like a crab under a rock, until his stepdaughter made a career writing about him. Even then he might not have seen the likeness, protected by vanity and the unlikelihood that he read her books. In the winter of 1948 the local paper reported that Mr and Mrs RH Kempley were staying at the Criterion Hotel in Rockhampton, Queensland, in search of warmer weather and possibly a business opportunity. He had taken to buying and selling properties for profit and would leave Margaret and Betty sitting in the car while he showed clients around. After waiting outside a house at Lindfield, Betty noted she'd 'Had it'.

Kempley bought a waterside weekender at Church Point, a small community on the placid shore of Pittwater, an hour's drive north of their Sydney home at Cammeray. A competitive fisherman in his sporting days, he still liked to drop a line off his boat in the salty estuary. Betty's isolated weekends allowed more time for reading, but her resentment was building like a pressure cooker. She later used this period in 'The Beautiful Climate', one of her most potent and popular short stories, first published in a 1966 anthology. Hector Shaw, a man of 'silent, smouldering violence', announces to his wife and daughter that he has bought a cottage on Scotland Island and insists they go every weekend to work on the house and take the boat out fishing. There is no joy in their natural paradise. Pale-skinned Mrs Shaw suffers migraines in the heat and glare. Del, the daughter, is a kindergarten teacher who makes soundless cries against being held hostage and having to preserve the peace. Even during Hector's rare good moods, mother and daughter are alert, frightened that complaint or enthusiasm could provoke his wrath. Del nervously examines his every 'supra-casual' gesture – his laughter and sighs; the way he crunches cashews and brushes salt off his hands.

Harrower plucked details from all over her life to create fiction. The migraines were her own, and they would flatten her for days of illness throughout adulthood. Del was her aunt Adell's familiar name. Hector, of course, the Trojan warrior. Was Shaw remembered from her father Frank's lover, Elvy Shaw? A homophone for the shore? Or a fitting name for a man so sure of himself? She chose Scotland Island – a residential island that is a short ferry ride from Church Point on the mainland – as an isolated offshore prison. The Shaws play poker with another visiting family, but when the son invites Del to a party across the bay, Hector ridicules him in an unwarranted show of snobbery and possessiveness. Del seeks solace in the library of books left by a previous owner. Normally she reads psychology in an effort to understand people but now she takes up leather-bound volumes of poetry and quotes Tennyson's 'The Lotus-Eaters' to describe their aimless existence. 'Let me *die,*' she protests silently.

Having subdued his captives, Hector shocks them with the news that the cottage is on the market and they will be travelling by sea to 'the Old Country'. Del is excited (secretly, for fear her perverse father will change his mind) that they are leaving their dull pretty city with the hope that 'Out in the world she would escape from them. There would be room to run, outside this prison.'

Hector Shaw in 'The Beautiful Climate' evolved into the menacing Felix Shaw in Harrower's fourth novel, *The Watch Tower*, which was also first published in 1966. The story was written several years before the novel but, despite her efforts to place it in Australia and the US in the early 1960s, Harrower had to wait until *The Watch Tower* made its companion story desirable. The *New Yorker* editors wrote to her agent in December 1961 that the story didn't measure up to the background. The editor of *Redbook*, an American women's magazine, also declined: 'The Harrower is very well written but I doubt very much that the average young American woman could possibly identify with this strange, ingrown Australian family.' Harrower herself described the story as 'mournful'. The Australian critic John Colmer would recommend 'The Beautiful Climate' in 1972 as an 'ideal introduction to Harrower's work' and

> a paradigm of her fictional universe ... a world in which selfish men manipulate their women and material possessions in a vain attempt to

achieve happiness; frustrated by their blind male egotism, they become subject to fits of smouldering violence and frequent relapses into bouts of alcoholism and morbid self-pity. The woman's role is to suffer, to pity, and to provide the innocent seeing eye for the narrative.

In his later, larger incarnation, Felix Shaw is one of the most intriguing villains in Australian fiction. While not a naturalistic depiction of Richard Kempley, the caricature is as recognisable as Dobell's disputed portrait of Joshua Smith. Betty and Margaret's suffering would not go to waste, and Kempley's love of travel would open an escape route for his stepdaughter. The ending of 'The Beautiful Climate' was almost literally true.

Kempley sold the Church Point cottage and in early 1951 the three of them embarked on a sea voyage following the same itinerary imposed by Hector Shaw: around the southern coast of Australia, up to Colombo, Bombay, Aden, through the Suez Canal, across the Mediterranean, through the Straits of Messina and on to Marseilles and Gibraltar, then London. Last news of Kempley as they sailed away was his application to the NSW Registrar-General to update title deeds to a block of flats on a subdivision called The Knoll in Kent Road, Rose Bay, a salubrious address opposite the Royal Sydney Golf Club. The lot may have been discounted, as were many properties near the harbour after the scare of Japanese submarines launching shells into the eastern suburbs in 1942. Some had blown up and damaged houses, while several unexploded shells created a lingering fear. One is still thought to lie under the golf club in Kent Road. As usual, Kempley saw a deal rather than a danger.

The Old Country

Betty Harrower stood on the deck of the *Mooltan*, facing into the warm wind, and gazing towards her future. But she hadn't let go of her past. She had cried and cried before leaving her employer, Miss Maclean, at the clothing factory. 'When you don't have many people it's hard to leave someone you are so fond of,' she wrote in her diary. With a mixture of childish despair and composed self-analysis, Betty told herself she always hated change, even though it often turned out for the best. She wrote down Miss Maclean's parting words of comfort in neat shorthand, as a secret keepsake: 'I couldn't forget you if you went away for twenty years. If ever you are in any trouble or want anything you can always turn to me, or if things go wrong come straight home to me. I cannot forget you any more than I could forget Margaret [her daughter] ...' As the *Mooltan* carried Betty away at the end of March 1951, 'The bottom seemed to have fallen out of the world – my whole inside feels flattened.' She was determined not to enjoy the voyage unless she had letters from Miss Maclean, and fortunately some reached her.

After rounding the southern coast of Australia, the P&O liner crossed the Indian Ocean and the equator. Soupy tropical heat brought out swimsuits, salads and sleepless nights. Betty recorded two 'hectic' days amid the boredom when 'Mum & UD had a quarrel – he was in a bad way and wanted to argue about anything. So he did. Then he marched off to have a drink. Mum nearly had a stroke – I've never seen her so annoyed. She decided we would get off at Colombo and go back to Australia.' They stayed on board after Kempley 'reformed again'. Betty had her first foreign experiences in Ceylon (present-day Sri Lanka): walked under an umbrella among statues of Buddha, photographed Uncle Dick holding a snake, inhaled the perfume of cinnamon flowers, and felt the press of the 'natives'. From Colombo the ship sailed to Bombay (now Mumbai), where she saw a street demonstration and heard people repeating Gandhi's famous words, remembered years later as 'We asked for bread, you gave us stones.' She saw there was a big, complex world beyond Sydney and felt an undirected missionary drive to help people: 'I was obviously needed. They needed me. That was when I thought, I'll never go home.'

Her sudden recovery from homesickness was prompted by a third passenger's arrival in Margaret and Betty's cabin. Over breakfast, 'Lady Bedingfeld' would tell Betty about her adventurous life of driving trucks during the war, seeing fashion shows in France, deep-sea fishing in the West Indies, and plans to tour Africa for six months with her husband. Betty was fascinated by her enthusiasm for travel and solemnly noted their conversation 'about Russia & Communism & the war & about religion'. Within days, she wrote: 'Since I've met her I don't feel a bit like going home after the holiday is over – I may stay in London & work there and travel round.'

The first sight of the English coast was a 'tremendously touching moment & very thrilling'. She was relieved when the ship docked at Tilbury on May 13 after six weeks and three days at sea with the Kempleys, and she was immediately more at ease in the British climate. London was a grey city still scarred by bombing and surviving on rations, but Betty was excited to meet her Scottish relatives – her mother's legendary Aunt Minnie and her husband, James Dick, and their daughter Stephanie. They had lunch at a hotel and Stephanie was mortified that the omelettes were made with powdered eggs.

When she recalled this life-changing trip, Harrower often edited out her mother and stepfather, as if she had travelled overseas alone at the age of twenty-three. However, Richard Kempley planned the route and paid the bills. Together they stayed in Scotland and England with Margaret and Betty's family, and Kempley saw the sons of his first marriage. They toured as a threesome for two months, with Kempley driving across the Continent in the English luxury of a Jaguar. As for the itinerary, which took in England, France, Switzerland, Austria and Italy, Harrower said later, 'I went everywhere.'

At the time she was embarrassed by the lavish spending, her pleasure dimmed by the company, but she allowed herself bursts of enjoyment. She wrote in 1973 to the Australian author Shirley Hazzard that she had been in 'beautiful Capri' for about a fortnight in 1951 and that her stepfather considered buying a house there. 'I thought it was heaven, and seem to remember having some Great Thoughts in Anacapri. There was only one hotel up there in those days, and it was out of season in September, so the place itself was wonderfully available.'

At Anacapri on the island's peak, where Graham Greene had a house, she may have stared into the infinite blue sky and thought about Europe's cultural riches, the ancient history vividly present, and the possibilities of freedom and learning ahead. Back in London, she waved farewell to Margaret and Richard Kempley as they embarked on the *Himalaya* in December, returning in the heat of January to Australia and the comfortable constraints of suburban life at Cammeray with tree-veiled views of Middle Harbour.

*

Betty had decided to stay in London. Knowing she would miss her mother, she also knew this was her only hope of a life of her own. 'I was so completely in the wrong element at home, & I would be again if I went back. Ruts are almost impossible to escape & I can see the old life stretching out like an octypus [*sic*] to engulf and drag me down. To have seen freedom and go back to that life would be madness.'

With the Kempleys' financial support, she planned to enrol at the University of London for a degree in psychology. She had even thought glancingly about psychiatry, but knew she had neither time nor money – nor stomach – to study medicine. For university entrance, having left school in Sydney without a certificate, she first had to matriculate with a basic knowledge of ancient Greek or Latin. She chose the former and while she applied herself to the language, she returned to Scotland to see her mother's family, and then moved to Edinburgh and on to a rented room above a shop in Kelso, a handsome riverside stone town in the Scottish Borders district.

When her grandmother Helen Hughes had migrated to Australia with her husband and children in 1920, she left behind her sister, Mary Reid, known as Minnie. Minnie married James Dick, a prominent mining engineer who managed mines all over Scotland and northern England.

Her great-niece was fortunate to arrive when they were living in Alloa, near Stirling, at Whins House, once the dower house of the Earls of Mar. Harrower remembered the place with affection: 'There was a beautiful garden, two gardeners, a glass house, a putting green, a billiard room, a view of the Ochils.' She was happiest at home with her cousins, and reading – from Jane Austen's *Emma* to Friedrich Engels' *The Origin of the Family, Private Property and the State*. Young Betty's blood pumped faster when she found a book of Scottish ballads, picked them out on the piano, and sang them through the house – 'My Heart's in the Highlands', 'Scots Wha Hae', 'All the Blue Bonnets are Over the Border'.

Helen Hughes adored her younger sister and had told Betty stories about Aunt Minnie, Uncle Jim and their three daughters, Margaret, Stephanie and Anne. Betty had exchanged letters with Stephanie during the war years and was ready to like her cousins. The youngest, Anne, was disabled by polio when she was eleven, lived with her parents, and had a long career as a teacher and deputy head of a Scottish school for students with cerebral palsy. Stephanie worked during the war at Bletchley Park, the secret code-breaking centre, where she was a Typex operator, frantically decoding signals intercepted by the Women's Royal Naval Service (none of which she could have told Betty in her letters). With a degree in Fine Art from Edinburgh University, she went on to catalogue the works of the Scottish architect Patrick Geddes, known as 'the father of modern town planning', and show her paintings in the Royal Academy Summer Exhibition in London. She had her small son, Robin, with her when she and Betty were together in London and Alloa, and at her home in Cheshire. In 1955 Stephanie and her family – which by then included a two-year-old daughter, Lesley – would leave for India, where her civil engineer husband, Alec Smith, had work for five years, so their face-to-face friendship was suspended for the rest of Betty's time in the UK.

Margaret Dick, twelve years older than Betty, was her first cousin once removed (first cousin to her mother), and they would become especially close as best friends and sisters in spirit. The two women would share the rest of their lives as they moved together to London and then to Sydney.

Like most of the Hughes and Harrower families, Margaret Burns Dick started life in the mining country of Fife. She was born on January 14,

1916, into the hollowed-out years of the Great War, and watched tanks rolling into her quiet village street to break up the General Strike of 1926. Her belief in social justice deepened during the Depression when she was surrounded by the hardships of unemployed mine workers. By the time she was seventeen the family had lived in fourteen different places, she had been to many schools, left friends behind, and turned to books for companionship. Isolation was the keynote of her youth. She thought of herself in retrospect as 'a terrible person' because of her 'one-sided interest in the intellectual' and in thinkers such as Socrates rather than in ordinary people. Yet her reading confirmed her pro-worker politics and she leaned away from her family's 'tremendously conservative' views to become a Labour Party stalwart.

At eighteen she left home and began a long civil service career in Glasgow and Edinburgh, and in London with the Department of Inland Revenue, where she was working when bombs fell on the city. She was poorly paid and felt she was misspending her life, so she devoted more time to the executive committee of the Staff Federation, and campaigned for equal pay for women and improved conditions for all workers. Her fellow members James Callaghan, a future prime minister, and Douglas Houghton, later in the House of Lords, thought she had a bright political career ahead, but she knew she had the wrong temperament. Instead she studied linguistics at night during the war years under a Hungarian-born scholar, Professor Stephen Ullmann.

Part of getting to know one another for Margaret and Betty was confiding family stories. Margaret's attitudes to politics, money and men were influenced by her father's background. James Dick's father – Margaret's grandfather – had been one of the richest men in Scotland and chairman of the governors of an elite school, where he fell in love with a much younger teacher. They married and lived in luxury with household servants until the City of Glasgow Bank collapsed in 1878 and they lost everything. In dire poverty, his wife struggled to bring up their eight children, and he drank heavily. The girls finished their education because their mother wanted them to be able to support themselves, which they did, as a nurse, a teacher and a seamstress. The five sons had to leave school to take home wages, one was wounded in the First World War, and four had professional careers. Most visible was the brother whose signature as chief accountant of the Royal Bank of Scotland appeared on Scottish banknotes. James Dick was damaged by his childhood but outwardly he was a gentle, quiet, diligent man and became a prominent mining executive. Margaret Dick absorbed the riches to rags story and her family's climb back to a conventional life of material comfort, and she chose a more intellectual path, meeting Betty Harrower on common ground. They agreed on almost everything important.

For both of them, books were at the centre of life, as Harrower recalled: 'I had never met anyone who had read as much as I had and Margaret had read more, and knew more. She had a lot of books in the house in the countryside in Scotland so I had access to her books, and I was studying. I loved ancient history and when I went to Greece I was extremely disappointed to see everybody was quite modern.' Neither had any religious belief. As a child, Betty went with her Harrower grandmother to the Church of England and heard there was no God from her Hughes grandmother, who had seen hungry people giving money to the church in Scotland. Margaret Dick remembered being chased home from school by boys throwing stones, because she was Presbyterian. Harrower would later recall, 'The Church of Scotland was tremendously strict, no singing, no dancing, none of this riotous behaviour. I don't think Margaret had any thoughts about it at all. She was so sensible, so bright.'

Margaret's left-wing political views were far more developed than her cousin's at that point. Betty knew the Australian Government, under Prime Minister Robert Menzies, was trying to ban the Communist Party when she left the country. But with her head in the books of the Sydney City Library, she'd taken no notice. In England she was awakened by hearing the Labour Prime Minister Clement Attlee give a speech on radio when she was at a hotel in Bath with her mother and stepfather. His policies of nationalisation and social services had helped to rebuild postwar Britain, and his foreign policy had decolonised India, a country that had left a mark on her. She was filled with lifelong admiration for this blunt, decent man who put ordinary people first in an unjust world.

While Betty was studying Greek, reading books, and writing home to her mother, she was also tinkering with fiction. The first story she completed was 'The Fun of the Fair'. On her tenth birthday, Janet tags along with her Uncle Hector and his nineteen-year-old girlfriend, Leila, as they swim in an ocean pool and take rides at a fair on the nearby cliffs. A simple story, at first glance, but sophisticated and unnerving in the context of Harrower's life and later writing. The scenario might be lifted from her childhood, the beach setting in Newcastle or Manly, the young man one of her uncles, and his mother the grandmother with whom she lived. Lightning knocks out the lights around the pool in the opening scene, briefly leaving the swimmers in darkness, like a miniature of wartime Sydney. There's the first incarnation of Hector, a young man with a Trojan hero's name to match Helen of Troy, as Helen Hughes would become in 'The Retrospective Grandmother'. Uncle Hector, whose name reappears as Hector Shaw, the glowering father in 'The Beautiful Climate', is bossy and self-absorbed. Wishing his niece would disappear so he can canoodle with Leila in the Tunnel of Love, he sends the tomato sauce–stained child into a tent to watch a freak show. Here, the raucous, neon-lit fairground gives way to a gothic fairytale, a surreal nightmare in which a giant professes his love for his blank-faced dwarf bride and invites Janet on to the stage to prove the wizened woman is tiny. She thinks of Jack and the Beanstalk, or Jack the Giant Killer, hints that she too can slay or outwit ogres. But she is unable to explain to Hector that it's not the giant who makes her burst into tears but what he reveals about her whole limited existence. Running away from her uncle, she screams that she will never go back to him and her grandmother, that she doesn't love any of them. The story ends with her no longer crying but 'brilliant-eyed'.

As a fully formed writer Elizabeth Harrower made a harsh assessment of her first short story – presumably this one – telling a journalist in 1966 it 'was ghastly. It was a complex introspective thing and was frightfully bad.' Perhaps editors agreed or, more likely, she didn't show them. 'The Fun of the Fair' was not published until Harrower's stories were collected in 2015, but it opens that book, fittingly as the youngest fictional version of herself, and also as one of the most striking metaphorical acts of compression in her body of work. The giant and dwarf are a grotesque representation of the imbalanced couples that will people her novels. Janet's breathless last-minute escape is repeated in future endings. On another level, the story mirrors Harrower's brilliant-eyed leap into her new independent life.

She may have written this hallucinatory tale of Australian childhood and summer storms while holed up in Kelso, the village by the River Tweed, which she found especially beautiful when it was white with snow. Margaret Dick had also been writing fiction privately but felt her stories couldn't be of interest to anyone else until Betty advised her not to compare herself with Dostoevski. Galvanised by her cousin's example, in 1952 she left her safe job and pension and joined Betty in Kelso. Margaret was first to be published, as it happened, with an ease that must have given them both unrealistic hope. Despite being told not to begin with the *New Statesman*, she sent a story to the esteemed weekly paper, where it ran in the issue of October 10, 1953. Her philosophical bent is dramatised in 'The Gift of Knowledge', which contrasts a seventeen-year-old boy consumed with anxiety about the brevity of human life, and his landlady's mother, a lively woman of eighty-four who infuriates him with her insouciant attitude to death.

Eventually Betty went down to London to pass her A-Level exams and receive the General Certificate of Education, which qualified her for university entrance. But in getting 'the confounded thing', she had strained her eyes and decided she was done with study. Having whetted her taste for writing, she was more interested in putting human psychology under the microscope of fiction than in the mechanics of theory and laboratories. Although she would forget all the ancient Greek she had swotted, she had read works such as Plato's *Republic*, which bolstered her emerging belief in an ideal society based on honour, merit and equality.

Elizabeth Harrower

Deciding to be a writer was one thing, but surviving as a writer in 1950s London was another. The city was starting to put itself back together, still home to many poor who could not afford electricity or proper nutrition, still shrouded in coal-fired pea soup fogs, and under the returned leadership of Winston Churchill. But rationing of sugar and sweets ended and the coronation of young Queen Elizabeth II in June 1953 brought fresh promise into the homes of the twenty million Britons who watched on new television sets. These were the years when Betty Harrower cracked open her chrysalis and flew out as the author Elizabeth Harrower. As a marker of her intent, she bought her first typewriter in London in 1953 for £20. She chose an Oliver, a heavy 'portable' machine in a square black carry case, which she noted was the British-owned brand used by the civil service in India. The constant tapping of her fingernails wore the keys as she worked at her fiction, and sometimes took in paid typing, at a series of tables in a series of rented rooms. When winter cold seeped around the window frames, she fed the small gas fire with shillings and typed on wearing gloves and a cap pulled down over her thick, dark, sensibly cropped hair.

For several years she was at 76 Lancaster Gate in Bayswater, part of an elegant row of white columned buildings that backed on to the lawns and ponds of Kensington Gardens. Well before her time, the Bloomsbury writer Lytton Strachey had lived with his parents across the street for twenty-five years, and Scottish-born JM Barrie had been around the corner in Bayswater Road when he created Peter Pan, inspired by his walks in the Gardens. Having cut loose from Kempley's control and most of his money, she took temporary office jobs again, one with an undertaker, an experience that did not show up in her fiction. She wrote at night and weekends, and saved for uninterrupted bursts of writing when she would keep a nine-to-five schedule, six days a week, and finish each day with at least four typed foolscap pages. When there was enough time and money she went to the theatre, and always frequented art galleries, cinemas and libraries.

*

Harrower was twenty-seven when she began work on a second short story, which grew almost spontaneously into her first novel within a year. She thought of *Down in the City* as 'a little love song to Sydney'. After years of absorbing material from life and books, distance from home and family released her memories onto the page. She had been reading Robert Browning's poetry and borrowed the novel's title from his poem 'Up at a Villa – Down in the City', which celebrates the vibrancy of a city square in Italy, compared with the serene isolation of a nearby villa. If Harrower was nostalgic for Sydney, she was not sentimental about her characters. Burning to write another novel about her childhood, she treated this one as her apprenticeship and hardly expected it to be published.

However, she told one interviewer that the first publisher who read *Down in the City* wanted to publish it. To another she said that she sent the manuscript to numerous publishers and after each rejection she rewrote and sent it out again. Both stories may be loosely true. She had found the British firm Cassell & Company in a publishers' handbook and Bryen Gentry, one of the directors, wrote in August 1956 – less than a month after receiving it – that they were enthusiastic about *Down in the City*. They offered a small advance of £75 against a 10 per cent royalty on home sales, and 5 per cent on overseas or export sales, which meant Australia. Most Australian books then, and for some decades after, were published by British companies that owned Commonwealth rights and gave Australian authors a poor deal in their own country.

Cassell had already published some Australian fiction and intended to fit Harrower's novel into their romance list, which did not please her. She wanted the book to appear under the pseudonym Antonia Reid, using her maternal grandmother's maiden surname. She had already sent a short story out under the name Claire Harwell, an upbeat play on her own name – 'well' rather than 'harrow' – when she was staying with her great-aunt in Scotland. The rejected pages were returned, as instructed, to Miss B. Harrower at Whins House, Alloa, and the story remains unpublished. 'Absent Friends' was part of a suite of three stories with 'The City at Night' and 'Summertime' about the fraught interaction of young women in offices. 'Antonia Reid' had an approach from Juliet O'Hea at Curtis Brown in London – literary agent to Patrick White, among many distinguished names – wanting to represent her after hearing about *Down in the City*. But the letter went via Cassell in Sydney and reached Harrower months later.

Before the novel's publication, Harrower asked Cassell to replace the nom de plume with her own name. Perhaps she could see future complications if she should have any success, and followed the lead of Margaret Dick, who had established her name from the outset. At this point she chose her adult identity by switching from 'Betty' to the more formal 'Elizabeth'. She would only make the change legal by deed poll in 2012.

The cousins shared the flat in Lancaster Gate for a time, and in 1956 could afford to take a cheap trip to Greece, where they luxuriated on the beaches of Corfu before leaving, 'desolately aware of our bliss', for Athens, Olympus and Delphi. The Kempleys visited London later that year, in time to celebrate Betty's newly signed book contract, check on her welfare, and stoke her desire to stay away. Soon after they left, in early 1957 she moved to 34 Sloane Gardens in Chelsea, a handsome Victorian red-brick mansion near the genteel shopping centres of Sloane Street and Knightsbridge with its famous Harrods department store. Her neighbours in the house were the Danish landlady, Gertrude Jensen, (Lady) Olga Livingston, some married couples and other single residents. Harrower climbed the stairs of the five-storey house to the furnished attic, with a shared kitchen and bathroom. She planned to be in the tiny room for a few weeks, and stayed for more than a year. Now she had some momentum, she was determined to race ahead with her writing.

*

Down in the City and its author, Elizabeth Harrower, entered the world in July 1957. This was Harrower's first interpretation of her mother's marriage. The novel dramatises the electric attraction of opposites between Esther Prescott, a refined young woman from a well-off family, and rough Stan Peterson, who operates shady businesses on the fringes of crime. To the disapproval of her lawyer brothers, Esther leaves their stone house overlooking the harbour at Rose Bay to marry Stan within two weeks of meeting and moves into his Kings Cross flat. Esther has been described as a Sleeping Beauty, and there is, as in other Harrower fiction, a fairytale quality to the unworldly woman awoken from bored comfort. Stan has the tarnished Hollywood glamour of a film noir antihero, a small-time gangster driving a Cadillac, sprinkling Esther with diamonds, and addressing his women as 'dame' and 'kid'. Soon after marrying Esther, he resumes his longtime casual affair with Vi, pub owner and barmaid, and mistreats them both. Writing in London, where the rigid class structure irked her, may have pushed Harrower to widen the social divide between Stan and Esther, but both Esther and Vi, from different backgrounds, are compliant with their bullying lover. Harrower makes an effort to show each of them, even Stan, as individuals deserving of some sympathy. Visibly bruised after a physical assault, Esther still excuses his drunken rages as the result of his orphanage upbringing, which scarred him with insecurity, resentment and material greed. To the frustrated reader, keen for Esther to leave, Harrower shows how people become trapped by intractable cycles of addiction, domestic violence and denial.

Harrower places the couple at the centre of an ensemble of Esther's brothers and stepmother, Stan's drinking and gambling cronies, and their neighbours in the Kings Cross block of flats. Laura Maitland (her surname a memento from Mayfield) is a pleasant but smug young wife and mother. Seventeen-year-old Rachel, another of the novel's many orphans, is a cameo of the Harrower high-minded girl who would be developed in her next novel, *The Long Prospect*.

Stan's illegal 'import export' and 'novelty' manufacture resemble Richard Kempley's activities, but he is the kind of dodgy small business-man common in Kings Cross during the restrictions of the 1940s and '50s. Bars and strip shows, servicemen and prostitutes, office workers and families, Italian cafés and fine restaurants, blocks of flats and mansions, mixed in a seedy cosmopolitanism that made everyone feel a little European. Harrower knew the inner-city suburb from her mother's time as a nurse at St Luke's Hospital, and from her own social life. Her home was always north of the harbour but friends lived in Rose Bay and Kempley considered owning property there. Harrower drew on her own life and family, as she always would, but she moved details around. Her years of working, watching and reading added to the urban kaleidoscope.

The point of view shifts constantly among the characters, even to a toll-booth collector on the Harbour Bridge and a restaurant waiter. Stan and Esther sit on their small sunny balcony, go to the local harbour pool and nightclubs; there are drives north to the Central Coast and west to the Blue Mountains, embracing the era of the motor car. Sydney's heat, storms, breezes, brilliant days and starry nights roll by with the turn of the earth, shaping and reflecting human moods. Harrower uses language as a camera to create dynamic patterns of light and shade and headachy dazzle: 'Sunlight exploded from every piece of nickel and chrome in the room. It fell refracted on walls and ceiling and floor. Vi's face was creamy in it, her arms pale apricot.'

Reviews were brief and dismissive. At least Harrower's arrival was noted. The *Times Literary Supplement* gave her a paragraph in a review with a French and an American novel. The anonymous reviewer said the books were more typical than usual of the national characteristics of their respective countries and then mistook Esther's brothers for farmers instead of city lawyers. In conclusion: 'The author has rightly sacrificed incident to convincing psychological detail, but the result is sadly pedestrian; neither genteel Esther nor her crude husband seems worth so much interest.'

Critic John Metcalf attempted a jokey plot summary:

> Shy Est married cocky Stan who still has an eye for plump Vi and hates Est's stuck-up family. They are all much less interesting than Miss Harrower thinks; it's a pity that the sincerity she's put into the book is incapable of bringing the so-ordinary-as-to-be-odd little people to life.

Back home, a paragraph in *The Bulletin* appreciated the 'intense feeling for the city' that animated the novel, at the expense of 'vague and sketchy' plot and character. The reviewer seemed disappointed that the story ended not with a shattering tragedy for dreamy Esther but with 'the damp squib of her acceptance'. And yet, 'there is enough of perception and understanding in the book to make one look forward to future work by its author'.

Ray Mathew, an up-and-coming Australian poet and playwright, wrote at more length for the *Sydney Morning Herald*. Finding the book no more than promising, he added: 'Having stated that, however, the reviewer is free to lose his head over Miss Harrower's immature but exciting novel.' He admired Harrower's 'searching scrutiny' of the city and said eastern suburbs residents would enjoy her fresh depictions of familiar people, places, seasons and social life. The novel's 'simple, unaffected observation' was its keynote, he wrote, its point of view 'fascinating', and its characterisation 'credible enough'. Most memorable, though, was the 'deep feeling for the charms of this city and the bird's eye view it gives of it'. Mathew's flashes of praise impressed Harrower, so his was the only review she remembered, and she kept the *Herald's* obituary after his death in 2002.

Down in the City earned back £65 from sales of 1144 copies (only 192 of them overseas) before the publication date. In the next three months, boosted by the *Herald's* review, overseas sales outnumbered British sales for a total of 2266 copies – and she received a royalty cheque for almost £30. This was no overnight success but enough to justify Cassell's decision to take on her second novel.

*

After finishing work on *Down in the City*, Harrower had taken a day off and then turned to the novel that had been forming in the space between memory and imagination. *The Long Prospect* took another year to write. The life of Emily Lawrence, daughter of separated parents and living with her grandmother in fictional Ballowra, closely follows the outline of Betty Harrower's unhappy circumstances in smoke-blackened Newcastle. The novel presents an ensemble of characters at Lilian Hulm's boarding house, lodgers and lovers drawn into her web of strife and gossip.

But more than *Down in the City*, this group portrait has a clear focus on Emily's troubled adolescent psyche. Readers experience the world's indifference through her tearful eyes, passionate crushes, half-understandings, and desperation to be loved. Lilian is a hearty host but a despot in her small domain, manipulating her victims into passive non-retaliation, and demonstrating that cruelty doesn't have a gender. Lilian always wins.

Emily is befriended by a decent, well-read boarder, Max, who opens her up to learning and kindness. Like many of Harrower's 'good' characters, he is a scientist and for a time he was involved with Thea, another chemist at the local chemical works and another lost object of Emily's devotion. Max may be modelled on one or more people Harrower knew – a boarder, a teacher, the beloved Miss Maclean – but more importantly he represents the intellectual and emotional nourishment she could only find outside her own family. Jealous Lilian would like Max for herself, if only to torture her latest lover, Rosen, whose Jewish surname complicates her power game with an implication of anti-Semitism. Married, separated, lonely Max and adoring Emily are both punished when a chorus of narrow-minded adults persuade Lilian to believe he means harm to her granddaughter. Harrower depicts a sensitive man managing a girl's attachment and his own affection, both teetering towards adult attraction, without a hint of sleaziness. Her own memory of heartbreak pours like molten metal into delicately wrought fiction that is alive with true feelings. As he prepares to leave the house, expelled by Lilian, 'Emily turned on her knees to watch him searching through his books, the urgency of her longing, her necessity to keep him, broke over her.'

The Long Prospect was accepted by Cassell for an advance of £100 just before publication of *Down in the City*. Harrower had written the second novel without knowing what reviewers would say about the first, and yet she had instinctively worked at strengthening her characterisation. A reader's report for Cassell judged the novel sensitive but loose and unsatisfactory. Harrower had signed with an agent, Paul Scott of Pearn, Pollinger & Higham in Soho, to handle negotiations and Cassell backed their new author. The only snag came when her editor suggested a change of title because *The Long Prospect* had been recently used by other authors. The alternative offered was 'Life and Emily Lawrence'. Harrower thought this was 'plain hell' and Scott agreed it was 'a stinker'. She wrote back politely with another option, 'The Narrow Look', which she admitted to Scott had no meaning. Fortunately that was found to be similar to another book's title, so they reverted to *The Long Prospect*.

Critics took this novel more seriously than the first when it was published in April 1958. Harrower was in Scotland at the time and missed the scattered British reviews, but Margaret Kempley alerted her to Australian reaction. She was still corresponding with her childhood friend, Barbara Johnson, now Barbara Ward with a husband and children in Newcastle. In a letter to 'Barb' that July, 'Bet' was bursting with news that her mother had sent a clipping of the *Sydney Morning Herald*'s excellent review.

> I was really astonished by the critic's praise, pleased, of course, but there was such a lot of it! Too exciting for me. The *Herald* was nice enough about *Down in the City* but this time they've really outdone themselves. And I was astonished, I suppose, because you forget about the things you've finished and concentrate on what you're doing at the present moment ... I often feel that something like ditch-digging would be a pleasant change.

Sidney J Baker himself, editor of the *Sydney Morning Herald* book pages, wrote the laudatory half-page review, which put Harrower in a 'prominent place among Australia's modern novelists'. Searching for comparisons, he could only think of DH Lawrence and Katherine Mansfield overseas, and Patrick White in Australia, because they called for slow reading to enjoy the 'exciting literary experience' of a novel with little action. Impressed by the sensitive portrait of Emily's developing personality, Baker wrote, 'That Miss Harrower has succeeded so triumphantly gives the book a distinction that puts it in a class of its own so far as Australian fiction is concerned.' He stumbled over some vague expressions of Emily's stream of consciousness but ended: 'To condemn the novel because of them would be comparable to condemning Patrick White for the poetic symbolism in his books; the cumulative rewards are much more important than the obstacles.'

Harrower must have been pleased and curious about the comparisons with White. She had read good reviews of his fourth novel, *The Tree of Man*, in English newspapers, and her mother sent her the book after queuing to get White's signature. Harrower found it marvellous. She probably knew that his fifth novel, *Voss*, had won the inaugural Miles Franklin Literary Award in 1957, but she may not have realised that this accolade followed years of sneering indifference from Australian critics. She still had no interest in reading Australian writers. Having travelled to the Old Country where 'real' literature came from, she was intent on making literature there, while looking over her shoulder to Australia. With the exception of Margaret Dick, she had no writer friends. She claimed not to have known any Australians in London, even though she joined the Society of Australian Authors and met some who were writing for television and radio. The society compiled *The Sunburnt Country: Profile of Australia* just before the Queen visited Australia in 1954. The anthology became a long-running bestseller with chapters by seventeen society members including its chairman Russell Braddon, Martin Boyd, Chester Wilmot, George Johnston and Dal Stivens; the only women were Judy Fallon on 'the Australian woman', and children's author Mary Elwyn Patchett on rural life and animals. Some writers had gone to Britain as war correspondents, others were chasing work for the theatre, the BBC, or the larger book market. Many had some success before the louder generation of Germaine Greer, Barry Humphries, Clive James and Richard Neville arrived in the 1960s. Harrower doesn't seem to have encountered Richard's sister, Jill Neville, or the poet Peter Porter, or Charmian Clift and George Johnston, who were all living in London in the 1950s.

A year after Harrower's novel appeared, the second Miles Franklin Award and its £500 went to the West Australian writer Randolph Stow for *To the Islands*. Two of the judges on the panel headed by Beatrice Davis preferred *Into the Morning* by Elizabeth Webb, and as a group they praised nine other novels, including *The Long Prospect*.

*

In mid-1958 Elizabeth Harrower left Sloane Gardens, Chelsea, for a flat in a white-trimmed brick house at 3 Dents Road near Wandsworth Common. The move came inconveniently in the midst of writing her next novel, but the less central address south of the river was quieter and more affordable, and Margaret Dick joined her there. Each December they went up to Scotland for a traditional Christmas with the Dick family. Elizabeth enjoyed visiting Auntie Minnie, but Margaret found her old-fashioned mother trying, so was always pleased to get back to London. There they had visitors from Sydney and Edinburgh, and some new friends, though when a Scottish friend moved to London, Elizabeth said, 'I like comparatively few people very much, so it's good not to lose touch.'

Their shared goals made the cousins companionable flatmates, and such was their synchronicity that both had books out in 1958. Margaret was forty-two when her first novel appeared and after years of full-time writing she was feeling the pinch of irregular income. In July Elizabeth wrote to Barbara Ward in Newcastle that Margaret would have her next novel finished and with the publisher in a month or so. Elizabeth herself would 'have to trail on with mine at least to the end of the year. It is slow!' She recalled earlier years when she had worked to a strict program and was always desperate for her one break a week but too tired to enjoy it. These days, she said, she was giving herself a much easier time. Knowing that Barbara shared her love of theatre, she wrote, 'It is a relief to get out to shows ... they really distract you and give your mind a rest, don't they?'

She had recently seen only one play: *Variation on a Theme*, at the Globe Theatre, written by Terence Rattigan, directed by Sir John Gielgud and starring Margaret Leighton. Kenneth Tynan wrote a scathing review for the *Guardian* in the voice of Rattigan's absent Muse. Harrower didn't express an opinion, but the play would have intrigued her for its cultural history: its story of a much-married-for-money woman in love with a young ballet dancer was a variation on the French novel and play by the younger Alexandre Dumas, *The Lady of the Camellias*, or *Camille* in English. Verdi had adapted Dumas's story as the opera *La Traviata*. The Paris courtesan who finds love, only to be abandoned and die of consumption, is one of the great tragic heroines, reworked over the centuries by writers, choreographers and filmmakers. She must surely have languished in Harrower's mind while she worked on her third novel.

The Catherine Wheel is a variation on Harrower's recurring theme of oppressive relationships, but this one is radical. Having looked back at her Australian past, as she was turning thirty she set this novel in contemporary London, so that it reads like a report from the frontline of her life. The story of Clemency James is a first-person, present-tense, emotional rollercoaster about a twenty-five-year-old Australian woman, Harrower's only novel written from inside the narrator's consciousness, recording her unsettled thoughts with the flickering speed of film. *The Catherine Wheel* – a spinning firecracker, an instrument of torture – is a portrait of mental illness, with Clem pushed from its sane centre to the edge of collapse. She lives and studies law by correspondence in an attic flat near Bayswater, where the wind blows in from Siberia. In the 'self-contained village' of the service-house, she chats to other residents while they cook their omelettes and hang their washing, and plays 'Constant Disciple' to her friends Lewis Grenville and his married sister Helen Reid (Harrower uses her grandmother's full maiden name), a government envoy and a doctor, paragons of British restraint and reason. But she lives too much inside her own mind.

Miss Evans, the landlady, upsets the peace when she hires an out-of-work actor, Christian Roland, as window cleaner and nightwatchman while she is out at spiritualist meetings. Christian and Olive, his older mistress, insinuate themselves into Clem's life, asking for free French lessons so Christian can revive his career at the Comédie Française in Paris – a delusional ambition, at best. Handsome, charismatic Christian is a narcissist, an alcoholic, a gaslighter, flirting with Clem to feed his ego and to unsettle Olive. Clem resists and sinks deeper, resists and falls into the well of his 'perversity and masochism'. She says without elaboration that in her past she had 'qualified with honours in those subjects', but has put the suffering of adolescence behind her, and hopes to be a 'stabilizing balance to counter his excesses'. In a drunken delirium he assaults Clem with a violent kiss and Olive with his hands round her throat, and is forgiven by both. Christian's name is cynical, or at least ironic, and the book's title recalls the wheel on which St Catherine was tortured for refusing to renounce her Christian faith.

Clem is attracted, in spite of herself, and *The Catherine Wheel* is Harrower's only novel to describe limbs tangled in physical sex. Yet Clemency, true to her name, acts out of sympathy more than desire and observes herself with a disembodied distance. The affair derails Clem's studious discipline and the mutual hot-and-cold obsession comes close to destroying her. Apart from outings to cold London streets in overcoats smelling of fog, the action is confined to circles of heat in Clem's small room with its shilling-meter gas fire and Miss Evans's sitting room, where the coal grate sends sparks flying. Like Harrower herself, Clem is forced to move when the house is sold, but she does not take her chance to evade Christian, who follows her to her tiny pink-walled nest in Knightsbridge. In all her novels the drama is shaped by houses, flats and rooms that act as both cage and stage.

The Catherine Wheel whirls with operatic extremity. Clem's decline into feverish headache, flu and despair mimics the consumption that kills Violetta in *La Traviata* and Mimi in *La Bohème*. Clem is hardly bohemian but she lives precariously on a legacy from her father, and her story touches Mimi's at many points. For one, she speaks French because she had a French stepmother called Mimi. (One of Harrower's friends at the Sydney clothing factory also had a stepmother named Mimi.) This is Harrower's novel about theatre, music, cinema, all the performance arts that filled her spare time and imagination.

Alongside an abundance of Shakespeare and genteel playwrights like Terence Rattigan, London was raising a new generation of writers and directors whose kitchen-sink realism showed working-class characters rebelling against traditional British society. The label 'Angry Young Men' began with John Osborne and his play *Look Back in Anger*, based on his own failing marriage and set in a one-room flat. The play premiered in 1956 at the Royal Court Theatre in Sloane Square, as did his next play, *The Entertainer*, with Laurence Olivier and Joan Plowright. The theatre became renowned for staging new plays, just a block from Harrower's Chelsea home, and its often-bleak dramas fed into her depiction of ordinary rooming-house lives.

'London was paradise,' she recalled fifty years later. 'I did see a huge lot of theatre in London. I saw Chekhov, *The Cherry Orchard*. I saw great, great actors and I loved their huge gifts – Margaret Leighton, Celia Johnson, Ralph Richardson. I was sitting in the front row when Laurence Olivier was *The Entertainer* in the little Sloane Street theatre – it wasn't one of his great things. I hated being at the theatre when people would eat noisily and I would want to shut them up.'

British and European fiction fuelled her imagination, too. She read all of DH Lawrence, and kept reading Henry James, Anthony Trollope, Stendhal and Proust. Contemporary novelists Rosamond Lehmann and, in particular, Elizabeth Bowen made a strong impression. She would forever remember Bowen saying in *The Heat of the Day* that 'all the people left in London during the war were in love' and 'To as much as dispute with him was to injure honour', lines that are relevant to *The Catherine Wheel*, and to all her own fiction, her personal life and her politics. Slightly misremembering the quotation, she wrote to Shirley Hazzard in 1974 about critics of the expelled Soviet writer Aleksandr Solzhenitsyn:

> Years ago I stopped arguing with anyone dead drunk, insane or drugged. Elizabeth Bowen said: 'to so much as argue was to injure honour', and there are times when you feel this so strongly that nothing could make you speak. Totalitarianism is ghastly insanity. The subject arises briefly, and hatred appears in the eyes, and your heart goes cold, and you feel deep surprise and disappointment, and realize that this person you've liked isn't ever to be counted on again. (This isn't to say I don't argue constantly!)

In London she also read the novels of Ivy Compton-Burnett, an eccentric Edwardian modernist whose terse, dialogue-driven novels read like plays. The Australian literary critic Geordie Williamson would see 'the forbidding' Compton-Burnett as the writer most like Elizabeth Harrower in her subtle, mannered, waspish-humoured investigation of family conflict and 'the abyssal depths of the psyche'. Harrower was a much less austere writer than Compton-Burnett, who lived nearby in Kensington, but she would have recognised the influence of Greek tragedy on her claustrophobic scenarios in which families are ruled by tyrants and torn apart by misdirected letters, inheritance, divorce and secrets.

Theatrical imagery is a constant through *The Catherine Wheel*. A 'stagy' Chelsea restaurant resembles the history-laden Café de la Paix, next to the Opera Garnier in Paris. Characters are self-conscious, in costume, playing a part, looking in mirrors. Clem's childish mouth disguises her as a 'nice quiet girl' and her overcoat is 'unintentionally deceitful'. Christian makes her laugh with his clever mimicry, and in his sunny yellow jumper looks like a Method actor from the New York Theatre Workshop. He calls out for his dead sister – 'Stella!' – like Marlon Brando, moody, drunk and violent in *A Streetcar Named Desire*. Their parents, Christian confides, were a tenor who hanged himself (his son found the body) and a small-time actress who abandoned her children. Stella was an opera singer and died of cancer, for which he blames himself. He has had roles at Stratford in *Hamlet* and *Macbeth*, and played Benedict, who in *Much Ado About Nothing* is the deceptive lover of Beatrice (also Christian's mother's name). The effect is of so many layers of pretence that no one can be trusted or believed. Christian – if his story is credible – is fatally damaged by childhood tragedy, a point Harrower makes in every novel. She used her reading of psychology to create a fragmented case study of a character who sparkles dangerously and leaves wreckage for the women who love him. Clemency has a room of her own but Christian breaks in and destroys her security.

The Catherine Wheel spins brilliantly, exhaustingly, unstoppably, a psychic war between ego and id, intellect and emotion, mind and body.

*

While she was working on *The Catherine Wheel*, Elizabeth Harrower was haunted by the Cold War tension building between the United States and the Soviet Union. The Second World War allies were dividing the world into a stand-off between Western and Eastern blocs, between capitalism and communism, a potentially explosive confrontation that infected both sides with fear and paranoia. A week after her thirtieth birthday, Harrower went to an overflowing meeting at Central Hall in Westminster, where the philosopher Bertrand Russell and scientist Linus Pauling denounced the build-up of nuclear weapons with a warning that London was a sitting target and could be flattened next week. Clusters of planes flew low over the city at night. She joined a crowd of four thousand for the first Aldermaston march against nuclear arms at Easter 1958, and walked the short distance from Trafalgar Square to the Albert Memorial. But her imagination was back in her Chelsea room. As the diminishing numbers marched on to Hounslow for the night before heading to Aldermaston, she broke away and rushed home to nearby Sloane Gardens with an urgent sense that she must write her novel in case the world was about to end.

Harrower first learned about Buddhism in London, and read a 1951 bestselling introduction, *Buddhism*, by Christmas Humphreys, an English barrister and Buddhist convert. He laid out the history and principles in a way that 'just seemed to make a lot of sense. It was straightforward and so I was interested but I wasn't surprised somehow.' This was one of many philosophical paths she would investigate, and much later she returned to Buddhism. She always described herself as a pacifist, and so does Clem in her confrontations with Christian. Novels were not the place to write about politics, Harrower thought, but the political atmosphere in *The Catherine Wheel* affects the characters' moods as much as the weather does. When Clem briefly emerges into spring sunshine and daffodils with Lewis, they soon descend into the café of a newsreel cinema, another den of illusion and bleak tidings. She indulges her obsession with Christian because a bomb could drop tomorrow. There are background references to crises in Africa and the Middle East – the Suez crisis of 1956 – which have the attention of Clem's friend Lewis, while Clem fails to resolve the microcosmic power struggle in her garret. Her generosity to Christian is described as satyagraha, Gandhi's philosophy of non-violent resistance; hate the sin and not the sinner; reach the heart of an opponent with the intention of converting not defeating. Harrower would wrestle again and again with this idea in her fiction and her personal relationships.

As always, Harrower pieced together the mosaic of her novel from countless fragments, real and imagined, personal and observed, read and transformed. She was neighbour to young women living between dreary rooms and dreary jobs, and to a woman who shared her prophetic dreams, as well as visiting shearers and cane cutters from Australia. By contrast, she 'began to feel what a free spirit I was'. She kept no drafts of her first two novels, but for *The Catherine Wheel* there are typescripts and foolscap pages of random ideas, many of them later discarded. 'Stepmother Mimi' are the first words on the first page. 'Ruth' (as Clem was then) likes Mimi but her father gave Ruth hell all her life because her mother died when she was born. In the notes, Ruth ponders a future as the unmarried daughter of Mimi's household. Harrower considers having her meet someone else who wants to marry her at the end, but Ruth believes she should never marry. She always loves people who do not love her. A con woman called Gina walks down the path one summer's day in an anecdote someone seems to have told Harrower. Gina becomes Mavis becomes Olive, who owns theatrical digs where Chris – not yet Christian – lives; she is a 'sex addict', her dialogue straight from the movies. Harrower considered making Chris and Stella of Austrian or Italian parentage, arrived in London at the beginning of the war. She alludes to an incident on a bus in Greece in which she had pretended to be fearful to make some frightened boys feel better but only earned their contempt. Brief notes range from Kierkegaard to frequent hair-washing as a hobby. More fully described is the '*Tonio Kröger* theme', a reference to Thomas Mann's novella about a writer's effort to balance creative life with the everyday world. Harrower saw the separation as intellect versus feeling, inquiry versus peaceful blindness, emotional turmoil versus emotional blank. From her psychology reading she noted that cats, like humans, become neurotic through frustration. She outlined a well-known experiment in which cats are given an electric shock each time they go to their food so that a conflict between attraction and repulsion results in neurosis.

A surviving page of a draft with the Hitchcockian title 'Tightrope', dated May 30, 1958, begins with the narrator, Ruth, out shopping for food in sunshine and gusty wind, which lifts her volatile spirits. Mimi, on the other hand, hated winds because they gave her headaches. In a crossed-out sentence she – Ruth and Harrower – warns against being a conscious character, because you can never forget anything. The opening page of a second draft, commenced November 18, 1958 and marked 'finished' on March 16, 1959, and again in April, is almost in the novel's final form and has put the Siberian wind before the shopping. Possible titles are scribbled across the pages. Some are shockers – 'Roses Round the Door' and 'Unlock the Cage, Darling' – and others better, such as 'A Head for Heights' and 'Island in the Air'. 'The Catherine Wheel' is circled and ticked, the right choice.

Inevitably the question arises, was there a real Christian Roland? If so, Harrower has buried the evidence of his identity. There are no giveaways in her notes. Late in her life she destroyed all her remaining diaries and the letters she wrote to her mother from London during this most important period in her personal and creative development. It was, she said, necessary to protect people. But she left crumbs. She told the writer Shirley Hazzard that her life had been affected by an alcoholic grandfather, an alcoholic stepfather who was possibly also mentally ill, and an alcoholic lover. Coming after Robert Hughes, her grandfather, and Richard Kempley, her stepfather, the unidentified lover was at least one too many dangerous drunks. She recognised the truth in a friend's comment about 'the charisma that is sometimes part of mental disturbance; that it has a sort of exceptional charm, exceptional attraction, magic, something quite special'. Years later she told her Sydney hairdresser, that traditional confidant, about her involvement with two men in London. Were they models for unruly Christian and dry Lewis? The hairdresser knew nothing more. But it would be surprising if a single woman in her twenties in London had no lovers or suitors. As always with Harrower, love and character are not simple. Christian's wild spending and histrionic behaviour remind Clem of an unnamed troublemaker who echoes Richard Kempley: 'the gambling losses, the cars wrecked, the cruises, the staterooms on Atlantic crossings'. Harrower gave the name Olive – a woman who once lived with Kempley in Newcastle – to Christian's shadowy, downtrodden, sallow-skinned mistress, who left her family for him. She was reworking, in a highly altered form, her mother's spirit-killing marriage yet again. When one interviewer asked an older Harrower whether her writing was autobiographical, she said she could not have survived all the drama in her novels. To another she said the truth had been worse than the fiction. *The Catherine Wheel* enacts Harrower's decision to choose the life of the mind, a dazzling metaphor for the liberation and exhaustion of creativity.

*

As a late starter, keen to make up for lost writing time, Margaret Dick had quickly turned out two novels back to back. The London-based publisher William Heinemann liked the first manuscript she submitted but asked to see another before they committed, 'as though it were a batch of scones'. Like Harrower, she kept regular long hours, writing from nine to five for six days a week when she could. But she also needed income, and for a time she worked two days a week with the London Council of Social Services.

She shared Harrower's active political concerns and in spare hours wrote letters of support or protest to newspapers and politicians. Both women were Labour supporters, abhorred the extremes of Stalinist brutality, and opposed acts of aggression by any nation. They wrote separately in November 1956 to Robert Allan, the Conservative MP for Paddington South and Financial Secretary to the Admiralty, to protest against Britain's involvement in opposing Egypt by occupying the Suez Canal. He wrote back thanking them but reporting that the government had stopped a major war in the Middle East and possibly a third world war. He regretted the United Nations had not intervened in Hungary before Soviet domination led to the revolution of October 1956 and its tragic repression. Harrower also had a letter in the *Sunday Times* expressing her shock that Britain, a UN supporter and a strong moral influence for peace, 'should have overthrown in a night all that she has so laboriously worked for over the past difficult years'.

Heinemann bought rights to both Margaret Dick's novels and decided to publish the stronger second story first in 1958. *Point of Return* is an elegant distillation of her misspent years in the civil service, transferred to 'the firm', a fictional business in which middle managers jostle for promotion and break the taboo of office affairs. Dick observes human absurdity with a touch of the Kafka-lite satire that Shirley Hazzard would develop in *People in Glass Houses*, her 1967 collection of stories based on her lowly career at the United Nations. Dick sensitively portrays young women at the mercy of male bosses who can pursue them, fire them and shame them. But there's a calm independence in her central character,

Marian Bonamy, a well-named personnel officer who has to sort out her own romantic tangle as well as the personal and industrial problems of her colleagues. The 'point of return' sees Marian and her married manager on the verge of an affair when he retreats from the potential damage to his career, with no thought for her feelings. The firm manufactures and sells clothing through its retail outlet, Grangers. Harrower's account of her clothing factory job and her good friends there, Marion and Claire, must have been some inspiration; she had seen them again in Edinburgh and London. There are scenes from English boarding-house life, of young women living on eggs in bedsits with shared bathrooms and kitchens. Dick's polished writing lacks the emotional and creative intensity that distinguished Harrower's work, but her clear prose and amused interest in ethical questions were made for thoughtful middle-class readers.

British critics were complimentary in trade papers, women's magazines and broadsheet newspapers. The writer JB Priestley doubly pleased Dick that year: first as a founder of the Campaign for Nuclear Disarmament that led the Aldermaston marches, and then with ambiguous praise in *Reynold's News* for her 'real talent for presenting ordinary dullish people in all-too-credible circumstances and suddenly lightening or darkening them with heartbreak or a touch of ecstasy'. Hilary Seton in the *Sunday Times* saw 'a clever book' in which 'different personalities unfold precisely and individually and their relationships are dove-tailed with skill and inevitability'. *The Scotsman* found the novel 'extremely well written and one to rouse more than ordinary interest in what the author writes next'. In Australia, *The Bulletin* reviewer admired *Point of Return* as a first novel that is 'mature in form and expression' and a sensitive portrayal of the growing love between a career woman and her boss.

Heinemann followed up a year later with the novel Dick had written first. *Rhyme or Reason* was a more obvious debut novel, a bildungsroman set in an unnamed northern university city, with the same character types and moral dilemmas as in *Point of Return*. Lisa, a sensitive young civil servant waiting for life to begin, bored by her work and potential suitors, is torn between friendship with a French girl, Renée, and the possibility of romance with Renée's fiancé, André. As in *Point of Return*, decency ends the potential affair.

Dick had connections with France. She had signed up with a women's organisation to 'adopt' a Free French Sailor, Joseph Ambrosine, in 1942. Before the war she had taught English literature to French students, setting assignments on Shelley, Hardy and Woolf. She continued for years to correspond with Louis Boireau in Cadillac near Bordeaux, whose letters complimented her French, corrected her mistakes, differentiated the words for love and friendship, and discussed art, architecture and music. In 1939 he invited her to France to celebrate his marriage to Jeannie Bompuy, with no mention of war. The warm but formal letters don't imply there was *amour* as well as *amitié* and *camaraderie* between them. It is tempting to think Margaret's memories were an ingredient in Clem's fateful French lessons in *The Catherine Wheel*. In reality, the poised, intellectual Dick was unlikely to have submitted to the extremes of emotional torment that Harrower portrayed.

As Heinemann prepared to publish Dick's *Rhyme or Reason* in mid-1959 and Harrower hurried to finish *The Catherine Wheel* for Cassell, both writers teetered on the edge of real success. Rather than consolidate their reputations in the London literary scene, they made a surprising decision. Harrower, for all her determination to build a life away from Australia and family, was always keen to hear news and have visitors from home. She wrote to Barbara Ward that 'UD' seemed not too sick though he was preparing to go to hospital for an operation. Richard Kempley was the benign-sounding Uncle Dick to Betty's friends. 'But he and Mum seem to be fine, really,' she wrote. That 'really' suggested an unspoken 'under the circumstances' or 'despite everything'.

Harrower worried about her mother and with her novel finished she planned to make her first trip home in more than eight years. She missed fresh fruit, steaks and showers, and couldn't face another winter of flu and deprivation. Cassell's lack of advertising for *The Long Prospect* in Australia had annoyed her, and both author and publisher were disappointed by sales of 2576 copies despite positive reviews. Even Australia House in London had failed to promote the novel. Cassell had first option on *The Catherine Wheel* and in August 1959 offered her £100 advance, the same amount she'd received for *The Long Prospect*. Her agent, David Bolt at the renamed David Higham Associates, had tried to broker a better deal but he implied that she didn't have a strong negotiating position and urged her to accept and give them the option they requested on her next two novels. He sheepishly told her they had agreed to a higher royalty if her sales exceeded 12 500 copies – 'which may be a little optimistic of course'.

Harrower needed to make an appearance in Sydney to establish herself there and, when she booked her passage, Margaret Dick decided to join her for the shared adventure away from London's damp chill and European war-mongering. In the postwar era of 'Ten Pound Poms', when British migrants had assisted passage if they would stay in Australia for at least two years, Dick nonetheless paid her own fare.

She and Harrower planned a visit of about a year. Certain that they would be back in London, they packed up their few household belongings – a Greek jug, a striped vase, blue dishes, bookcases and books – and left them with Reg and Phoebe Chaloner, the amiable owners of the Wandsworth house where they had rented rooms for the past year.

There was one more chapter to the story of Clemency and Christian. Harrower would write 'The Last Days', a short story, a year or two later, as an unnerving coda to *The Catherine Wheel*. In their attic bed-sitter, Clem and her friend Kate, a new character, pack their trunks for a voyage to Sydney. Clem moved a year ago from fashionable Knightsbridge to unfashionable Wandsworth to escape from 'one person'. She has earned her law degree and begun to recover from a dark period of cynicism when she did not eat and hardly breathed. Obliquely she explains the reasons they want to leave London, including, for Kate, 'the lack of that one face to turn to any more' and for Clem, 'a face I wanted to turn away from'. But Christian has her phone number. When the phone on the landing rings, his voice emerges from the past asking why she didn't answer his letters, if she still loves him. He insists they will have dinner and plan their future together, charm turning to sarcasm as she says no, no, no, no. Christian's disembodied presence is a powerful force, haunting, seductive and evil – a stalker, an intruder, a ghost. Clem could succumb to her old addiction but this time she hangs up on his con-man tricks. Rushing to look at the date on the newspaper, she counts the days until her escape to Australia.

Homecoming

When Harrower's ship sailed into Sydney Harbour on Wednesday, July 1, 1959, the press was ready. *The Bulletin* announced in its 'Women's Letters' that day:

> Great preparations are in hand at the Mosman home of Mr. and Mrs. R.H. Kempley to welcome back her daughter, Elizabeth Harrower, and her friend Margaret Dick, who are arriving in the *Southern Cross* from England. Both girls are writers ...

This was the only time Harrower and her stepfather would appear together in print. Amid the fanfare the journalist mixed up 'the girls' (who were thirty-one and forty-three years old) and wrote that 'Margaret' had published several books during her eight years in London. Other journalists were waiting on that sunny winter morning to interview 'Miss Harrower' and 'Miss Dick' for the afternoon papers, and they made much of the cousins' each having published two books. Dick said politely that she was pleased to leave home and see Europe from another perspective, and that she might write a novel with an Australian background. Harrower was happy to be in Sydney but wanted to go back to London – 'I like the life there'. Both women wore their dark hair clipped short for the voyage and dressed in neat jackets for the photographs. Neither bohemian nor glamorous, there was nothing about these poised newcomers to alarm readers or North Shore neighbours. They welcomed the attention after being invisible in London, but gave wary half-answers, apparently in unison to one journalist, who wrote: 'Neither believes in using a lot of autobiographical material in their books – "You'd soon run out of ideas," they said.'

Elizabeth had left Australia eight years earlier as Miss Betty Harrower and she returned as Miss Betty Harrower, according to the passenger list on the SS *Southern Cross*. But her passport had been officially amended in 1957 from 'secretary' to 'writer'. Nostalgic scents of the Australian bush had wafted off the west coast when they pulled in at Fremantle. Waves of joy and dread had tossed her as the ship entered the harbour between North and South heads before docking in sight of the Harbour Bridge. For Margaret Dick all was marvellous, new and yet familiar, low light slanted on the golden sandstone of colonial buildings under a sky she'd only seen in Greece.

Margaret and Richard Kempley drove them across the Harbour Bridge to their home at 5 Stanley Avenue, Mosman, on the north side of the harbour. They had recently bought the property, a twentieth-century bungalow on a steep block of land that ran from the quiet street down a rocky slope. The white house was named Headlands Ho (once House) and had a Mediterranean air, with living rooms opening through glass doors onto a curved terrace. Guests were led through the house to emerge at the spectacular view over tree-framed roofs to the crescent of Balmoral Beach, and across the bay to the crouching headlands and the ocean.

Margaret Kempley was excited to have Betty home, to see her namesake cousin again, and proud to host the writers. One of her first gifts to her daughter was a regular copy of the *New Yorker*, which started a habit of many decades. Richard Kempley was almost seventy and in declining health after a lifetime of alcohol, nicotine and distemper. With thunder always threatening, the new arrivals planned to find their own accommodation as soon as money and manners allowed. But Harrower remembered the atmosphere being so dark that they moved out in a week. 'We couldn't stay there. He was a poisonous man.'

In January 1960 Kempley took off alone by ship for England and stayed away for seven months, visiting his sons in Essex. His motive might have been generous, giving his wife space to enjoy her family, or he might have left in a tantrum. Perhaps the women threw him out. Harrower and Dick made the most of the house by the bay, sitting with 'Auntie Daisy' on the terrace and inside among her displays of silver and china ornaments. They walked down the hill to Balmoral Beach, swam in the lapping sea, caught green-and-yellow ferries and went sightseeing around the city of Betty's youth. But the trip was not a holiday and work began straight away.

Sidney Baker, the *Sydney Morning Herald* literary editor and admirer of Harrower's fiction, was keen to have her write for his pages. In the first six months she reviewed a dozen books, mostly British middle-rank fiction. Her clear comments were never harsh but her strongest criticism was that a novel was a psychological study observed from outside with characters too contrived to hold attention or sympathy. One of her favourite books was the novelisation of a French film she adored, Jacques Tati's almost-wordless comedy *Monsieur Hulot's Holiday*, in which the well-meaning but bumbling Hulot creates havoc at a seaside hotel. Harrower appreciated absurdity and even silliness, and she loved people, books and films that made her laugh. She would forever picture herself as a character in *Monsieur Hulot's Holiday* when she was among crowds of would-be happy holiday-makers. In a review of a non-fiction book about the writers of the American Beat Generation and Britain's Angry Young Men, she drew on her knowledge of London theatre to argue that the disparate 'AYM' were often more petulant than angry. John Osborne of *Look Back in Anger* fame had more in common with DH Lawrence than with his contemporaries, she wrote. His protest was timeless, against 'the stock response, the phoney, the pretentious, the unfeeling heart, the wilfully blind', much like the vanities she protested against in her own writing. She didn't enjoy reviewing but continued to accept a few commissions. As she told Patrick White's biographer, David Marr, many years later, after declining to review his selection of White's letters: 'Writing about books, as opposed to writing about people, is Chinese torture to me.' However, the pocket money and association with Baker and his network were welcome. She and Dick attended the 1959 Christmas party for members of International PEN, the writers' organisation that defended freedom of speech, at the York Street offices of William Collins publishers. They were among fifty guests, including the writers Margaret Trist and Olaf Ruhen, bibliophile, publisher and ALP stalwart Walter Stone, and Gwen Meredith, creator of the long-running *Blue Hills* radio serial. Dick became a more active member than Harrower. She joined the PEN Committee on Censorship with Stone and Alex Sheppard, a Sydney bookseller and one-man publisher, who would go on to print the banned books *The Trial of Lady Chatterley* in

1965 and James Baldwin's *Another Country* in 1966 from pages sent in instalments by friends overseas.

The erosion of free speech in books, radio and television was the great concern. In one infamous instance, Alan Ashbolt, producer of the ABC's current affairs program *Four Corners,* was removed from his job for exposing political pressure on the government from the Returned Servicemen's League. The ABC denied that his transfer was connected with the RSL, but Dick and her PEN colleagues published a letter saying the 'alarming' denial brought to mind 'familiar and well-tried totalitarian tactics'. Ashbolt was returned to his job until he attacked another sacred cow and became the most censored man in the ABC.

After a six-month wait, Harrower signed a contract for *The Catherine Wheel* with Cassell in February 1960. According to her agent, the publisher had held up negotiations with niggling questions about subsidiary rights. Harrower made final edits so late in the process that the printer received a typescript with her red ballpoint marks. Her editor, Hilary Cox, had asked her to make the long novel slightly shorter by cutting out five thousand words to speed up the first half and to reduce production costs. Harrower obediently dropped two pages of Clem's conversation with a cleaning lady vacuuming her room, removed three pages of background about Clem, and made numerous nips to tighten the text and heighten the tension. 'Deletions are always an improvement,' she said after the book appeared. 'I sometimes think if everything were deleted one might have the perfect novel.'

In order to move away from the Kempleys, Harrower and Dick both needed a reliable income. Harrower took up office work in 1960, this time in the programming department of the Australian Broadcasting Commission, an environment closer to her ambitions than previous jobs. As she had done in London when she wanted to write full-time, she resigned less than a year later, before she could be tempted by interesting work and promotion. Dick, the more natural critic, was also reviewing books for the *Sydney Morning Herald* and writing for ABC radio literary programs. At the same time, she was moulding her impressions of Sydney into a novel.

The Catherine Wheel was published in October 1960 and the first brief review came from the *Times Literary Supplement*. The characters of Clemency and Christian 'emerge with abrupt life, but their love is not communicated', wrote the reviewer. 'If the author fails to touch the heart she is, however, successful in her precise exploration of London's bed-sitting rooms, home of the rootless thousands without homes ...' The literary weekly *John O'London's* declared 'really excellent' this 'almost frighteningly well-perceived and subtly-told tale of what is really a rather sordid love affair'. Miss Harrower, the female reviewer concluded, came close to answering the question, 'What does she *see* in him?' In Belfast the novel was declared 'A strange one, but good' and in Aberdeen, 'A fine study of human emotions and failings'.

To her dismay, there was no review in *The Observer* and Harrower promptly wrote to the newspaper's deputy editor, John Douglas Pringle, with a copy of the novel. She had reasons to feel emboldened. Scottish-born Pringle had been editor of the *Sydney Morning Herald* for five years while she was in London. He had taken an enthusiastic interest in the paper's coverage of books, even commissioning and writing reviews. He had sent Patrick White's *The Tree of Man* to the poet AD Hope, who trashed the novel as 'pretentious and illiterate verbal sludge'. She had seen him give an amusing talk to the Society of Australian Writers in London and in her covering letter thanked him because 'Life in London wasn't always hilarious.' She had been too shy to speak to him then. Pringle wrote a cheerful letter back to Harrower, pleased to receive her book and letter, sorry they had not met, and committing to read *The Catherine Wheel*. He waffled sympathetically about the difficulty of giving attention to the enormous number of novels published but assured her that the good ones were not ignored for long. Their correspondence did not result in a review.

In Australia, two influential writers expressed opposing views. Nancy Keesing in *The Bulletin* placed *The Catherine Wheel* in a growing class of novels about intimate relationships between lovers, whose best practitioners included Colette, Rosamond Lehmann and Simone de Beauvoir. But she found Harrower's prose 'clumsy and irritatingly mannered' and Clemency 'too mixed up and self-centred to depict herself or her feelings in the round'. She suggested an outsider viewpoint would have been more interesting. In the *Sydney Morning Herald* – too late for Christmas shopping – Barbara Jefferis appreciated the novel

Harrower had actually written, with 'no secondhand emotions ... no faked solutions, none of the emotional clichés most writers use to spare themselves the trouble of profound thought'. She complained about the slow opening but praised Harrower's characterisation, economy of plotting, and the depiction of 'the mechanics of loneliness' in all her novels. Few Australian novels had matched this one in 'understanding the way in which anguish leads to the gradual getting of wisdom', she concluded. Other reviewers found Christian 'one of the most remarkable character-creations in recent fiction' and recognised Harrower's 'gift for sensitive and accurate character analysis and an incisive clarity of style'.

Harrower had been drawn to Cassell partly because they published some other Australian books. But the Australian novel they advertised on the dust jacket of *The Catherine Wheel* was a very different creature. *Unlucky Dip* by Margaret Henry was a murder mystery set on a cattle station and conformed to the stereotypes expected by the British. This made Harrower's writing seem all the more sophisticated, or more esoteric. No one repeated Sid Baker's comparison of Harrower with DH Lawrence in his review of *The Long Prospect*, even though *The Catherine Wheel* could be likened to *Lady Chatterley's Lover* for its depiction of a tempestuous affair across class lines, minus graphic sex scenes and obscenities.

When in 1961 Sidney Baker wrote a historical survey about the importance of women writers in Australian literature, Harrower was the youngest on his list of notable novelists that also named Henry Handel Richardson, Eleanor Dark, Katharine Susannah Prichard, Christina Stead, Kylie Tennant, Helen Simpson, Eve Langley, Mary Durack and Ethel Anderson. (Dozens more were not far behind, he added, including Ernestine Hill, Helen Heney, Barbara Jefferis, Ruth Park and Elizabeth O'Conner.) Her first long interview, with Melbourne journalist John Hetherington, appeared in both *The Age* and the *West Australian*, nudging her towards a national profile. This came about because Olaf Ruhen, who knew Harrower through PEN, wrote to Hetherington recommending he read *The Catherine Wheel* in spite of *The Bulletin's* negative review. Hetherington raised the question of why Harrower's novels had roused so little notice outside Sydney when 'many authors whose work is less arresting than hers are better known and better respected than hers'. He placed her in a small but growing school of Australian novelists interested in people more than places and in the city not the bush, unlike those writers who described setting 'in conscientious, and often tiresome detail'. Hetherington revealed the address at 12 Hayes Street, Neutral Bay, of a pleasant small house where the Misses Harrower and Dick shared a bedsit 'in complete amicability'. Harrower worked on her seven-year-old portable typewriter at a table in the kitchenette, while Dick typed in the bed-sitting room, six days a week. Both were writing novels set in Sydney and Harrower expected hers to be more about people and less about the city than *Down in the City*. 'Perhaps that will make it a better novel,' she suggested. She had come home to refresh her knowledge of Australians and moved out of her mother's house with its panoramic view because – she half-lied:

> I've concluded I can't write in comfort. I was comfortable for the first twenty-three years of my life, and also bored all the time ... From the time I was on my own in London, I was never bored, though rarely comfortable, and I found no difficulty at all in working.

She would return to London because she feared becoming a 'mental beachcomber' in Sydney, and 'learning always has to be done the hard way'. Her ruthless writing did not please everyone, she said. 'The truth about people is never hard – it is simply true', and people who didn't like the truth reminded her of a woman who sang 'I want to hear of beautiful things' in *The World of Paul Slickey*, John Osborne's 1959 musical satire about Fleet Street gossip columnists.

Harrower told Hetherington that she liked theatre, ballet, opera and reading, and her favourite authors were Stendhal, Tolstoy, Mauriac, Saul Bellow, Truman Capote, Elizabeth Bowen and Nadine Gordimer. Not an Australian among them. Did she notice on the reverse side of her interview in *The Age* a review of a book about Patrick White's writing by Geoffrey Dutton? If so, she might have thought she could get on with this granite-faced Anglo-Australian whose fiction, according to the reviewer, was admired in Europe but often condemned at home, whose writing did not pull punches and was concerned with the meaning of truth, love, beauty, and the difficulty of staying sane in life's tragicomedy.

Photographer Jill Crossley shot portraits of a serious-faced Harrower for the article and future publicity. One would fill the back cover of her next novel. For some, Harrower sat in the kitchenette at her Laminex-topped table typing (or pretending to type) a story, 'The North Sea', about a doctor who retreats from London to a Scottish hotel while shaken by her recent divorce. Crossley, at the age of ninety-six, remembered Harrower as 'sensitive, gentle, a bit self-effacing and modest about herself'. They talked little because, she said, 'we were both very shy, quiet and not socially outgoing'.

Word of mouth persuaded Harrower that there was growing international interest in Australian writing since the US publication of White's novel *The Tree of Man* and a Hollywood film of Ray Lawler's play *The Summer of the Seventeenth Doll*. She had kept American rights to her novels out of her contracts with Cassell, and now asked her London agent to send *The Catherine Wheel* across the Atlantic and she began contacting literary agents in the United States. Nine American publishers had turned down *The Long Prospect* and several agents could not see any market for her books. Polite rejections of *The Catherine Wheel* came in one by one from Harper, Simon & Schuster, William Morrow and others. One agent in New York, Willis Kingsley Wing, was nonetheless pleased to represent her and see her new work.

Harrower had written half a dozen short stories, which she gradually sent to Wing in the hope that they were easier than novels to sell to the American market. In the next couple of years he reported rejections of at least six stories by magazines from *Ladies' Home Journal* and *Good Housekeeping* to the *New Yorker, Atlantic, Harper's* and *Gentlemen's Quarterly*. The *New Yorker* passed on 'The Last Days' – the tense finale to *The Catherine Wheel* – with the comment that Clem's telephone conversation with her ex-lover Christian was good but the story wasn't sharp enough. Wing advised that one story, 'The Expatriate', was unsuitable for women's magazines because 'the other woman' was the winner. 'The Cornucopia' lacked plot and, he moralised, the central character, a manipulative society woman called Julia, got away with too much given that 'shoddiness of character is usually easily recognized and dealt with'. This was the whole point of Harrower's fiction, that people got away with appalling behaviour, and that wives did not always win nor even deserve to. Her hard-learned understanding of human nature did not fit with the commercial desire for happy endings. Most of her stories would remain unpublished for another fifty years, and some forever. With long-delayed justice, *Harper's* magazine would publish an abridged version of 'The Cornucopia' in 2015.

Harrower was making progress on a new novel and trying her hand at writing plays, which were in demand for theatre, radio and the new medium of television. Her first attempt was an adaptation of *The Catherine Wheel*, which followed closely the novel's dialogue and its claustrophobic bedsit and coffee lounge settings. None of the critics had remarked on the obvious theatrical qualities in her writing, yet the prose was still difficult to remake for the stage. At first she dismissed the result as amateur and too wordy, but later she told Wing she had put it aside without showing anyone because she had no confidence in local standards of acting. She sent an original play called *The Bosom of the Family* to her London agent, David Bolt, who made a valiant effort to help. Eventually he wrote back apologising that the theatrical agents at David Higham and Theatrework had not considered it 'vigorous' enough for production in London, but they thought the characters were well handled, some scenes moving, and Harrower had a 'feel' for theatre. They urged her to contact Sydney directors John MacCallum at Williamson Theatres, Hugh Hunt at the Elizabethan Theatre Trust and John Carson, son of the actress Sibyl Thorndike. Harrower either ditched the play or reworked it into *Beginners' Class*, which began with a squabbling family fixated on a new television set and quickly devolved into a soap opera about their corruption by postwar affluence and happiness measured in harbourside apartments, car ownership and electric toasters. The play is an examination of her feelings about returning to Sydney, her proxy a poor male artist who went to Europe for heart surgery, beleaguered on his return by a conventional wife, a mother-in-law who is like 'holding the Olympic Games in a canary cage', and a drunk sister having a disastrous affair. Her sugar daddy, a married advertising executive, bullies the artist to join his agency and make bacon commercials. Harrower entered *Beginners' Class* in an Australian competition, whose judges ranked it 'about third' among a hundred, and passed it on to the Elizabethan Theatre Trust, where interest stalled. From New York, Wing responded that *Beginners' Class* might work better for television than stage but he warned that materialism as the root of evil was a well-worn theme. She agreed the play was 'the least original and least feeling piece of work I had ever written'. In April 1963 she wrote to Wing that she wasn't surprised he had been unable to place yet another story, 'The Beautiful Climate', and that there was no point trying to sell it in Australia, where the fee would hardly cover paper and postage. She might privately have hesitated to publish at home the too-recognisable story about the island weekender where a girl and her mother were held hostage by her father. Anyway, she added, she was now working for Macmillan and using her spare moments to finish a novel. After that she would try to send some more saleable stories. Impatience crept into her letters and behind his back she referred to Willis Kingsley Wing as Wee Willy Winky.

Harrower would shape her pent-up disappointment into an essay titled 'The Short Story: Australia' – the only time she wrote about the publishing industry – for the *Kenyon Review* International Symposium on the Short Story. This survey of the market and the art of the story by leading writers from every continent occupied three issues of the American literary magazine in 1968–69. She put the question directly: 'Is there a paying market for serious short fiction in Australia? The only answer at this time is: emphatically not.' Since the heyday of the short story, some time between settlement and the Second World War, she wrote, magazines such as *The Bulletin* and quarterlies had become more interested in non-fiction, criticism, qualifications and money-making than in creative work by living writers. Her argument became a personal manifesto: 'Australia is not a metaphysical country,' she complained, and young people who were 'good at English' were turning to journalism or television, where producers and technicians had control. Even so, it was easier to publish novels or poems than a collection of short stories. Where once writers would first offer their stories overseas, 'Europeans and Americans frequently feel an understandable resistance to the idea that human beings in Australia have the same significance as those in centres of power, or backwaters made familiar by art'. There were paradoxes in Harrower's protest: she had until recently been one of those uninterested in Australian writing, and here she was being published in the United States as a non-fiction writer for US$100 after failing to sell her fiction. She ended on a melodramatic note that no writer would abort a story for lack of a market. 'Having placed so much of himself in jeopardy, he [sic] waits for understanding, or the news that he would be well advised to commit suicide ... for he has no other way of spending his life.'

Harrower interrupted her novel to write this piece, responding to an invitation that came via Geoffrey Dutton from the editor seeking his advice. She was in good company with writers including William Saroyan, Mordecai Richler, Nadine Gordimer, Maurice Shadbolt and Christina Stead, who wrote her lyrical essay about the importance of stories in her own life, 'Ocean of Story'. However, when Laurie Hergenhan at the University of Queensland asked to reproduce Harrower's piece in *Australian Literary Studies* in 1981, she refused, with a hint of embarrassment at its tone, because so much had changed for writers in the Whitlam years.

New connections

Joseph Heller's satire *Catch-22* came out in 1961, putting a phrase into the English language that perfectly fitted Elizabeth Harrower's dilemma. She had written nonstop for almost a decade, published three novels in quick succession, and attracted admiring attention in Britain and especially Australia. In her thirties she could just about call herself an established author. But she wondered if she could keep up the pace and make a living from her writing. Book sales were still small, royalties limped in at a few pounds twice a year, and each title was remaindered after two or three years. The American market remained a solid wall of indifference. An application to the Commonwealth Literary Fund for a fellowship to write her fourth novel was unsuccessful. Exactly when she and Dick decided to stay in Australia is unclear, as it was to them. They kept saying they would leave soon but they were working without a break to establish themselves in Sydney, and there was nothing waiting for them in London. There were practical questions, too, such as a letter from David Higham in March 1960 suggesting that if Harrower planned to stay in Australia she should fill out British paperwork to avoid paying tax in both countries. Undecided, she kept the blank form as a kind of insurance.

There was enough happening in Australia to keep them engaged and hopeful of a breakthrough. Sid Baker, as book pages editor at the *Herald* until 1963, was well-connected and sociable, despite suffering from multiple sclerosis and having a 'reputation of fractiousness and irascibility'. Even to Harrower he could be blunt, sending a deflating note to say *The Catherine Wheel* was skilfully done but not as good as her first two novels, especially *The Long Prospect*. In the next sentence he invited her and Margaret Dick to a party. They became regular guests at the home of Baker and his wife Barbara, and for Harrower he set off a chain reaction that formed some of her most life-changing friendships.

Dick shared his interest in linguistics and learnt about Australian usage from his book *The Australian Language*, as well as becoming one of his frequent reviewers.

Harrower dared to write a letter to Sir Allen Lane of Penguin Books in London with the hope of bringing her past novels back to life in Penguin's quality line of orange-and-white paperbacks. Boldly she pointed out that her name had been linked by Australian critics with Patrick White, but that her novels had been issued in London with no publicity. She knew this was a long shot but it turned out to be a timely move as she flushed out two more champions. Max Harris and Geoffrey Dutton were among Adelaide's most energetic literary entrepreneurs, with confidence, charm and cross-fertilising activities that gave them significant influence. A poet and editor, Harris had survived the embarrassment of the Ern Malley hoax in 1944 when he published nonsense poems submitted under the pseudonym by the young poets Harold Stewart and James McAuley to ridicule his modernist taste. He bounced back to run the Mary Martin Bookshop and co-found the literary and art quarterly *Australian Letters* with Dutton, Bryn Davies and Rosemary Wighton. In 1961 he started *Australian Book Review*, devoted to criticism of Australian books, and he and Dutton were appointed by Sir Allen Lane as the local editorial committee for Penguin Books. Elizabeth Harrower was advised by the Sydney manager to contact Harris and wasted no time writing to him with copies of *The Long Prospect* and *The Catherine Wheel*. Harris had not heard of her books but wrote an encouraging letter saying '*The Long Prospect* represents one of the really major achievements in the postwar Australian novel.' He intended to help with Penguin and do a feature on her in *Australian Letters*, and suggested that her work, 'of singularly intellectual and reflective character', had been misdirected to the commercial market. She replied, almost giddy with gratitude, that she was in need of a literary knight errant and confided that she had dreamt of him telling her how bad her short stories were. She offered him a section of her novel in progress, which he declined in favour of running an excerpt from *The Long Prospect* and one of six short stories she sent him. He chose 'Lance Harper, His Story', which he summarised as the life of an effeminate young man, a reductive description of a gentle character whose mission was to self-educate by reading and learning what made 'a classic'; Lance might have been any bookish young man or woman.

Harrower's fiction was introduced by Harris's unsigned but glowing overview of her work in *Australian Letters*. He was the first of many in decades to come who complained that her novels had received 'perfunctory critical attention on the one hand, and an almost non-existent market demand on the other' in the 'inchoate mass of contemporary publishing'. She deserved far better, he argued:

> Along with Patrick White, albeit of slighter range and power than Australia's dominating literary genius, she stands head and shoulders above the current pack of sociological realists in the national novel. Way below her, Randolph Stow and Christopher Koch are groping for the kind of penetrating humanism that she has realised fully and beautifully.

In his many cultural roles Harris promised to open endless doors along a hall of mirrors. He urged Elizabeth Harrower and Margaret Dick to attend Adelaide Writers' Week in March 1962, not as speakers but to enjoy the talks and social gatherings. They went by car with some friends from PEN, two days' driving and singing across western New South Wales, across the endless flat Hay Plains, across northern Victoria and into South Australia. Harrower was marked forever by the shared adventure and outback landscapes. She remembered: 'Olaf Ruhen sang, "We're going back to Yarrawonga, where the skies are always blue. Life is longer in Yarrawonga …" He sang a lot of First World War songs. The amazing thing was he had sold some stories in America, unheard of. Only Morris West had sold things in America, just didn't happen.'

Ruhen was a New Zealand-born writer, a hardy sailor and adventurer, who worked in Sydney as a journalist and author of books based on his travels in Australia, New Guinea and the South Pacific; as a prolific short-story writer, he was well paid by the popular American magazine the *Saturday Evening Post*. After they'd got on well at PEN writers' meetings, Ruhen had championed Harrower's fiction, and his success encouraged her to pursue US publication, though she learnt that men's tales of war and exploration were in more demand than women's domestic struggles.

Adelaide Writers' Week was Australia's first writers' festival, launched in 1960 as a biennial offshoot of the internationally known Adelaide Festival of Arts. The program for the second Writers' Week, at Adelaide University, was heavy with scholarly earnestness and cultural defensiveness. Geoffrey Dutton gave a bright opening speech, followed by West Australian writer TAG Hungerford's address on 'The infiltration of canned overseas culture on Australian writers'. There were talks on poetry, fiction, education, contemporary English theatre and English television. Frank Dalby Davison, author of the beloved novels *Man-Shy* and *Dusty*, lectured on 'The problems of Australian writers' and poet David Rowbotham led a public forum that asked, 'Is the short story dead?' Fiction was represented by Olaf Ruhen and John O'Grady, who had written the comic migrant novel *They're a Weird Mob* under the pseudonym Nino Culotta. Xavier Herbert spoke about his epic novel *Capricornia*. Max Harris chaired an afternoon poetry reading by Kenneth Slessor, Colin Thiele, Chris Wallace-Crabbe, Ian Mudie and others. Mary Durack, known for her 1959 family history *Kings in Grass Castles*, was the only woman on the program, chairing a session. Harrower and Dick were billed with local newspaper journalist and author Ted Smith and his wife Nancy, whose Brighton house was a hub of boozy conviviality. At a festival party they mingled with writers such as Kylie Tennant, Nancy Cato, Patsy Adam-Smith, Nene Gare, and the influential Angus & Robertson editor, Beatrice Davis. Harrower would form the long-lasting opinion that Davis had no interest in her or her novels and became an obstacle to her progress.

After the festival, Harrower wrote to Harris that she was glad to have met him and that Adelaide had been instructive because she learnt that you will, and should, make enemies in the literary world. She'd been seen as the

> representative of Max Harris, Patrick White, literary quarterlies, complexity as against a 'normal' view of life, of the city as against the outback, Europeans as against aborigines, of meaning as against sales,

and the world as against Australia ... I was treated to a great, endless, boring bombardment of words. In a way, you can only argue with people you agree with. When Greek meets Red Indian he might as well save his breath ...

Without naming the bores, Harrower sounded hypersensitive, as if she'd never been in a room full of writers before. Harris ignored her gripes. He asked her to write reviews and do research for a documentary he was writing, *The Land That Waited;* suggested showing her books to the managing director of Faber and Faber, and her play to Harry Kippax, theatre critic at *Nation* magazine. She replied too late that Margaret Dick would like the research job, always trying to advance her career too. While nothing came immediately from his enthusiasm, Harris remained a friend who visited Harrower at home in Sydney and praised her books at every chance. She would always credit him with having 'discovered' *The Long Prospect*. His *Australian Book Review* ran a biting review of *Son of Mars*, a novel by a well-known journalist and broadcaster, which began, 'At his best Mungo MacCallum can write like a poor man's Elizabeth Harrower ...' In contrast to his 'puffed-up egotism', she was held up with Patrick White, George Turner and Hal Porter as 'formidable exponents of "literary" writing', with a lovely compliment: 'Her eye is always on the sparrow – the essential detail that exposes character and motive ...'

Harrower told Harris with some irony that her 'abortive attempts to make a fortune' from short stories in America had held up her novel. Having written a draft, she was about to put it aside for some time and take a job.

By the middle of 1962 Harrower and Dick were renting a flat at the back of a Federation-style house at 6 Want Street, Mosman, a pleasant yet poignantly named address for struggling writers. Harrower wanted to be near her mother's house but far enough away from her stepfather, who was hostile to her and most visitors. Instead, Margaret Kempley would go to the flat once a week, and the three women talked and laughed with a relaxed freedom that was impossible at Stanley Avenue. Harrower cared deeply for her mother, but her love was mixed with pity, frustration and boredom at her narrow existence. She could not see Margaret Kempley as a whole person, and she was determined not to give up her own identity for a man or anyone else.

*

At one of Sidney Baker's parties, Elizabeth Harrower had her first conversation with Kylie Tennant, a highly regarded writer and larger-than-life fixture in Australian publishing. Tennant by the age of fifty had published eight novels based on people and places she'd encountered during research in the hard years of Depression and war, ranging from *Foveaux*, set in the slums of Surry Hills, to the roving unemployed of *The Battlers*, and *Ride on Stranger*, about a country girl's move to the city. With a disabled husband and two children to support, travel and writing had become more difficult, so she had taken on work from home as the reader of Australian manuscripts for Macmillan & Co., the publisher of her books, and a role that extended to becoming an influential literary adviser and advocate. The London-based company had recently established a Melbourne office in the hope of expanding its local list and improving distribution.

The self-described 'Great Australian Bottleneck', Tennant was both hardworking and chaotic, kind and bossy. She remembered meeting Harrower with Margaret Dick, 'both very charming people', among other guests at Sid Baker's house in Double Bay and almost immediately swept her under her large wing. When she learnt that Harrower – still failing to sell her stories and plays – needed another source of income while she worked on her novel, she recommended her to the Macmillan bosses in London as a capable manager for their planned Sydney office. So began a fateful friendship. Tennant would recall many years – and many dramas – later that Harrower was both 'very, very efficient' in the job and 'rather took me over and did good deeds for me for years ... She's the kind of person who doesn't let me get away with anything.'

Harrower joined the new office of Macmillan publishers on December 10, 1962, and returned to the familiar city streets near Sydney Town Hall. This time she sat in a showroom for Macmillan books, waiting for occasional customers while receiving orders from booksellers, typing invoices, sending out books, answering phone calls, and reporting to both Melbourne and London. Never keen on housework, she dusted the display books only when essential, shamed once by a browsing priest who asked where he could wash his hands after handling some of them.

The children's author and educator Maurice Saxby asked his students in the writers' group at Alexander Mackie Teachers' College in 1963 if anyone would like to interview a very good writer called Elizabeth Harrower. Mary Quinion and Ellen Nixon volunteered and went upstairs to the Macmillan office in Pitt Street, a bare space on the first floor, where Harrower gave them coffee and an interview for the college literary magazine. She impressed them as being alone but not lonely, friendly but restrained, and answering their questions without gushing. Nixon was struck by Harrower's comment that her years as a writer in London were 'like living on a knife edge'. She told them,

> I would not have taken this job if I had not had a novel three-quarters finished. I rush home, have dinner and work from seven till nine. On Saturday and Sunday I work all day ... I take two nights off each week ... My novels have been written and rewritten until I have felt I have said what I intended ... No, you cannot write about what you do not know.

Harrower built strong relationships with booksellers but also became caught up in the new venture's tedious problems such as lazy sales representatives and excessive phone bills, to which she applied her 'Scottish blood' when asked to cut costs. There were many pleasures, too. She got on extremely well with the top executives, first with Tony Rudkin, who returned to London soon after hiring her, but continued to write personal letters about his reading of philosophy and his young family as well as office matters.

Among her confidants were two English gentlemen who became her friends – Robert Cross, head of the Australian operation in Melbourne, and Alan Maclean, the company's director in London, attentive editor of Rebecca West, CP Snow, Muriel Spark and Shirley Hazzard. Maclean had joined the company in 1954 after his brother Donald's exposure as a

Soviet spy required Alan to leave the Foreign Service. Harold Macmillan returned to the family publishing business as chairman in 1963, after seven years as prime minister, and rewarded Maclean's commercial and diplomatic elan with promotion. Both Maclean and Cross wrote Harrower frequent appreciative letters, asked about the progress of her novel, and when in Sydney took her out to lunches and dinners with Kylie Tennant or alone. As well as her basic office duties, she sent a Christmas garland to Maclean, and Christmas greetings to Sir Harold Macmillan, which he read out at the staff party.

Tennant recognised Harrower's talent for organising company dinners and parties. One of her early tasks was to make arrangements for Dame Edith Sitwell's Sydney visit, putting her up at Fernleigh Castle in Rose Bay, a private hotel that had hosted stars such as the ballet dancer Robert Helpmann, and acting couple Laurence Olivier and Vivian Leigh. London office considered Tennant 'the only person of suitable stature' to meet the grand old poet and critic Sitwell, but Harrower was a welcome presence at their meetings. A horde of journalists and a few Macmillan authors were invited to meet the frail Dame Edith, 'lying on her bed like a great porcelain doll, wearing a long black dress and black picture hat', in the words of author Nancy Phelan. Harrower would get to know Phelan at Macmillan, and as a colourful, funny, well-connected friend in Sydney and the Blue Mountains.

Despite the solitude of her office, some of Elizabeth Harrower's closest friendships began there. One day an enormous man in a suit and hat came up the stairs unannounced. She wondered if he was going to arrest her. Judah Waten, a Russian-born Jewish communist, whose books were published then by the left-wing Australasian Book Society, was up from Melbourne and had come especially to introduce himself. Harrower noted the date in her diary, June 14, 1963, because she was flattered that he had sought her out after hearing of her, and possibly reading one of her books. 'We were friends from that day,' she remembered. 'He was a subtle, kind, life-enhancing man.' Waten was 'the first Australian writer to write "from the inside" about non-English-speaking migrants' and a leading name on lists of 'realist, left-wing or migrant writers' in Australia. Born in Odessa, Ukraine, in 1911, he had come to Australia from Palestine with his parents as a small child and joined the Communist Party of Australia as a schoolboy in 1927. When he met Elizabeth Harrower, he had revisited his personal history as fictionalised stories in *Alien Son* and *The Unbending*, which were praised for their vivid storytelling more than their prose.

Every time Waten was in Sydney for a political or literary meeting he took her to dinner at a Greek restaurant in the city or she cooked at her place. Waten liked to walk around the city, visiting the sites of his youth, talking about politics, writing, people, giving advice on her career, health, and life. Between visits they kept up a warm correspondence. After their first dinner, Waten wrote that he had 'enjoyed your company very much' and sent a copy of his detective novel *Shares in Murder*, which critics hadn't liked but the English poet Robert Graves had, with some chiding about poor writing.

'I am a clumsy writer and I can't help it although I am always trying to lift my writing,' he said modestly in a letter full of blotches and crossed-out words. She replied that his book was 'new and surprising territory to me' and that she had at last read and admired Henry Handel Richardson's *Maurice Guest*. As for her own writing, between work and caring for a visiting friend who'd had a 'crack-up', she'd only had time to change the line 'She thought she suffered' to 'She suffered'. She hoped in another month to underline the sentence. 'I've been involved for months now in the business of rescuing (really, failing to) someone from a nervous breakdown,' she wrote. The unnamed friend was Christine Cooper, an Oxford Classics scholar from London who knew no one else in Sydney. She recovered and went home, but the 'crack-ups' of others would recur surprisingly often in Harrower's life as interruptions to her writing.

*

Kylie Tennant was soon central to every part of Harrower's life. After bringing her into the office, she became an advocate for her writing with her superiors at Macmillan. She wrote to head office in London in 1963 urging the general manager, 'Rache' Lovat Dickson, to revive *Down in the City* and *The Long Prospect* as Pan paperbacks after their poor treatment by Cassell. He replied with a roundabout knock-back that summed up so much of Harrower's publishing history. He felt warmly towards Harrower and would do more for her than for most authors, he wrote, but her out-of-print novels would not be commercial in the competitive paperback field where Pan made its money from the likes of Ian Fleming, author of the James Bond spy thrillers. He hoped they might publish her novel-in-progress and, if that were successful, possibly consider the paperbacks, and went on to say:

> I haven't any doubt that Elizabeth has had a hard deal, and I can well believe that Patrick White's books overshadowed hers. I can also understand that the reprinting of them would be warmly received in Australia, but the kindness and generosity of your heart betrays you in this case … There is no-one in Australia, except you, whom I would rather see succeed.

Harrower lost Dickson's distant kindliness when he retired in 1964 but Tennant didn't give up. When she volunteered to create an Australian version of Macmillan's annual collection of British short stories, she made sure to feature new stories by Harrower in two volumes of *Summer's Tales*. She also chose stories by Hal Porter, Mary Durack, Patsy Adam-Smith, Nancy Phelan, Patricia Rolfe, Margaret Dick, Kay Brown, herself, and others – mostly friends – from about twelve hundred submissions. Judah Waten wrote a story at her request, but she knocked it back as rushed and below par. Intent on finishing his new novel, *Distant Land*, Waten good-naturedly promised to review the book for the left-wing press and told Tennant privately that he most liked her story and Harrower's, but disliked Porter's as 'devoid of any human affection'. The predominance of women in the collection Tennant put down to women being more reliable, and writing more stories based on realist experiences. She differentiated her authors from the academic writers dominant in the 1963–64 edition of the anthology *Coast to Coast* edited by Leonie Kramer.

Tennant wanted a cheerful collection, or in the words of her husband, Lewis Rodd, 'she wants to strike a note away from depravity and gloom – [towards] humanity and humour …' Neither of Harrower's stories was cheerful but each was certainly rich with humanity and dry strokes of humour. 'The Cost of Things', published in 1964, made a critique of contemporary consumerist society through a man torn between memories of his former lover – a single woman he worked with at a film unit – and the comforts and demands of domestic life with his wife and children. Her second story in 1965, 'English Lesson', was a psychological study of a woman's shock at receiving an insulting letter from an unnamed person on an unspecified subject. In her office job Harrower also had to send out review copies and help make up orders of the books. *Summer's Tales* came out in Britain, Canada and the United States, at last presenting Harrower to American readers. Tennant was anxious that the venture should create a new market for Australian short stories (and 'long' short stories), which were being squeezed out by *The Bulletin* and many quarterlies in favour of criticism. She advised prospective writers to 'adjust themselves to new forms' by reading stories in the *New Yorker*, and especially those by Shirley Hazzard or Frank O'Connor. 'The plots may not alter but the style of telling must be 1966 not 1930.'

Reaching far beyond her role as reader of Australian manuscripts, Tennant was a prolific letter writer and generous adviser to authors, always giving feedback on submissions whether accepted or returned. She pushed Macmillan to consider books for publication in Australia that might not suit the UK market, and gradually wrenched open management minds to more adventurous thinking about Australian fiction and creative non-fiction.

*

In addition to her professional advocacy, Tennant also extended Harrower's social circles, most importantly by connecting her with Patrick White. Harrower liked to say she met White in the early 1960s through the theatre director John Sumner while White was focused on playwriting. She would soon give up her own efforts to write for the stage and revert to her lifelong role as enthusiastic theatregoer. British-born Sumner had made his mark in Melbourne with the Union Theatre's 1955 premiere production of Ray Lawler's *Summer of the Seventeenth Doll* and a London production, which Harrower may have seen. The play about

Queensland canecutters and their barmaid girlfriends in Sydney was hailed as a landmark for Australian theatre as *Look Back in Anger* was for British theatre. When Harrower was in Adelaide, the Adelaide Festival of Arts had whipped up outrage and publicity by turning away White's much-rejected play, *The Ham Funeral*, for the 1962 program. Perhaps she did then see the 'epoch-making' production, directed by John Tasker, at the Palace Theatre in Sydney. Along with Tasker, Sumner became one of the champions of White's plays about ordinary and often unpleasant people. He directed the suburban satires *The Season at Sarsaparilla* and *A Cheery Soul* in Melbourne in 1962 and 1963 with mixed success.

Harrower moved into White's orbit during that period. But the friendship really began when Kylie Tennant drove her out to visit White and his partner Manoly Lascaris at their Castle Hill property, Dogwoods, on the outskirts of Sydney. The two men had met in Alexandria during the war while Lascaris was serving with the Greek Army and White with the Royal Air Force; they moved together to Australia, and to semi-rural Castle Hill, in 1948. Tennant blew into White's life in 1956 after taking offence at AD Hope's notorious review of *The Tree of Man* as 'pretentious and illiterate verbal sludge'. She proposed to Sid Baker that she should interview the author for the *Herald* and, unstoppable force that she was, Baker and White at first resisted and then agreed. White told her he had been dejected after the failure of his previous novel, *The Aunt's Story*, until *The Tree of Man* began to take shape in his mind 'down by the cowbails' on the farm. Although the book was topping bestseller lists, he said he would have felt like putting his head in a gas oven if not for the enthusiasm of American critics. Tennant told White she'd had a terrifying dream about him with a blue face, and likened his novels to stained glass and to the paintings on the walls by his London friend Roy de Maistre. He found both her and her interview crazy but she was amusing company and serious about books, and she had championed his novel without a mention of Hope's name. She would review his novel *Voss* the following year and pick up his first Miles Franklin Literary Award on his behalf.

Tennant and her family were regular visitors to Dogwoods by the time she drove Harrower out there in 1964 for an impromptu visit. White and Lascaris emerged to meet Harrower in the car.

White was born in London in 1912 and, after an Australian early childhood and a Cambridge education, he had begun writing there, decades earlier than Harrower and backed by family money and connections. But they quickly found common ground in the extraordinary coincidence of having just missed being neighbours in Gertrude Jensen's house in Sloane Gardens by a matter of weeks in 1958. That year White and Lascaris had made their first visit back to Europe since settling together in Castle Hill. In August they arrived in London from Greece and rented the large ground floor flat, No. 10, at 34 Sloane Gardens, as a base for visiting White's frail mother and other relatives and friends. Mrs Jensen mentioned to them that a young Australian writer called Elizabeth Harrower had been living upstairs in the attic until a few weeks earlier. White would remember the name when they met at Castle Hill.

He and Lascaris stayed with Mrs Jensen twice in 1958 and he recommended her rooms to other friends such as Geoffrey Dutton. Harrower remembered her as a 'pretty appalling' landlady who 'watched everyone coming and going like a concierge', made her son share her bed when he came home on school holidays, and dispensed 'negative charm round her unfortunate guests'. Mrs Jensen had told White the young Australian writer had 'very expensive cosmetics', a detail he recalled in a 1972 letter to Harrower about 'that warren where we all lived and you were doing things with the cosmetics.'

London had injected both White and Harrower in their youth with European culture that they remade, in their own styles, into Australian literature. His intellectual ambition and scepticism were exactly what she hungered for among the lotus eaters of Sydney. She was dismayed, but also slightly comforted, that with six books published he still had delayed shipments from England, harsh words from critics, and difficulty selling his work. Their friendship would take off after White and Lascaris left the outer suburbs and moved to Centennial Park in Sydney's east in 1964. On January 2, 1965, he invited Harrower, Tennant and Sumner to dinner. Kylie was soon complaining that Elizabeth saw more of Patrick than she did.

*

Through the 1960s, Harrower spent more time with Tennant than with anyone except Margaret Dick. As well as working for the same company, in early 1965 they jointly bought a property named Hillside Farm, a ramshackle fibro cottage on three acres at Blackheath. Margaret Kempley gave Elizabeth her half of the money, assuring her anxious daughter that tax had been paid on it when she and Kempley sold out of a business. 'Silly things may have been done in the past, Bet darling, but with the Taxation Dept. NEVER', Margaret wrote from the *SS Himalaya* in Penang. In an earlier letter written in Cornwall, she authorised 'Bet darling' to take money from her bank account and told her to stop worrying. She agreed it was nice for Betty and Margaret Dick to have separate outings, and added: 'I know exactly what you mean. I'm a different person on my own. I know it!' The Blue Mountains, west of Sydney, were a favourite holiday place and health retreat for city people seeking clear, bush air. Elizabeth had been there many times since childhood and on her return from London, she and Margaret Dick went with the Kempleys to visit her Newcastle schoolfriend, Barbara Ward, who was holidaying with her family in the mountains. Barbara had made 'Bet' godmother to her two daughters, Toni and Robyn, born in the 1950s while she was away, and they joyfully reconnected. For Elizabeth the mountains linked her past and her future. The cooler weather, forested slopes, and sheer sandstone escarpments shared a touch of drama with the Scottish Highlands. Kylie Tennant persuaded her that getting away to the country for weekends would give her peaceful time for writing.

But Tennant was a whirlwind. Sixteen years older than Harrower, she had published eight novels, mostly with Macmillan, as well as history, biography, children's books, plays and criticism by the mid-1960s. She had raised her young children – Benison, born in 1946, and John in 1951 – in Laurieton on the New South Wales north coast where her husband was a school principal for thirteen years, and had done much of her travel and writing from there. Back in Sydney, Lewis Rodd's depression worsened and he made several suicide attempts. In 1961, soon after Kylie had told him about a long-ago brief affair, he suffered a breakdown and threw himself under a train at Circular Quay, fractured his skull, lost an arm and a foot, but survived. Tennant coped in her joking way by calling him

'Privet Hedge Rodd' when he was semi-conscious, because he had clipped himself around the edges. But she felt that their marriage never recovered, and that she became a nurse rather than a wife. Mostly housebound, Rodd continued to type one-handed, write his own books and edit manuscripts by Tennant and others, managing their business affairs, often taking charge of the teenagers and their house at Hunters Hill while she travelled and worked harder than ever to support the family.

The children brought their own complications. Benison, or 'Benno', was artistic but had dyslexia, and though physically small she was a passionate horsewoman, so she saw Hillside as a place to ride her horses. Kylie had given her the name of a character in her novel *Lost Haven* that she thought too good to waste. John, always known as 'Bim', was academically inclined until he drifted into trouble. Tennant had given him the nickname at birth, after a eucalyptus tree called Bimble Box, with the quality of being 'bimbly' or an aimless wanderer. From the age of three he ran away from home; at high school he won the Latin prize, had the longest hair, and started taking drugs. For Tennant, the Blackheath cottage shared with Harrower was meant to give her writing time away from family and the desk in her bedroom.

Tennant and Harrower were as unalike in writing style as they were in personality, which made them complementary and uncomfortable friends. Tennant couldn't have been more Australian in her direct, humorous, practical style. She was born in 1912 and grew up in Manly, where Harrower had lived as a young teenager. Her mother was a devout Christian Scientist, a believer in spiritual healing, and although Tennant converted to her husband's High Anglicanism, she retained an optimism about her problems that Harrower would come to see as infuriating denial. Tennant was linked with an older generation of writers, many of them anti-fascists or communists, and she exchanged letters with Katharine Susannah Prichard, Jean Devanny, Nettie Palmer and Alan Marshall. Harrower had respect for them but little interest in their books. As an old-style documentary novelist, Tennant went out on the road to interview unemployed workers and prostitutes, getting herself arrested for soliciting a policeman in order to experience a night in Long Bay Gaol. Compared with Harrower's introspective psychological studies, her novels were outward-looking adventures, scrutinising Australian history as well as human character and experience. By contrast, she told an interviewer years later, 'I can't think of any of Elizabeth's books that aren't autobiographical.'

When Harrower was working at Blackheath on her fifth novel, *In Certain Circles*, Tennant wrote to her old friend Mavis Cribb, the senior librarian at Maitland Library: 'Elizabeth is typing industriously at her novel. If it is about a young woman suffering I will hit her with a brick. I don't dare ask.'

As a child in the 1930s, Betty, as she was then, celebrated a birthday at her grandparents' Mayfield home. Fancy dress transformed the serious little girl into a nurse, and on other occasions a Spanish dancer, or a fairy with wings and a wand.

Above left In the 1940s, teenage Betty and her mother, Margaret Kempley, caught the Manly ferry from Circular Quay.

Above right Frank Harrower's work on the New South Wales railways took him away from Betty and her mother in Newcastle.

Right Margaret and Richard Kempley with Barbara Ward, Betty's lifelong friend from Newcastle, c. 1960.

Betty with her aunt Adell Harrower at the Newcastle Baths, where she became a strong swimmer.

In her twenties, Betty cut a glamorous figure on the beach.

A city girl at heart, Betty loved the Australian bush by the time she left for the UK in 1951.

Elizabeth and her cousin Margaret Dick holidayed in Greece and on the island of Corfu in 1956.

The press met Elizabeth Harrower and Margaret Dick when they sailed in to Sydney Harbour on July 1, 1959.

In 1961, Elizabeth worked on *The Watch Tower* and short stories at her Neutral Bay flat.

Elizabeth at the Hunters Hill home of her friends
Ferdi and Helene Nolte, c. 1973.

In 1973, Elizabeth set out on an ill-fated cruise to Japan
with Kylie Tennant (centre).

Elizabeth and Shirley Hazzard on the terrace
at 5 Stanley Avenue, Mosman, in 1984.

Elizabeth with Shirley's husband, Francis Steegmuller,
and Japan scholar Donald Keene on Capri in 1984.

Elizabeth with Ferdi Nolte, a South African-born architect, in the 1990s.

Elizabeth in her Cremorne study in 2014, when her novel *In Certain Circles* was published.

The Watch Tower

A few blocks from Richard and Margaret Kempley's Mosman house, Elizabeth Harrower sat over her typewriter, imagining them into the novel that would immortalise the brutality of their marriage. There were weekends in Blackheath but mostly there were days in the Macmillan office followed by long nights writing at her flat in Want Street. Almost under the subject's nose, she created the villainous Felix Shaw with a mixture of fury and cool analysis. This was the culmination of the emotional trauma she had to write out of her system, and although she told a tale of two sisters, they stood unmistakably for her mother and herself.

The Watch Tower opens with the line 'Now that your father's gone–'. Another lost father, this one dead at forty-five from a heart attack while driving, sets in train events that will strangle the lives of sisters Laura and Clare. Their English mother, Stella Vaizey, raised in colonial India, removes the girls from a country boarding school and takes them to live in a flat at Manly. The name of their headmistress, Miss Lambert, echoes Miss Lambert's School for Young Ladies, situated a few blocks from Harrower's first London flat in Bayswater, and Laura is another version of Esther Prescott, the hoodwinked wife in *Down in the City*. Here, clever Laura's ambitions to be a doctor like her father and to sing opera are thwarted by her indolent mother's demands that she run the household, go to business school and take a job at Shaw's Box Factory. Already this recalls Betty Harrower's move from Newcastle (where the Vaiseys commercial building stood in the main street of Mayfield) to Manly with her divorced mother, her removal from boarding school, and her first job folding boxes at a box factory.

Mr Shaw is a short, swarthy, nuggety man in a brown suit and brown hat atop his thick black hair, and to Laura he looks like a pirate. Like the erratic men in Harrower's other stories, he appears jocular but laughs in the mirthless, self-conscious way of pantomime characters. In the background, the Second World War begins and eleven-year-old Clare wishes, as Betty did, that she could tell Hitler to stop, while Mr Shaw boasts of admiring the dictator. When their mother abandons them to live in England, Laura becomes surrogate mother to her sister, seven years younger, and is persuaded by Mr Shaw to enter a businesslike marriage that will support them. But like the merchandise at Vaiseys store, the Vaizey girls are commodities to be traded, and eventually Clare is also removed from school and both are working like slaves in his factory and house. Mr Shaw is a terrible businessman, dealing with black marketeers and selling the factory cheaply, only to buy 'an almost defunct home-made chocolate factory', a reminder of Kempley's fraudulent confectionery college. He repeats this stupidity, buying an artificial flower factory, a clothing factory and a partnership in a hotel, losing money to younger men in pathetic bids to win their friendship. He also buys without warning a white colonial house in Neutral Bay. Laura loves the house with its 'embroidered' wrought-iron verandahs, large cool rooms, flowering gardens, and view though French windows to the harbour and city. There is such a house, Honda, built in 1858, at 55 Shellcove Road, not far from the Neutral Bay flat Harrower had shared with Margaret Dick while beginning her novel. The fictional house stands in for various houses where Richard and Margaret Kempley lived along the middle arm of Sydney Harbour, and Shaw's sudden decision to sell and buy another in the same street recalls the Kempleys' move from one house to another in Cowdroy Street, Cammeray. In retrospect, the house is also a light disguise for 5 Stanley Avenue, Mosman, where the Kempleys were playing out the last act of their Punch and Judy show.

But this is a novel not a memoir, a work of powerful compression and rising tension, recognisably real and mythically heightened. The metaphor that gives this story its otherworldliness is a gift to Felix Shaw from a business colleague – a china ornament of a swarthy turbaned man holding an assassin's knife. '"Bluebeard!" Felix cried. "Me!"' Almost naively, Felix enjoys being likened to the leering figurine: '*He* knew how to treat his women!' Harrower does not explain, but Bluebeard is a well-known murderer in tales from many cultures; first named in Charles Perrault's 17th-century folktale, 'La barbe bleue', he is a wealthy man whose wife finds the bodies of his former wives in a locked room of their castle. Bluebeard is only passingly mentioned in *The Watch Tower*, but he remains a sinister presence on the mantlepiece overseeing, or conjuring, the descent into turmoil. Even with its specific setting in pre-feminist Australia of the 1930s and '40s, here is a timeless dramatisation of coercive control and domestic violence. As Felix fails in business, he becomes drunk and abusive, smashing his loving wife and their lovely house, pulling the financial reins more tightly on Laura and Clare to render them prisoners. The neighbours, Blanche and Dick, ignore the noise next door and thank God they are 'normal'.

Harrower shifts the point of view back and forth between the sisters, building sympathy and horror as one sinks into submission and the other begins to rebel. Laura tries to excuse her husband's cruelty as the result of his harsh upbringing, which closely resembles Kempley's: English boarding school for naval cadets, Royal Navy until invalided out, accountancy in Sydney, racing car accidents, bad luck in business. Clare has studied psychology but finds no comfort in its formulas of cause and effect. As well as taking a job in the city, she finds an ally and possible escape route in Bernard, a Dutch man sick from overwork in Felix's clothing factory, who comes to convalesce at their house and tells his own tragic family history. Even on a quiet day, every detail of domestic life with Felix is threatening. After three beers he taunts Laura, who fears she has lost the diamond ring he gave her, and after accusing Clare and Bernard of theft, he 'finds' the ring on the floor. Sentence by carefully controlled sentence, Harrower creates an atmosphere of suffocating isolation, the breathless expectation of a Hitchcock psychological thriller. *Spellbound. Vertigo. Rear Window.*

But her intention was deeper. Beyond fear and hopelessness, Clare wishes 'to be in the presence of someone good'. In early drafts of the novel, including the one Harrower first sent to her agent, there was lengthy musing about good and evil. Her theme had to be dramatised and humanised before it could work as a novel rather than a philosophical essay. A one-page outline dated July 1961 laid out a large cast of characters such as neighbours, television producers, and a visiting American sociologist researching a project, wryly titled 'The Single Woman in Australia'. There were at times pages of exposition, excursions around Manly, ferry rides to the city, and Clare's office work. Harrower deleted most of this, leaving enough to let in a gasp of air, while maintaining the pressure at gothic levels. Clare, the reader of the family, relishes *The Fall of the House of Usher*, Edgar Allan Poe's horror story of death, dread and stormy nights, and she feels closer to characters in the works of Chekhov, Dostoevski and Tolstoy than she does to people around her. She is, she thinks melodramatically, 'the only Russian in Sydney'.

Before settling on *The Watch Tower* as her title, Harrower considered 'The Vantage Point' – a less sinister, less pungent option, referring simply to a place with a clear view. Clare watches the world and ordinary humans from her bedroom window, 'her look-out tower', and feels she is watching through windows everywhere. Harrower, too, was an observer – sometimes from on high – searching for sympathetic souls among the insensitive masses. She describes Clare as craving help and understanding, apprehending other people with clarity, an intuition she often claimed for herself. Clare also feels 'pusillanimous, vicious, sustained only by a peculiar sort of pride and insurmountable determination'. Harrower's title alludes to the climax of Perrault's tale, when Bluebeard threatens to cut his last wife's throat. She calls on her sister Anne to go up to the watch tower of the castle to look out for their brothers, who are coming to save her. But for the well-read Harrower the image of the watch tower could also refer to a John Donne elegy: 'up into the watch-tower get, / And see all things despoiled of fallacies'.

It would be nice to see a link between *The Watch Tower* and Bob Dylan's song 'All Along the Watchtower', which he wrote and released in 1967, a year after the novel appeared. His riddling lyrics about a joker and a thief are said to draw on the Book of Isaiah, Chapter 21, verses 5–9, with its moral theme of the judgement of oppressors and restoration of righteousness to Jerusalem: 'Prepare the table, watch in the watchtower ...' Harrower may well have turned to Isaiah, as Harper Lee did for the title of her novel *Go Set a Watchman*, which was published in 2015 but written in the 1950s as a first draft of *To Kill a Mockingbird*.

Harrower gave *The Watch Tower* all her creative power and all of herself. Everything she had written was leading to this. Felix Shaw is a brilliant, complex work of characterisation, misogyny in all its masculine force, weakness and banality. Whether Kempley was quite as malevolent as Shaw can't be proven. There are no police records or charges of violence against him, no letters from Harrower that detail his sins, and no one still alive who remembers her talking about him. But physical assault is often unreported and emotional abuse invisible. Neither man was a cartoon monster. Shaw weeds the lawn in his shorts, jingles keys in his pocket, reads the newspaper after work, and laughs at his own jokes. While there were endless men Harrower could observe to create her antagonist, Richard Kempley was her reason for doing so. She would insist, as she always did, that *The Watch Tower* was pure fiction, but at the end of her life she told at least one friend the novel was autobiographical. And another that 'Richard' was 'a monster. A real monster. A poisonous man.' Mostly she couldn't even bear to refer to him by name. Whatever suffering Kempley inflicted was transformed into a masterpiece. Unlike her earlier novels, each written within a year, this one took five years because she was working full-time; and also, she knew the stakes were high professionally and personally.

*

Kylie Tennant read the first draft of *The Watch Tower* and reported to Alan Maclean in London that 'it is very good, though I thought she should rewrite the last sixty pages'. Her formal report on the manuscript likened Harrower in tone and style to Christina Stead, both at 'their best with a situation that is tight-knotted with conflict on several levels'. She put the novel in a broader social context:

> While women remain economically and socially inferior to men, books like *The Watchtower* [sic], with its independence and powerful spirit, will from time to time flash out exploding from the volcanic depths underlying the thick and callous layers of masculine superiority. It is a powerful study of the neurotic man who passes as successful and the society which makes his pretences possible.

She was worried about Cassell's 'peculiar option clause', which gave them right of first refusal on this and Harrower's next novel, but she asked Maclean to give a speedy decision if Harrower allowed her to send the manuscript to Macmillan. 'Her work has reached the stage when the critics in Australia want to hail her next book as a masterpiece. This was the position with Patrick White when *Voss* came out.'

In early 1965, Harrower wrote to her new London agent, Michael Horniman at AP Watt & Son, sending him a copy of the manuscript and asking his advice about publishers. Cassell had first option but she hoped to do better, because they had never liked her novels. 'Whatever my books are like, they are not really light romantic fiction, which is what Cassell's imprint suggests.' Macmillan was a possibility but changes were afoot in the company's management; their list was still very technical and in Australia concentrated on textbooks. She knew it was important to be well received in England and that depended on having the right imprint. Eyre & Spottiswoode published Patrick White, Faber published Hal Porter, Macmillan and Gollancz both published Kylie Tennant. Desmond Briggs, a partner with Anthony Blond in Blond & Briggs, had made an offer, even before the book was finished, but she hesitated because his list 'does have an aura of pornography'.

A decision was made within months, after Cassell relinquished its option. Alan Maclean brought good news when he visited Harrower in the Sydney office in September with Macmillan's managing director. Three professional readers of *The Watch Tower* in the UK had delivered positive reports. Maclean had read the novel on the plane from London and liked it. He made a firm offer with an advance of £250 and publication the following September, after she made his suggested cuts and revisions. Even while recognising Elizabeth Harrower as a fine novelist, Macmillan tied her to her office job for survival. At the same time as trimming her own book, she was editing for Macmillan – or as she put it, 'having a hack at his prose' – the manuscript of *The Roo Shooter* by Keith Watson, which was championed by Tennant and would eventually be published to positive reviews.

The energetic Max Harris and Geoffrey Dutton were doing their best to boost Harrower's sales and reputation through Sun Books, a small press they started in 1965 with Brian Stonier. After failing to interest the local arm of Penguin in publishing Australian books, all three left the company to become independent publishers of 'quality paperbacks for the sophisticated reader'. In 1966 their list included Geoffrey Blainey's history of Australia, *The Tyranny of Distance*, which became a bestselling classic, and books originally published in the UK such as Harrower's *The Long Prospect* and several titles by Christina Stead. This gave Harrower the second chance she had been striving for, but only for one book, and only in Australia. The comeback wasn't quite what any of them hoped for.

At last her Newcastle novel attracted attention in Newcastle, with a 'book of the week' review by academic Julian Croft, but his interest was parochial. Identifying the novel's main setting as Birmingham Gardens, a suburb adjoining the University of Newcastle, he quoted approvingly from the 'embarrassing' descriptions of run-down Ballowra, and thought

> the most intriguing thing is the environment in which the characters live, where there is an overall feeling of sterility and of the purposelessness of urban living which is reinforced by the ugliness of the city and the reliance of the inhabitants on the drugs of beer, prawns and the races.

If the publishers were hoping to reach a new generation of readers, they weren't helped by Monash University's student newspaper, which ran an unflattering review by Richard Murphet, who described the novel as 'a diluted Lolita'. Unwisely, the book's press release said *The Long Prospect* 'anticipated the Lolita situation' – Nabokov's novel about a pedophile was published in 1955, three years before Harrower's first appeared – and the reviewer said this comparison 'only points to the book's mediocrity'. Harrower had been careful to avoid salacious implications between the emotional child and the kind man, but now *Lolita* was seen as a selling point. Unfortunately, *The Long Prospect* was released in March 1966, months before *The Watch Tower*, so there was no cross-fertilisation and, despite Harrower's request to Dutton, no mention of the new novel in the blurb, so reviewers were oblivious of the mature work to come.

*

Harrower was underwhelmed by the cover planned for *The Watch Tower*. The designer in London had gone for the most obvious cliché, a black-and-white aerial image of Sydney Harbour Bridge spanning the dust jacket. Calmly she wrote to Alan Maclean,

> I was totally blind to any special relevance it might have to THE W-T. Like those psychological tests where you can choose to see either a white urn on a black background or two black profiles with a white space in between.

Short of time and money, Maclean – and the marketing minds – compromised. The Harbour Bridge stayed on the UK edition but for Australia there was no picture, just the title and Harrower's name in large pink lettering on a purple background – a striking and brave choice, as it gave nothing away about the contents except their intensity.

Nicholas Byam Shaw, a rising international sales executive with Macmillan (later CEO and chairman), wrote to Kylie Tennant that Harrower's book was good but would have to be carefully sold. 'Elizabeth is of course hopelessly modest,' he said, and he thought readers might find the narrative depressing, so promotion should emphasise qualities of perception and character study. Kylie Tennant rang Patrick White asking him to read a proof copy of *The Watch Tower* and give a comment for use in publicity, if he liked it. He said he would rather not, but rang back and asked for a copy with no promises. Tennant told her Australian boss, Robert Cross, that she had been 'very subtle' in changing his mind:

> Patrick and I never agree on anything and he thinks my literary taste poor save that I admire his books. So I said that I thought Elizabeth's book was slightly inturned and soulful. Patrick bit. He said this did not mean that it was necessarily bad.

Byam Shaw was visiting from London and over a 'merry meal' with Tennant and Harrower discussed whether to ask Alan Maclean to approach White formally for an endorsement of the novel. Tennant decided this was too much fuss and she was right. Within weeks White sent a sentence. Byam

Shaw was grateful that Tennant had 'worked on' him to produce a 'very jolly' quote, which they would use on promotional postcards and in trade magazine advertising. White's gnomic comment read as if it had been extracted like a tooth: 'Elizabeth Harrower's characters don't fornicate under the reader's nose, but what they do and say is always true, sometimes subtly so.' If he was implying a general lack of sensual earthiness in her head-in-her-books protagonist, Harrower didn't object.

*

In October 1966, Gavin Souter reported in his news column in the *Sydney Morning Herald* that three Brisbane booksellers were refusing to stock the book because of the cover blurb, written in London based on notes from Tennant, and with the opening sentences: 'The central character of *The Watch Tower* – outwardly a successful Sydney businessman – is wicked. One could say, perhaps, that he suffered a deprived childhood, is a homosexual, or offer any one of a number of excuses for him.' Souter noted, 'That word "homosexual" did it,' and quoted a 'baffled' Harrower: 'There are no homosexuals in the book.' Could homosexuality be what White had been hinting at? Harrower's denial might have been self-defence. Others have read an undeclared homoeroticism into Felix Shaw's dumb attraction to young men, but the blurb was clumsy. There are other possible connotations – the pull of male mateship for a man who can't relate to women; the ageing man's nostalgia for his own youth; vanity blinding his business sense.

In December, Alec Chisholm in *The Age* also took issue with the blurb writer for branding Felix an entirely wicked, destructive sadist, and argued the character was far more complex. He judged the novel 'a patient, sensitive, indefatigable study of the mind's contradictions and mysteries, and should win the author a very high place among the novelists of today'.

When considering his own comments on *The Watch Tower*, White had been distracted by his seventh novel, *The Solid Mandala*, which came out in February that year, and coincidentally was a double portrait of simple kindness and unforgiving hatred in the twin brothers Arthur and Waldo Brown, whom he saw as the inextricable halves of himself. Their love-hate had an almost sexual intimacy, which might have coloured White's reading of Felix Shaw. He and Harrower rarely discussed their own writing with each other but a shared interest in the struggle of good and evil shaped their novels. White was rereading *The Brothers Karamazov* as he wrote, and had Arthur read the Dostoevski novel at the Mitchell Library, to his clever brother's annoyance. Harrower gave Clare the Russian writers in the same way, to represent the full-blooded extremes of human experience. If she had known that White's publisher paid him £1500 advance, she might have been dispirited, or spurred on by the remote chance of making real money as an author.

While she waited for her book to appear, she moaned to Margaret Dick about the quietness and boredom of the office, and dreamed she was typing a new novel. But she later said in an interview, 'It's necessary to have a job unless you are a Morris West or have a private income.' White lived on his inheritance but West was her particular bugbear, an Australian living in Rome whose novels about the Catholic Church's power, most recently *The Shoes of the Fisherman*, each sold more than a million copies. She complained about her publisher having taken out commas and changed 'which' to 'that' throughout the novel, all of which she had changed back. When flattered by the interviewer as 'one of Australia's most sensitive and psychologically perceptive novelists', she said pedantically she had never studied psychology. 'Because I am interested in people, it doesn't mean that I go around consciously analysing them. Sometimes it is years afterwards that you remember an occurrence which, when it happened, just flowed past you.'

Speaking to journalist Gavin Souter, who would become a close friend, she danced around his questions and excused herself as 'flippant off the typewriter'. More seriously, she said:

> A book and its characters choose you. You don't choose them. When I start writing a novel, I have no message in mind, but, at its end, something seems to be resolved. I hope I am saying to someone in a difficult situation: 'There are ways out.' And I am saying that it is too easy to judge others in unfamiliar circumstances.

On her first trip to Melbourne at the end of the year, an *Age* journalist saw she had a notebook in her handbag. 'My ideas for a novel or a story just come to me,' she told him:

> I never quite know what inspires an idea but I do know that it cannot be forced. Anyway, once it comes I find myself noticing all sorts of details and incidents that add to it and build it up. So, as I go along, I jot down notes and keep them by me. Not elaborate notes, just an occasional phrase, maybe only a word.

She was gathering thoughts for her next novel, which she knew must follow *The Watch Tower* as soon as possible. With her interview and her first visit to the Macmillan head office, she had no time to contact her Melbourne friend, Judah Waten. Shortly afterwards he sent her the newspaper clipping with a handwritten note: 'If you had rung me I might have bought you a cup of coffee or even a Greek meal. Ever, Judah.'

*

In Britain the critical response was sparse but positive. The *Irish Independent* praised the novel as 'powerful, intelligent and very well written' but might not have helped sales with its simplistic summary of a 'study of a particularly repulsive monster, a man without any redeeming features, who has almost total control over two girls'. The *Yorkshire Post* took a narrow view of colonial manhood: 'This excellent novel is totally free of the masculine Australian mawkishness of "mateship".'

There were no books in Australian bookshops when reviews of *The Watch Tower* began to appear. They were stuck on a ship and the official publication date was pushed back two months to November 1966. In *The Australian* the writer Laurie Clancy found the novel 'extraordinarily compelling reading' with 'complete fidelity to the truth of the author's experience'. All her novels

> seem to be written out of a personal vision so anguished as to be almost unique among Australian writers ... Every drop of significance, every

grain of meaning is sifted from even the most apparently trivial event
so that by the time the novel is ended the reader is almost physically
exhausted ... It is a measure of Miss Harrower's integrity as a writer
that she is prepared to be unpleasant in order to tell the truth.

In the *Sydney Morning Herald*, Harry Kippax wrote the serious rave review every writer hopes for, seeing the complexity of Harrower's achievement.

To create a monster as continually credible, comic and nauseating
as Felix is a feat of a very high order. But to control that creation, as
Miss Harrower does, so that Clare remains the centre of interest is an
achievement even more rare. *The Watch Tower* is a triumph of art over
virtuosity ... This is a dense, profoundly moral novel of our time, not
just an exercise in suspense ...

He concluded: 'In a year which had not produced *The Solid Mandala* I should have no hesitation in proclaiming *The Watch Tower* as outstanding. As it is, one can be grateful to have had in twelve months two such additions to the small body of distinguished Australian novels.'

Having the two novels out at the same time led to frequent comparison, mostly complimentary for Harrower. When likened to White *and* Jane Austen, she said: 'I admire both writers tremendously but they are so different and I certainly see no similarity in my books and theirs. Mine are strictly novels – straight fiction – and I haven't consciously cultivated a specific "style".'

The poet Geoffrey Lehmann in *The Bulletin* wrote that conflict between sensitive and insensitive people was a dominant theme in recent Australian novels, naming White and Harrower. But he added:

Elizabeth Harrower's prose has a quality of intense compassion and
suffering. Here she differs from Patrick White, for where White
is savage she is resigned. Her writing has an elusive femininity ...
something which most very good women writers such as Virginia
Woolf or Katherine Mansfield have. It is a quality of 'sympathy'.

An ABC reviewer said on radio: 'I can't help hoping that Elizabeth Harrower ... is not writing about herself in *The Watch Tower* ... This brilliant book is written in a style like the more lucid passages of Patrick White, and it is one of the best Australian novels I have read for a long while.'

Strangely, Max Harris focused his appreciation of *The Watch Tower* in seeing Harrower as 'the first Australian writer to have dared to use some of the stylistic devices of Patrick White – in particular the use of parenthetical comment and the illuminating aside'. The two names appeared together in many lists of the year's best books.

Kippax repeated that he had read 'no more memorable modern novel this year' than *The Solid Mandala*, and 'in *The Watch Tower* Miss Harrower clinches her claim to be regarded as one of the most accomplished of Australian novelists'. *The Age* rounded up the best of 1966 in an impressive international list that included White and Harrower, Shirley Hazzard's first novel, *The Evening of the Holiday*, Truman Capote's *In Cold Blood*, Paul Scott's *The Jewel in the Crown*, Graham Greene's *The Comedians*, Anthony Powell's *The Soldier's Art* and Peter Matthiessen's *At Play in the Fields of the Lord*. Stephen Murray-Smith, editor of *Overland*, paired Harrower's novel with her friend Judah Waten's *Season of Youth* for attention. He described *The Watch Tower* as 'a simple little plot, but an extremely effective and frightening novel, one of the most astute studies in depth of the mind under stress that I believe any Australian writer has yet achieved'.

Max Harris named four novelists as the year's best: Australians Harrower, Waten, and Judith Wright for *The Nature of Love,* and British writer Iris Murdoch for *The Time of the Angels*.

Even Nancy Keesing, who had reviewed *The Catherine Wheel* harshly (and was 'soundly castigated' by other readers for doing so), was convinced that '*The Watch Tower* is a rare, and in every way expert, book'. In her 1967 review in the literary journal *Southerly*, she defended her opinion that the earlier novel was 'distasteful' and that a trend towards novels about personal torment accounted for much of the recent decline in novel reading. But she had found *The Long Prospect* a better, more poignant book, and admired *The Watch Tower* for its characterisation and tension that build to the archetypal truth of a fairytale or myth. 'In a final chapter of great force and some beauty the book not only ends, but is complete.'

Geoffrey Dutton also mentioned *The Watch Tower* and *Season of Youth* in his Australian 'best of' list topped by *The Solid Mandala*. He was the only critic to include *Trap* by Peter Mathers, a novel whose 'richness was almost indigestible at times'. But Dutton's round-up of the year's prose in *The Bulletin* had the greater purpose of explaining that 'writers in Australia are a depressed class, in terms of finance and prestige'. Artists could make more money from one exhibition than novelists could make in five years, he wrote. A bestselling non-fiction book might make its author $1500 in three years for a hardback edition of three thousand and $2500 for a paperback edition of 30 000. Whereas in the United States a paperback publisher would pay half a million dollars, and in the USSR more than three thousand writers lived on their writing, more than a thousand of them poets – and many were national heroes. 'For us sardonic Australians, however, accustomed to bitch rather than enthuse, the first rays of talent are enough to make us narrow our sun-squinting eyes; at a glimpse of genius we call for our dark glasses ...'

Although she was not a joiner by nature, Elizabeth Harrower was a member of the Fellowship of Australian Writers and PEN Australia for reasons of solidarity and socialising, alongside Margaret Dick, and would benefit from the Fellowship's earlier work to expand writers' grants from the Commonwealth Literary Fund. She had joined the Australian Society of Authors in 1963, when it was formed largely to lobby for better pay rates for writers, a perpetual worry. With short-story writer Dal Stivens as president and poet Jill Hellyer as secretary, bestselling expat Morris West and publisher PR 'Inky' Stephenson as vice presidents, the society's first campaign was to remove the 'colonial royalty' that meant British publishers paid Australian authors 10 per cent royalty on UK sales of their books but as little as 3–4 per cent on 'export' sales in Australia. That success brought Harrower slightly more income from *The Watch Tower*, but she was unlucky in other familiar ways.

As an insider at Macmillan as well as an author, Harrower saw the factors that worked against her. *The Watch Tower* was published at all because of the new company strategy to expand beyond textbooks and build a strong Australian fiction list. But the practice was flawed. Harrower contained her frustration for years but eventually 'moaned' to Alan Maclean in a letter after the novel was remaindered, with no paperback edition planned. The problems as she saw them began with Robert Cross still settling in as general manager in Melbourne, so in spite of his goodwill the book was published from London and he was not on top of its progress. There were no salesmen in Sydney or Queensland for six months before or after the book came out. The 'excellent' reviews appeared before stock arrived from England, so sales were delayed even though the office received more inquiries and pre-orders for *The Watch Tower* than for any other novel since she had been working there. She had 'always felt a little sad about the timing of the novel's appearance. Not a world tragedy, but novels can have happy or unhappy circumstances.'

On the strength of her writing and the critical response, *The Watch Tower* should have vaulted Harrower to the next level of recognition. But there was yet another unhappy circumstance. In 1967 Patrick White resolved to accept no more prizes for his novels. He had won five: the Gold Medal of the Australian Literature Society for *Happy Valley* in 1941 and in 1955 for *The Tree of Man*, Britain's WH Smith Literary Award for *Voss*, and the Miles Franklin Literary Award for *Voss* in 1957 and *Riders in the Chariot* in 1961. When the *Encyclopaedia Britannica* committee, which included Geoffrey Dutton and ABC executive Clem Semmler, chose *The Solid Mandala* as winner of the 1966 Britannica Award for literature, he refused to accept the $10 000 prize. Semmler, who took the news to White in person, wrote in his diary that he gave no reason but said if they publicly gave it to him he would publicly refuse.

In April 1967 White's British publisher called to congratulate him on winning the Miles Franklin Award. White protested that he had not entered his book, but apparently his publisher, Eyre & Spottiswoode, had. The Miles Franklin trustees pushed him to accept the prize and donate the money to their fund, so he contacted Beatrice Davis, a judge, and insisted he would not. He suggested sharing the prize between Harrower and Peter Mathers for *Trap* – 'both well above the average book which wins'. After days of discussion the judges took half his advice, choosing

Mathers. White told his agent he was glad because he considered *Trap* 'one of the few creative novels about Australia'.

This was the last straw in White's troubled relationship with his 'ex-publisher' and he would change companies for his next novel, *The Vivisector*. Macmillan was an early contender, after a tip-off from Tennant to Maclean. Perhaps the mishandling of Harrower's publication and Tennant's meddling had a negative effect. In the end he went with Jonathan Cape for an advance of £5000 and 15 per cent royalties, and assurance from managing director Tom Maschler that, if he had to choose, he would prefer to publish White than Graham Greene, who happened to be the uncle of the other managing director, Graham C. Greene. White was nearing the pinnacle of his career.

For Harrower, the disappointment of the Miles Franklin was also career defining. While she never boasted and was careful not to whinge to anyone except her closest confidants, she knew she had written her best novel so far. What more could she do? Knowing she'd been a real contender for the prize, Robert Cross wrote that he was sorry about the 'proper mess up' of the Miles Franklin, and that *The Watch Tower* should have won. He accepted Harrower's invitation to dine at her place with Patrick White next time he was in Sydney. She did not let her feeling of being let down damage relations with two of her strongest supporters.

Peter Mathers' *Trap* was an experimental novel inspired by the South American magical realists, written in the form of a diary by Jack Trap, an Australian with Irish-English-Aboriginal-Tierra del Fuegan roots, an angry man who forms a community on a mining lease at Cape York. English-born Mathers received $1000 in prize money, but hardly any boost in sales. A year later a journalist called *Trap* a 'highly praised worst-seller'.

Allies and impediments

Elizabeth's staunchest friend remained Margaret Dick, who felt her cousin's loss in the Miles Franklin debacle keenly. Soon after Mathers' win, she wrote an outraged letter to the editors of *Australian Book Review* decrying the judges' decision. Given her close association with Harrower and White, this was highly inappropriate and an odd move by one who was usually so tactful. She must have thought a great injustice had been done.

Writing from their shared flat in Want Street, Mosman, she did not say who should have won the prize nor mention Beatrice Davis, the Miles Franklin judge who praised *Trap* as 'a literary tour de force' with 'great comic talent'. Instead, Dick took exception to 'pathetic' critical overstatement that *Trap* would change Australian writing, and Australia, forever. She argued that the novel had deceived those blinded by chauvinism with its technical peculiarities and fashionable political views that its style was 'new'. In fact, the satire was 'applied with a wooden mallet', the sex and humour were 'at the level of the lavatory joke', the characters were 'galvanised cardboard', and reading the book was 'like running a three-legged race in a ploughed field'. To emphasise her point, she compared *Trap* with Joseph Heller's *Catch-22*. 'The difference is, of course, the difference between originality and gimmickry, but it is one that those who lack critical standards, or whose critical standards are parochial, find it all too difficult to apply.' She ended with the despair the Miles Franklin has periodically provoked: 'It is sad that a prize which should be the major prestige award of the year is in growing danger of falling into disrepute.'

By this time, Dick's own ambitions as a novelist had come to something of a halt, and she had shifted her focus to non-fiction, publishing *The Novels of Kylie Tennant* earlier in 1966.

Margaret Dick had given up everything to come to Australia, but she didn't consider the move a sacrifice. Harrower said her cousin had always felt she should have been born and lived her life in France, and that 'the shock of Scotland was something she could have done without'. Sydney was not Paris but neither was it Edinburgh. Dick basked in the Australian sunshine and relaxed class structure, and found enough literary work and friendship to decide this was home. Having arrived in Sydney as Elizabeth Harrower's cousin, she was soon known as a respected writer, critic and teacher in her own right. Her ambition was to keep writing fiction and she began work immediately on a novel as Harrower edged her way towards *The Watch Tower* by writing stories and plays.

Dick's novel 'Southern Latitude' brought together Australian, British, and American characters in Sydney to reflect on Australia's changing place in the world. This was a national obsession as the country began to lurch out of postwar conservatism. The sceptical mood and catchy titles made bestsellers of John O'Grady's migrant comedy *They're a Weird Mob*, architect Robin Boyd's *The Australian Ugliness* and Donald Horne's *The Lucky Country*, his ironic label for a lazy, British-derived society run by second-rate people.

Dick embedded her commentary in a light-hearted social comedy intended to evoke the city 'in the eye of its own people and of the sophisticated European or American newcomer'. The Jane Austenesque novel had many familiar details in the story of Frances Elton and her widowed mother Constance, living in a house with a wide sundeck looking over a beach to grey-green headlands that shield the harbour from the sea. Charles Loden, an American expat writer, has come from Italy to work on a translation and is in an 'unserious' relationship with Frances. He is a kind of alter ego for Dick and Harrower: writing a novel, reviewing books, translating from French and Italian, pedantic about language. His previous books have been praised by critics and sunk without trace, no one will look at his play, and he lives on the generous proceeds of a single short story sold to an American glossy magazine.

Charles falls in love with a married woman; Frances falls into a 'dangerous affair' with a 'professional charmer', Roland Antrim, whose name and nature echo Harrower's dissolute actor, Christian Roland, in *The Catherine Wheel*.

When Max Harris asked Harrower to write book reviews in 1963, she was not keen but recommended Margaret Dick as a reviewer. She enclosed British reviews of Dick's first novel, *Point of Return*, and said she had just finished a third. Dick sent 'Southern Latitude' to William Heinemann, who had published her first two novels, but no book emerged. Harrower told Shirley Hazzard later that it 'didn't come off' and Margaret 'was inclined to think she was happier with non-fiction'. Sitting unpublished among her papers in the National Library of Australia, her intelligent, polished novel reads more as dialectic than drama, a set-up for debate about ideas, slightly patronising in its affection for Australia yet no match for the scathing commentary of contemporary Australian writers.

She had always written short stories, many of them subtle and moving, and often ending with an unexpected act of self-effacing decency. A wife pays £5 to keep her abusive husband out of gaol. A boy pretends he has fallen over and reaches out his hand for help to the girl who pushed him. Some stories depicted the hardships of people in mining communities, and others drew on her own family's financial losses. Dick was encouraged by winning second prize to Hal Porter in the 1962 *Adelaide Advertiser* Literary Competition – AD Hope was a judge – with her short story 'Summer Sunday', which Tennant included in *Summer's Tales 1*. The story isn't as cheerful as its title might suggest: members of a middle-class family gossip about a girl who has killed herself after becoming pregnant to her married lover, and blame her for her own tragedy; only the daughter who was her friend is sympathetic. The *Bulletin* reviewer of the collection singled out Dick's 'beautifully constructed' story for its 'piercing clarity and subtlety'.

The following year Dick sent another story, 'Choosing', to the Adelaide competition. This one reads as a retelling of Harrower's novel *The Long Prospect*: after being left by her lover, Bea gets a flat of her own and reluctantly takes back her daughter, eleven-year-old Sadie, who has been living with her grandmother. Bea wants to be alone with her new lover, Martin, but in a gentle twist he shows Sadie kindness, to the distress of her jealous mother. Couples retreating from unconsummated infidelity appear so often in Dick's fiction that they suggest some personal experience with married men in all those years of being single. She sent other stories out under pen names – 'Greville' and 'AB Siddon' – and offered at least one to the *New Yorker* but had no more success in the US than Harrower did.

Within weeks of landing in Sydney, Dick had her first assignment for the Women's Session on ABC radio, writing and presenting a talk titled 'Festival for the Old People's Clubs in London'. She formed a strong association with the ABC and would write many radio features, especially for the poetry programs *Poet's Tongue* and *Quality Street*.

She also worked for seven years from 1963 as an English mistress at SCEGGS Redlands, a private girls' school in Cremorne, not far from home. Dick had no formal teaching qualifications but her writing and knowledge of literature had impressed the headmistress, Miss Isobel Humphery. Many of her senior English students received excellent marks in the Leaving Certificate and, from 1967, the Higher School Certificate. Dick described teaching as 'quite a revealing experience. It has had its rewards, it's also been very trying.' She became restless about not writing and resigned at the end of 1969, telling Miss Humphery she wanted to finish a novel and possibly move overseas.

Elizabeth Harrower and Margaret Dick lived together on and off in Sydney as they had in London, for companionship and to save money. Harrower had a driver's licence but she was a nervous driver, and mostly content to catch ferries, trains and buses. Dick made travel easier by always owning a small car, a Volkswagen Beetle or other old model prone to break down. She was the driver for shared outings, and invitations were often for 'Elizabeth and Margaret'. People who saw them together wondered about their relationship, some assumed they were a couple, but those who knew them well understood their familial symbiosis. They understood each other intimately, spoke teasingly in the way of siblings and shared private jokes, addressing each other for a while by the mysterious nicknames 'Pot' and 'Net'. Harrower's only complaint was that, when one of them was away, her cousin did not miss her enough, or write often or emotionally enough.

Standing together they looked like a heron and a robin. Compared with the long-limbed Harrower, who was 'five feet 10 inches in medium heels', Dick was physically smaller and rounder, with an engaging wide smile and a softly burred accent. Harrower described her as having 'the disposition of a scholar', and at every opportunity promoted her as more intelligent, better read, and a more talented writer than she was. Others found her quieter, calmer, more self-contained, less scrutinising, and even 'nicer' company. Her niece Lesley thought the Dick sisters, Margaret, Anne and Stephanie, were 'lovely people, women of quality and substance', but 'reserved like their father' rather than 'warm and fun' like their mother, Minnie, sister to Harrower's irrepressible grandmother, Helen Hughes. All the same, Dick had been a skilled public speaker in the British civil service and, as her response to the Miles Franklin Award showed, she wasn't afraid to express strong opinions in person or print.

*

Through Harrower, Kylie Tennant became a friend and a subject for Dick, who occasionally went up to the cottage at Blackheath and visited Tennant and her family at Hunters Hill. When her novel failed, Dick turned to writing a critical study of Tennant's novels for two years at weekends and holidays, while Harrower was deep in *The Watch Tower*. In her usual straight-spoken tone she argued that Tennant had been misread by previous critics who saw the obvious realism, social critique and earthy comedy in her novels about ordinary working Australians, but missed their deeper metaphysical search for meaning. Dick was first attracted to Tennant's work by reading her 1946 novel, *Lost Haven*, a fictionalised portrait of Laurieton, the north coast town where her husband had been school principal and where she had learnt how to build a boat while writing about the community. Dick's advocacy was most effective when she discussed *Tell Morning This,* which she considered Tennant's finest novel. Tennant had submitted the manuscript at a huge two hundred thousand words, which Macmillan insisted she cut by a third and published as *The Joyful Condemned* in 1953 with great success. Dick read the original manuscript, which she judged to have been badly impaired by the removal of its high-spirited wit.

The Novels of Kylie Tennant came out with the Adelaide publisher Rigby in 1966, shortly before *The Watch Tower*. Margaret Dick's attention urged Angus & Robertson to publish a full-length, 446-page edition of *Tell Morning This* a year later.

Reviewers had mixed opinions of Dick's book. Dorothy Green, a Canberra academic, valued the sympathetic, insightful reading by a 'visitor from overseas' but found the attempt to place Tennant among modern European novelists unconvincing and 'a dubious compliment'. Dick acknowledged: 'We are extremely different temperamentally, our whole approach, whole nature, whole mode of writing, mode of experiencing life is entirely different, and so I think this was a valuable experience for me, to extend myself in this way.' Tennant was too down-to-earth to agree with Dick's intellectual thesis but she didn't object. She thought of herself as 'a political journalist rather than a novelist', a book reviewer not a critic, and she didn't lecture readers: 'If you entertain people they may be in a better mood to listen to what you are saying, so it's no use telling them what they should think; they either pick it up from the book or they don't.'

Tennant was busy with her next books and protests against the Vietnam War. On the October day in 1966 when President Johnson was in Sydney, she recruited Harrower to join her in the city at a demonstration of women. They dressed in black clothes but not the veils worn by some. As the president's car went by, Tennant held up a large sign made by her son that said 'STOP VIETNAM WAR', and Harrower held a smaller one saying 'Support the United Nations'. They hurried to the Art Gallery of New South Wales to repeat their messages and finished with sandwiches and coffee in the Domain. Tennant thought her throat was sore from shouting but was diagnosed with scarlet fever. She was back at work by early November, 'full of penicillin' and editing a 'charming but sometimes scatty' manuscript by Melbourne society dynamo Dame Mabel Brookes, which was published in 1967 as *Riders of Time*, a title Tennant suggested while unwell.

Margaret Dick educated herself in Australian literature as a way of understanding the country, and she was often asked to give talks and to teach courses. At a Writers and Readers seminar in Armidale in 1967, she gave a lecture comparing Christina Stead's *Seven Poor Men of Sydney*,

Kylie Tennant's *Foveaux* and Brian Penton's *Landtakers* as examples of the different kinds of writing in Australia in the 1930s. That year, Tennant, Harrower and Dick judged a short story competition for the Society of Women Writers of New South Wales. Dick's book about Tennant elevated her reputation as a critic and she reviewed important books such as EM Forster's posthumous novel, *Maurice*, and Nadine Gordimer's Booker Prize winner, *The Conservationist*.

Like Harrower, she had a strong following in Adelaide, and Professor John Colmer of Adelaide University named her as the only *Sydney Morning Herald* reviewer of note among the best in the country. Harrower wrote to Shirley Hazzard, 'I was v. pleased because she is extremely modest about anything she does, and mixes with people who are more assertive ...' After reviewing Hazzard's novel set in Naples, *The Bay of Noon*, Dick put on her francophile hat and was thrilled by the biography of writer and filmmaker Jean Cocteau by Hazzard's husband, Francis Steegmuller. Both were among her best books of the year. She also reviewed Steegmuller's collected short pieces in *Stories and True Stories* and received his gracious note of thanks.

Work and friendship overlapped in more and more complex ways for Harrower, weaving a fabric of favours, obligations and disillusionment.

*

Elizabeth Harrower's long-distance and life-shaping friendship with Shirley Hazzard began almost incidentally. Australian-born Hazzard had lived overseas since her teens, first with her parents, Kit and Reg, who was a trade commissioner in Hong Kong, New Zealand and New York; then working for the United Nations in New York and Naples, and finally with her older American husband, Steegmuller, a distinguished biographer and translator. The couple moved between rented apartments on the Upper East Side of Manhattan and in Naples and Capri, keeping up a relentless pace of writing, travel, social and cultural events. She published her first book, *Cliffs of Fall and Other Stories*, in 1963 and her first novel, *The Evening of the Holiday*, in 1966, with Macmillan, so Harrower handled the books in the office and read early copies.

Among Harrower's many acquaintances in the book business was Norma Chapman, owner of Clay's Bookshop in Macleay Street, Potts Point, often the only bookseller in Sydney to stock some overseas titles. Divorced from her unfaithful husband in 1954, by 1966 Kit Hazzard was living alone in a tiny flat in The Chimes, a newly completed apartment building in Macleay Street. When Chapman met 'Shirley Hazzard's mother', she put her in touch with Harrower. The two women got on well over coffee at the Macmillan offices; Kit was entertaining and funny, shortly to leave Sydney to stay with the Steegmullers in New York. Harrower wrote to Kit there in August 1966 with Macmillan news of Alan Maclean's visit to Sydney, Robert Cross's arrival in Melbourne, her own stay at Blackheath with the company of horses, cats and birds. She complimented Hazzard on a story in the *New Yorker*, 'Nothing in Excess'. Kit replied with gratitude and flattery, reports on Shirley and Francis's dinner with the Macleans in London, their trip to Stockholm and her own sea voyage, signing her letter, 'Your very sincere admirer'. Hazzard added a note of thanks to 'Dear Elizabeth – (if I may call you that??)' and said she looked forward to reading her work, and perhaps to meeting in London or New York.

In the three months before Harrower replied, *The Watch Tower* was reviewed with *The Evening of the Holiday* by the Adelaide academic John Colmer for *Australian Book Review*, commissioned by Max Harris. Colmer gave Harrower qualified praise for 'her unsuccessful excursus into London bed-sitter life in *The Catherine Wheel*' and, in both *The Long Prospect* and *The Watch Tower*, 'a failure to integrate the character who provides the innocent seeing eye into the imaginative structure of the novel'. However, he was sensitive to her great achievement in creating Felix Shaw to embody 'the evil, life-denying forces that dominate the modern business world' and reduce 'all human relations to a matter of property ownership'. On the frequent comparison of Harrower with Patrick White, he agreed she had 'as deep an insight into evil and the blight that afflicts Australian suburban life'. She lacked his 'apocalyptic fervour, his massive structural cohesion and surface brilliance', but she was also free from the obsessive images of distaste that marred his writing. 'In *The Watch Tower*, the images are perfectly controlled,' he said, concluding that the novel marked a great advance in her career if she could deal with her structural problems. Colmer gave less space but high praise to Hazzard's 'exquisite novella' about a brief love affair between a married Italian architect and a half-English, half-Italian young woman. The 'consummate artistry of this remarkable first novel' brought to his mind Flaubert, Turgenev, Chekhov, Henry James and – he said, to cut her down to size – Françoise Sagan.

Harrower responded to congratulations from Nicky Byam Shaw with the wry comment that 'Max's professor would obviously have liked a touch of high life in the middle [of *The Watch Tower*], but you can't expect too much of professors. Kylie thought he was awful. Patrick rang to say how good he thought the review was.'

Neither Harrower nor Hazzard mentioned in letters to each other their shared review, which gave both of them serious attention but suggested that Hazzard was a fully formed, sophisticated novelist. Harrower must have felt somewhat deflated by the juxtaposition, and in her subsequent letters she did not mention *The Evening of the Holiday*, though she told Hazzard she found her writing 'extremely congenial' and her short story collection, *People in Glass Houses,* very good and pleasing. She sent a copy of *The Watch Tower* and Hazzard wrote warmly that she felt she had got to know the author, was absorbed in the story 'told in your very special, clear, poetic voice', and admired her for tackling a powerful theme so successfully. She enjoyed Harrower's evocation of the city atmosphere, which was fresh in her memory after twenty years' absence. Like Harrower, she had spent her childhood on Sydney's lower north shore, specifically in Mosman overlooking Balmoral Beach, a few streets from the house where Harrower's mother now lived. Between continents the two writers found many points of connection and their letters were immediately alive with discussion of books, travel, world events, friends, and Kit. She had set out by ship for London and wrote excited letters to Harrower, who sympathised with her restless loneliness and also with Hazzard's concern about her travelling the world alone. In a rare mention of Margaret Kempley, Harrower wrote:

... (I have a gentle, intractable mother who worries me, too, and am apt to run on, giving her good advice which she listens to with interest and takes no notice of.) It's rather hard all round. To be fair, I suppose it's life and circumstances that are intractable rather than mothers.

When Kit eventually returned to Sydney she took up their fateful friendship as Harrower was trying to will her next novel into being.

*

After *The Watch Tower*, Harrower had the continuing dilemma of no time to write while working for Macmillan and no money if she left. Writing after work demanded more sacrifice and stamina than she could give for a fifth book. Kylie Tennant and Judah Waten urged her to apply for a fellowship from the Commonwealth Literary Fund, which had benefited them. Each had endured attacks in parliament on their right to funding in the 1950s because of their association with communism, but had been awarded fellowships after rapid reassessment and letters from the prime minister, Robert Menzies. Tennant bought a truck with her grant money so she could drive north to research *The Honey Flow,* and Waten wrote his second novel of migrant life, *The Unbending.* The fund was still politicised by its structure, with a literary advisory board and another, with right of veto, made up of the prime minister and leaders of the Opposition and Country Party. After Harrower's application for a grant to write *The Watch Tower* had failed, she took the proud stance that she preferred to write without pressure and obligation from unearned money. Even now, she hesitated for so long that her application arrived three weeks after the closing date. 'My friends were ready to murder me because of the indecision and alarm all round,' she told Shirley Hazzard.

Her publishing record made her an outstanding candidate, but it can't have hurt that Tennant was now on the mostly male advisory board headed by the poet Douglas Stewart. In October 1967, Harrower was awarded a twelve-month fellowship worth $6000 for the following year. The National Librarian, Harold White, wrote to her pleased that her proposed contemporary novel set in Sydney would help redress the imbalance created by earlier writers who preferred the country. He also signalled an interest in collecting her papers for the library. She told him she felt 'puritanically, that it was better to do everything the hard way' but was pleased to have a year of 'worry-free freedom to write'. The eight fellowships were reported in Brisbane under the headline 'Woman writer gets $6000', but the woman was Queensland resident Nancy Cato – 'Mrs Eldred Norman, mother of three' – and among the recipients were George Johnston for the sequel to his bestselling Miles Franklin winner, *My Brother Jack*, and the young novelist Thomas Keneally and poet Les Murray.

Her grant obliged Harrower to give up full-time work and would be paid in monthly instalments, contingent on her progress reports. Equivalent to about $95 000 in 2025, the money was generous even after tax, but with no other income ahead she felt she would have to live as plainly as ever. The prospect was far from worry-free, and she told Hazzard, 'the future seems dark and precarious, and the application quite reckless and silly'. Among many letters of congratulations came a card from 'Mum' enclosing money for a gift and suggesting she buy a little clock. Harrower stayed at Macmillan until the end of March, at Robert Cross's request, to organise a visit from Harold Macmillan. Tennant was sick with the flu, so Harrower took her place beside the ageing chairman at a company dinner, relaxing into his amusing conversation. She and Tennant helped orchestrate a social visit by Macmillan to Patrick White's home with the unstated hope that he might be wooed if he decided to change publishers. In a personal letter of thanks, Macmillan warmly told Harrower he was sad she was leaving the company and pleased about her fellowship. Her bosses in Melbourne and London would miss her diplomatic presence, but they were eager to see her manuscript.

She had made a symbolic start on the novel in the debilitating heat of January 1968, opening windows in the Mosman flat to search for a sea-cooled breeze. Work was slow in her least favourite season, but turning forty on February 8 added to her sense of urgency. As she advanced through the winter, she wrote to Cross that the work was 'marvellously difficult and interesting'. She had declined his offer of half a day's work a week for the company when she resigned. After some months a sense of loyalty made her offer to do 'extra-mural tasks' such as proofreading, but Cross questioned whether it was wise to risk disrupting the flow of her writing. There were distractions at home from her landlords and their children, who lived noisily in the front of the house, and from a neighbour's cat called Marmalade.

*

Elizabeth escaped to Blackheath whenever possible but life intruded there, too. As well as working nonstop as an editor, adviser, lecturer and member of many boards, Kylie had decided to write a biography of HV 'Doc' Evatt, the late Labor Party leader, when she could not find another writer brave enough to take on the controversial subject. Under his leadership the Party had split in 1955 over attitudes to communism, and after losing three elections Evatt had retired from politics to be Chief Justice of New South Wales. Kylie often laboured on this massive job at Blackheath, with her husband 'Roddy' researching, fact-checking and reading chapters at home in Hunters Hill, while Elizabeth was trying to inhabit the minds of a new cast of suffering women, as Kylie feared.

The old house and overgrown garden at Hillside were forever in need of repairs, cleaning and clearing, which cost time and money. Migraines took days from Elizabeth's work schedule when she was laid out with headaches, backaches and sleepless nights. Kylie's arthritis was worsening. Both of them often needed to lie down with a book. Kylie's daughter, Benison, came up for holidays from art school to ride her horses and Bim, her son, wandered in and out, physically and mentally, in his last years of school. Kylie was the practical one, while city-raised Elizabeth made an effort but was not used to the gritty side of country living. She was hysterical when bats flew through her bedroom, and Prince the dog terrified her by chasing one across her bed. For a while she retreated to a smaller 'cell' where she could shut them out.

Roddy sent daily letters addressed to Kylie and Elizabeth, sometimes also to 'Dog' or 'Hound, Lizards and Water Lilies', reporting on work, children, home duties, reading, gossip and accidents in sardonic detail with misspellings of the name of their Polish house cleaner, 'Mrs Pluzcnzck'.

He could be pompous in his advice to the writers, but helpful too, sending reams of typing paper when Elizabeth ran short, editing notes for Kylie, and encouragement for both. He was also working on his own book about an old friend, John Hope, who was a Christian socialist like Rodd and retired rector of Christ Church St Laurence near Central Railway in Sydney, the Anglican Church where the Rodds had married in 1932 and attended for years. Amid the church's High Anglican rituals and music, Hope had built an impressive practical ministry caring for the poor and destitute of the inner city. Rodd's fine biographical portrait would be published in 1972, a year after Hope's death.

In bursts of ecstasy between bouts of work and anxiety, Elizabeth restored herself by standing under the Blue Mountains sky in sunshine or misty rain, watching boronia and wisteria bloom, leaves turn copper and gold. Nature calmed her and strengthened her resolve. There was also the pleasurable interruption of trips to Diamond Head, where Kylie was researching another more personal book. When she and Roddy had lived at Laurieton on the mid-north coast, they became friendly with Ernie Metcalfe, locally nicknamed 'the mad hermit', but known to Kylie as a gentleman living in harmony with his environment. He gave her an acre of his land, where she put up a one-room shack for writing and rusticating in true isolation. She still occasionally drove up to the slab hut among red gums, paperbarks and she-oaks, and would fictionalise the story of that time in *The Man on the Headland*. Elizabeth loved going there with Kylie for days or weeks to work, read and walk down a steep track to a secluded beach where they swam and lay on sun-warmed rocks. She thought of it as 'an eternal place' that meant 'the happiest of days to me' and she was fond of old Ernie, too.

In 1968 rutile miners moved in to ruin Diamond Head and break their hearts. Kylie returned the company's insulting cheque for forty cents rent on her land and went to court to stop the mining lease. Elizabeth joined her as a witness, wrote a supportive essay and sent it to her friend Helen Frizell, a journalist who had succeeded Sidney Baker as the *Herald's* literary editor. As she suspected, it was 'too moody and descriptive for a newspaper' to publish in full, but her lyrical writing made a moving elegy to paradise and a tribute to Tennant. Frizell quoted at length from

Harrower's piece in her own article. Harrower wrote from her European sensibility of earth 'so hot and dry that trodden grasses turn powdery and smell like incense'; 'a deserted orchard by the sea, and somehow pastoral and Greek. It seems legendary as few places do in this country not overrun with gods.' She couldn't help adding a judgement: 'It wasn't everybody's sort of place: humans find happiness in such different things – fast cars, applause, power over another person.' Kylie's legal action saved her own land, but her campaign couldn't stop the mining company from gouging profit out of pristine sand dunes along the coast.

As a schoolgirl and an art student, Benison Rodd loved going with her mother, and sometimes Elizabeth, to Diamond Head, where she collected coloured earth and quartz crystals to use in collages. She had less blissful memories of the long drive on winding roads, a storm that blew buildings away, and a trip she made by train with Margaret Dick when Kylie and Elizabeth couldn't get away. Neither she nor Margaret had lit a kerosene lamp before, and Benison's finger got stuck in the opening to the base while she was checking for kerosene. In the dark the two of them walked across a paddock to ask Ernie's help but even he couldn't free her. Benison slept with the lamp attached to her hand and in the morning they went to the rutile works, where the men brought out their tools and worked for two hours to release her – a small favour in return for their destruction.

Orphan Betty

If Elizabeth Harrower was reticent about her mother, she was silent about her father, as if he had vanished like the fathers in her fiction who died suddenly from heart attacks or accidents. But Frank Harrower was alive and following his daughter's progress from a distance. After he and 'Daisy' divorced in 1941, he kept moving between country towns, sending money for Betty's school fees, unsettled and single, until he was appointed railway station master at The Rock, a tiny town overlooked by a rocky hill near Wagga Wagga. There he met a young woman, Elma King, who was the eldest of nine children and had been pulled out of school from sixth class to help her mother with the younger ones. After a short time working in Junee she was called back to look after her grandmother. When she became pregnant to Frank, they married and had two sons, Francis and David, and a daughter, Lolita Catherine, who died at five months old. Another daughter, Yvonne Adell, named for her Newcastle aunt, was born in 1954.

From London, Elizabeth had written to her father and sent a copy of each of her novels, signed 'Betty'. Yvonne saw him go away to read the letters by himself, but she was not told she had a half-sister, and her brothers knew but said nothing because the subject was taboo in their mother's house.

Soon after Elizabeth and Margaret Dick arrived in Sydney in 1959, they caught a train up the coast of New South Wales to Taree and stayed a few days with Frank and Elma and the children at their home in Mount George, on a quiet bend in the Manning River. Frank was pleased, if overwhelmed, to meet his grown-up daughter as a sophisticated author. Elma was on her knees cleaning the kitchen floor when the visitors arrived and she was angry that Betty stepped over her rather than getting down and scrubbing with her. It didn't occur to her to stand up and greet them. She was jealous of her stepdaughter, who was only four years younger and seemed to have done very well for herself. When Yvonne spoke years later about Betty's visit with her elder brother, Francis said, 'I think she was a lesbian, because she came with that girl.' She had to correct him: 'No, that's her cousin.'

That was the last time Elizabeth saw her father. She didn't feel welcome to visit again, but they exchanged letters privately and she sent him *The Watch Tower*. Her half-brother David thought to ring her once when he was sixteen to tell her he had passed the Intermediate exams at school and was starting work on the railways, like his father. 'He called me Elizabeth!' she told Margaret Dick, with surprise. Yvonne's memory was that 'he did ring Elizabeth once, he was quite under the weather and she told him politely, don't ever ring back again'. Hardened by her harsh upbringing, Elma dominated her husband and children, until she walked out on them for another man when Yvonne was thirteen and the boys nineteen and twenty-one. The following Saturday, Frank got up to go to work and found one of his sons still in bed with a hangover. In a rare show of temper he shouted, 'Get out of that bed, you're going to work. You don't stay home because you've been drinking.' Frank was not a heavy drinker. His only tangle with alcohol had been years earlier when he drove home after a day's work and a few drinks and rolled his truck at a sharp bend that became known as 'Harrower's corner'. Yvonne regarded her father as a quiet man, a diligent worker and union member who wanted a simple life, liked to have a smoke and read his newspaper. By then he was a line manager and jack of all trades for a manufacturing company near Wollongong, and both his sons had jobs with the railways. He was keeping the household going but he had leukaemia. Two years after Elma left he was feeling unwell at work and was rushed to Wollongong Hospital, where he had a massive heart attack and died on November 2, 1968.

Once again Elma was forced to go home, pick up the pieces of her life, and see her daughter through school. Yvonne remembered: 'She came in, I threw my arms around her and her words to me were, "I don't know why you're crying. I'm the one who should be crying because I had to come back to look after you." God love us, she was a hard hard hard woman.' Elma inherited everything from Frank, which amounted to a modest red-brick house in Dapto, a Datsun Bluebird sedan, a small life insurance policy and some cash. There was nothing for Betty.

Elizabeth lost her father for a second time and gained a 'wicked' stepmother, a scenario she could have written. With a stepfather already damaging her peace of mind, this was more bad luck than she deserved, but she did not suffer deeply for this family of strangers. She had her mother, her friends and a life of her own in Sydney, and she had a deadline for her novel.

*

Her fellowship officially finished in April 1969, and in August 1968 the secretary of the Commonwealth Literary Fund had inquired about her progress. She replied that she had finished the novel and was working over the manuscript. But privately she knew something was wrong and she was struggling to fix the problem. She told her agent that Macmillan's newly elevated managing director, Nicky Byam Shaw, hoped it would be 'very plotty and extraverted: it isn't'.

She was also struggling with the old Oliver typewriter. After rejecting the latest Olivetti models as too frail, too red or too turquoise, she overcame her old prejudices and bought a German-made Olympia, which in turn gave her trouble and never 'wrote' well. 'Everyone was heartily sick of my moral dilemma,' she said of her dark feelings about Germany. Migraines slowed her down until she went, on Judah Waten's insistence, to a 'genius' specialist who gave her effective medication, dietary advice, and other instructions that ended six weeks of pain and illness. Another nervous year passed before she sent typed copies of *In Certain Circles* to her agent and the Literary Fund in June 1970. In her final report, she expressed disappointment that 'minor illnesses and one or two other things' had extended the time taken to complete the book. She was grateful that the fellowship had 'made the difference between never writing another book, and deciding to write more, regardless of the odd difficulties: and to a person to whom words, and ideas, and books matter, this is a very big difference'.

Alan Maclean received the manuscript at Macmillan as he was

leaving London for Florence to holiday with Shirley Hazzard and Francis Steegmuller. Macmillan was publishing Hazzard's second novel, *The Bay of Noon*, and Steegmuller's *Cocteau: A biography* that year, and Maclean's professional relationship with the couple had developed into a high-flying and genuine friendship. While Elizabeth was eager to read their books and fond of all three, she must have felt a multi-pronged stab of jealousy. Shirley's mother, Kit Hazzard, told her that a trade journal had declared *The Bay of Noon* 'a practically flawless book'. Elizabeth passed the news on to Margaret Dick, away at Adelaide Writers' Week again, with the comment: 'How clever! Takes some bringing off. Anyway, we must just persevere with this flawful one.' Since Kit's reluctant return to live in Sydney after trips to New York and London, Elizabeth saw her occasionally for coffee and a chat. She asked her own mother to join them once, to brighten the occasion and lighten her load. Margaret Kempley was worn down from caring for her demanding husband, who was in and out of hospital, but she still went to Elizabeth's flat in Want Street, Mosman, sometimes with cooked meals for her hard-pressed daughter. Elizabeth was torn between feelings of love and gratitude, boredom and guilt.

Maclean had sent Harrower's manuscript out to an independent reader, as he had with *The Watch Tower*. He often used CH (Christopher) Derrick's critical services, coincidentally in 1963, when Derrick advised against publishing Hazzard's first novel, *The Evening of the Holiday*, because she was 'not by temperament a creator of large positive things' and should stick with short stories. Fortunately, Maclean was undeterred then and Macmillan became her British publisher. In 1965 Derrick had also judged as 'an interesting and perhaps marginal failure' Jessica Anderson's second novel, 'A Question of Money', which would never be published, and suggested that she, too, write short stories. (She was highly acclaimed for later novels, such as *Tirra Lirra by the River* and *The Impersonators*, and her collection *Stories from the Warm Zone*.) On August 24, 1970, he wrote a tepid report about *In Certain Circles*, which Maclean read on his return from Italy and sent to Elizabeth as the book was being considered in London and Melbourne.

*

While Elizabeth was waiting for a decision on the manuscript, her mother suffered a severe stroke at home in the dark hours of a Saturday morning. Elizabeth heard nothing from her stepfather, but a neighbour rang her to say an ambulance was coming to the house. Margaret Kempley died the next day, September 13, at the Mater Misericordiae Hospital in North Sydney. She was only sixty-one.

Elizabeth's shock was compounded by learning that her stepfather had been slow to seek medical help, and treatment was delayed because Margaret's doctor was on holiday and the hospitals were disorganised on a weekend. A long correspondence with the health authorities and insurance company dragged on for years but brought no comfort. Meanwhile, Elizabeth had to organise the funeral, held two days later, and then settle her mother's affairs. Richard Kempley, seventy-eight and in worsening health, forgetful and taking frequent 'turns', was unable to live without Margaret's constant care. Elizabeth was relieved to send him back to England and hand over responsibility to his brother and sons in Grays, Essex. Everyone had thought he would die first, and she saw his final cruelty in not only surviving his wife but hastening her death. She blamed herself, too, for not being more aware of her mother's needs. She wrote to Judah Waten:

> It doesn't help to have neighbours saying he is a 'cruel man' and that my mother was so gentle and selfless and never complained. (Actually, she was full of life and fun. She said recently she felt like an oil well that had been stoppered up all its life. A pity. Such a pity.)

Harrower would write a finely crafted diary of this time in the form of a short story, using real events, feelings, and even her mother's name. 'It Is Margaret' opens with the funeral of Clelia's mother, Margaret, a few days after she has made the two-hour visit to Clelia permitted by her husband, Theo. Clelia remembers calling her into the kitchen to see the branches of spring blossom she had brought home from a three-week stay in the mountains. 'I do feel old tonight,' were Margaret's final words before Theo picked her up to go home. This was all true. So were Harrower's descriptions of Margaret as innocent and trusting, accepting without bitterness that she had made a grievous mistake in her marriage, and of Theo as 'a great figure in his imagination', so jealous of his wife that she was allowed no friends, relatives or pets. To Clelia he had been 'a tyrant, terrifying in her childhood and girlhood, a man who tortured and smiled and, after her escape, continued in this role in her mother's life'. She had not seen him for ten years until now.

In the story, Clelia is taken out to dinner by her friend Sam, tells him about the mismanagement that led to her mother's death, and then listens to his long account of the Russian Revolution. Large, considerate Sam is an exact copy of Judah Waten, who took Elizabeth to dinner and distracted her with a Russian history lesson. Judah had insisted she must not do her stepfather's washing herself, the same advice that Sam gives Clelia. 'I took your advice and put R's washing into a laundry,' Elizabeth wrote to Judah.

The rest of the story follows Clelia and Stephanie, her mother's cousin – Margaret Dick, given her sister's name – as they visit Theo every day to make dinner and help him prepare for his journey to his children in England, whose mother had left him when they were small. 'He didn't ruin *their* lives,' Clelia says bitterly. Reduced, tearful and ingratiating, Theo asks Clelia to go and live with him, an offer she resists. He hands her Margaret's diamond jewellery, dug out from under the bed like buried treasure, and tortuously relinquishes the rest of her possessions in a final transaction. His unwanted parting gift is a set of studio photographs of himself as a young man.

Clelia muses on the mystery that has pursued her through life: how should human beings treat each other? How to treat those who have treated you badly? 'She would have known much less about good and evil without his lessons, but she had paid a great deal for them.' Not knowing how to explain this excessive character to others, Clelia has said nothing about him to friends and lovers. Elizabeth, too, was silent about Kempley. But now she could write some of the truth. Three drafts sit among her papers, the first titled 'The Wicked Stepfather' and changed to echo the last line of Gerard Manley Hopkins' poem 'Spring and Fall': 'It is Margaret you mourn for'. The story, unpublished until 2015, bears powerful witness to the destruction wreaked by one man and by many like him.

Orphan Betty

On the eve of her ninetieth birthday, Elizabeth's sorrow and regret about her mother's death were undimmed:

> I only feel I knocked myself out for other people and I wish I had given my mother more attention. You take your mother pretty much for granted. You know that. They would die for you ... I was missing for a long time. She never ever put pressure on me. This is what very good mothers are like – they sacrifice themselves; you are lucky to have had them ... I saw her the night before she had a stroke, she said 'I do feel old' and I said 'No, no' and was hugging her. She just had a stroke and never woke up. I did see her just before she died in the Mater hospital. For about two years after that I felt nothing about anyone. It was a huge shock. I felt she was immortal. I then felt I understood in a completely different way how soldiers came back from the war, they saw their pretty little wives and children wanting to go to a dance or something, and they had had this shock that was in some cases never going to leave them. I felt no affection for anyone for a long time, and I would dimly know I had been fond of these people. It was very strange. You have to feel it, if you tell someone they don't understand. Patrick looked at me and said, 'You're too thin' – I lost weight immediately. He said, 'Your hair is very ...' He thought I had a lot of hair, and I did – shiny and dark. Maybe he was advising me to get it cut. For Patrick to make personal comments, he really was very fond of me ... Judah came and took me to dinner and told me the story of the Russian revolution; he wanted to get me to eat.

Harrower was in no state to fight for her novel when she wrote to her agent, Michael Horniman at AP Watt & Son in London, asking for advice at the end of September, 1970. There was still no word from Macmillan about *In Certain Circles*. They had published many worse novels in her time there, she said, but she had never written a novel she liked less than this one. She was inclined to take it back and try to give it the organic 'something' that a good novel needed, or to scrap it altogether. She pleaded: 'What do you think? Should I withdraw it?'

With terrible timing, Robert Cross, her local champion, left Melbourne for London that month to become managing director of the publishing house Thomas Nelson – perhaps relieved he wasn't the one to give the verdict. His replacement, Gordon Ross, was courteous but clear that Macmillan was not interested in publishing the novel in Australia. He added, 'From what you say, it does not seem that you will be unduly sorry about this.' Having delivered the bad news he dropped dead suddenly, too, a fortnight after Margaret Kempley.

So it was up to Alan Maclean to decide the fate of Harrower's novel. Despite Christopher Derrick's discouraging report, he was steadfast that the British company wanted to go ahead, and made an offer in October of £250, the same advance he'd paid for *The Watch Tower*. Horniman explained that the small sum was due to most novels 'selling very poorly of late'. Harrower felt Maclean was merely being kind, but she decided to accept on the condition that she could produce a manuscript that pleased everyone better. The ambiguous messages from him and Derrick were in fact unkind, encouraging her to proceed while further undermining her faint belief in her book. She could see the trap when she wrote to Shirley Hazzard:

> Whether it will be more inhibiting in the long run to publish and face justified harshness from critics, or to write off two years' work and the CLF's $6000 is the choice. There was an interesting book to be written, but I blocked it for all sorts of reasons and my concentration disappeared. People.

Starting work again in the quiet discipline of a new year, she began cutting and retyping on January 1, 1971. But her stepfather had not quite done with her. News came from England that Richard Kempley had died in a London hospital on January 19. With some justice from the universe, he had collapsed as he left his bank, felled by a ruptured abdominal aortic aneurysm, for which smoking was the main cause. There could hardly be circumstances more surreal or less conducive to creative thought, but Harrower pushed on with no excuses. When Alan Maclean flew to Sydney for a working visit in March, they met with undiluted mutual affection at a Macmillan party and a lunch. She handed him the revised manuscript as he left for London and told Shirley Hazzard:

I did my best to turn him against it: his decision will be the right one, whichever way it goes. Meantime, now that I am less involved with solicitors and legal affairs following my mother's death, and having finished the weeks of typing and cutting, I must think of new work. There are piles of notes already.

Kit Hazzard was first to tell her daughter that Elizabeth had finished her novel, and Shirley responded to 'the exciting news' with hope that the book would be in print soon. The Steegmullers had found *The Watch Tower* an 'unforgettable book' and Francis added that it was 'very strong and impressive & I am its and your great admirer'. They sent thanks for her friendship with Kit, who was planning to sail again from Sydney to London.

Elizabeth's letters in early 1971 made only brief mention of her own mother's death, focusing instead on Kit, whose restless mood swings were worrying her. They met one day at a café near the St James Theatre in Elizabeth Street and over their coffee Kit fell limp in her seat. Elizabeth led her to the GPO in Martin Place, where she rang a friend who suggested contacting Lifeline, the crisis support service. Over the following weeks she took Kit to a series of doctors, and to Callan Park Mental Hospital for a prescription for antidepressant medication in the form of 'little yellow pills'. They went to the Erskine Street Clinic in the city, where Kit was counselled by Andrew Robertson, a psychiatric nurse who would become a friend and ally. Elizabeth wrote to Shirley with a long report on Kit's treatment and improvement, trying to be frank but reassuring. She also sent congratulations on Shirley's being nominated for a National Book Award for *The Bay of Noon*, and Francis's win for his Cocteau biography. Such grace can't have been easy in her state of grief for her own mother and anxiety for her own novel. Her letter ended with a declaration that there would be no more letters once she began writing her next novel. The Fates were laughing silently.

Christopher Derrick read Harrower's revised manuscript fast and wrote his second one-page report. He noted that the author had produced 'a more distilled, sharpened, polished version' of the same novel, which he described as 'a sharp, sad, intense, abstract study of personal relationships within and without marriage, among well-to-do Australians, with some emphasis upon the destructive effects of (a) egoism, and (b) pity, self-pity included'. He gave patronising 'Very good marks' for the author's intelligence, observation of people, and wry, precise, economical use of language. Overall, though, the novel gave him 'a feeling of unreality, of diagram, of theory' because the characters talked about their relationships rather than demonstrating them, and their introspection was unconvincing. He backed off slightly, wondering if 'the author's mode of perception is simply too feminine to connect with my hairy old mind', and suggested that an intelligent, sensitive female reader who was also an Iris Murdoch fan would probably respond differently. But he concluded: 'The subtlety and even brilliance of the author's mind is obvious: I find the book at once empty and stifling. I can only fumble, as above, in search of a reason why.'

No one sought that female reader, and Maclean told Harrower he reluctantly agreed with Derrick that the novel still didn't work. At the beginning of April she wrote back:

> Your assessment is more than just and kind ... I do know the difference between a good and a bad novel, and it is a model of what a novel should not be. – All I regret are what I can only call 'the true things' scattered through it here and there, that I am as addicted to as a physicist might be addicted to quarks.

She was 'interested and not irritated at all' by Derrick's comments, having 'warned my two readers here that it was like a blueprint, a theoretical thing, that – breaking my own rules – everything was told and nothing demonstrated, that the people were not differentiated or visible, and that it was dead'. Maclean still did not withdraw his offer to publish, but suggested she show the novel round and come back if she did not find a more enthusiastic publisher. Harrower told her agent a few days later that she felt bound to withdraw the novel from circulation. Regretting the time and effort wasted, she promised like a penitent schoolgirl: 'Next time, I must make sure to do better.'

Maclean admitted he was 'relieved' that she had taken the criticism well and decided to put the book to one side. Horniman assured her that he and Maclean retained a warm respect for her gifts, and it was the right decision to put the old novel behind her and move on. Indeed, Maclean generously offered her a 'token' advance of £100 on the unwritten next novel or even the full £250 he had offered for *In Certain Circles*. But Harrower insisted that she wanted to work off the $6000 fellowship money before accepting an advance. Outwardly calm, she took full responsibility for the unpublished novel, telling Shirley Hazzard that Maclean had written 'so kindly, such considerate, morale-building letters, that it almost seems nothing bad has happened. But it does make you hesitate to dash in to the next thing.'

At the time, she told friends that she had notes for her next novel and was ready to start writing again, an effort to convince herself as much as them. Looking back from old age on the decision to withdraw *In Certain Circles* and all that followed, she said, 'That's when I decided to destroy my life.'

*

In the midst of the indecision about her manuscript, Elizabeth helped Kit Hazzard make her erratic plans to sail to England for an indefinite stay, and farewelled her at Easter. Her correspondence with Maclean referred to Kit as well as the Steegmullers, the professional-social circle knitting more tightly. Despite her 'no letters' warning, Elizabeth told Shirley to stay in touch if her mother returned to Sydney. She wasn't sure why she had become so involved: partly because she had finished her novel, and her mother died, and she had time between tasks when Kit needed help. She may not have seen that Kit filled a complicated need for her to give and receive kindness, and to procrastinate as she looked uncertainly ahead.

After a series of accidents and disasters, Kit was back in Sydney by mid-1971, and Elizabeth took up her role as proxy daughter: helping to find accommodation and medical care, urging her to install a telephone, reporting to Shirley, and mediating between Kit and her other daughter, Valerie Barnes, who lived in Sydney but was in endless conflict with her mother and sister.

Kit may have fascinated Harrower as potential material for a future novel. Her fiction was full of charismatic but unstable characters, and she was often drawn to complex people who needed help. *In Certain Circles* did have more young women suffering, as Kylie Tennant had irritably predicted. But in this novel she stepped back from the memorable intensity of *The Watch Tower* and its villain, Felix Shaw, and rather than focusing the drama around one dark figure, she created a circle of mismatches and cross purposes among families, friends and lovers.

The novel begins as if it will be a lighter social comedy in the style of Margaret Dick's 'Southern Latitude', opening at a square stone house on the north side of Sydney Harbour where drinks are served on the verandah and tennis balls bounce across the private court. Zoe Howard is the pretty, wealthy, carefree daughter of well-known academic scientists who encourage her to believe in her talents and shiny future. Her brother Russell has returned from a prisoner-of-war camp and is about to marry Lily, a German lecturer. Scarred by war, illness and drowned friends, he is determined to save lost souls and brings home brother and sister Stephen and Anna Quayle, who have been raised by relatives after their parents died in a level-crossing accident. Harrower's design was to show how the chance of family shaped personality and opportunity. She had always seen the difference between rich and poor, successful and strugglers as partly a matter of luck. By this time she had observed society in ever-widening circles and plucked details for her characters from a multitude of sources, even including Marmalade, the neighbours' cat. She seems to have given parts of herself to the female protagonists. In a sense she was as privileged as Zoe Howard, living in her house by the sea, but Zoe has the advantages of family, education and confidence that she had lacked. Harrower identified more with orphaned Anna, made fragile by growing up with her 'neurasthenic' aunt and 'extinguished' uncle. The novel's optimistic set-up descends into misery after Zoe marries Stephen, attracted to his difficult, frustrated soul; Anna falls in love with Russell, and like Anna Karenina contemplates suicide because she can't have him; Lily gives up her career for her daughters, only to despair when they leave to dance in London; even altruistic Russell hurts those close to him. Once again, Harrower portrays unhappy marriages, except for the well-matched Howard parents.

Zoe, dragged down by conforming to Stephen's dark moods, decides there are no happy marriages and notes, 'It was often suggested these days that the institution would have to change or go.' The women have careers in academia, war photography, film and so on, but as Zoe tells Lily:

> 'What I do understand is that at any point in a woman's life she may come across something like a cement pyramid in the middle of the road. Another person. People ... What makes men superior is that they don't – on the whole – stop functioning forever because of another person.'

The difference from Harrower's earlier novels is that, in a kind of happy ending, the characters are not trapped in their marriages but agree to part. This is the first glimmer of social change in her fiction, set in the postwar years before Australia introduced no-fault divorce in 1975. Her novels clearly showed the conditions that led the women's liberation movement to erupt in the 1970s, but like many women of her generation, she refused to call herself a feminist.

In Certain Circles contains big ideas and fine writing, evokes Sydney's lush beauty and subtle class differences, and tracks the transition from youth to middle age through love, success, disillusionment and renewal. However, as Christopher Derrick said in his reader's report, there is a diagrammatic quality to the narrative and each character represents a type of psychological damage. The couples, Russell and Lily, Zoe and Stephen, move between their two houses at opposite ends of a small beach. They interact like chess pieces and become difficult to distinguish from one another: who is brother and sister, who is married to whom. They talk about their relationships and emotions without stirring deep feeling in the reader. The static scenes and wordy dialogue recall the formality of the English writer Ivy Compton-Burnett's English drawing-room novels, which Elizabeth had read in London, and might have worked better on a stage.

But the real fault seems to be that Harrower was reworking her old material, attempting to stretch it into new shapes. She was squeezing in everything and everyone she knew, in dispersed and sublimated forms, rather than telling an urgent story driven from deep within her. There is also the problem of a melodramatic suicide note that Anna mails to her family by mistake in a bundle of envelopes, years after she decided not to kill herself and put the letter away in a drawer. The letter turns the plot, forces everyone to reveal true feelings, but feels like a device from an old bag of tricks. The flaws make sense in the context of Harrower's personal losses and emotional stress when she wrote the novel. Despite all this, and her own doubts, she had enough belief in her novel to bury the manuscript in the National Library of Australia so that another publisher could discover *In Certain Circles* many years later.

Although the novel's suicide letter feels contrived, suicide and mental distress concerned Harrower in her writing and often in her life. There's no evidence that she attempted suicide herself after the time she lay on the road as a child, but she had been close to emotional collapse, and she was hypersensitive to the anguish of those around her. She would have heard of the writer Charmian Clift's death by overdose in 1969 at her nearby Mosman home, overwhelmed by family problems, overshadowed by her writer husband, George Johnston, and unable to complete a novel. Too many women writers took their own lives, most famously Virginia Woolf in 1941 and Sylvia Plath in 1963. Elizabeth had spent months in 1963 trying to rescue a woman she knew from London, Christine Cooper, who had a nervous breakdown while visiting Sydney. As her only acquaintance, Elizabeth had been 'sitting at death-beds and visiting four hospitals and doing no good at all to her, or myself, or anyone else'. Elizabeth recalled Christine's condition when Kit Hazzard was 'pre-suicide' at her lowest ebb of depression and telling 'sad stories about herself for four hours'. She knew from Kylie about Roddy's frequent hospitalisations and suicide attempts, culminating in the breakdown that led to his mutilating fall under a train and the consequences it had for his family. Kylie explained in her no-nonsense style that he had given up trying to kill himself by the time Elizabeth knew him, but he was forever fragile.

Having tried to dramatise the hopelessness that could lead to suicide and the hope that could save someone from the edge, Harrower put her manuscript in a drawer. She had already written a short story that examined the suicidal impulse from the inside and had sent a version of 'A Few Days in the Country' to her London agent, Michael Horniman, along with 'Alice', in April 1969, tentatively hoping for overseas sales, before offering them to Australian quarterlies. Again, both stories were returned.

'A Few Days in the Country' came from the same material as the suicide scenario in the novel. *In Certain Circles* focuses on the other characters' panic after receiving Anna's letter, which confesses that she and Russell have been secretly in love for many years but did not want to hurt his wife, Lily, and their daughters. Death seemed the only way to end her pain of longing. They rush around looking for her, expecting to find a body. When Anna arrives home and realises that she has unwittingly sent out the old suicide letters, she explains to Zoe the surprise of turning into a suicidal person: 'one morning I woke up and my mind was still sound but suicide had chosen me'. She had gone to stay with a friend, a doctor, in the country and planned to end her life in the bush. But finally she made a choice: to eat a stale piece of apple pie and stay alive. In 'A Few Days in the Country' the character is a different woman, a lapsed pianist called Sophie, who visits an acquaintance, Caroline, a doctor in a country town. The city was getting her down, she tells her host, but in her mind: 'The universe was hostile. The sun rose in the west. She was in danger. Only strangers might not be malevolent.' Sophie does not name the problems that have brought her to this point, other than 'grief' and a 'psychic knife'. She too is surprised that 'suicide thought of her'. Before leaving the city she posted a letter or two, to be read after her death, and she plans to find a secluded place where she will swallow her tablets. But there are glimmers of comfort in the wordless company of Caroline's cat and the radiance of 'Caroline's small valley from sky to dandelion'. As Sophie boards a homeward train, the two parts of her mind, suicide and instruction, are still in a tug-of-war and the future is unresolved. As with Clare's departure by train at the end of *The Watch Tower*, there is hope.

The story would eventually be published in *Overland* magazine in 1977, and much later in her collected short fiction. It can be read as a universal portrayal of heartbreak, caused by a painful love or betrayal. Harrower must have tinkered with the story several times before the final version to reflect particular events in her life. She was surely thinking of poor Christine Cooper when she used the surname Cooper for Caroline's dinner guests. There is much of Blackheath in the setting, and some of Kylie Tennant in Caroline herself. At least one detail suggests a personal response to Margaret Kempley's death: Sophie's detachment from life is manifest as she listens to Caroline's heedless chatter and places branches of japonica from the garden in a vase, reminiscent of the blossom Harrower had brought home from Hillside Farm the last time she and her mother spoke.

*

After her mother's death, as usual, Elizabeth hid her inner pain from most people behind an outer shell of normal behaviour and concern for others. Patrick White, Kylie Tennant, Judah Waten and Margaret Dick were her strongest supports, in different ways. She socialised, went to Blackheath, read books, helped Kit, and made noises about writing. There were also the final duties of death to perform.

Richard Kempley's will, written in England shortly before he died, asked for his ashes to be shipped back to Sydney and placed beside his late wife's at Northern Suburbs Memorial Gardens. Elizabeth had the unpleasant task of reuniting them. After a lifetime of deal-making and money-worship, Kempley's estate was meagre. In Australia he left $7545.13 in his bank accounts, all to his elder son, Richard John William Kempley. In England he left £1008, also to his son. There was nothing for Elizabeth, but she did not miss out. Margaret Kempley left everything to her daughter in her will written in 1960, the year after Elizabeth returned to Australia. Her estate was worth $44000, including a block of four tenanted flats at 113 Middle Head Road, Mosman, valued at $40000 (more than $500000 in today's money), which gave Elizabeth an income of about $5000 a year in rent, and a small amount of cash. She also received Margaret's famous diamond jewellery, valued at $545 – a wedding ring with twenty-five stones, two other large rings, a wrist watch with fifty-four diamonds, and a pair of single-stone earrings – and all the contents of the house at Mosman. Her mother seems to have been meticulous in listing every item to prevent Kempley from claiming even a cushion, though she probably expected to outlive him.

The inventory describes the three-bedroom house that became her prison as if it were a museum of mid-century middle-class Australia: the furnishings included a wing-back lounge suite upholstered in tapestry, an Admiral TV set (superseded model), eight-piece cedar period dining suite, Oriental tables, verandah chairs, a Laminex kitchen table, a Crosley refrigerator, a cake mixer, numerous sets of china, cutlery, glass and silver, the pedestal desk and revolving office chair from Kempley's den. Among the ornaments in the lounge room were two Royal Doulton figures, leaving the tantalising question of whether one was the Bluebeard china figurine made by Royal Doulton from 1932 to 1949, which exactly matched Harrower's description in *The Watch Tower* of 'a swarthy turbaned man' in red and blue robes and 'drawing a long assassin's knife from the low-slung girdle at his waist'. Did she take pleasure in smashing him?

The bigger mystery is why the house at 5 Stanley Avenue, Mosman, did not appear in either will, even though Harrower always said she had inherited her mother's house. There's a possible clue in Margaret Dick's unpublished novel, 'Southern Latitude'. The widowed Constance Elton, who lives with her daughter Frances in their harbourside house, says:

> this *is* my house as long as I live. Daddy bought it in Frances's name because of death duties, but I have a life-interest in it … Frances furnished the place, of course. As I told her, it'll be hers in the long run, anyway Daddy tied up most of the capital and I couldn't be expected to furnish it out of my income.

This sounds like the future the Kempleys expected when they moved into Stanley Avenue, though they paid to furnish the house, and fits with Richard Kempley's lifelong efforts to skirt taxes and ethical financial dealings. The house may have been in Elizabeth's name all along, and Kempley may have bought the block of flats in Margaret's name for the same reason. Death duties (an inheritance tax) took a slice of every deceased estate in Australia until they were abolished in 1979, and there was much discussion about how to minimise if not avoid them. Patrick White had urged his mother in London in the 1960s to give her jewellery, furs and furniture to daughters and granddaughters so they wouldn't be consumed by death duties. A decade later he was reviewing his own will and doing 'an enormous amount of research to see how one can reduce death duties'.

By April 1971, Harrower was still dealing with solicitors and accountants, writing cheques for state and federal death duties, her mother's final income tax, and rates, taxes and repairs to the block of flats. Meanwhile, she was seeing friends off on their travels and wrote to Judah Waten, 'I am rather wishing myself one of these travellers. As I'm not keen about ships (boring) or planes (too high) (and too expensive), must think of a third way.' She ended her letter:

> Had better go off now and do something like the washing or shopping, or even considering the next book. Because there had better be one. I have one in mind, notes and all, but don't want to make another false start. The worst of it is, in a way, having that ghastly CLF [Commonwealth Literary Fund] thing in the back of your mind. If the one written for it doesn't come off, I mean. Because, of course, there are always sixty people who feel they were more deserving. Ah, well!

Before she went anywhere, she had a visitor from the past. Yvonne, the daughter of her late father, Frank Harrower, was too young to remember Elizabeth's visit to their home a decade ago and her mother, Elma, did not allow her name to be mentioned. All these years Yvonne had not known that Elizabeth existed. But after Frank's death in 1968, Elma's sister threatened to tell Yvonne she had a half-sister, so Elma grudgingly broke the news and arranged for her to visit Elizabeth in Sydney. Sixteen-year-old Yvonne was excited when she caught a train from Dapto to Central Station in the spring of 1971. She clearly remembered the day:

> Elizabeth was standing with arrangements to meet under the big clock, and there she was. You couldn't miss her because she was so tall, but she was so like my dad in the face, because Elizabeth had a big nose and so did my dad. It's quite funny because one of my sons has the same nose – every time I look at my son I think, gosh, there's your grandfather's nose.

Yvonne knew Elizabeth was a writer and was struck by her dignity and loveliness, but smaller details impressed her most. They caught a taxi to the flat in Want Street, Mosman, where they had a cup of tea and Yvonne looked through a kaleidoscope. Talking about their parents, she remembered Elizabeth simply saying, 'my mum and your dad, it wasn't working any more, so that's why they got a divorce'. Back in the city they sat in the bay window of a café and ordered pancakes. Elizabeth asked if she wanted lemon and sugar or maple syrup, and warned that maple syrup was an acquired taste so she may not like it. 'I had lemon and sugar, she had the maple syrup … Every time I have maple syrup I think of that.'

Elma's hostility stopped the half-sisters from seeing each other again, to Yvonne's regret. 'I would never ever go and visit her because that would have created world war three.' Yvonne had a career in nursing, married and had four children. Several times a year she would secretly ring Elizabeth to talk for an hour or so and confide problems with her mother or children. Elizabeth sent Christmas cards but Yvonne had to hide them. Their hunted correspondence faded out in the 1990s as Yvonne was taken up with family and work. Elma had married again and lived until she was ninety-seven in 2022, domineering but loved by her daughter to the end.

PART TWO

1972 to 2020

La vie bohème

Cynthia Nolan gave Elizabeth the reason she needed to travel again. Her well-timed invitation in late 1971 was just the kind that worked with Elizabeth, posed more as a request for help. Would she care for the Nolans' house and garden in London while they were travelling, and at the same time have a much-needed holiday?

Patrick White had sent his friends Sidney and Cynthia Nolan to see Elizabeth in the Macmillan office when they were visiting from London for a retrospective exhibition of Nolan's paintings in 1967. There was business to discuss as Macmillan was publishing the latest of Cynthia's travel books, *Open Negative: An American Memoir*, and a book about Sidney's art. Elizabeth attended the retrospective, timed for Nolan's fiftieth birthday, at the Art Gallery of New South Wales, with Patrick and Manoly, Robert Cross, and Cynthia's friend Ida 'Bill' Cantwell, a lively figure in Sydney's arts, social and left-wing political circles. Elizabeth found the Nolans were 'immensely likeable and added much to the Sydney landscape for those few weeks'. She felt a particular affinity with the plainspoken but sensitive Cynthia, who had avoided the exhibition opening.

Their friendship grew during the annual visits the couple made to Australia. Sidney Nolan was considered one of the nation's great modernist artists, in demand for his paintings of history, mythology, the outback, and especially the bushranger Ned Kelly, as well as theatre and opera designs in London. Patrick White had connected with Nolan in 1957 when he asked him to design the covers for his great, tragic explorer novel *Voss* and then a new edition of *The Aunt's Story*, his 1948 novel about a spinster losing her mind as she travels a world on the brink of war. He met both Nolans for the first time in Florida a year later when they were all travelling in the US. White thought Sidney 'completely honest and without nonsense' and Cynthia 'forthright and intelligent, perhaps a little ambitious', but jealous and protective of her younger husband. They became friends in Australia, and after sending the Nolans to meet Elizabeth Harrower, White had them together around his table at 20 Martin Road, Centennial Park. He spent some of his happiest times in London with the Nolans, at the theatre, the opera, and their riverside home.

Elizabeth and Patrick were also friends by now, sharing meals and outings, and regularly speaking by phone to exchange thoughts about books, theatre, films, friends and gossip. White could complain to Elizabeth, trusting that she was sympathetic and discreet, and she saw through his grim-voiced pessimism to his perceptive humanity and humour. She greatly admired him but was not in awe as some women friends were, nicknamed the 'lady disciples' by the quietly observant Manoly. White had boosted *The Watch Tower* and encouraged her writing, and, along with Bill Cantwell, he was frank to the Nolans about her need to get away after stressful years of adversity.

Shirley Hazzard and Francis Steegmuller, frequent visitors to London, also knew the Nolans and wrote to Elizabeth in mid-1971 that they had shared an evening at the home of the Macleans, which was 'heaven', and that 'Harrower is loved'. Elizabeth replied that the feeling was reciprocated, and that she enjoyed the Nolans' spring visits to Sydney and her erratic exchange of letters with Cynthia. By the end of the year she decided, after much hesitation and encouragement, to go to London for three or four months, staying at the Nolans' house. By chance she was sailing on the ship that had recently delivered Kit Hazzard home from her latest escapade. Patrick and Manoly had sent Elizabeth a postcard from Europe warning they were 'alarmed to hear Mrs Hazzard had broken a leg & was returning to Australia. Keep well away, or you'll be landed with her forever.' Ignoring the omens, she was adamant that when she returned from London, she would not have much time for Kit. There were many reasons to leave Sydney, including the hope that a change of scene might induce some writing. Since retiring her novel, she had 'written two poems and seen people and wasted my time badly which is why I had better be exiled'.

She embarked on the *Fairstar* in January 1972 for the return to London that she'd intended to make a decade earlier. A small group of friends saw her off, among them Margaret Dick, Kit Hazzard, Kylie Tennant, Lewis

La vie bohème

Rodd, and Bill Cantwell. There was also David Cleaver, an American-born, radical left-wing publisher who had been a sales representative at Macmillan. He had recently dined at Elizabeth's place and taken her to see a film of *The Brothers Karamazov*. She was startled by how seriously he responded to her goodbye kiss at the wharf and the telegram he sent mourning her departure. 'Heavens! I'll be silent after this to disillusion him,' she wrote onboard to Margaret. Kylie's husband, Roddy, too, saw her departure as 'a field day for goodbye kisses' as if he 'were in a brothel. Grr.' Roddy sent letters accompanied by love poems – good poems, by real poets – while she travelled, a symptom perhaps of his depression and strained marriage, but also of the exasperating dominance of Kylie and her family in Elizabeth's life. Before she left, she had stayed a while at their Hunters Hill house, where Kylie berated her for going away without consultation, and Roddy interrupted every conversation they attempted with his 'clammy pervasiveness'. She was desperate to leave the pressures of home, yet she spent much of the sea voyage composing letters to her many friends and waiting impatiently for their replies. She wrote diligently to her grandmother Helen, 'Mummum', who was, naturally, shattered by the premature death of her daughter. All the way she confided to Margaret Dick, apologising for 'being a trial to you' and reprimanding her for not having a letter waiting in every port. Travelling alone was especially hard in her limbo state, the desiccated past trailing behind her, the future unknown. To Margaret she wrote:

> I'm not at the moment unduly depressed; as long as I keep my mind off the many misinterpretations inflicted regarding this whole enterprise and in general, I'm OK, like an engine in neutral ... And perhaps the desire to set the record straight, the feeling of misinterpretation, is the irritant that might help a novel along. Novels exist to put the record straight. Even if very few people know what record, or no-one.

Kylie and Roddy saw her adrift in her grief but she rebelled against their attempts to guide, or control, her. On the ship she did not harness her mind to writing, but chatted to other passengers, formed a friendship with Darryl and Judy Henderson, English migrants headed for study leave at the university in Canterbury, took some Italian lessons, and observed the *'Monsieur Hulot's Holiday'* bubble of amusingly tedious shipboard life. Australians became more aggressively Australian as they approached England, she noted; men threw punches, girls got plastered on the deck, and one threw a chianti bottle that cut a child's head open.

Among her constant reading from the ship's bookshelves were Joseph Conrad's *Lord Jim*, Kingsley Amis's newly released *Girl, 20*, and a self-help bestseller, *The Power of Your Subconscious Mind* by Joseph Murphy. As a teenager in Sydney, Betty had been given Conrad's *Nostromo*, which set her off on a passionate period of reading Conrad. His seafaring novels were far from the fiction she would write but taught her about great prose and individual moral challenges – on a sinking ship in *Lord Jim*. In Fremantle she met up with Leslie Schenk, an American she and Margaret had befriended as a self-important would-be writer in Corfu and Paris in 1956; he worked for the United Nations, knew writers such as James Baldwin, and would later write literary criticism and several novels. When Elizabeth met him again, he had recently moved from Tangiers to Perth with a young man named Mohammed. 'Leslie's accomplishments still weigh very heavily on him, I'm afraid ... He was quite – not quite – extremely disagreeable.' He spoke of the 'chemistry' he'd had with Margaret and dropped hints about looking for an agent, while making snide remarks about 'the illustrious Elizabeth Harrower' – she insisted on Elizabeth, not Betty – and his amazement that someone had done a PhD thesis on her work. Elizabeth, the reluctant traveller, had threatened she might leave the ship in Perth but, perhaps goaded by the prospect of more Leslie, she sailed on.

The worst of the voyage was a severe storm that battered the *Fairstar* off the coast of South Africa near Durban, tossing people and furnishings across the ship, and confirming Elizabeth's decision to fly home at the end of her trip. As always, she was acutely aware of the weather at sea: a misty red sun and a pale moon in the sky at dawn, a violet dusk like 'Omar's bowl', warm days giving way to a cold north wind as they approached Tenerife. 'It's strange and exciting in a way to change hemispheres slowly.' She wrote again to Margaret:

Heaven knows if I'll be able to write; I'll get myself organized first. You don't start a book in an odd hour. Perhaps everything I know is too sad to pass on. Not sad exactly. And I am not sad. I just don't know about writing. We'll see. I don't want to be another Leslie, perpetually not writing but always thinking of myself as a Writer, and everything else being second-third and fourth-best. I'll find out …

Cynthia and Sidney Nolan left London as soon as she arrived, with an itinerary that would take in Athens, Africa, Australia and New York; they travelled mainly for work, to find subjects for his paintings and her accompanying travel memoirs, and for his exhibitions. Elizabeth settled in to their rambling house at 79–81 Deodar Road in Putney, alone except for the dogs, the cook, Winifred Fox, and a cast of gardeners, cleaners and tradesmen. London thrilled her with its familiar buildings and spring weather, despite the election of another Conservative government under Prime Minister Edward Heath, and train go-slows, heavy traffic, and daily blackouts as Britain switched over from coal to North Sea gas. Grey skies and cool days were preferable to Sydney's summer heat to an Australian who felt genetically programmed for Scottish weather. She walked across the Putney Bridge to buy groceries, caught the bus to her 1950s haunts in Chelsea and Knightsbridge, shopped for classic Jaeger clothes, saw Harley Street doctors for her migraine headaches and skin cancers left by x-ray treatment for teenage acne. She took pleasure in galleries, lecture halls and theatres refreshed from postwar fatigue, but with performances curtailed by blackouts, or advertising their own generators for emergency lighting and heat. *Hair* and *Godspell* and *Oh! Calcutta!* were playing, and she could have seen John Gielgud and John Mills in *Veterans* at her old Royal Court, or Kenneth More in Alan Bennett's *Getting On*.

There were reunions with old friends, such as the once-suicidal Christine Cooper, who still seemed lost and worried about money. Her request to borrow £20 for a weekend away offended Elizabeth, who gave it with a lecture. Perhaps there was some of Christine in Christian in *The Catherine Wheel*. Elizabeth made several visits to Reg and Phoebe Chaloner's house in nearby Wandsworth, where she and Margaret had rented an upstairs flat in the year before leaving for Sydney. Reg picked her up in his MG sports car and the couple was as kind and likeable as ever. Elizabeth wrote to Margaret: 'I saw the famous round table on which I wrote *The Catherine Wheel*. The furniture was different. The lavatory wouldn't pull properly; I seem to remember there was a knack to it, which I've lost.' She reclaimed the Greek water jug and striped vase that she'd written into her London novel, but left the rest of their few stored possessions behind again. Reg and Phoebe were so pleased to have Elizabeth's company that one Sunday they invited her over for roast duck, drove her in the MG to see stones that marked the site of Caesar's Camp at Royal Wimbledon Golf Club, and took her to visit Edith Crapper, a renowned painter of miniatures, illustrated manuscripts and woodcuts. Curious about everyone she met, Harrower described her as a character in an Edwardian novel: 'She is a tall lady, with white hair, a white beard (little), black stockings, beautiful skin, and very intelligent blue eyes like her mother's eyes in the miniature.' The butcher and his wife in the flat downstairs 'persecute her' by playing their television loudly; 'she was on the verge of passing away that very day'.

Shirley Hazzard and Francis Steegmuller made sure to be in London on their way to Italy in March so they could meet Elizabeth after six years of exchanging letters. They all had dinner with their publisher at Macmillan, Alan Maclean, and his wife Robin, at Boulestin, a famous French restaurant in Covent Garden, and carried on until after midnight at Brown's Hotel, where the Steegmullers were staying. For tea at the Ritz with Shirley and Francis, Elizabeth had her hair done and brooded about what to wear – both frequent preoccupations – deciding on new beige wool slacks with turn-ups, a white polo-neck sweater, suede jacket, and a striped scarf she'd bought in Venice in 1951. To her delight, Francis guessed which shop it came from. 'Anyway, they are very, very nice, which we both knew already. They are just like their letters,' she wrote to Margaret. 'Shirley is almost as tall as I am ... with very pretty eyes and a genuine smile.' They thanked her for helping Kit and for 'the little yellow pills' that seemed to have transformed her. She recognised them as a happy couple, though Francis said Shirley had barely any time for him in the past six months while she finished her book about the corruption of the United

Nations, *Defeat of an Ideal*. Shirley, exhausted and steeled for criticism, said, 'I wouldn't like you both to know how I feel about work. I'd like to sit on a sofa and eat chocolate creams all day.' When the Steegmullers returned to London in July, the three of them travelled to the Macleans' house in Kent for a day of 'white wine, hilarity and talk'. Kit Hazzard sent sixteen letters to Elizabeth in the months she was away, with news of mutual friends and enthusiastic wishes to see her in Sydney.

Elizabeth tried to contact Shirley's friend Patricia Clarke, who had worked for British Intelligence in Cairo, and more importantly took care of Kit when she was in London, but she was away in Tangiers. She did see Margery Williams, who had been Patrick's adoring friend when she and her husband worked in Sydney with the British Council promoting British-Australian cultural ties. Patrick also gave her an introduction to the Irish novelist Edna O'Brien, which led to a meeting at a poetry reading, a pleasant lunch and a signed copy of her novel *A Pagan Place*, as well as a connection with her manuscript typist, who was a neighbour in Deodar Road. There were pleasant times with Patrick's former publisher, Maurice Temple Smith, and his writer wife Jean. Judah Waten put her in touch with his daughter Alice, an accomplished violinist and music teacher, who had studied in Moscow, and his writer friends Gerda Charles and Christina Stead. Concerned as ever about her health, he provided the name of a professor of medicine should she need a doctor.

*

Christina Stead became an important friend for Elizabeth. They had already met in Sydney, when Stead visited from London in 1969 after the death of her husband, Bill Blake. Ron Geering, a literary academic who had written the first full-length study of Stead's work, and his wife Dorothy held a dinner for her at their home in Gordon on Sydney's North Shore, and invited Elizabeth Harrower. Curious to read Stead's fiction, she especially liked the 1940s novels *The Man Who Loved Children* and *For Love Alone*. She felt empathy with the author, whose introspective writing had drawn on an unhappy childhood, conflict with her father, and a young woman's move to London for an unworthy man. At dinner

Harrower admired Stead's dignity and lack of self-importance. Later she told Stead's biographer Christine Williams: 'We got on well, we talked and I could see that she was still very devastated by her husband's death. I felt she was wondering what to do now with her life, and I said that I was sure a lot of people would welcome her back to Australia. I urged her at that first meeting to come back.' Soon after that encounter, Stead read Harrower's novel *The Long Prospect* and wrote to her: 'You have a remarkable, sober acerbity, an almost historical view ... and the fragrance and nuttiness of the kernel, with the nutshell dispensed with ... You are unique, a writer on your own and your future is no doubt, a long prospect.'

Patrick White wrote to Elizabeth in London, wondering how she would get on with Stead this time. He had found her 'rather forbidding' and thought she didn't like him when she lunched at Centennial Park. Elizabeth rang Christina and went to see her in Surbiton, an outer suburb of London, where she lived in a derelict block of flats next to an empty demolition site. Born in 1902, she had spent her adult life overseas since 1928, the year of Elizabeth's birth, and published her books in New York and London. White had sent a letter of protest to the *Herald* when the 'Higher Junta of Australian Intellect' denied this 'novelist of genius' the $10 000 Encyclopaedia Britannica Award for Literature in 1967 because of her long absence. She had met her European-Jewish-American husband, Bill Blech (later Blake) in London, where he was a banker, and joined him in the odd pairing of banking and Marxism. Although they couldn't marry until his first wife gave him a divorce in 1952, Blake was the defining love of her life. Living on their writing between Europe and the United States, she was dogged by Australian censors and ASIO for communist sympathies until Blake's death in 1968. At the age of seventy Stead was impoverished, unwell and alone, with an international reputation but little recognition in Australia. Elizabeth might have imagined herself in the same predicament in future: she had published most of her novels as an Australian living in the UK and been almost invisible in both countries. She caught the train several times to Surbiton, taking food up to the desolate flat, which reminded her of places where she had lived in London, and often spoke to Christina by phone.

There were fun times, too. Christina had a playful sense of humour, she enjoyed good food and took Elizabeth to a splendid lunch at Le Petit Club Français in St James's – a dining club for the Free French during the war – with her bookseller friend, Paul Koston. He had paid for her membership and was one of three men whom Elizabeth described as 'her chiefest friends' but not lovers. 'She really loves men as someone like Judah loves women, in a most unusually straightforward and generous manner with no – to use the ghastly term – hang-ups.' At Fortnum and Mason Christina bought Elizabeth an Easter present of glacé fruit in a china dish, and then had to stop and take medication for her heart condition as they were walking through a tunnel in the Piccadilly Tube station. At her urging, Elizabeth bought copies of *Private Eye* and *Oz*, the underground magazine edited by Australian Richard Neville and others that had been subject to a famous obscenity trial in 1971. 'Pretty horrific they are, too!' As in Australia, Elizabeth mostly had older friends, and her London did not intersect with the Swinging London generation of Neville, Martin Sharp, Jim Anderson and Germaine Greer. But while she was considering what to do with her mother's squirrel coat and how to style her hair, she noticed with interest that young people were wearing coats with sheepskin collars, no longer teasing their hair, and using expressions such as 'It's not on'. Christina told her she was a natural writer and must remove herself from any situation that stopped her writing. She offered to send Elizabeth's books to her New York agent, and invited her to use a room and a typewriter in her flat. Though she did not accept the depressing room, Elizabeth was deeply grateful.

Writing to her after their outing, Elizabeth referred to Christina's desire for a boyfriend, and she added: 'I had a letter from one yesterday who is travelling in New Zealand at the moment; he said he looks at everything twice, once for me and once for himself. What a pity I don't love him! He's nice, too. But, but, but ...' This was David Cleaver, who had seen her off on the *Fairstar* and whose work as a sales rep with the Australia and New Zealand Book Co. took him across the Tasman. His aerogrammes, signed 'affectionately', were hardly love letters, but he said he missed her very much and wanted to help her move when she got home. Elizabeth had once told him he neglected his friends, and he promised to reform, especially in her case, if she would allow him. Yet he encouraged her to stay in London and hoped the 'electric' atmosphere would inspire her to start a new novel. Writing and politics were the only things that mattered, he said, and the finest thing happening in the world was 'the eclipse, the decay, of the Anglo-Saxon world; once their hegemony is ended the human race may be able to bring some sense into the world'.

Christina's non-boyfriend, Paul Koston – a committed Marxist – had argued 'scornfully' with Elizabeth over lunch about her praise for Francis Steegmuller's biography of Jean Cocteau, and asked her to define a work of art. She gave a considered reply to his question in a letter to Christina:

> The long-sustained analysis of virtually unanalysable states of mind, ways of being, when the writer seldom makes direct statements but produces by a most curious and subtle accumulation of words a true impression of a living person – this delights my mind extremely and I call it a work of art. It's as if the writer writes, but also concentrates on the paper and makes magic pass over it, and then, as I say, one's mind has the extraordinary pleasure of rushing up and down stairs and along corridors at top speed and there, in the end, is someone alive and breathing. Marvellous! This is what you can do. And on a good day, what fun!

Elizabeth was not writing at all, other than copious letters, but she was buoyed by her hectic social life. She often told Margaret she was pleasantly surprised that people liked her and didn't want to knock her down. Her movements were constrained by Cynthia's insistence that she must be in residence for the whole time they were away – which was extended to nine weeks – in order to walk the dogs, read the mail, pay the staff, oversee the gas installation men, and so on. She didn't mind, but various friends were outraged on her behalf. This was further complicated by the request that she should be discreet about being in the Nolans' house, with the amusing result that her former landlords, Reg and Phoebe, came to visit and dismissed the Sidney Nolan paintings on the walls as amateur and childish.

Alan Maclean was furious that Elizabeth couldn't stay for a whole weekend at his Kent country house, and complained directly to Cynthia about her unreasonable demands. Instead, Elizabeth caught the train for a day to lunch on chicken and plum pudding in the kitchen of the Macleans' converted oast house, a building originally used to dry hops, with windows opening on to rolling hills. Another time they took her to Sissinghurst, the National Trust–owned home of Vita Sackville-West and Harold Nicholson, where she marvelled at the garden with its bluebell woods. She thought Alan and Robin Maclean were a happy couple, their two small sons 'luckily' liked her, and 'Alan is an angel. A nicer man you just couldn't meet. His concern for me, for everyone, is far above the call of duty.' At the end of her long, ecstatic letter to Margaret, she wrote: 'Sorry I left it so long to report all this. I've been so busy and in such good spirits. Everything is interesting. I feel so much freer and braver and more independent. I hope no tests arrive; I've had so many!'

While she couldn't yet visit her relatives in Scotland, Auntie Minnie – her great-aunt – sent a welcoming bunch of tulips, daffodils and hyacinths. Margaret's sister Stephanie went down from Cheshire to stay with Elizabeth at Deodar Street for a weekend. They got on warmly, even though Elizabeth recognised their political differences, Steph's unconscious snobbery towards Australians, and 'vast gulfs ... between our experience of life'. Stephanie, her husband Alec, and her sister Anne, took Elizabeth on car trips to Richmond Park and Hampton Court, and she swooned over fields of daffodils and bluebells, deer and dairy cows. They walked through the city from St Paul's Cathedral one Sunday morning, and saw *Under Milk Wood* and *The Threepenny Opera* at Festival Hall.

Her pleasure was diluted by hearing from John Kempley, the younger brother of her late stepfather, whose voice on the phone was disturbing because he sounded 'faintly' like Richard Kempley. John or 'Jack' had left Australia and settled back in England years earlier and wanted to see 'Betty'. She assured Margaret this would be her only meeting with any Kempley. On a beautiful blue March day he and she both arrived early at Leicester Square. They sat for two hours over lunch, for which she paid, and then walked to Hyde Park and sat in the sun. She listened while the 'poor old thing' spoke with tears in his eyes about Richard and their family. Richard's sons wanted to know whether Betty had brought photos of the plaque she'd had made for his niche next to Margaret Kempley in the Sydney cemetery. She hadn't had time and was annoyed by their impatience. However, the sons weren't sentimental about their father. Elizabeth's report of the conversation to Margaret Dick was sketchy but suggested Richard Kempley was as volatile as Felix Shaw in *The Watch Tower*. One son had told Jack that if he were Margaret Kempley he would have stuck a knife in him and Jack thought his brother was 'born that way'. Yet John and Richard had never quarrelled as boys or men. The worst that passed between them was his telling Richard when he returned to England months before his death that he wasn't a 'tin god', 'whatever he thought he was in Australia'. When they were young, their mother had thought Greenwich Naval College would be good for Richard, and their ex-Navy father agreed grimly, 'It will break him or break his heart'. Before Richard left home for Greenwich, his father whipped him for some reason and Richard ran up the stairs shouting, 'I'll kill myself when I go to my room.' Anger, discipline, rebellion, violence and self-pity were built into Richard Kempley by nature and example. Elizabeth ended her letter with one uncomprehending word: 'Strange.'

Between social engagements, Elizabeth was content to be at the house in Deodar Road, which was two semi-detached houses joined by a connecting door. They were part of a plain but handsome row of late-Victorian gabled houses with long back gardens that ran down to the south bank of the Thames near Putney Bridge. The other side of the street was gap-toothed where houses had been bombed. Elizabeth had a self-contained upstairs flat consisting of bedroom, living room, kitchen and bathroom in the second house. For most of her time there, she endured long electricity cuts and dark nights with no television, but she listened to BBC radio broadcasts such as Strindberg's play *The Father*, with Trevor Howard and Peggy Ashcroft – 'Awfully good, but "harassing" like my books, to use Mrs Fox's word'.

At the same time she was reading *Married to Tolstoy* by Cynthia Asquith, a biography of the writer's wife Sofia, which was 'harassing like my life, too, with madly contradictory people loving each other and driving each other crazy'. She still identified with the Russian novelists, whose intense books she had found as a teenager in the Sydney City Library. Among her other reading were two books that dealt with Freud: *Black Ship to Hell,* a study of human destructive and self-destructive behaviour by Brigid Brophy, and *My Sister, My Spouse*, a biography of Lou Andreas-Salome, writer and friend of Freud who, she told Margaret, 'was extremely beautiful and drove numerous men to distraction – Rilke and the superman philosopher whose name begins with N. I can't spell it.' (She meant Nietzsche.)

Mrs Fox, or Winifred, turned out to be a talented, generous cook and a fascinating character. Her mother was Scottish, her father Viennese-Jewish, her ex-husband a 'promiscuous' German millionaire-lawyer who agreed to a divorce only if she left one of their sons with him. He joined the Nazi party, her sister Isobel joined the Communist Party, and her brother-in-law, Cecil Powell, was a Nobel Prize winner in physics. Winifred was 'a non-joiner' like Elizabeth, but a supporter of miners and of Labour, if not its leader, Harold Wilson. Astringent, intelligent, and something of a bully in her household management, she was 'won over' to Elizabeth by a bottle of Dubonnet and after reading *The Watch Tower* and *The Catherine Wheel*. ('Said it was a chef d'oeuvre. What is that??') Elizabeth, also won over, often left her attic in the evening and went through the labyrinth to Winifred's flat, separate from the house, to talk, watch television and play Scrabble, sometimes with Isobel, too. Having always been a tenant with no experience in home decorating, Elizabeth was in awe at Cynthia's ability to create a casual artistic blend of faux-bamboo furniture, blankets as curtains, and photographer's spotlights. 'One room for entertaining is grand, but all the rest is books, beads, flowers, pottery, paintings (I'm not supposed to say that! ...).' From her breakfast table she looked down at flowering magnolias and ducks on the river, and luxuriated in her 'vie bohème'.

When the Nolans returned at the beginning of May, Cynthia was 'absolutely furious' that a rose bush had been over-pruned, and downcast that Elizabeth was leaving for Scotland the next day. Even Patrick White heard the news from Cynthia and wrote to Elizabeth: 'What of the Nolans? Has there been a confrontation between Cynthia and Mrs Fox over the mutilated rosetree?' Elizabeth told Cynthia she'd been apprehensive about her return, and to Margaret she wrote she 'was amazed and irritated to find myself yet again with someone who (so it seemed) wanted to terrorise me'.

On the train to Scotland she stewed about Cynthia's coolness and decided, 'I've been insulted!' This was a feeling she had analysed in minute physiological detail in her story 'English Lesson', published in Macmillan's *Summer's Tales 2* in 1965. The story preceded her close friendship with Cynthia, and the shock for the young woman, Laura (a favourite name), comes from a rude business letter in reply to a letter her friends had urged her to send. The circumstances are deliberately vague but Laura experiences a mixture of physical shock and self-critical surprise at how shaken she is by a callous remark. With pounding heart and burning body, she realises: 'She had been insulted. Someone almost a stranger had hit her across the face. *Why?*' Incidentally, the self-important American lodger who observes Laura's shock is named Leslie and bears a strong likeness to Leslie Schenk, whom Elizabeth had re-encountered in Fremantle. Always trying to keep the peace and please her friends, Elizabeth was hypersensitive to their criticism. Scarred from conflict and raw with grief when she arrived in England this time, she had no resilience. Her response was silent flight. Unfortunately, Cynthia was hypersensitive too, another friend with fragile mental health, and she reacted to perceived offences with emotional outbursts and withdrawal.

Elizabeth stayed in Edinburgh for a week with Margaret Dick's parents and her sister Anne. Later she would spend two weeks with Stephanie and Alec in Cheshire, and visited their daughter Lesley, who was at university in Nottingham. She found her great-aunt Minnie 'exactly the same – light-hearted and scatty, constantly feeding me, in very good spirits ...' On a bus trip by herself to Oban, she was rapturous about the mountains patterned with shadows, snow, gorse and sheep. 'I thought I was having a good time before, but oh God!' She yearned to see more remote parts of Scotland, and even New Zealand and Tasmania – 'highlands if not Highlands'. There was family discussion of unhappy childhoods, which prompted Elizabeth to write to Margaret a soul-searching insight:

> I feel bound to say that I must have cast off mine (and it really leaves me unmoved and has for years) partly because of writing, and partly because I told you and you listened and thought it hadn't been right

or fair. I don't know if my listening had quite the same effect on yours, but it probably made a difference.

Back in Nolan land, all was calm and loving. There seemed to have been a misunderstanding. Elizabeth regretted taking Cynthia's mood too personally, and sympathised with her dismay at seeing her rose reduced from a tree to a twig. She stepped carefully but enjoyed being drawn into her hosts' busy home and social life. Among many dinners and cultural outings, they took her to an Edward Albee play, *All Over*, with Peggy Ashcroft and Angela Lansbury; to Festival Hall for a piano recital by Rudolf Serkin, where they met Charles Osborne, the Australian-born critic and literature director of the Arts Council of Great Britain, and afterwards – just as much fun – home to drink Ovaltine and talk about books in the kitchen. There were gatherings with the visiting Australian writer, editor and publisher Geoffrey Dutton, his wife Ninette, and their children. Elizabeth and Cynthia went on shopping expeditions, walked the dogs along the riverbank tow-path, and pottered in the garden. Cynthia, a passionate, energetic gardener, had created 'the prettiest, most packed and least formal small private garden you could see'. When the tide was low they climbed over the wall down a ladder to walk on the Thames mud, where someone had recently found a Roman sword. In the evenings Sidney often listened to music or read philosophy while Cynthia went up to Elizabeth's sitting room for conversation. Not everything was shared. Elizabeth resumed dog-walking duties in June while the Nolans went off to classical music concerts at the Aldeburgh Festival in Sussex. And while she watched a repeat of Kenneth Clark's *Civilisation* on television with Winifred Fox, the Nolans watched at the home of Clark himself, the great art historian who had introduced them into the British art world.

Most days, Sidney went out to his studio to paint for a coming exhibition at the Marlborough Gallery in London, or to work on his vast multi-panelled *Snake*, to be shown in 1973 for the opening of the Sydney Opera House, or to collaborate with filmmakers on two documentaries about his art. He had worked so hard before their travels that his hands had swollen. Cynthia assisted him or did her own writing, which she called her 'knitting', turning her travel diaries into illustrated books about the places they explored, the people they met, and the paintings that emerged from them. She'd had many careers – as a gallery owner, actor, novelist, nurse, single mother – before meeting Sidney when he was in a ménage à trois with her brother and sister-in-law, the art patrons John and Sunday Reed. Since then they had been complementary and symbiotic: Sidney adopted her daughter, Jinx, who had been born after a brief love affair in the United States; she organised and promoted his career and fended off unwanted attention.

But there were strains between them, with Sid more gregarious yet self-absorbed, and Cynthia unable to get money for household basics such as sheets and towels while subsuming her work into his. The marriage would unravel in the next few years as he had affairs and she sank into depression. She told Elizabeth about her grand but isolated upbringing in Tasmania, with a father who had a religious mania. She was a glamorous young woman and a handsome, almost manly, older woman, but in a photo as a child she had 'enormous light eyes, and such a timid pleading smile'. She told Elizabeth, 'You're asking to be trampled on, if you look at people like that'. Elizabeth concluded: 'We are just beginning to get to know one another again ... She is as diffident about hurting people as I am.'

After the rocky start, Elizabeth found them both kind and interesting, and Sidney often funny. Her presence was a welcome buffer, and they encouraged her to stay another six months, enticing her with a trip to see a Beckett play in Paris and a trip to Aix-en-Provence to see Sidney's goldsmith collaborator François Hugo. Cynthia asked Elizabeth to write her biography, which Elizabeth thought an interesting vote of confidence but impractical because she would have to settle in for too long. Besides, she only wanted to write fiction. At the same time, Cynthia 'wanted to know if I'd done the three or four skeletons (of books) she had asked for when she went away, and I said yes, but of course that only means sentences. God knows, I could write 12 vols in red bloody ink, if I got the right way in.' Talking to her about art and work, Sidney said 'you just had to make something up and start from there and keep on, and not stop working'.

When Elizabeth began to talk about going home soon, Cynthia pushed her to have at least a first draft written when she left. Patrick White urged her not to hurry home: 'it would be better to stay longer & store up plenty for when you are reduced to sitting drearily in Sydney. Take this advice from one who burned his bridges too rashly.' She didn't bother contacting Michael Horniman, the literary agent she felt had done little for her. But she did accompany Cynthia to the office of her agent, Richard Scott Simon, and gave him a copy of *The Watch Tower*, minus the dustjacket with the 'homosexual' blurb that misrepresented Felix Shaw's character. Simon enjoyed the novel, praising Laura and Clare as two good characters, with no mention of Felix. He asked to read her new novel when it was ready. Francis Steegmuller tried to help by sending *The Watch Tower* to his New York agent, Cyrilly Abels, who was also Christina Stead's agent, but he was embarrassed to report back that the Australian setting was a problem. In Sydney, while writing *In Certain Circles*, Harrower had met Peter Grose, an agent with Curtis Brown, over a meal with Cynthia Nolan at the Sebel Town House, and he followed up enthusiastically to offer himself as her agent. Again, nothing resulted, because there was no new novel to sell.

Although Elizabeth was conscious of conserving her money, she had more than the hard-working Margaret, and sent a cheque for her much-needed holiday in the country, encouraging her to go somewhere nice. Margaret had a full-time office job again, as a student adviser with the Chartered Institute of Secretaries. She needed to work but couldn't face school teaching again, because 'the reluctance to learn got her down'. At some point she also worked for the British Information Services. She was writing reviews again for the *Sydney Morning Herald* and had enough income to move into a rented flat at 34 Hopetoun Avenue, Mosman, when Elizabeth gave up their shared flat in nearby Want Street. With Elizabeth away she had a full social life with her own and mutual friends such as Patrick and Kylie, as well as keeping an eye on Kit. She also had a 'swain' – Elizabeth's term – but showed little enthusiasm for this nice man, Ron Ferguson, never heard of again. Elizabeth wrote sympathetically after meeting the Steegmullers: 'Ron Ferguson. Why aren't there lots of Francises about? Not fair.' Margaret had the task of paying bills for Elizabeth, who had to manage rents, rates and other new responsibilities as an absentee property owner. Money in, money out in both countries was still a balancing act and Elizabeth knew she couldn't stay away indefinitely.

Soon after arriving in London, she had told Margaret, 'Cynthia said she had to insult me to get me here! True; but as I said, I was ready to go <u>anywhere</u> if someone insisted.' The trip had been exactly the tonic she needed, but she had been obsessed since leaving Sydney with what she would do, and where she would live, when she returned. She tossed and turned in her letters to Margaret:

> Above all, what sort of situation am I going to be in when I get back? Kylie is one thing, the situation is another. I can't stay away forever because of it. I would like to have started a book before I return.
> I don't quite know what to think about the return. I dare not sink into that destructive situation again ... Undoubtedly you and Kylie are the people who would care most if anything happened to me ...

She didn't quite spell out 'the situation' but it was clear that although she loved Kylie, their friendship was inextricable from Tennant family dramas. The shared house at Blackheath had never been the haven she wanted. Kylie's son Bim often arrived with a struggle of hippie friends who were meant to work on the property but hung around taking drugs and taking advantage of Kylie's liberal-mindedness. 'I am relieved not to be there, part of the unimportant background.' Margaret and Kylie were the friends to whom she wrote most often but she was frustrated by Kylie's lack of interest in her happy London life. In another letter to Margaret she explained her concerns in more detail, the visitors mentioned just some of the constant parade at Blackheath:

> I had another shot at writing to Kylie. You know she never ever says she's received a letter from me or makes a single comment about anything I say. Once she did that week long ago when I felt ill; and once when I mentioned a rubber rake in the garden. That is entirely all. Apart from that my letters might fall into a hole between here and there. So now I don't comment on what she says, either. I used to go assiduously through, but I don't any more. And Monday's letter ... saying: 'And when is Elizabeth coming back? We need that tower of strength.' And saying all about [visitors] arriving and getting stuck in

drive at Blackheath, and staying overnight, and looking for somewhere to live there, and poor children. Roddy was enraged and seemed to think it was her fault. So she didn't dare take Petra's mother to the hospital to have one of the children's arms X-rayed. 'You know how I suffer if I have to <u>not</u> help people. I suppose it's lucky that Roddy (and you) have firmer minds. Otherwise you would be dithering about in a whirl of other people's troubles like me.'... I can only say I must have fooled an awful lot of other people into thinking I did take an interest in people's troubles. However. Consistency, or seeing a true thing was never her strong point. Which is not to say I don't think she's marvellous in her way, but I just can't have my life taken over again, and listen as though to tales of wondrous heroes, to the tales of Bim and Co. Everyone has woes, but at least the woes I hear here are of interesting people, not tiresome kids.

Kylie and Roddy had been asking all along when she would be home, and were urging her to move in with them at Hunters Hill with quasi-parental concern for her welfare. But as Kylie admitted, she and Roddy were getting old at sixty and nearing seventy, and she could no longer sweep up leaves with her arthritic limbs. Elizabeth sensed that she would become trapped as an unacknowledged housekeeper and carer. She worried that Kylie would be hurt by her decision not to live at Hunters Hill, and conceded she'd had lovely weekends there and good times as well as bad with her friend. At Roddy's request, she had sent his new biography of John Hope, the late rector of Christ Church St Laurence in Sydney, around to London publishers, but she kept her letters to him brief and businesslike, 'because I refuse to be interpreted, misinterpreted, any more'. In an odd case of Chinese whispers, Elizabeth wrote to Margaret that their mutual friend Bill Cantwell had told Cynthia in Sydney that Kylie had asked her, 'Bill, you're a woman of the world. Is Elizabeth in love with me?' Elizabeth's only comment was 'Poor Bill! And poor Kylie! It's all of no consequence.' In the same paragraph she declared she was 'going to practise getting meaner and meaner'.

Benison Rodd, Kylie's daughter, would remember years later that Elizabeth had told Kylie she should leave Roddy, but she wasn't clear about when or why, and the reason may have been a simple concern for Kylie's wellbeing. 'It was just a feeling,' said Benison in 2024. 'But Mum would not leave Dad until he died.' She and Elizabeth both felt Kylie did not listen to them, focused on her impossible men and relentless work. The only conversations she recalled between her mother and Elizabeth were about books. Perhaps jealous Roddy implied there was something more than close friendship between the two women, which led Elizabeth to feel misinterpreted. But she tied herself in knots managing all her friendships with kindness and tact. She mailed a copy of Henry James's novel *The Spoils of Poynton* to Patrick White, who was writing his own story of an iron-fisted matriarch in *The Eye of the Storm*, and she collected thoughtful presents for everyone at home. While she wrote to Margaret about the delights of London, her letters to Kit Hazzard said she was longing to get back to Sydney – a strategy aimed at preventing Kit from boarding another ship. She swore to Margaret that she did not tell Cynthia anything about her personal life or family, but Cynthia was aware of her worries, as she told Bill Cantwell she hoped Elizabeth would stay on to break her bondage with Kylie and Roddy; perhaps she could take the flat in Bill's house when she got home.

Everyone, except Elizabeth herself, seemed to have an idea about her future. Robert Cross, her former boss from Macmillan in Melbourne, was now running Thomas Nelson publishers and offered her a job as his personal assistant if she wanted to live in London. Shirley and Francis invited her to travel home through New York. David Cleaver in Sydney urged her to go cheaply via Leningrad, Moscow, Siberia, Japan and Hong Kong, or Budapest and Bulgaria, and offered to send money for the detour. She took none of their suggestions, insisting that she missed her homeland, her friends and her routine. After eight months away, she flew directly to Sydney on August 18, agonising to the end in letters to Margaret: 'Where will I go when I land?'

Whitlamania

On landing in Sydney, Elizabeth went to Kylie's place for two weeks and then moved into a flat at Hunters Hill, the old suburb on the north side of the harbour where the Tennant-Rodd family had their house in a quiet cul-de-sac. All her resistance to Kylie and Roddy collapsed under the need for a home. Flat 8 at 20 Joubert Street was upstairs in a ten-year-old plain red-brick building set among historic sandstone houses with water views. Kylie's sister Dorothy – 'Doff' – owned a rental flat downstairs and knew about the vacancy. The Rodd family lived further along the Hunters Hill peninsula between the Lane Cove and Parramatta rivers in Garrick Avenue, and they were Elizabeth's only friends in the area. Margaret Dick was still at Mosman, and others were scattered round the northern and eastern suburbs. Patrick White would send her clippings of the *Herald* classified ads for flats nearer to him at Centennial Park, hoping to save her from her bossy friends, to no effect. She wanted to leave behind memories of her mother's wasted existence in Mosman, but her only reasons for choosing Hunters Hill were Kylie's company and the ease of travelling together to Blackheath. She lamented that none of her groups of friends especially liked each other. Margaret firmly told Kylie and Roddy they were selfish in wanting Elizabeth to live with them, because she needed to start a new life altogether. Roddy said that was all right if she had a happy life.

Happiness? Elizabeth had rediscovered the elusive feeling in London and, after a long period of sorrow, she looked ahead with her 'genetic optimism'. Friends noticed tired grey streaks in her dark hair. In Sydney, the essential ingredients were a home of her own, a quiet place to write, friends who cared but didn't try to control her, a stimulating social and cultural life. Most important of all, she needed to write, to be a writer again. Home was modest and practical, $36 a week rent for a bedroom and a study, partly furnished with pale carpet, a couple of chairs, bookshelves and wardrobes, to which Elizabeth added two beds and bedcovers, books, a filing cabinet and lamps. 'But it does look out on trees and water, and is in every way an improvement on poor little Want Street.'

In September 1972, after her 'uncharacteristic nest building', she and Kylie left for Blackheath, where she wrote nothing except letters, one of them telling Shirley Hazzard in Europe of Sydney's great radiance and of the Blue Mountains, 'also radiant, smelling of clover, violets, cut grass, and buzzing, alas!, not only with bees but blowflies'. Her elation continued in October when Margaret drove them west over the mountains to Bathurst, Parkes and Cowra. The countryside reminded Elizabeth of Sidney Nolan's Dimboola paintings,

> with little mop trees scattered sparsely over the landscape, each with its shadow, and little dams seeming to run uphill. There is a drought, needless to say ... And yet it was, to me, enchanting and magnetic and I couldn't bear to turn back to the city.

Australia had changed since Elizabeth returned from London the first time, and was about to change more quickly, carrying her along with it. Even under unbroken Liberal–Country Party governments since the 1950s, and the rapid hotchpotch of prime ministers who had followed Robert Menzies in the 1960s, the country had modernised and urbanised, swung attention from Britain to the United States, switched from pounds to dollars, absorbed American popular culture, sent troops to Vietnam, built high-rise towers, while also becoming more confidently Australian, effectively ending the White Australia immigration policy, and finally numbering Aboriginal people in the Australian population. Women's and gay rights movements, and protests against the Vietnam War, sent ripples across the surface of daily life, catching a breeze from the storm of civil rights movements in the US and Europe. Elizabeth listened to her activist left-wing friends and supported policies that promised a more equal society, but she was hardly radical. People had warned that she would find Australia provincial after being away and getting her news from the BBC, *The Guardian* and *The Observer*, and to her surprise she did. She told Shirley Hazzard two months before the federal election:

Even now I can't look at a newspaper and care much about what's
going on. The General Election will be held on Dec. 2nd, it was
announced today and perhaps, perhaps, Labour [*sic*] might win
after about 25 years. That's all I know of current events here.

In the next sentence, she gasped that the city department store David Jones might close down in four years because of land tax and water rates. 'It is the only place, just about, that was here when I was 17 and if any more of the background changes it will be too much.'

She was about to be surprised again when her vote for the Australian Labor Party succeeded for the first time in her adult life. On election day, she went to watch the results at Kylie and Roddy's place carrying champagne, balloons, streamers and little trumpets, and on the local bus was surrounded by friendly, hopeful Labor voters. Having recently lamented with Shirley the re-election of the Republican President Nixon in the US, she shared her excitement:

I, and my Mob, and half the population are THRILLED about the
change of government. At last. And they are speaking so rationally,
simply, unaggressively, unoratorically – it's heaven. It can't last perhaps,
but it has started very, very well. From not being able to read an
Australian newspaper, I am reading four a day. You become so used to
living in a condition of public shame, vicarious shame, that you forget
what – no, have never known what – it might be like to agree with
those who speak for us.

For the first time since she had admired Britain's Labour prime minister, Clement Attlee, and marched against nuclear weapons in the 1950s, Elizabeth became politically engaged. This opened up friendships in her new community. At an art exhibition in Hunters Hill soon after the election, she met Helene Nolte, a potter and a Labor Party supporter, who insisted that Elizabeth must meet her husband, Ferdinand Nolte. The Noltes were an old Dutch/German family from Cape Town, where Ferdinand had studied architecture and joined the anti-apartheid movement. He'd been among a small group of activists who were smuggled into Nelson

Mandela's township to teach him English. Hating their country's injustice, he and Helene moved to London, where he had a successful practice, but they disliked the cold so brought their two daughters, Karin and Linda, to Sydney in 1971 with government assistance and a job designing public hospitals. The Noltes' house was around the corner from Elizabeth in Figtree Road and they were looking for new friends. She and 'Ferdi' hit it off immediately, first through their shared political enthusiasm, and more deeply because he was a cheerful, kind, gregarious man who would become one of her most reliable and loved friends. 'They were very close and I'd say she was probably his best friend,' said his daughter Linda. Despite Elizabeth's resistance to joining any party, group or organisation, Ferdi persuaded her to sign up with him at the tiny Hunters Hill branch of the ALP – because 'what moral legs did I have to stand on, so approving, a freed slave and all that, if I didn't join?' She told people they joined, not out of anger, but out of happiness at the election of Gough Whitlam and Labor.

Elizabeth already had other South African friends. John Brink owned the Anchor Bookshop in the city, specialising in politics and race relations, and supplied her with all kinds of books, including the novels of South African novelist Nadine Gordimer, whom she admired as a rare writer able to 'transmute' (a favourite word) politics into fiction that was not didactic. John and his wife Margaret, an English teacher at Alexander Mackie Teachers' College, had been prominent anti-apartheid activists and had moved to Australia in 1961 after he was imprisoned for three months without trial. They were founding members of the South Africa Defence and Aid Fund in Australia, with support from Patrick White and Judith Wright, and as chairman John asked for donations from Kylie Tennant, Elizabeth Harrower, Margaret Dick and other writers. Through the Brinks, Elizabeth had met two South Africans in London, one of whom had been imprisoned for eight years for a bomb-throwing incident. In Hunters Hill she was often invited to the Noltes' house, where the Brinks were guests and the circle extended to other like-minded South Africans, such as Jane Harris, an English teacher and librarian who took an interest in Harrower's books, and her partner, James Mohr, an Australian accountant. Ferdi took a lot of photographs of Elizabeth, and a

lovely series shot in their garden in 1973 with the Nolte dachshunds, Zoe and Gina – all three looking slightly anxious – would much later become her favourite publicity portraits.

By moving from Mosman to Hunters Hill, Elizabeth joined another sedate middle-class community, one which mobilised to protect its heritage buildings and natural environment in an area sullied by factories and a radium refinery. Kylie Tennant had written in support of saving a remnant of foreshore bushland near her red-brick bungalow from high-rise development by the building company AV Jennings. The women of Hunters Hill (Elizabeth pointedly called them 'ladies') had led the campaign to preserve Kelly's Bush with the backing of the NSW Builders Labourers' Federation and its communist secretary, Jack Mundey, who imposed the first of many green bans on the site in 1971.

Mundey and the BLF also stepped in to stop the NSW Government from building a sports complex on the Centennial Parklands, a project proposed in the hope of winning the 1988 Olympic Games for Sydney. Patrick White, reluctantly at first, fronted up as a persuasive spokesman for that campaign, which saved swathes of land around his white house on a hill overlooking the park. He even made his first nervous 'telly' appearance for the cause, and recruited Kylie Tennant to speak at one of the rallies. His letters to Elizabeth in London had been full of his gloom about the prospect of bulldozers and vast expense on a stadium rather than hospitals, schools, art galleries, museums, and the needs of Aboriginal people and the poor. 'Thanks for your letter, as lively as I feel dead at the moment,' one letter began. Elizabeth watched admiringly from the sidelines as her friends demonstrated a talent for public speaking that was unimaginable for her. But she went with Ferdi and Helene to local Labor Party meetings, often tedious, voted in preselection ballots for state and federal candidates, and evangelised about the government's good works to friends and strangers.

She was especially enamoured of the prime minister, Gough Whitlam, for his sharp wit and erudition ('he reads Greek and Latin for pleasure'), as well as for rapid-fire policies that launched universal healthcare, removed tertiary education fees, withdrew troops from Vietnam, ended conscription, supported Aboriginal land rights, advanced women's equality and, within its first term, sent the government into debt as the world slumped into a recession. Elizabeth enjoyed passing on the news to Shirley, sometimes sounding like a breathless fan, and even as her 'Whitlamania' gave way to some disillusioning realities, she remained faithful: 'I haven't been swayed by a charismatic leader; Whitlam just simply stands against the fanatics of the left and right; he is stable, consistent, brilliant, good-hearted and has commonsense. Brave and witty.'

Some friends thought she was politically naive, less interested in policies than in heroes and villains, and she agreed that she simply wanted a fair, kind world. She accepted the reasons for Judah Waten's communism and his support for the Soviet Union, even when the Stalin regime's brutality was exposed, but he didn't try to recruit her and she would not have been tempted. Among her other friends were Jack and Audrey Blake, long-time activists and Communist Party of Australia members who split with the Australian party in the 1950s. In Judah's words, 'they ran out of puff'. Judah had been expelled several times before leaving the party in 1972 to join the pro-Soviet Socialist Party of Australia. The Blakes, knowing he was a dear friend, did not comment to Elizabeth on their vehement disagreements. Both Judah and the Blakes would come in for criticism from Stephen Murray-Smith, the editor of *Overland* magazine, another of many who left the Communist Party after the Soviet invasion of Hungary in 1956. With time Murray-Smith became more conservative, to the point that he judged the Whitlam Government a disaster. After speaking about the party's history and current Soviet writing at a conference in 1980, he wrote a friendly letter to Judah and Hyrell Waten that said, 'anything I said about your views was minor compared to what I had to say about e.g. the actions of Jack Blake or [writer] Frank Hardy'.

They were complicated times and Elizabeth Harrower stood back from the intricacies of factional disputes, seeing herself at the sensible centre of the Labor Party. Politics came along when she needed a break from the introspection of writing, and gave her an outward-looking purpose. On a personal level, Kit Hazzard did the same.

*

Elizabeth had come home from London in a mood of relative lightness after years of work and family problems. The friendship forged in happy encounters with Shirley Hazzard, mixed with the aching absence of her own mother, opened her to giving Kit some of the care she had failed to give Margaret Kempley. She seemed, though, to be using Kit as another excuse for postponing work, and Shirley was grateful but taken aback by the intricacy of her care. Elizabeth wrote long reports about her mother's mental swings, doctors' appointments, plans to move flats, problems with her cat, fights with her other daughter, Valerie, and on and on. Shirley and Francis sent generous amounts for any expenses but then asked further favours.

Meanwhile, Shirley was working intensely on the first of her two book-length diatribes on the failure of the United Nations. When *Defeat of an Ideal* was published in early 1973, she sent a copy to Elizabeth, who privately praised Shirley for a 'tide-turning' work of philosophy. Commissioned to review the book for the *Herald*, Kylie Tennant borrowed Elizabeth's copy, and asked her for the American and British reviews, which Elizabeth picked up from Kit and delivered to Kylie. Later that year, Kylie favourably reviewed *The Eye of the Storm* by her old friend Patrick White for the *Sydney Morning Herald*, at the request of the literary editor, and Shirley reviewed the novel for the *New York Times*. No one seemed to worry about conflicts of interest in this circle of friends and presumably the admiration was genuine. Kylie declined to review the next White book she was offered, concerned about improper appearances.

Kylie remained central to Elizabeth's life now they were near neighbours, though she did not often overlap with the South African crowd. They were up and down to Blackheath, for social gatherings as well as physical and mental work. Nancy Phelan – a Macmillan author of travel memoirs, novels, food and yoga books – and her husband Peter were charming hosts at their Blue Mountains property in Lawson, where lunches extended from the elegant stone house across the garden and into the afternoon, with guests including cultured Russians and a Japanese university professor who would undertake translations of Australian fiction. By contrast, the atmosphere up at Hillside Farm was increasingly alien to Elizabeth as Bim Rodd and his mates took over:

> A week of Blackheath in heavy, heavy rain, with four, five and sometimes six of us confined to what is scarcely more than a fibro tent with very few amenities. What was once meant to be a place to work has become a sort of halfway house for hippies. Long-haired boys who take drugs and think (and worse, keep telling you) that they're The Universe drift tiredly from bed to table. Twas somewhat chaotic and unexpected because visits are usually planned not to coincide. By some miracle or other – with all that mud, rain and close confinement – the situation didn't deteriorate; but I tottered away from a week of Ritual Magic, I Ching, Tarot cards, Om, Rolling Stones, assorted mystics and Great Teachers, with my mind slightly mazed. They talk in blocks of words, slogans and curses, and show no sign of pausing to think at all. My mind, such as it is, seems to sit about thinking profound thoughts like: Oh, the pity of it!

When Shirley Hazzard heard from Kit that Elizabeth was searching for tarot cards, she asked no questions but posted a pack bought near the British Museum with instructions on how to use them – almost the least imaginable exchange between these rational women. Elizabeth explained, without naming Bim, that since returning from London she had witnessed 'dreadful dramas and traumas' affecting two boys who had addled their brains with drugs. She had tried over months to persuade one of them to seek professional help but the traumas resumed, 'like going through the mincing machine twice'. She continued to humour them at Blackheath, and when they visited her at Hunters Hill she would offer Nescafé, sandwiches, and tarot cards to divert them and protect herself. And yet there was beauty mixed in with the madness. Elizabeth later recalled a letter Bim had once written to her from India, describing the view from his window: 'such a brilliant, complex picture of everything in life happening simultaneously ... Afterwards I looked out at Hunters Hill: it was like a terrifying, super-real, empty painting of suburbia, no sign of life.'

Tennant gave an account of her family troubles in her 1986 autobiography, *The Missing Heir*. She blamed Benison's inability to spell on the trauma of Roddy's breakdown and suicide attempt when she was a child.

After starting life with his parents' great expectations, Bim's decline into addiction, reckless adventures, and psychosis may also have had a genetic or psychological link with his father's condition. When Elizabeth told Shirley there had been 'crises' at the end of 1972, she was skirting the terrible facts. In a long series of misadventures, Bim had left university several times, hitchhiked to Queensland, broken his neck in a car crash, broken a leg flying off his motorbike, travelled to Bali and India, been caught carrying hashish, and with a fellow student had a baby boy. The child was adopted and removed from their lives, to the distress of Kylie, who would search but never find him. After years of using cannabis and LSD, hearing voices and becoming aggressive, Bim was diagnosed with schizophrenia.

While Elizabeth was struggling to write *In Certain Circles*, Kylie managed to finish and publish the biography *Evatt: Politics and justice* in 1970, and the short novel *The Man on the Headland* a year later. Fiction was harder for her to write and sell, too. She hadn't published a new full-length novel since *The Honey Flow* in 1956, and after *The Man on the Headland* there would be another long break before her next novel in 1984, *Tantavallon*, which compressed elements of her life into a satirical fantasy about Balm Point, a suburb resembling Hunters Hill, peopled with developers, miners, hippies, mystics, drug addicts, and a church warden who becomes suicidally depressed.

These upheavals, as well as her own, had driven Elizabeth overseas and escalated while she was away. She knew her absence relieved Kylie of juggling everyone's time at Blackheath to keep Elizabeth separate from Bim. This was 'the situation' in her letters from London that she couldn't return to, and yet her concern for Kylie kept her close.

In early 1973 she agreed against all her defensive instincts to go on a six-week cruise to Japan with Kylie, her father, and Benison. Thomas Tennant, a character known as 'the Parent', lived alone at Patonga Beach on the New South Wales central coast, where Kylie visited him, and he was as keen a traveller as Kit Hazzard. Kylie wanted to please her ailing father with a last ship voyage at the age of eighty-four. She also needed respite from Roddy and Bim, and she invited 'the devoted' Elizabeth for company on the 'hellship', and a break from the chaos they inflicted on her. Each woman thought she was looking after the other. But a week before they embarked on the cruise in March, a clash of wills broke out. Cynthia and Sidney Nolan arrived from London for their annual working visit and Cynthia was horrified to learn that Elizabeth was planning to travel with Kylie. She had heard her wail in London about being trapped with Kylie's family, and vow never to travel by ship after fearing she'd drown off the coast of South Africa. Cynthia had felt then that she was in a forced tug of war with Kylie over their friend, and in Sydney she gave another sharp yank. Elizabeth was excited to have the Nolans back in town and spoke warmly to Cynthia on the phone several times. Cynthia had visits from Patrick White and Bill Cantwell, but she refused to see Elizabeth because she was so opposed to her going on the cruise. In an elliptical letter to Shirley Hazzard, Elizabeth wrote that Cynthia said she was as upset as she had been when her daughter Jinx 'was wrecking her own life'. Cynthia was also unwell, suffering from depression and back pain, and losing weight. Elizabeth wrote:

> I'm sad about it, but she is fragile, and I've seen her ill, and down physically and psychically – all ways. She thinks I am used, apparently, and credits me with a rather frailer and simpler character than I possess. If I want to be compassionate, C says, I should be a nurse or a doctor.

Other friends, and even Elizabeth herself, thought she was unwise to go on the cruise, for which she was paying her own fare, but she felt obliged, as she put it, to 'wring some advantage from this self-inflicted adversity'. She sent around the long itinerary of the *Nieuw Holland* that encompassed Japan, Taiwan and Hong Kong, soon to be irrelevant when Elizabeth left the ship at Brisbane after two days of hesitation. She fled home and disappeared to a guesthouse in Katoomba without telling Cynthia or their mutual friends.

She wrote miserable, guilty letters to Kylie in every port, and admitted to Shirley that she should have had the brains to refuse the trip in the beginning. 'I hoped someone would rescue me, see how desperate I was, and say firmly, "She cannot go, and it isn't her fault." However, this desire to be faultless and blameless turned out to be my undoing.' She admitted, on the other hand, that she would have stayed if someone had insisted. Her indecision was disabling. Shirley expressed sympathy and relief that Elizabeth had rescued herself: 'there is a disorder of the soul, combined with actualities, that is like having physical wounds' and she ended, 'I know how you felt, not wanting people buzzing at you'.

Shirley couldn't predict that her own buzzing would one day chase Elizabeth away.

Kylie, undeterred, sent Roddy and Elizabeth vivid, funny letters about Japan and ship life. Benison enjoyed the sightseeing and shopping, despite a constant cold, and was panting to go on another trip after learning from Japanese students how to travel cheaply. The Parent, however, was a regular patient of the ship's doctor for bronchitis aggravated by the smog of the Japanese ports, and for a worsening hernia. He wanted only to sit in a deck chair with whisky and cigars. Kylie took Japanese lessons, assured by the teacher that she would be fluent in eleven years. Having accidentally locked herself in a toilet cubicle, she ruined her suit trying to climb under the door, yelled for help until Benison heard her, and then locked the purser in with her. Nothing wasted, she turned her misadventure into a comic article for the *Sydney Morning Herald*.

Back in Hunters Hill, Kylie and her sister Doff threatened to move their father from his house at Patonga into the flat below Elizabeth's at Joubert Street. Elizabeth got on well with Thomas Tennant but, she half-jokingly told friends, he had been proposing to her for years and she wanted to keep her distance. In the end the incursion was cancelled. The Tennant-Rodd families were looking at ways to reduce their expenses, to consolidate several properties, and to give Benison a place of her own. They began to talk about buying Elizabeth out of Hillside Farm. Their friendship recovered but the contest between Kylie and Cynthia over Elizabeth's soul made everyone more wary. Elizabeth saw Cynthia at a dinner given by Patrick but otherwise Cynthia avoided her, and their letters and phone calls had a porcelain fragility. Cynthia told her friend Bill Cantwell she believed Elizabeth was not writing because she wanted to write about Kylie but couldn't do so. That may well have been true. Although Kylie's family supplied rich material, loyalty would have required genius to transmute them into fiction; she'd already made an oblique attempt in the marriage of Zoe and Stephen in *In Certain Circles*. At the same time, Roddy saw Kylie trying to write a light-hearted book about her cruise to Japan, but distracted by Bim, Elizabeth and him. Torn between optimism and doom, Kylie wrote to her friend Mavis Cribb:

> I wouldn't be too sorry for Bim, who is rusticating up at Diamond Head. He is no more insane than some of his mates. Just silly I would say. He no longer hears voices so I gather he has given up the more poisonous drugs. He has a new girl. He wrote a coherent letter saying that he wishes to return to the University next year. Poppycock! Long may he delude himself with the thought that he might use his brains. He has blown them for keeps I'd say.

*

Elizabeth was hoping that Cynthia Nolan's agent, Richard Simon, whom she had met in London, would be interested in her work. He had enjoyed *The Watch Tower* and asked to see the new novel when it was ready. At Alan Maclean's unwise suggestion, she sent Simon a typescript of *In Certain Circles* from Sydney with the warning, 'It was written out of will-power when life was not going well.' She received a blunt reply, fortunately while she was high on Whitlam's election:

> Actually I agree with you all, and I don't think this one is really at all successful. I think the basic trouble is that the family is just not interesting enough, so you have started off with a great disadvantage. Unlike the other book it seems to me to lack life and conviction. So, I think you are right to absolutely put this one out of your mind and get on with the new one.

Observing that she had fallen back into allowing other people's needs to keep her from writing, Patrick White spoke 'sternly' to her as 1973 began. 'He thinks that I should be writing more books, which knowledge encourages me.' Elizabeth was able to turn Patrick's bullying into encouragement, never admitting she was offended as she was by other bossy friends. Her respect for him, and his steady regard for her, made her see kindness where others saw bad temper. She continued the task she'd set herself of re-establishing work habits by typing from old diaries and notebooks, 'with the hope that my mind might begin to stir, wake up and take an interest'. White set his friend a fine example of discipline, working from dawn to lunchtime as he prepared his novel *The Eye of the Storm* for publication. He told Elizabeth she must 'do something', by which he meant write, and to a mutual friend he said, 'She is living a novel instead of writing one.' Shirley Hazzard responded guiltily when Elizabeth passed on Patrick's remark: 'at least some macabre passages of that novel you are living must be designated "KIT"'.

That year the new Literature Board made its first rounds of grants to writers. One of the Whitlam Government's most important moves for Harrower and her friends was to replace the old Commonwealth Literary Fund with the Literature Board, an autonomous arm of the Australia Council for the Arts, with funding and advisory powers no longer subject to veto by the prime minister and opposition leader. Margaret Jones, literary editor of the *Sydney Morning Herald*, wrote that this would create what a board member called 'a climate of "economic tranquillity" for Australian writers'. Indeed, the number of Australian novels published annually would rise from nineteen in 1972 to two hundred in 1986 and 'veteran Sydney novelist' Elizabeth Harrower was quoted by a British newspaper article in 1988 about the effect: 'Writers were thin on the ground when I began writing. The Australia Council changed all that. It's much easier now than it used to be.' As Elizabeth knew, money could help a writer but couldn't *write* the novel.

The board members attending the decisive meeting at the University of Queensland Press offices in Brisbane on September 26, 1973, were Geoffrey Blainey, AD Hope, Geoff Dutton, Tom Shapcott, Judah Waten, David Malouf, Richard Walsh, Richard Hall, Nancy Keesing, Elizabeth Riddell, and the director of the Literature Board, Michael Costigan. Manning Clark was overseas. They had received more than 1100 applications from individual writers for assistance, of which 134 were successful. Elizabeth Harrower received a $6000 fellowship for two years – a total of $12 000 –

after confirmation that she had acquitted her previous grant by delivering the manuscript of *In Certain Circles*, even though it was not published.

Hers was one of the more generous grants that year; others were given smaller amounts or shorter periods. Costigan, who was not involved in the decision-making, recalled in 2024 that 'part of the thinking was she had this famous writer's block and people said she has written superb books, we should do what we can, if we can do anything'. He also knew the grant 'didn't thrill her, in a way'. In her acceptance letter she thanked Costigan for the 'generous offer' of the fellowship and said, 'While I would not have applied for one, I must say that – after great thinkings – I feel this could be a life-saver for me.' After explaining the fate of her previous novel, she added: 'Now I suddenly feel hopeful again and as if I have a good many books yet to write.'

Elizabeth was determined when she wrote to Shirley Hazzard, with an unspoken message about her mother, Kit:

> In an effort to save me from myself, or for some reason I'm not sure of, I'm being given a grant to get on with a novel. (This was not my idea.) When this happens, at the beginning of November, there are going to be changes in the Harrower regime. I'll only be sociable at night; and, as the phone can't be switched off, I'll have to warn everyone to lay off. So this grant is one of the crimes I've had to answer for. The others recently are a) not inviting someone to dinner when Patrick was coming, and b) not being a Christian. About the grant, I said to P, 'If I'd just written a wonderful book, I'd feel it was justified.' He said, 'You might write a wonderful book …' While I can afford to stay home and not go to an office, I have to be very careful with money, so this will mean a certain loosening up, which will be nice; but much more than that, it will provide a spur, and an obligation of the kind that most people can recognize. It could be – quite non-financially – a lifesaver. Margaret could do with it more. She has to go out to work. I don't like to be the one on whom all the goodies shower, but it wasn't a matter of either/or, so such feelings aren't very useful.

The Literature Board was able to grant fellowships by invitation, but Harrower surely had to sign an agreement and explain her project. Her passive attitude towards receiving grants must have frustrated the friends who pushed and helped her to receive them. Kylie Tennant had retired from the Commonwealth Literary Fund and was not on the Literature Board, but Elizabeth had several supporters there. Judah Waten, in particular, would have championed her as a strong candidate. Geoffrey Dutton admired her even though she had not made money from the Sun Books edition of *The Long Prospect*. She had got to know Richard Hall at ALP meetings as an adviser to Gough Whitlam; he would pilot the Public Lending Right program that paid authors a fee for their works held in libraries as compensation for lost sales. Nancy Keesing had liked *The Watch Tower* and she was Kylie's next-door neighbour in Hunters Hill. There's no question that Harrower was deserving of recognition, and the board members might have decided to give her generous time to produce the novel they were waiting for, but not so much time that she would procrastinate further; so not a full three-year fellowship. She might have seemed well-off with her inherited house and block of flats bringing in rent, but the small rents were eaten up by long-delayed repairs on both buildings. As she said, she did not need a job, and did not want one, but she worried about money as she worried about everything, so two years of subsidised writing was a gift from the literary community.

She would have to tame her doubts, her friends and her political fervour to finish a manuscript by the end of 1975. Off she went for a week in Blackheath and a visit to Jenolan Caves, pretending she would be clamped to her desk for the next two years. A full year after her return from London, she told Shirley, she had typed up her notebooks and ten years of diaries, but had done no real writing. And now she had so much material. 'I said to Patrick: "I feel like Oscar Wilde when he left Reading Gaol. That I wrote before I knew about life. Now that I know …"'

Even in her forties Elizabeth was tormented by her own proud independence and modest insecurity. She needed her friends' approval and was sensitive to every perceived slight. This was often a way of not taking responsibility for her own actions and a waste of nervous energy. In this case she feared not all her friends were pleased about her writing grant. Roddy, for example, did not mention the fellowship to her but averted his face and went to bed at five in the afternoon rather than staying up for dinner when she visited. (She should have known he often felt unwell and retired early.) On the other hand, their neighbour Nancy Keesing rang with congratulations and when Elizabeth thanked her she said not to thank her. 'I said I was thanking her for being pleased.'

Before she could settle into the planned writing came the long-expected news that Patrick White had won the Nobel Prize for Literature. The process had begun years earlier when Artur Lundkvist, a writer and member of the Swedish Academy, became determined to champion White for the prize, reviewing each of his novels from the 1960s onwards. In 1969 the Academy chose another of his favourites, the Chilean poet Pablo Neruda. Lundkvist and his poet wife, Maria Wine, travelled to Australia in 1970 to learn about Australian writing, and in particular to meet White, who invited them to dine at Centennial Park and introduced them to Elizabeth Harrower and Margaret Dick. White wrote with amusement to Geoffrey Dutton that in a taxi with Dick the 'earnest' Lundkvists had asked her, 'Explain to us this word "booger" which is always coming up.'

Lundkvist took home a copy of *The Watch Tower*, hoping to have it translated for publication in Sweden, but Elizabeth told Francis Steegmuller, who had tried to interest his New York agent, it was 'resistible there too'. Lundkvist wrote a newspaper feature article headed (in Swedish) 'Australia – impossible to write about!' in which he referred to the contemporary novels of Randolph Stow, Thomas Keneally and Hal Porter, but gave most attention to White and Harrower, 'a middle-aged novelist' who was his most important successor. He sent a clipping to Dick, who had impressed him intellectually, and she passed the article on to Harrower and Tennant, neither of whom could make out the Swedish beyond a few words such as 'charmfull parasit' and 'psykologisk tortyr'. Lundkvist had told a Melbourne journalist that the socialist realist school of Australian writing did not appeal to him, and that he had read one of Tennant's novels 'but it was not my kind of book'. Clearly miffed, Kylie spoke later in an interview about Elizabeth's close friendship with Patrick and her style of writing in 'very subtle nuances of feeling. This is very much appreciated by erudite Swedes, French, Germans who come out here and want an article for their newspaper about Elizabeth Harrower.'

White put aside his usual refusal of prizes for the Nobel. He really wanted to win, but he had almost given up after being shortlisted and sidelined several times, including in 1969 because some Academy members disliked his brutal depiction of an artist in *The Vivisector*. Lundkvist made a final push in 1973, sending four advance copies of *The Eye of the Storm* to his English-reading colleagues. He gave the book a very favourable review, which proclaimed the portrait of a dying matriarch in Centennial Park 'a universally valid enquiry into the terms of human existence'. The final choice between Patrick White and Saul Bellow came down to one vote, and the prize would go to 'the new land of Australia'. Not even the winner was informed ahead of the public announcement. On the night before the news broke, Elizabeth cooked dinner for Patrick, Manoly, Margaret, and Alice Waten, Judah's 'marvellous' violin-playing daughter. She ruined the paella because she was too engrossed in the conversation, in which no one mentioned the prize. She and Margaret found out from the Swedish Consulate that the decision would be announced at 10 o'clock Sydney time on the night of October 18. Hearing on the radio that White had won, she rushed to the phone and found him calm after learning of his win half an hour earlier when an onslaught of journalists banged on the door of the dark house. He and Manoly went back to bed and made them wait until morning. Elizabeth stayed up all night, more excited than he was. Another time she might have wanted Saul Bellow to win, as an author she had long admired, often quoting his novels *Henderson the Rain King* and *Herzog*, about a compulsive letter writer. (He would win in 1976 after his next novel, *Humboldt's Gift*.) But Patrick's prize was a personal joy. She wrote to Shirley: 'Next day there was a tremendous delight loose everywhere. Everyone seemed so generously delighted that it was an extra sort of happiness to feel the responsiveness of strangers as well as acquaintances and friends.'

In that week of wonders, Queen Elizabeth officially opened the Sydney Opera House 'with doves, balloons, bands, millions, F111s flying past, big and little boats with flags and decorations', and a shower of fireworks over the Danish-designed sails. Shirley and Francis had sent tickets to

Kit for Prokofiev's operatic adaptation of *War and Peace*. They invited Elizabeth to join her and, after tactfully suggesting Valerie should go with her mother, she accepted and did a reconnoitre to make sure the night was easy for Kit. 'We drank champagne and investigated Sydney's Elsinore,' she told Shirley. 'It was – opera, and building, and first production – thrilling. The theatre itself has little to distract the eye. You concentrate on the stage. At last we have a <u>building</u>. To whom should we give thanks that our first building is not dedicated to sport?'

She had watched the slow construction from Circular Quay and on ferries, telling sceptical taxi drivers it was a Good Thing, as she now told them about Gough Whitlam. The day after the opening, she and Margaret went with Patrick and Manoly to a concert by the Moscow Chamber Orchestra, where, in the swarming crowd, 'probably for the first time in the history of Australia, a writer was recognised in public'. Elizabeth went again for a performance of *Hamlet* in the presence of 'the Honourable EG Whitlam', and was for a time euphoric.

White wanted to avoid both publicity and a cold winter that might damage his lifelong weak lungs, so Sidney Nolan flew to Stockholm to accept the prize on his behalf from the newly crowned King Carl XVI Gustaf. Instead of receiving his medal at a formal dinner in Canberra, White chose to cook at home with Manoly for the Swedish Ambassador, Per Anger, and his wife, Sidney and Cynthia Nolan, and Elizabeth and Margaret. Pleased to be there, Elizabeth felt 'listless' at the prospect of seeing the Nolans, but affectionate and relieved in their presence. She would benefit decades later from White's long-considered decision to use his A$81 862 prize money to establish an annual award for an Australian author who had made a significant contribution to Australian literature but had not received due recognition.

Elizabeth and Shirley took heart from world news of a ceasefire in the Middle East, and the resignation of the US Vice President Spiro Agnew as President Nixon fell further into disgrace over the Watergate scandal. The multi-layered celebrations, however, only marked a brief pause in the drama of Kit. Shirley, while excited about Elizabeth's fellowship, had also asked her to help Kit with the complicated application for the age pension, and there were hearing aids to be fitted, flats to be inspected, and travel plans to forestall. As well as all the practical tasks she took on, Elizabeth was helping Andrew Robertson, the psychiatric nurse who was Kit's regular adviser, to manage Kit's extreme moods, the lowest of them turning her violently against caring friends. She had, at some point, been diagnosed with manic depression, or bipolar disorder.

In her letters to Shirley, Elizabeth was gloomy about any prospect of long-term recovery for Kit, and concerned about the stress she caused – for Shirley. By this time Kit was so often discussed that they used the shorthand 'MM' and 'YM' for 'my mother' and 'your mother'. Elizabeth wrote: 'YM doesn't ever think that anyone else has a tether to come to the end of. Her daughter, for instance.' But she was also writing implicitly about herself. In one of the most revealing statements of her own emotional scars, Elizabeth went on in this long letter:

> They say that every difficult soul affects the lives of fourteen others. As one whose life has been affected by an alcoholic grandfather, step-father (possibly also mentally ill), and lover; by a few genuinely depressive bosom friends; by acquaintances who were raving mad; by several youthful drug addicts; and, almost worse, having had to witness others having their lives affected, others who were lovable, gentle, intelligent, considerate, talented, with capacities for life and laughter, I can only say that my wholehearted sympathies lie with the fourteen damaged, rather than with the person causing the destruction. (And I have really cared for some of them.)

Plenty of evidence showed how the grandfather, the stepfather, the friends, acquaintances and addicts had damaged Elizabeth, though the lover remained elusive. She seemed never to write or talk about this memorable cad, except in her fiction. But old wounds still hurt. Ever private, in her letters to Shirley she kept deflecting from herself, laying down resentment that would surface years later:

> You know I understand the sadness of your mother's life. In a way, I must love her or I couldn't put up with her on bad days. But I can't bear to see all this damaging your life and Francis's more than it

already has. You say Andrew is right and that you are afraid, because the outbreak of emotions is more than you can bear, and because your mother is able to go so much further in total statements, depression and so on ... While I defended myself, saying 'not afraid' to Andrew, it's true of me as well. Uncontrolled, violent, negative emotions are intimidating. Many people don't mind what they say, as if words had no meaning and no effect and their hearers no memories and no feelings ... But, no, you are both so good to Kit. We do our best out here, and you're both heroic. None of us can do more. Like you, I don't feel I can combat the trip to England forever. <u>Of course</u> you must think of Francis and his work, and your own work ... Forgive all this vehemence.

At the same time, on Shirley's behalf, she was writing to Elizabeth Reid, Gough Whitlam's adviser on women's affairs, about the appalling employment conditions of Australian women at the United Nations, and lobbying Geoff Dutton to invite the Steegmullers to Adelaide Writers' Week. She was angry about industrial chaos in New South Wales, with the airport shut down, mail unsorted, electrical blackouts, and a Liberal state government under Premier Askin that, in Elizabeth's view, was refusing to take any action so that blame would fall on the federal government. At a local ALP meeting before the state election she was unimpressed by their candidate, who lost the vote despite her efforts with Ferdi Nolte as volunteers at the polling booth. She was worried about Whitlam too.

The gloom weighed heavily in Blackheath, where she was back and forth with Kylie, and where Benison Rodd was living full-time with a growing menagerie of horses, cats, ducks, hens and more. The spring beauty of pear blossom, boronia and wisteria was dampened by heavy rain, mud and a box of chickens in the spare room. Bim was back in Gladesville Hospital in a terrible mental state. No wonder, then, that Elizabeth was suffering from an enlarged heart and high blood pressure. Judah Waten, jumping into his habitual role as medical adviser, consulted a professor of medicine who recommended seeing a cardiologist for an x-ray of her heart. Elizabeth did so, pretending only to placate her concerned friends, and 'Dr Fisher's pills' brought her symptoms under control. She told Judah, 'I hope to lead a less dramatic life. It has always been, always, something like an opera, but that hasn't always been my fault.' To Shirley she wrote, almost laughably: 'When I start writing, I'm not going to be available by day.'

White's Nobel Prize had a cascade of effects on his reputation and Australian writing. The pompous citation read: 'To Patrick White for an epic and psychological narrative art which has introduced a new continent into literature.' Reviews of *The Eye of the Storm* were mixed in the UK, where the novel was published before the prize announcement, and the ship carrying books to Australia arrived late because of a strike. But worldwide sales of his books boomed and Viking reissued six of his novels in the US, which his agent admitted had been a 'dismal' market for him. Shirley Hazzard wrote to Elizabeth for reading advice before she reviewed *The Eye of the Storm* for the *New York Times* in a rousing essay that lamented American self-centred ignorance of Australian writers. She named Hal Porter, Elizabeth Harrower and Judah Waten as worthy of attention, and their Australianness as 'both essential and irrelevant'. Accepting some flaws in the novel's execution, she wrote: 'White's magnanimity, his logic, his poetry are not incompatible with the spirits he invokes by name – Shakespeare, Stendhal, Redon. Splinterings of James, of Joyce ...' With worldwide attention from journalists, critics and publishers, White was at last earning a handsome income from his books.

His grand fury of a novel tracks the dying of Elizabeth Hunter, a monstrous matriarch based on his own late mother, Ruth White, and the family battles after she dies in her Centennial Park mansion. White described Ruth as 'one of those domineering, dominating characters who couldn't help having power over people'. Elizabeth Hunter's psychic clash resonated with Elizabeth Harrower, victim and creator of her own domestic power struggles. How inspiring and yet daunting it must have been for her – and other Australian writers – to measure themselves against the new laureate's Shakespearean achievement.

Yet Elizabeth could take some small credit for the metaphysical underpinnings of his writing. When White was first thinking about *The Eye of the Storm*, she had given him for Christmas 1969 a book called *Existentialism and Religious Belief* by David E Roberts. In a letter to the ABC's Clem Semmler about his own religious philosophy, White said the book 'is full of interesting things, particularly a chapter on Gabriel Marcel. Elizabeth Harrower who gave me the book thought he might be the one who would interest me, and he does.' He had since found Marcel's book *Being and Having*. He was, he said, trying in his novels 'to give professed unbelievers glimpses of their own unprofessed faith', which frightened people who considered themselves intellectuals. 'Gabriel Marcel ... may help me more in the novel I am working on at present ...'

Elizabeth had read Marcel when she wrote *In Certain Circles* and considered his ideas about hope and despair in the godless modern technological world – her character Stephen Quayle reads a book about Catholicism and existentialism by an unnamed author, most likely Marcel. Among her papers is a long typed summary of his life and philosophy, and she was still interested in him in 1982 when she wrote to Christina Stead that she had spent a weekend 'with my typewriter and a good book – *Problematic Man* – Gabriel Marcel'.

*

The Literature Board's public record doesn't show what Elizabeth Harrower was intending to write during her fellowship time, but later correspondence referred to a novel and some short stories. As the clock began to tick at the end of 1973, she told Shirley she was locking herself up 'in the hope of either boring myself to death or bringing about a confrontation with the typewriter'. Shirley replied, knowing she was part of the problem:

> VERY GOOD NEWS that you are thinking of working, and also working. When I am thinking of working, that is when most gets done. When I make the hideous effort to get to the typewriter, quite a lot seems to have gone through the hoops in my head. You have two well-wishers here for your thoughts and their outcome.

By mid-1975 Elizabeth reported: 'Yes, some writing is happening. Not very euphonious, quite cement-blockish, but going on anyway.' She told Christina Stead: 'I have enough foolscap pages covered to make, I hope, at least one peculiar book. So much keeps happening. Information keeps coming in and I keep sorting it out.' Kylie Tennant observed that Elizabeth was exhausted from working hard on 'that Penelope's web of a book. She must have it almost clean-typed by now. I don't ask.'

In August 1975 she sent two stories to the assistant features editor of the Melbourne *Herald* newspaper. Judah Waten and Kylie Tennant had alerted her to his search for stories for a planned series, the *Herald Weekend Story*, and she told him she might also have others more suitable, published and unpublished. The stories were 'Alice', the sad fairytale that alluded to her mother's early life in the thrall of a harsh mother and two husbands, and 'The Retrospective Grandmother', in which she reassessed her childish feelings about her two grandmothers in an adult and lightly fictionalised voice. Keith Connolly accepted the grandmothers, paid a hundred dollars and published the story across two tabloid pages in January 1976. By now the 'Colonial' grandmother, Catherine Harrower, had died but the 'Old World' Scottish grandmother, Helen Hughes, who had raised Elizabeth, lived on. Mummum, or Helen of Troy in the story, or Helen Wilson after the last of her several marriages, had gone to live in Maryborough, Queensland, with her son James, and was ending life in a nursing home. She sent sad notes to her granddaughter in tiny writing, with fears that she was going blind, and Elizabeth wrote to her with affection. Time, distance, and visits to Auntie Minnie, Helen's sister in Scotland, had enabled Elizabeth to rethink the diminished figure who had once been fierce, entertaining, dangerous, the life of every party, and the model for Lilian, the grandmother in *The Long Prospect*.

Harrower's writing about her grandmothers might also have been influenced by Margaret Dick's first trip back to Britain. In 1975 Margaret 'turned herself into an Australian', as Elizabeth put it. 'No, she didn't marry her swain; she made an affirmation. Now she has dual Australian/British citizenship.' (There was no clue to the identity of her swain, whether the 'nice' Ron Ferguson mentioned earlier or another.) Approaching her sixtieth birthday, Margaret was looking ahead to retirement and the need for a pension, and she wanted to see her family at least once more. Her student adviser job became ever more demanding, and she was trying to write in her spare time, but she was battered by respiratory illnesses and knew she couldn't work full-time forever. Soon after becoming Australian,

Margaret scraped together enough money to spend a month in London, Cheshire and Edinburgh, visiting old friends, staying with her sister Stephanie, and with her parents, Minnie and Jim. Her mild nostalgia only confirmed that she'd made the right choice in committing to Whitlam's dynamic Australia. In October she returned to Sydney in time for the turmoil of his dismissal.

During Margaret's absence, Elizabeth set herself a quota to write four pages a day, though she was producing stories rather than her novel. She'd always said the long form of the novel suited her better but short stories broke through her writer's block, and some of her earlier stories had grown into novels. Not really a smoker, she told Margaret she had taken up Sobranie cigarettes, a brand considered a luxury, and 'I think they help me concentrate. We'll see. No sacrifice too great.' So serious was she about work that she slowed down her social life and often unplugged the phone. When Patrick finally got through to her he said he'd given up ringing because she was never there. Elizabeth learnt he had been working hard, too, finishing a book that he was now rereading before packing up four copies of the typescript for his publishers, while talking of the next one. His tenth novel, *A Fringe of Leaves*, a sensual, historical story based on the shipwreck of Eliza Fraser, came out the following year, despite the political turmoil and dental problems that would distract him for months.

Elizabeth's more fragile concentration was shattered again by pressure building on Gough Whitlam and his Labor government. Whitlam had called a double dissolution election for May 18, 1974, after the Opposition threatened to stop the Budget passing in Parliament. She had an angry letter published in *The Australian* just days before Labor was reelected, condemning the 'dictatorial' leaders of the Liberal and Country parties, Billy Snedden and Doug Anthony, and urging: 'Let us hear a little less about Mr Whitlam's supposed arrogance, and more about the insult inflicted on the electors of 1972 by an Opposition prepared to use any means to gain power.'

However, as 1975 wore on, rising inflation and unemployment, political missteps and personal scandals were stoked by the media, and the Opposition pushed for an early election. In October they did block supply, meaning the government would run out of money within weeks.

The stalemate ended in a constitutional crisis as Harrower's fellowship deadline approached. She happened to become an eyewitness to history while visiting Christina Stead in Canberra.

*

Christina had decided to leave London the previous year, as her home was cracking and collapsing around her, soon for demolition. At the age of seventy-two she moved into a barn-like flat that her brother Gilbert Stead had built for her, attached to his bungalow in southern Sydney. With her love of puns and black humour, Christina quickly renamed the suburb Hurstville as 'Curstville' because of its isolation from the city, the summer heat, and the screams of low-flying planes from the nearby airport. Elizabeth Harrower caught the train out there in October 1974 on a secret mission, asking her to accept the first Patrick White Literary Award, which came with $6000. White had personally chosen Stead with agreement from the judges he appointed, historian Geoffrey Blainey and librarian James Allison. As Elizabeth recalled, Christina cooked lunch and was happy to accept the award, for 'the gesture of friendliness from another writer she admired, not the recognition, which she didn't care about much at all'. Her novel *The Little Hotel*, written in the 1950s, was published around this time in Australia, Britain and the US to good reviews. But like Elizabeth, she was struggling to produce a new novel, as she told a friend in New York: 'Why does all I write seem tripe, I wonder? Because I am not writing THE work – and what is the work? I don't know. Something that fills me with love but so far has no shape ...'

While Christina was in Sydney, Elizabeth took her out to lunch with Kylie Tennant, surprised that her two dear friends had never met. For all their common ground, they were not an easy match. 'K and C and I all exceedingly different from each other; they were united anyway in hating *Herzog*. Ah well ... It made me quite nervous to have brought these so-different consciousnesses face to face.'

Needing a break from 'Curstville' and her 'kind but not congenial' family, as Elizabeth described them, Christina took up an offer from the literary critic and poet Dorothy Green to stay in her house in Canberra while she was away. After persistent invitations from Christina, in November 1975 Elizabeth went down by train for a few days' visit and a welcome change from Sydney. She found Canberra 'sweet-smelling and spread out in a great shallow saucer surrounded by hills, and the circle of hills under a circle of purely decorative flat-bottomed clouds. Lovely.' She and Christina, once a Marxist true believer, always had lively conversations about politics and their respective passions for Gough Whitlam and the Premier of South Australia, 'dashing Don' Dunstan. Expecting the Opposition to back down and pass the Budget that week, Elizabeth was eager to visit Parliament House.

On Tuesday, November 11, she and Christina joined Canberra friends Patricia Walker and Clare Golson for a picnic by the Murrumbidgee River with 'lots of optimistic political talk' and arrangements made for Elizabeth to sit in the Visitors' Gallery the next day. Soon after they got home, Elizabeth heard Christina answer the phone and repeat, 'But that's terrible. That's terrible.' The governor-general, Sir John Kerr, had sacked the prime minister, dissolved Parliament, and put in the Liberal leader, Malcolm Fraser, as caretaker prime minister.

Elizabeth's reaction was, 'Horror. Horror and stupefaction.' She remembered later, 'I stepped back like somebody in a terrible film, going backwards and saying "No, no, no",' and Christina spoke to her as if she were 'an unexploded bomb'. In a ground-zero report to Shirley Hazzard, she wrote:

> Switched on radio which was dooming away in stunned voice. Chris offered gin, brandy, sherry, while I paced about holding head and listening to reports. Finally knocked off some Nescafé and took taxi to Parliament House. People surged there from everywhere. It was so AWFUL. Everyone was outraged. Our votes meant nothing. Moderate reform is not allowed to take place here. The new leaders came out on the balcony and laughed like Nazis. Then our deposed mates came outside to the front steps where we all were, to talk to the crowd, and were hugely cheered. Whitlam came out and it was a relief to see him still alive and valiant in the face of all this. To say that Kerr and Fraser have welded the Labor Party together is an understatement.

Telephone calls to and from Sydney where my mates were running temperatures, marching in the city, collecting money for the campaign, signing protests, sending telegrams, talking of Chile and Greece and the death of democracy.

On Wednesday I went again to Parliament House. A great rally in the space opposite the House, the police out in force. They don't understand. It's good feeling that brings these people together. People only clapped and cheered and called 'Shame!' from time to time. Police moved the crowd from around the steps and doors of PH and directed us across two roads running in front of the building. Whitlam and most of the Cabinet spoke from the back of a truck. The sun blazed down. People handed up ten and twenty dollar notes to Whitlam, who put them in his shirt pocket. I met Manning Clark. We all got sunburned. Labor staff went round handing out little squares of paper, hastily roneoed, to pin on fronts, saying LABOR WILL WIN.

Anxious that her inflamed emotions were putting too much strain on her friend's weak heart, Elizabeth caught the train back to Sydney. Her own heart held up, but with blistered feet she went from Central Station to the home of journalist and writer Craig McGregor to sign a petition protesting against the coup for a full-page advertisement in *The Australian* newspaper. Arriving home at one in the morning, she went later that day to ALP headquarters to give them Stead's donation to the cause, a cheque for $50. Stead wrote a wry account of events to Dorothy Green:

> Had a delightful time with that lovely (innocent too) girl Elizabeth Harrower. She had the great good luck of supernatural foresight to be here exactly in time to see her god (Gough W) in the flesh and manfully speaking from a lorry-end after his ignominious and ignoble dismissal, laughing (he) and all-embracing. She has gone home filled with the Message!

Elizabeth admitted, to herself and others, that Labor had made some mistakes. But she was evangelistic in her praise of their achievements, and their efforts to redistribute wealth and make up for years of conservatism during a world recession. Living on a fixed income, she was poorer than she had been. But she was proud to hear the ABC radio stations play 'Advance Australia Fair' instead of 'God Save the Queen' as the national anthem. She wanted to defend this new Australia against attempts from the right and the extreme left to undermine the country's progress. With Helene Nolte she went to a lunchtime rally at Sydney's Capitol Theatre organised by a group called Arts for Labor and attended by a crowd ranging from venerable artist Lloyd Rees to young actors Jacki Weaver and John Bell. There were speeches from Gough Whitlam and his wife Margaret, and from Patrick White, despite the removal of more teeth. Harrower wore a 'Shame, Fraser, Shame' button, once an inconceivable display for her. With Ferdi Nolte and Margaret Dick she went to a People for Whitlam dinner, attended by the Whitlams, at architect Harry Seidler's house in Killara – 'a thoroughly enchanted evening' – and a series of rallies and meetings.

But all was hopeless when an election in December confirmed a Coalition government with Malcolm Fraser as prime minister and heavy losses for Labor. Harrower went to bed with a virus and began 'to grieve for the books I haven't written'.

Stanley Avenue

By 1974 slow-brewing plans for Shirley Hazzard and Francis Steegmuller to attend Adelaide Writers' Week were finally in place. Elizabeth had connected them with Geoffrey Dutton, the founding director, who issued invitations for March 1976, which they accepted. In the long lead-up to their visit and her review of Patrick White for the *New York Times*, Shirley had asked Elizabeth in December 1973 to add to her knowledge of contemporary Australian writing. She thought a few Americans had heard of Daisy Bates or Henry Handel Richardson, or more recently of Christina Stead, AD Hope, and Thea Astley. Elizabeth replied at length but with little more enthusiasm than she had ever shown for Australian literature. 'In fact, there is not a great deal of it,' she began.

Apart from *The Eye of the Storm*, she had not read a new Australian novel for a long time. With uncharacteristic hostility, she responded, 'None of us (US, whoever WE are) much like Thea Astley's work or, indeed, Thea Astley.' She was partly channelling Patrick White's choppy relationship with Astley, which had begun in 1960 when she dropped in at his Castle Hill home as an admirer seeking encouragement, and developed into a friendship that required her to absorb his tough criticism of her novels and character. He wrote to congratulate her on winning the first of four Miles Franklin Awards for *The Well-Dressed Explorer* in 1962 but said she looked sour in press photos. His irritation burst after Astley complained that Geoffrey Dutton had ignored that novel when he was selecting Australian books for Penguin paperbacks. Defending Dutton, White damned her 'wretched book' and told another friend she resented his move to Sydney and 'resented anybody's having a vacuum cleaner until she had one herself, when she had, she forgot about the vacuum cleaner and went on to something else'. They did not speak for decades until he softened at the end of his life. Astley's use of complex language, metaphor and satire were often compared with White's and, with his endorsement, she won the Patrick White Award in 1989.

Astley, in turn, found Harrower's novels 'a bit miserable at times'. Although Harrower's writing was likened to White's, she was also dismissive of another 'Patrick-copying' admirer. She told Shirley Hazzard in January 1974 there had been 'a huge fuss about Thomas Keneally ... but that is over'. Keneally had published seven novels by then, most recently *The Chant of Jimmy Blacksmith* in 1972, and he went on to be one of Australia's most prolific and successful authors of the twentieth century. Harrower named Hal Porter, Judah Waten and Randolph Stow, whom she had met not long ago at a dinner at Patrick's house. Struggling to think of others, she added, 'Barry Oakley (facetious), David Martin (much better), Frank Moorhouse (trendy sex), David Williamson (playwright), Alex Buzo (playwright)' and David Foster – who was admired by Dutton, White and Tennant, though she had trouble remembering his name. Among poets, she said Patrick liked Les Murray, and she listed RD Fitzgerald, Kenneth Slessor, Geoffrey Lehmann, Judith Wright, Francis Webb and Bruce Beaver. To explain her poor list, she added:

> There is a sort of wistful looking out for new people (the same anywhere, I know, but there are fewer of us here and the climate is so against literary effort – physical and mental climate) and so when something that <u>isn't bad</u> arrives everyone thinks: perhaps this one will keep on and develop.

While Harrower had every right to her own taste, her negative summary of the literary scene revealed her as uninterested in Australian writing beyond the books of her friends, and out of touch with the younger generations pushing at their backs. She had, in fact, enjoyed David Williamson's most recent play, *Jugglers Three*, though she'd found *The Removalists* and *Don's Party* crude and violent. Many of her opinions seemed secondhand, passed on by Patrick, Kylie and Margaret, and there was a sour-grapes suggestion of insecurity about her own writing, or non-writing.

She was, however, excited about planning a party in Hunters Hill to introduce Shirley and Francis to her circle of friends. She offered to invite Ron and Dorothy Geering, Nancy Phelan, Geoffrey Lehmann, David Malouf, Rodney Hall, Bruce Beaver, Nancy Keesing (now chair of the Literature Board) and her husband, Mark Hertzberg, as well as Margaret, Kylie, Kit, and Kit's psychiatric nurse, Andrew Robertson, and friend Yolanda Davies – and anyone else Shirley wanted. Kit had threatened to leave Sydney, as Shirley told a friend, so that they could be 'free to enjoy ourselves without her'. Elizabeth did her best to include Shirley's mother in their social events, but Kit remained icy towards her daughter. Twenty-five guests was the most she could entertain in her 'little white cubes', which Francis kindly said reminded him of their place in Capri. Among those at the party was Christina Stead, an 'unforgettable' pleasure for Shirley, who met her for the first time.

Elizabeth also organised a small dinner at her place with Patrick and Manoly, and another at theirs, and she helped with all kinds of social and professional arrangements. This was Shirley's first return to Sydney since a short stay in 1951 when she was twenty, and she was to write a 'Letter from Australia' for the *New Yorker*. For months Elizabeth sent her informative letters with piles of clippings, and facilitated interviews with Patrick and Gough Whitlam while she was there. The bond between Elizabeth and Shirley was strengthened by this intense time of shared pleasures, Kit-troubles, and quiet conversations at the Sebel Town House in Elizabeth Bay, a hotel that Elizabeth recommended because the Nolans stayed there. Shirley's thoughtful and deeply researched *New Yorker* essay celebrated the political and cultural changes she experienced at first hand in Sydney and Adelaide, largely brought about by the Whitlam Government, and she went home fired-up to boost Australian writing in New York. Privately she told Elizabeth that her 'Letter' owed much 'to Elizabeth, Eliz-docs, Eliz-chums, & the atmosphere of Eliz's Australia'. But the article itself mentioned Elizabeth only as a friend of Patrick White.

*

The visit was an important reconnection for Shirley with her birth country and with the streets of Mosman, where she and Elizabeth had each at different times spent some of their early years overlooking Balmoral Beach, a counterpoint to the tensions in their respective homes. She wrote to Elizabeth that Balmoral, with its memories of school and swimming, had turned out to be 'the most poignant and pleasant of all places of return' and she imagined the two of them together as schoolgirls in boater hats. Driving past her former family home in Stanton Road, she had also shown Francis where Elizabeth's mother and stepfather had lived in nearby Stanley Avenue: 'a pleasant place to have a house'.

As it happened, Elizabeth had recently, reluctantly, decided to give notice to the tenants in her inherited house and move back in while she prepared the property for sale. When her accountant spoke of finances, her head felt like 'an unassembled kaleidoscope', but she understood that with no job, no book, no prospect of another literary grant, and inflation eating up her rental income, she needed to liquidate some assets. 'I must go because last year I managed to spend more money than came in.' She also needed to liberate herself from the Tennant-Rodd family by leaving Hunters Hill and Blackheath, where she had sold her half-share of their shack to Kylie as a home for her daughter, Benison. The Mosman house near Chinaman's Beach where Margaret Dick rented a flat had just been sold, too. Wanting to scale back her expenses, Margaret agreed to move into Stanley Avenue to save Elizabeth from floating round the ghost-filled house alone.

As soon as they had moved, in June 1976, there were workmen repairing, painting and recarpeting the cavernous rooms. Elizabeth and Margaret, both used to living alone, intended to 'camp' until the real estate agents took hold of the house on desirable 'Balmoral Slopes'. 'We'll ask people over. I intend to work, write, whatever else,' Elizabeth said. Meanwhile, high on the hill, she was seduced by beautiful autumnal weather, 'and every day the brilliance of the sea and sky surprises me, I wake up and see the sun rise without having to get up. It is intimidatingly a sunrise.'

In July, when they were still settling in, Elizabeth developed shingles, a painful eruption of blisters on the right side of her face, caused by reactivation of the chicken pox virus and often a reaction to stress. Tension had accumulated from the Whitlam dismissal, the house move, and years of trouble with Kylie's family, but there was also the strain on her nerves of returning to a house she'd been desperate to escape. Memories confronted her in every room of battles with her stepfather, her mother's shrinking presence, the night she was taken away to die. Time and travel might have eased the post-traumatic stress of her mother's death, but her body held her grief. There was the secret knowledge that Kempley's dirty money had bought the house that gave them physical comfort and psychic pain. Elizabeth had put Edgar Alan Poe's story *The Fall of the House of Usher* in the receptive hands of Clare in *The Watch Tower*, and now she was in her own haunted house that was threatening to collapse around her.

While she was unwell that July, Elizabeth had a letter from Sandra Forbes at the Australia Council inquiring about her progress on behalf of the Literature Board.

In February Elizabeth had reported to Michael Costigan, the director of the Literature Board, that since her fellowship began she had written a number of short pieces, enough for a collection. The novel she was working on was nearing completion and Macmillan had an option on it. She had notes for another novel. Such a list of accomplishments must have boosted everyone's confidence.

But now here was a request for a further update, and aside from the publication of 'The Retrospective Grandmother' in January, there was nothing to show – or nothing she was prepared to show. She turned for advice to Judah Waten, asking if she should give back her grant money. Typing with difficulty on her old Olivetti portable while she couldn't sit at her desk, she wrote:

> I know I've been slow, u and I know why, too. What a pity I didn't migrate from Hunter's Hill as soon as I got it [her grant]. Only Marg. and perhaps Patrick have any idea of the day to day and week to week and month to month (why stop there?) merciless frazzling I underwent there. If I'd had any brains, I'd have evaporated much soon [*sic*] from there. Ah well! However, I can't expect the Australia Council to understand that I was EXPERIENCING LIFE at quite a level. Out of which comes – eventually – work.

Judah replied in exasperation that the Australia Council letter had been a formality and that the Board, from which he had retired, 'took into account the possibility of a writer being frazzled by life to use your expression' and was flexible about delivery. If she were to write that

> I have sinned I haven't finished my novel and I am returning my grant then you would not only throw consternation into the ranks of the Board but you might open up the possibility of a change, a return to the CLF [Commonwealth Literary Fund] days, particularly as the high authorities are anxious to cut down on grants etc.

Elizabeth recovered from her shingles within a few weeks but her novel did not survive. Whatever she was writing then remains a mystery: there is no record of a submission to the Literature Board or to Macmillan or another publisher; there is no manuscript nor notes towards a new novel. Mixed in with the old drafts of *The Watch Tower* are pages of writing about characters and scenarios that did not appear in the final drafts of that novel, some of them set in 'the Department of Information', a television or filmmaking organisation, which vaguely resembled Harrower's past workplaces at the ABC or the Macmillan office. They were wisely deleted to create a tighter ensemble. It's possible Harrower tried to rework those or abandoned parts of *In Certain Circles*, because she often said she had wasted good material. But her disillusionment over that stillborn novel would more likely have made her turn in a new direction. So it must be assumed that she was unsatisfied with the longer fiction she was attempting and did not want to repeat the humiliation of offering substandard work. If she were using the experiences of Kylie's family and other friends, she destroyed the evidence at some stage. During this period, with only a few changes, she adapted the section of *In Certain Circles* about Anna's suicide note into a self-contained short story. The story was not published in that form, but may have been a stepping stone back to the internalised story about suicidal Sophie, 'A Few Days in the Country', which was written in the late 1960s but would first appear in Stephen Murray-Smith's literary journal, *Overland,* in 1977. Christina Stead had suggested he ask for a story from Elizabeth, who was grateful and quick to respond. 'That was kind,' she wrote to Christina. 'I'll type something out and give him a choice. I'm not sure what *Overland* likes, but we'll give it a go.'

In the same letter she shared the news that Cynthia Nolan had died a week earlier at the age of sixty-eight. She did not say the cause was suicide but Sidney Nolan had rung Patrick White in the middle of the night after Cynthia killed herself by taking a drug overdose in a London hotel room. Elizabeth wrote that she 'really loved' Cynthia, as did three other people she knew in Sydney, meaning Patrick, Manoly and Bill Cantwell.

> We are grieving away and don't know what to do with ourselves. She was wonderfully unsentimental and direct, meant what she said, said what she meant. This was a marvellous relief to me because I'd been much in the company of a couple of people who made a virtue of never meaning, never saying etc. That is really a sickness, I think now. Anyway, Cynthia's truthfulness was fresh air and spring water. But (as who knows better than you?) a few words about a complex person, an intense and feeling person, can only be misleading. Still, it's sad and not right ...

That 'couple of people' were probably Kylie and Roddy, the source of so much discomfort for Elizabeth, set in contrast to the Nolans since her trip to London and the aborted Japan cruise that followed. She had overcome the distress Cynthia caused her by refusing to see her in Sydney in 1973, understanding how depressed she was then.

Cynthia's suicide was prominent in her mind by the time she sent her story to Stephen Murray-Smith. Her depiction of Sophie's fragile mind ended with an unresolved struggle between her rational and irrational thinking, but she saw how easily the equivocation could tip into a lonely scene in the bush with an overdose of pills. She may have done some further revision in the rawness of grief. Cynthia had pleaded with Elizabeth in London to write, or to become a doctor or nurse if she wanted to be compassionate. The published version of 'A Few Days in the Country' echoes that plea when Sophie's friend Caroline urges her to practise the piano, 'or we'll turn you into a medico and send you overseas to do good'. After it was published in 1977, Elizabeth wrote to Christina with a clue to what the writing had cost her, creatively and personally. 'Thank you for saying something about that story of mine in *Overland*. I hope you did think it was all right. I had some wrestling with it.'

As Judah Waten had implied, the Literature Board was more lenient towards writers than the Commonwealth Literary Fund had been. Flush with money in the first years, the board only cut short monthly grant payments if a writer earned so much from their work that they no longer needed help. Having published two stories and expressed her intention to keep writing, Elizabeth Harrower is unlikely to have been asked to repay any of her $12 000. She would have known, with some relief, that she would not be offered another fellowship when needy writers, organisations, small presses and journals were straining the Literature Board's budget.

*

Once the expectation of a novel was lifted, Elizabeth returned her attention to her friends. If nothing else, she was writing reams of letters, reporting on everyone to everyone else. They all seemed to be travelling: Patrick White had been to Europe with a stealthy visit to Stockholm, Judah Waten to Russia, Nancy Phelan to Morocco, Ferdi Nolte to Cape Town, Jerusalem and Athens. Margaret Dick took time off from her office job to visit the Snowy Mountains. Elizabeth and Margaret had toured the countryside for two weeks when she was recuperating from shingles. They had ended up in Murrurundi, the town where Frank Harrower was living in 1939 when Betty and her mother visited before their divorce, the last time the family of three was together. Perhaps Elizabeth gave her cousin the 'unhappy family' tour of her father's railway postings. They had done a few driving trips in New South Wales and up to the Queensland rainforest, but Margaret had seen more of Australia than Elizabeth, who was more and more reluctant to leave home.

The big Mosman house demanded care and money. Elizabeth postponed plans to sell once she saw how much work was needed, but she was always watering the parched garden or having something fixed. As promised, she began entertaining more often at lunches, dinners and parties. Her guests always remembered the outlook from the terrace, where sky met sea and trees, and they could imagine themselves on holiday. 'The balcony', Elizabeth romantically called the semi-circular concrete area above the garden with its chairs and white railing. On rainy days, Elizabeth felt she was living in a submarine. Inside, she had removed most of her mother's silver and glass, and some of the old-fashioned formal furniture left by the Kempleys. She had never had to furnish more than a room or two and, although she had loved Cynthia Nolan's bohemian clutter, she had a minimalist approach to her own homes. She recalled in an interview the anticlimax of buying something she'd wanted when young, and

> it dawned on me once and for all that mine was not a life in which buying things would make me happy ... I'm not really all that interested in objects and in a way for me all my happiness comes from either work or people and not from startling people with my new this or that, and not from impressing people by my ability to spend a lot of money, which I haven't got.

Almost no art hung on the walls at Mosman but Elizabeth liked to show visitors a print of a nineteenth-century painting by Conrad Martens that captured her view of Balmoral Beach before houses pitted the green slopes. Dinners were served from the dark timber sideboard to the dark timber dining table, where Elizabeth did her best to banish the past with the conversation and laughter of her friends. There was often a case of champagne in the house, and she enjoyed a glass or a gin and tonic. She was no gourmet cook – friends rarely remembered the food – but she made one-pot curries, lamb shanks, soups and, for special guests, a crab, prawn and artichoke heart casserole. Her Sunday morning phone calls with Patrick were often about recipes as well as politics, books and friends. When her lentil soup was too solid, he advised adding stock, parsley, tomato paste, garlic and a ham bone. The rescued soup (minus ham) was delicious.

She remained a willing guest, too, accepting a constant flow of invitations from friends, and going to art exhibition openings, films and plays. In 1976, she saw two plays by the South African Athol Fugard;

Australian playwright Ron Blair's *Mad, Bad and Dangerous to Know*, starring a young John Bell; an American documentary film about the Depression, *Brother, Can You Spare a Dime?*; and *Dersu Uzala* by the Japanese director Kurosawa, before going down with shingles.

Afterwards her friend Ruby Madigan wrenched her from her seven-week slump by ringing to say the Labor Party needed help – and Elizabeth was her first call. Ruby had helped organise the People for Whitlam dinner at the Seidler house that Elizabeth had found so heartening, leading to a friendship with Ruby and her husband, Col Madigan, the architect of the new High Court and National Gallery buildings in Canberra. So now, rather than despair, she rallied for Labor Party meetings and anniversary events for Whitlam's sacking, which evolved into an annual Republic Day event at Sydney Town Hall on November 11. She and Margaret went to a conference aiming to change the Constitution – 'depressing and cheering at the same time' – where Whitlam and former Liberal prime minister Billy McMahon were on the platform together. McMahon 'carried on like a comedian', to which she silently responded: 'Where were you on Nov 11 and why didn't you say this then???' At every election she optimistically pushed flyers for local Labor candidates into voters' hands outside the polling booths, and was indignant when a woman with a Central European accent refused her paper, saying, 'I don't vote for communists.' Everywhere, she sought sympathisers. After a podiatrist working on her feet made positive comments about Manning Clark and Patrick White, she confided to Christina Stead: 'I suspect she must be One of Us – that is, a Labor voter. It's like a secret society. Yet there must be millions of us. Why should we feel like an oppressed underground?'

Elizabeth's Labor principles were still centred on class-based workers' rights and had not embraced race and gender issues that were coming to the fore. She was not unusual among white Australians in having no direct contact with Aboriginal people and had only an abstract idea of their lives and history. In 1977 she went to the Bondi Pavilion with Ferdi and Helene Nolte to see Aboriginal writer Robert Merritt's play *The Cakeman* with Aboriginal actor Bryan Syron. 'Like many plays, it could have been better,' she told Judah, 'but hearing <u>his</u> story and Bryan's story, the miracle was that they had done so much.' A week later a friend asked if Syron could come to a party at Elizabeth's place – probably the first time she entertained an Indigenous person. She thought the Aboriginal rights movement at its most radical was counterproductive and inflamed by 'neurotic and trendy characters looking for causes …' The limits of her understanding were exposed in a terse exchange with Shirley Hazzard during Bicentennial celebrations of the British colony in 1988, when Labor was again in power. Elizabeth complained about

> the irrational and sentimental attitude taken towards aborigines and the founding of the colony by self-righteous (but irrational) white Australians who always like to be 'agin the government'. No one really plans to give his own house to an aborigine, or to sail back to Europe, but they rage and rage about something that happened in 1788.

Again, not an uncommon view. Shirley snapped back from more racially mixed New York that

> surely there is something between giving up one's house to an aboriginal or 'sailing back to Europe' … and reverting to ignorance or, wildly worse, the sort of thought and talk about native peoples that blighted the world of my childhood?

*

An unusual request came from Christina Stead at the end of 1976 to spend a day at Palm Beach. The artist Bryan Westwood was going to paint her portrait, surrounded by the sea creatures studied by her marine biologist father, David Stead, who was the model for the father in *The Man Who Loved Children*. Christina was dubious and wanted moral support. Westwood suggested she invite two more writers to join them for lunch, so she arranged for Michael Wilding, an author, academic and publisher of experimental 'new writing', to drive Elizabeth up to the northern beaches. In the English department at the University of Sydney, Wilding had reviewed Stead's novels, and included her in an anthology of anti-Vietnam essays. They had lunched at her London club around the time

Elizabeth was also there. Christina wrote a teasing letter to Elizabeth in 1975, enclosing a copy of *The Short Story Embassy*, Wilding's comic fantasy about the literary world. An inveterate playful flirt, Christina pointed out, 'Your pin-up is on the back of this book and naked to the amiable trapezius. Someone has told him – or else he has noticed – that he is beautiful. But he is a very charming, good, kind man.'

Christina was less enamoured of his writing and told Elizabeth, 'I should like to see MW come off that counter (culture) and write straight!' This was in response to a letter from Elizabeth, who had been given copies of *Tabloid Story*, the magazine he had co-founded with Frank Moorhouse and Carmel Kelly. 'Don't tell anyone,' Elizabeth wrote, 'if I tell you that what impressed me most was a photograph of Michael Wilding: he is very very beautiful to look at. Can he possibly be as nice as he looks?' Like Christina, she hadn't got on 'terribly well' with his stories and, while she alluded to 'extenuating circumstances', she would have put him in the 'trendy sex' category with his friend Moorhouse. In 1975 Judah Waten and Stephen Murray-Smith had put Harrower's 'English Lesson' with stories by Wilding, Moorhouse and Peter Carey – the youngest writer – in a wide-ranging anthology, *Classic Australian Short Stories*. Before the Palm Beach lunch, she confided to Shirley: 'Not sure what MW and I will have to say to each other, though Judah says some good things about him.'

The atmosphere between driver and passenger in Wilding's car must have crackled. Not surprisingly, the odd quartet at Palm Beach had plenty to talk and laugh about, including Westwood's once-planned portrait of Whitlam's nemesis, John Kerr. The Stead portrait did not go ahead either. In 1994 Wilding would republish Harrower's story 'The Beautiful Climate' in *The Oxford Book of Australian Short Stories*. The story appealed partly for its setting on Scotland Island, where Wilding had gone to live from inner-city Balmain. Despite his respect for the author, he tried to read her novels and did not get on terribly well with them.

*

The grey-haired spinster, almost fifty years old, and the long-haired charmer in his thirties were separated by more than years. Elizabeth's reaction to Wilding's stories was intensified by his casual depiction of sex, drugs and bohemian living, while she was watching Bim Rodd's addiction destroy him and his family. Earlier in 1976 Kylie had moved her husband and son away from Hunters Hill to an old apple orchard at Shipley in the Blue Mountains, where she thought she could create a calmer, safer atmosphere as well as make some money from the gnarly apple trees. She was undeterred when the body of a murder victim was found at the back fence, and when she realised the rundown Cliff View Orchard would need even more rehabilitation than Hillside Farm. Kylie employed two men, who turned out to be alcoholics, to help her, and Bim continued to bring in homeless and addicted youths, ostensibly to work. In an unpublished memoir, 'The Curse of Cliff View', Benison Rodd recalled that Bim was becoming more aggressive and argumentative, throwing stones at trespassing kids, and driving the tractor dangerously. She felt bitterly resentful towards him and her mother, who she thought indulged his worst behaviour at everyone's expense.

When Kylie wrote to Mavis Cribb, her librarian friend from Maitland, about her plan to visit Cliff View for a weekend in 1977, she added:

> If you can persuade Elizabeth to come so much the better but it is more than I can do. I have issued invitations and lures of all sorts but she vaguely says she has: 'Things to do in Sydney'. I suspect she is still determined that if I cannot be with her alone she does not want me with my family. I don't blame her. The dreary Rodds are a bit much to take in a lump.

Elizabeth was indeed avoiding Shipley, but when Kylie was diagnosed with breast cancer that year, she was quick to give her a bed at Mosman each time she travelled to Sydney for doctors' appointments, a mastectomy and ongoing treatment. While Kylie was making a promising recovery, she was about to face much worse.

Bim, at twenty-seven, was on a permanent invalid pension, unable to study or work. He was trying to write and took some pages to Elizabeth's place for her to read, but became angry with her when he lost them. In the autumn of 1978 he planned a trip to Nepal and when he was leaving, Kylie dropped him at the train for Sydney and gave him some travel money – a dangerous combination, but no one was able, or had the will, to stop him.

A detective rang Kylie the next morning with the shocking news that Bim had been found unconscious from head injuries in Kings Cross after being attacked, his money, guitar, watch and sleeping bag gone. At St Vincent's Hospital he was kept alive on a respirator for days. On the day Bim died Kylie had to take Roddy home to Shipley because he was collapsing from stress.

Elizabeth went to identify Bim's body in the morgue and was glad his mother didn't have to see him. The funeral was held at Christ Church St Laurence, the Anglican church in Sydney where Kylie and Roddy had a lifelong association. After the wake at her sister's home in Chatswood, Kylie returned to exhausting herself at Shipley by tending to the orchards, flower and vegetable gardens, geese, chickens and ducks. As friends made their pilgrimages to show sympathy, Kylie cheered them up with food and conversation by the fire. When the visitors were gone, Elizabeth was relieved that she let down her usual coping facade and allowed herself to grieve honestly for her son.

'K and R make it easy for everyone,' she wrote to Shirley. 'But Bim's life for years and years has been tragic and terrible. He used to be an affectionate, smiling boy. Kylie loved him greatly.' For herself, she said, 'You can imagine that, while walking through the days with apparent calm, there's a sort of awful reaction that overtakes you when life supposedly settles down to normal again. Everything's a bit of an effort.'

Elizabeth sat through the inquest at the Coroner's Court in June for Kylie, who was still seeing doctors and went only to give her own evidence. She looked ill again when she finished. Bim's watch, a gift from his mother, had led to the arrests of three people – 'all black, of no fixed address' – who were charged with murder. The police said they had robbed Bim, the woman hit him on the head with a wine flagon, the men threw him from an upstairs window to a concrete courtyard and dragged him into a laundry. He was found moaning when officers went to investigate another robbery in the building. What Bim was doing at the derelict house was not clear, but probably involved drugs.

Six months later Kylie and Elizabeth, with other friends, sat on hard benches in the airless Central Criminal Court in Darlinghurst for the trial. Elizabeth thought the defence used Bim's experimentation with drugs and his mental illness to make him sound like 'a disturbed person who jumped out of the window for no good reason'. Even so, Kylie was not vengeful towards the three on trial and Elizabeth told Judah Waten, 'No doubt, if you knew their lives from the beginning they would hardly turn out to be favoured children of fortune.' When they emerged into the pre-Christmas shopping crowds they felt 'like visitors from another planet. All the week we'd been in the world of life and death, and truth and lies, and that real world made this seem so flimsy and nightmarish.' The jury found one man guilty of murder and he was sentenced to life imprisonment, but the other two defendants went free.

Bim's death ended a slow, sordid decline and was a sad release. His sister, Benison, was so worn down that she wrote of his attackers:

> I think they did my family a favour as he would have killed someone sooner or later. It was better this way. There were times when I could have killed him myself and I think my father could have too, because he made our lives hell.

*

Kylie gave Elizabeth a silver flute that had belonged to Bim, a memento of his gentle side. For months Elizabeth gave Kylie the calm support she always mustered for friends in a crisis, but this time she kept some self-protective distance. She had 'an unremitting social life' of lunches, dinners and entertainment. With Ferdi and Helene she went to Andy Warhol's film *Bad* ('*Bad* was good') and another night Ingmar Bergman's film *The Serpent's Egg*, which was so grim she closed her eyes. With Patrick she spent a day at the Sydney Film Festival seeing a Greek film and a Spanish film: 'It was fun. He's a good companion.' She saw Quentin Crisp perform at the Theatre Royal, and went on an anti-uranium march, only her second march after the Aldermaston protest against nuclear weapons in London twenty years earlier.

At the request of a woman she knew from the Mosman branch of the Labor Party, she attended a women's class at the Workers Education Association (WEA) to talk about books, writing and human nature. So enjoyable were the hours of 'idle conversation, not speech-making' that she would go back once a year for a long time. The group had been reading Christina Stead's novel *The Man Who Loved Children* and they asked how Stead knew about children, not having had any. They were too polite to ask Harrower the same question but she answered for both of them. As she reported to Christina: 'I said you had been a child, which was the best possible experience from which to write, but anyway, being yourself, you knew things instinctively that other people had to struggle with endlessly.'

Her friend Ken Levis, head of the English Department at Alexander Mackie College of Advanced Education, had often asked Elizabeth to meet students at his house, and she had always said no. This time he asked her to be writer in residence at the college's campus in Paddington. Tom Keneally, by now the celebrated author of a dozen published novels, was to have been there but he had to go overseas. Elizabeth decided after 'all the death and devastation of Bim's event' that she would enjoy the nine-week commitment, which began in September 1978 and filled the time until the murder trial. There was the helpful sum of $4000, too, half paid by the Literature Board. Levis craftily put the invitation just before his retirement as a plea to help the college keep the funding and the position. She told him she didn't want to be 'an imitation academic' and set her own conditions:

> No lectures or formal talks. You just take your typewriter and write in your own office ... 'Available for conversation' (one must be), the rules say. Apart from English Dept. everyone speaks Jargon, I'm told. By not understanding Jargon, I'm to persuade them in directions of English. Friends lecturing there say cheerfully, 'You'll suffer!' The last thing I intend to do!

She arrived at the college with the seed of an idea for – what? She wrote to Christina just before starting:

> In spite of numerous interesting outings, the time spent just thinking about things, people, the how, why and is of things, feels more necessary. I guess it's the non-writing part of writing. I've been noticing two people and remembering Thomas Mann's <u>Tonio Kroger</u>. One true-heart is knocked down and passed over by fate again and again; the other with good looks and the <u>appearance</u> of other qualities conquers all over the place. 'Twas ever thus but, from the sidelines, I've just seen a series of new examples. There's nothing to be done about it (out in the world); you certainly can't go round explaining in conversation …

Thomas Mann's novella about the development of the artist's nature had been in her working notes for *The Catherine Wheel* twenty years ago. She had interpreted the theme then, in the tortured relationship between Clem and Christian, as the difference between 'the one who understands and knows but does not relax or warm; the other who doesn't know or care and attracts partly because of this'. These ideas about human nature, inequality and fate had replayed in different forms throughout her work, and her life. She didn't say who raised the memory in 1978 and she left no further written evidence.

Elizabeth had fun with the students – many of them bound to be teachers – and was grateful for her colleagues' courtesy and friendliness. Some took away copies of her novels to read, some invited her out, a few remained friends. Sitting in classes on creative writing, children's literature, world literature, teaching and curriculum, and in private talks about students' writing, she 'used every opportunity to speak for plain English and the printed word'. This made a bright interlude between court appearances. One lecturer was so enlivened by Elizabeth's literary and political conversations that she developed a brief crush on the more worldly writer, but settled into being her driver when she began house hunting. Predictably, too, by keeping her office door open, Elizabeth found concentration on her own work impossible. She managed only some 'pieces of novel and pieces of short story', as she wrote in her official report to Michael Costigan at the Literature Board. She concluded:

> To me the college was a privileged and rather enclosed place where people on the whole were occupied with tasks they enjoyed: this made them agreeable company. I felt I arrived with news of an outside world where life was – at least superficially – much harder and less secure and comfortable.

She told Judah more bluntly: 'In the rather rare vacant spaces between events, I just wasted the hours and felt imprisoned … Writing fiction, even thinking of writing fiction, seemed a strange thing inside a university, college.' To Shirley and Francis, knowing she had sympathetic readers, she complained:

> I say, friends, I had no idea that English and literature were in such frightful danger till I stayed at A. Mackie. If something was too difficult to be expressed in words (and, to the students, almost everything was) they could travel across the city to a building filled with radio, television, film equipment and fiddle around with technical things for a couple of hours, utter something spontaneous and fade out. It all counts towards a degree!! No doubt I've told you about leaving college with wonderful flowers, presents? I did get on very well with the eighty staff members. They were gentle, modest, intelligent. But – to revert – books are in danger. However, that's all the more reason for everyone who knows that and cares to work and work.

Slowly spreading circles

The mid-1970s marked a turning point for Elizabeth Harrower. Twenty years after the appearance of her first novels and a decade since *The Watch Tower*, all the novels were out of print and she was slipping out of view as a contemporary writer.

In her feminist history of Australia, *Damned Whores and God's Police*, Anne Summers argued that women writers had been physically and critically excluded from Australian literature. She wrote:

> Elizabeth Harrower must possess a very special strength and conviction to be able to continue to write her splendid books about women for a world that mostly fails even to acknowledge their existence. Other women have lacked her tenacity and, when their offerings have been ignored, have disappeared.

Those respectful but alarming words were published in 1975 when Harrower still saw herself as a working writer and, despite the Sisyphean effort of pushing every book into the world, did not feel she had been ignored. Yet this image of neglect had taken hold early in admiring reviews from Max Harris and others, and was reinforced by Summers' bestseller, which helped to drive a new round of attention. Interestingly, Summers saw a likeness between Harrower's Emily Lawrence in *The Long Prospect* and Kylie Tennant's Shannon Hicks in *Ride on Stranger* as girls who each suffered 'the pain and intellectual frustration of being denied books by the Philistines in whose charge she has been put'.

That year, too, the United Nations held the first conference on the status of women and, as part of International Women's Year, the Australia Council featured Harrower on a poster of women writers. In a lecture on 'Images of Women in Australian Literature', the eminent poet-activist Judith Wright spoke of *The Watch Tower* as a portrayal of the ownership and subjection of the person, as well as the economic dependence of women ... Her analysis of the forces that drive the awful Felix, in that novel, is direct, intelligent, and as relevant today as in the early '60s ... a more powerful analysis of what really happens to women in such situations than many women writers, even today, venture on.

Wright saw that *The Watch Tower* was 'not a narrowly feminist novel' but a 'very feminine novel', written from the interior of its female protagonists. Harrower was asked many times of *The Watch Tower*, why Laura did not leave Felix but remained a passive victim of his control. She explained that women in distress then, in the 1930s and '40s, could go to the police or the Salvation Army, but had none of the refuges, pensions and other supports that came later. And who would believe them? She felt she had understood all this before women's inequality was spelt out by writers such as Simone de Beauvoir in *The Second Sex* in 1949 and Betty Friedan in *The Feminine Mystique* in 1963.

Even if no new books were coming from Elizabeth Harrower, as the decade went on there was one publisher keen to bring her old novels out of obscurity. As chief executive of the revered but ailing Angus & Robertson in the 1970s, Richard Walsh tried a more commercial approach to save the country's oldest publisher. He also started two cheap paperback imprints to revive old A&R and other titles that had fallen into obscurity. Walsh worked with Christina Stead on new editions of her early A&R books, *Seven Poor Men of Sydney* and *For Love Alone*, and some others, as well as a late new novel, *The Little Hotel*. While he was keen to publish *The Long Prospect, The Catherine Wheel* and *The Watch Tower*, Walsh remembered that Harrower 'was very reclusive and I left all negotiations with her to the paperbacks publisher'.

Reclusive was an odd description for this sociable woman, but showed how her profile had disappeared from the mainstream. *The Watch Tower* came out as an A&R Classic in 1977 and the others as Sirius Quality Paperbacks two years later, with a small flourish of publicity and reviews. Writing for the *National Times*, Jean Bedford thought *The Long Prospect* and *The Catherine Wheel* 'a delight' and Harrower 'such an intelligent writer, if a bit painstakingly ethical ... like the improbable combination of Doris Lessing and Iris Murdoch ...' The ABC magazine *24 Hours* juxtaposed Stead's old line about *The Long Prospect* as 'Elizabeth Harrower's masterpiece' with the double-edged compliment that she was 'an under-estimated – within the context of Australian fiction hardly known at all – novelist'. Walsh arranged for Harrower to do an interview with Jim Davidson, the editor of *Meanjin*, but she was tongue-tied, he was verbose, and the result was excruciating. Between them they slashed the lopsided conversation into a readable piece, but she wrote to Judah:

> I told him we had no golden opinions for that interview – my friends all failing to find the person they've known for years. He was crestfallen, but he had the same reaction. Mary [Lord] said most of the interview consisted of the writer saying a few words and Jim giving a long interpretation of the writer's <u>real</u> meaning. However, apart from not enjoying being put in the dock over characters invented long ago, I quite enjoyed Jim's company.

So far as getting the books beyond Australia, every step forward ran into another blockage. In 1981 Carmen Callil, the Australian-born founder of the feminist Virago Press in London, expressed some interest in republishing the novels but took forever to read them and stepped away when she learnt Australian rights weren't available. Elizabeth was at least able to give the A&R books to friends who hadn't known her when they were first published. She sent *The Long Prospect* to Shirley and Francis and responded to their praise with a spontaneity that eluded her in interviews:

> Your call and all the lovely things you said ... made me feel happy. It was published in London in 1958 when things Australian were (to the rest of the world) still lost in primaeval mists and slime. Patrick and Sidney Nolan had just begun, at that time, to clamber out of it, surprising people. But all along the way, over the years, single persons have come across it and been fond of it. Patrick and Christina, before they knew me, liked it. Max Harris 'discovered' it and wrote some reams. That's all long ago. What nicer thing could

you possibly have said than that you wanted to know what happened to Emily, and wondered. Really, thank you.

Elizabeth was flattered that Shirley's friend Donald Keene, an American scholar of Japanese literature, visited her while in Sydney in 1981 and bought a copy of *The Watch Tower*. After reading it, he wrote to compliment her, sorry she had persuaded him not to buy her earlier novels. She told Shirley:

> I didn't want to exploit him! And I didn't think he'd like them, anyway, since I was still finding my way. However, after he wrote to me, not to seem mean, I sent the others to him when I thanked him for his book. A&R did me no favour with that tatty Australian Classics edition.

As Harrower and Hazzard's paths diverged further, Shirley's 1980 novel *The Transit of Venus* won the National Book Critics Circle Award in the United States and was loved (and sometimes mocked in Australia) for her filigree sentences that weave an intricate story of women and men seared by love, deception and war. The Australian film director Gillian Armstrong wanted, but eventually failed, to make a film of the novel, at the same time as a filmmaker showed fleeting interest in adapting *The Long Prospect*. The film that did get up was *For Love Alone*, produced by Margaret Fink, forty years after the novel came out and three years too late for Christina Stead to know.

While Shirley was flying high, Elizabeth had to be content with the retrospective interest of academic writers and editors. Feminist scholars including Anne Summers, Frances McInherney, Sneja Gunew and Carole Ferrier took her work into women's studies journals such as *Refractory Girls* and *Hecate*. A young scholar at the University of Western Australia, Nola Adams, learnt about Harrower by reading *Damned Whores and God's Police* and was struck by Summers' argument that Harrower, like other Australian women writers, had been denied serious critical consideration. In a perceptive review, she took up Nancy Keesing's challenge that Harrower 'awaits the critical assessment that her four novels deserve.

She is a perfectionist of small output, but her rare books display equally rare qualities of style and depth of understanding and interpretation.' Adams wrote her MA thesis, 'A Dark Realism', on Harrower's work and spoke about 'The Gothic Sensibility in Fiction by Australian Women' at a conference in Adelaide. Nola was thrilled when Elizabeth agreed to meet her at Stanley Avenue. They shared a darkly wry sense of humour and talked about her planned PhD on Janet Frame, New Zealand's great author of mental anguish.

As she turned fifty, Elizabeth was coming to be regarded as an elder of Australian literature, held in high esteem for past work, and the subject of study and rediscovery. She accepted, even welcomed, the interest but was detached from analysis of books she had not read since writing them; she disliked the label 'feminist', and other limiting theoretical terms, for herself or her fiction. But the scene was changing.

Helen Garner's first novel, *Monkey Grip*, was published in 1977 by a small Melbourne press started by Hilary McPhee and Diana Gribble. In a way, Garner's story about a single mother obsessed with a heroin addict was not so different from Harrower's toxic relationships, but she wrote about a casual bohemian community in a direct Australian voice. Older writers such as Elizabeth Jolley and Olga Masters had broken through and Thea Astley had won three Miles Franklin Awards and a string of others. If Harrower wanted to continue her career, she urgently had to publish some substantial new fiction that connected her with contemporary readers.

Was she still a writer? Friends kept trying to help. At Patrick White's suggestion, the Michael Karolyi Memorial Foundation, founded by a Hungarian writer's widow, invited Elizabeth to stay in one of their artists' cottages near Vence in the south of France. After declining the offer in January, in February 1979 she accepted a residency for three months beginning in May. But then someone advised her strenuously that the accommodation was isolated and primitive, like a boy scout camp, and that residents were expected to work in the gardens. Most of the writers and artists were American, Hungarian or Russian, and little English was spoken. In her typed record of the unattributed warning are notes such as 'Desperately lonely. Place for geriatrics.' She sent another cable apologising that 'family events' would prevent her from going, and a letter with a tortuous explanation that she'd had 'a sudden responsibility descend within a day of the arrival of your invitation' and while she had thought she could still travel, this turned out to be untrue.

> Patrick White, who has been a kind and encouraging friend for years, had every reason to think I would at least respond in a reliable manner and, even more probably, with delight. I am sure he hoped something good would come of the venture.

*

Guilt-stricken again at her unreliability, she did have at least one practical family reason to be at home in those months of 1979. Margaret Dick had decided to retire from her office work in July, and after 'camping' at Stanley Avenue for three years, she had bought her own tiny flat at Elizabeth Bay with her savings, money from her parents, and some from Elizabeth, on Margaret Kempley's instructions to 'look after Margaret'. Finding the place, packing up and settling in was intense work for both of them.

As it turned out, Kylie's husband Lewis Rodd died at Shipley that same July, aged seventy-four, weakened by the trauma of Bim's death and his own multitude of health problems. At his crowded funeral at Christ Church St Laurence, the minister, their old friend Alf Clint, especially remembered his work with the unemployed and evicted during the Depression. Two days after the funeral, Elizabeth drove up to Shipley with Kylie's sister, Doff, taking fish and chips, gin and tonic, cigarettes and matches, pad and pen for lists. Glad to be helpful to Margaret and Kylie, she nevertheless wrote to Judah that 'having got all that organised, I turn once again to my own affairs, feeling like someone about to resume – say, cooking an omelette that I started six months ago!'

Without the stresses of Blackheath, Bim and Roddy, Elizabeth resumed a more placid, equal friendship with Kylie. That year a successful ABC television miniseries based on Kylie's 1943 novel *Ride on Stranger* attracted interest from a new literary agent. When she left her chooks to come down for a meeting, Kylie stayed the night at Mosman. Elizabeth wrote to Judah about her 'heroic' friend:

> We've been through so many extraordinary and tragic times, and know each other so well, that she relaxes and is more herself with me than with most people and places. We have good discussions, up hill and down dales, mostly agreeing about life and reality.

*

Christina Stead had been away from Sydney for a long time. As well as making visits to New York, she lived at a residential hall at the Australian National University in Canberra, where she formed a coquettish (on her part) friendship with the chancellor, Herbert Cole 'Nugget' Coombs, and dubbed him 'King Cole'. She stayed for almost two years in Melbourne with her friend Mary Lord, a lecturer in the English Department at Monash University, who was editing a book on Hal Porter and was distracted by Christina's restless, talkative presence. From there Christina filled out a form for Elizabeth to be listed in 'some *Who's Who*' and praised her friend to Lord, who asked Elizabeth to be writer in residence at Monash in 1980. This was simply another invitation to be declined.

'If Christina had only asked me,' she complained to Judah:

> I'd have told her I have my own plans for next year. A holiday in Melbourne seeing friends would be fun, but no office is a good office for one who spent so many ill-paid years in offices. And as I know from my enjoyable experience at Alexander Mackie, I can't write one word surrounded by hundreds, thousands of people.

Not wanting to return to her brother's house at Hurstville, Christina asked Elizabeth if she could rent a room in the house in Stanley Avenue. But Elizabeth, for all her affection, could not take responsibility for Christina, who was drinking too much and becoming frail as her heart failed. She told her she was likely to sell the house and go overseas.

Christina told a friend that Elizabeth had wanted Margaret to leave the house in order to dispel 'an undeserved reputation' for being lesbian. Elizabeth may have emphasised this as an excuse to discourage Christina. There's no doubt she and Margaret were subject to speculation, as independent single women often were. Other friends heard and dismissed the rumours. Christina herself had to fend off occasional whispers that she was a lesbian and a man-hater, despite her long, loving marriage to Bill Blake. According to her biographer, Hazel Rowley, she could be quite hostile to lesbians. As with Elizabeth, she did not accept the label feminist, disliking the divisive politics of the movement. 'I LOVE men,' she said and demonstrated it in her marriage, affairs, friendships and crushes. She was emphatic that Elizabeth couldn't ignore such a rumour and, perversely, she also refused to accept that Patrick White and his 'friend' Manoly were gay.

Elizabeth loved men, too. Thanks to Christina, she came to know Nugget Coombs after they met in 1982 at their mutual friend's eightieth birthday party in Canberra. 'I liked your great good friend so much, your Cole,' she wrote on that occasion. For years afterward he would visit Stanley Avenue and take Elizabeth to lunch at the restaurant on Balmoral Beach; he sent her cases of wine and copies of his books. To her annoyance, he proposed marriage, despite having a wife and a lover, the poet Judith Wright. But he was one of the most fascinating men Elizabeth knew, a former governor of the Reserve Bank, a champion of arts funding and Aboriginal rights, and an adviser to Whitlam. Many of Elizabeth's male friends were married or gay, possibly 'safer' and more interesting than the available single men. 'I certainly knew some very nice men and a few who would have, yes, been quite happy. But I wouldn't,' she said on the subject of marriage in 2017. Close friends from her later years came up blank when asked about her love life, with men or women, unaware of romantic relationships ever. They just didn't think of her as a sensual being. She was elegant, smartly dressed, conscious of her appearance, and yet had a 'maidenly' air. For all her warmth, she did not like presumptuous intimacy and could overreact as she did to gratuitous unkindness. Roddy had given unbearable 'brothel' kisses as she sailed for London, and Elizabeth was startled when her dear friend Gavin Souter kissed her goodbye on the lips. Her recoil was old-fashioned propriety with an extra protective layer that told people not to touch, not to ask, not to intrude.

She was, in her way, in love with her married friends Judah Waten and Ferdi Nolte and talked adoringly about both as kind, intelligent, politically active men. Some wondered if – even hoped – she crossed a sexual line with one or other, but the ambiguity seems to have settled on the side of deep platonic love or at most 'an emotional affair'. Both were rocks in her life, advisers and helpers she could trust, the kind of friends a single woman needed. For many years she had seen good-natured, talkative Judah alone on his trips to Sydney, having dinner at her place or at the New Hellas Greek restaurant in the city. Asked if he was in love with her, she said: 'He thought I was very nice, let's just say. There was something about me that he liked.' After Hyrell, his wife, retired as principal of a Melbourne school, she began to travel to Sydney with him in the 1980s and was admitted as an associate friend. Elizabeth also appreciated the bright company of their daughter, Alice, who was a founding member of the Australian Chamber Orchestra and had taught Richard Tognetti her Russian style of violin. But Elizabeth's love was reserved for Judah. Despite his communism, his personal decency and generosity had helped him become an establishment figure in Australian literature, and in 1979 he was made a Member of the Order of Australia (AM) in the Queen's Birthday Honours.

Ferdi Nolte, too, was an amiable, happy man. As an architect who designed hospitals, he was outside the intellectual, literary world, but he was practical and quick to travel from Hunters Hill to Mosman to do or oversee house repairs. Elizabeth went out for movies, meals, Labor Party events and driving trips with Ferdi and his wife, but Helene could be demanding, jealous and less easy to like. At one point Ferdi left her, not for Elizabeth, but for a woman in Germany who changed her mind when he turned up to marry her. Elizabeth gave a sympathetic ear to both Ferdi and Helene, while saying she wanted to divorce both of them, and remained loyal when he slunk home.

She was fond of their daughters, Karin and Linda, who wrote her letters about their adventures and misadventures. For Linda, 'Elizabeth was like a second mother to me. She gave me a lot more support growing up than my own mother ever did.' When she and her partner Barney had a baby girl in 1990, they named her Kasavere after the place in Pakistan where she was conceived while they were photographing and writing about wolves and snow leopards. Back in Sydney, they made Elizabeth her godmother. Neither Linda nor Kasavere thought the love between Elizabeth and Ferdi was sexual; in his granddaughter's view, he preferred more glamorous women. But Linda understood: 'He was a lovely man and I can see why she was totally besotted with him.'

*

The main reason for Margaret's move from Mosman was nothing scandalous, but simply because Elizabeth kept talking of selling or renting out the house and, close as they were, both women preferred to live alone. Margaret loved her small flat at 43 Elizabeth Bay Road in an elegant 1930s building, suitably named Scotforth, with a café and shops on the ground floor at the crossroads of Elizabeth Bay, Potts Point and Kings Cross. Relieved of work, she was happier than she'd been for years and promised friends she would never complain about anything again. Eve and Ken Levis – he the former head of English at Alexander Mackie College – held a party to celebrate her retirement, and Nancy Phelan welcomed her to 'the Cross' with a lunch at her flat in Macleay Street. Elizabeth was less enthusiastic, as she told Judah: 'Nancy is a great propagandist for that area; all the eccentric, poor, addicted, elderly, lonely people in the street there trouble me and would give me a nervous breakdown if I encountered them every day.' With its apartment buildings, restaurants and cafés, strip clubs and bars, the area was much livelier and seedier than Mosman, and home to many friends, such as Bill Cantwell, Jessica Anderson – and Kit Hazzard at The Chimes in Macleay Street, regardless of her threats to leave. In 1979 Anderson published her fourth novel, *Tirra Lirra by the River*, about a woman who escapes her constrained family life in Queensland for bohemian poverty in prewar Potts Point. Her vivid evocation of the inner suburb's rundown mansions overlooking the docks of Woolloomooloo helped make this her most successful book, then and still. Anderson had been published (and once turned down) by Macmillan when Elizabeth and Kylie worked there, and had written drama scripts for the ABC in the 1960s when Margaret was writing poetry programs. They got on well enough for Anderson to ask Margaret in 1976 to be her literary executor.

Elizabeth, too, had set her novel *Down in the City* around Kings Cross after the war, based on the time she spent there as a child, when her mother was a nurse, and later when she worked in offices and became a confirmed coffee drinker in the European cafés of Macleay Street and the Queen Victoria Building, home of the old City Library. She visited a friend at St Luke's Hospital in Potts Point in 1979, the first time for decades she'd been inside the small private hospital that held layers of personal memories. Her mother had been a sister there in 1939–40, working in the maternity wing at Lulworth House, which had been Patrick White's long-ago family home before his education in England.

Patrick himself, approaching eighty, was in and out of nearby St Vincent's Hospital with his lifelong asthma and bronchitis, crumbling bones, failing eyes and heart. In his last decade, however, he was writing freely and personally. *The Twyborn Affair*, published in 1979, explored gender fluidity in a character of White's generation, followed in 1981 by *Flaws in the Glass*, an episodic self-portrait in which he declared his homosexuality. Christina Stead disapproved, believing novelists should not write autobiography. The last book seen in his lifetime, in 1986, was *Memoirs of Many in One*, supposedly the papers of an actress edited by her friend Patrick White. While his body weakened, White's mind was firing the final cannon blasts of imagination. His friends had always known they were at risk of excommunication if they offended his political or moral values, and in old age he shed more. Sidney Nolan was publicly reviled when he married Mary Perceval too soon after Cynthia's death. Geoffrey Dutton's review of *Flaws in the Glass* in *The Bulletin* provoked a scathing letter that ended, 'I'm sorry, but I've had enough of Duttonry, and ask you not to ring me ...' White dropped his English acolyte, Margery Williams, after arguments about Vietnam and Whitlam, and he snapped at Christina Stead when she drank and declined in her last years. Shirley Hazzard, once a great admirer, thought he had become a bully after she read *Flaws in the Glass* and received some acidic words for *The Transit of Venus*. In a letter that began with praise for her 'impressive insights and solid detail' he flung at her: 'You are still inclined to strike attitudes and pirouette round yourself ... your chief lack is exposure to everyday vulgarity and squalor.'

The wonder was that Elizabeth and Patrick remained close until his death. She and Margaret were regulars at his table, and he and Manoly at hers. He gave her tickets to the Sydney Film Festival and to his own plays, and they exchanged books; he sent Margaret his weekly *Observer*, airmailed from the UK, and she passed it on to Elizabeth. A snapshot of their friendship in early 1980: she went to his place for cups of tea and a walk in Centennial Park with his dog Nellie; they had dinner and went to a Roger Woodward concert at the Town Hall; she had lunch at his place; Cynthia Nolan's daughter, Jinx, took them out to dinner in Paddington; they were both at a political conference dinner at the University of New South Wales. She had her Sunday slot at 9 am for an hour-long phone call, immediately after the theatre designer and artist Desmond Digby, so she heard some of their gossip. She also had her own amusing friendship with Desmond and his partner, the librarian James Allison. In *Flaws in the Glass* Patrick mimicked Desmond's phone manner and said they roared with laughter together. For him the telephone was a lifeline, while Manoly regarded it as the great disrupter.

Elizabeth thought of Patrick and Manoly as her brothers, always emphasising that she ranked friends as highly as family. With Patrick she shared a quiet intimacy that was not demanding on either side. 'We certainly didn't praise each other, God forbid,' she said. When Lizzie, his beloved childhood nurse, died at ninety-six, he dined at Elizabeth's place after the funeral and later showed her through a chest of her photographs that stirred emotional memories. This is not to say she escaped Patrick's bitchiness. He hurt her unnecessarily in 1981 at a dinner held by the poet and journalist Elizabeth Riddell with guests Patrick and Manoly, David Malouf, Murray Bail and his wife Margaret – all people she liked. Riddell told the table about a chance encounter with Elizabeth, who had said she wasn't going to be a victim any more, and they all laughed and joined in the cruelty. Elizabeth told Shirley, without further context, that the story was a lie and the 'massacre' was depressing. She added, naively or disingenuously, that she had imagined she would escape malice because she avoided literary groups – 'where friends write reviews for each other, organise publicity and promotion'. Patrick simply told her to toughen up. Thanking Francis for his sympathy, she wrote:

> Perhaps I made heavy weather of that occasion, but I was certainly laid low. I thought Patrick would be satisfied to complain about me to myself.

Yet she defended Patrick from Shirley's anger, saying she saw 'the more homely non-famous person', and the friend who had 'tried to rescue me from bad situations when no-one else did'. Even this late, he inscribed her copy of *Memoirs of Many in One*: 'To Elizabeth, luncher & diner extraordinaire. Sad you don't WRITE.' To Shirley he implied that she and her mother were at least part of the problem: 'Elizabeth keeps her principles. Whether she is also writing, I have given up asking in case I get the wrong answer. Too many vampires make too many demands on her ...'

Kit was still a friend and a burden to Elizabeth, one of Macleay Street's 'elderly, lonely people', and Margaret Dick became more entangled now she lived nearby. When she dropped in to The Chimes one day, having not seen Kit for a while, Margaret 'found her exceedingly distraught and angry. She had seen no one for ages and had thrown her clock across the room.' Margaret let her talk and left her in a better state, and a few days later Kit was ecstatic over reviews of *The Transit of Venus*, which was being received as Shirley's greatest work. Elizabeth and Margaret visited every Christmas Day and drove her over to Stanley Avenue for lunches with Kit's friend Yolanda Davies and other women who had also become their friends. But Elizabeth had lost any hope of recovery for Kit and her exchanges with Shirley were resigned or even gloomy.

Shirley had sent her early copies of *The Transit of Venus* and Steegmuller's translation of Gustave Flaubert's letters. When Elizabeth told Judah with pleasure that she had received the books, she added a brutal image: 'Shirley's mother still runs around the Cross, bad-mouthing (the only word) the few who've exerted themselves for her. She is not improving with age, our Kit.' By late 1980, after suffering a stroke and fading into dementia, Kit was in hospital and then a nursing home. While Shirley was promoting her novel, Elizabeth and Margaret packed up Kit's flat, a 'monstrous task' that Shirley called 'a sort of last straw of ultimate largeness of heart'. Elizabeth remained a regular visitor to the Mosman nursing home, which was conveniently close, shopping for nightgowns and other items the nurses requested. Within a short time Kit barely recognised her. On a long list of tasks and expenses (always paid by the Steegmullers) that Elizabeth kept at the time, two stand out: 'send S. necklace of cut crystal beads' and 'burn S's letters'. She couldn't find the beads and, sadly, she destroyed the letters.

*

Elizabeth enjoyed having an inner-city base with Margaret and didn't hesitate to cross the harbour by bridge or ferry, but she remained a committed resident of the Mosman peninsula. Unable to sell or find tenants for 5 Stanley Avenue with its outdated kitchen and cracking walls, she 'camped' on and instead sold the block of flats she'd inherited for a low price she would always regret. International oil crises were causing petrol shortages, transport disruptions, inflation, and collapsing property values. Lunches, dinners and Sunday afternoon parties gave the house and its owner their purpose. At the Geerings' 'regular spring lunch' in 1980 she met Christina Stead's friend Mary Lord for the first time with a pang of discomfort about 'my faulty and indecisive character' over her offer of the Monash residency, which wasn't mentioned. Rather, they enjoyed the al fresco gathering: 'wisteria, bees, freesias, azaleas. We ate food, not flowers, of course, but we did have petals falling into our hair and wine. So it was all very idle and enjoyable.'

As her dearest friends were ageing and slowing down, her gregarious nature created ever-widening circles. She was often at parties and dinners, sometimes with Christina Stead, at the Lindfield home of lawyer-poet Geoffrey Lehmann and his wife, Sally McInerney. Through them she met generations of poets from Peter Porter to Robert Gray. After a dinner there, she told Kylie she had never known anyone to talk shop as much as poets did. She became especially close to the poet-academic Vivian Smith and his wife, writer Sybille Smith, and the painter Salvatore Zofrea and his partner, Stephanie Claire. One weekend the Smiths drove her to Manly to visit the poet Bruce Beaver, who was mentally and physically unwell and not writing; she felt he needed to see old friends. An artist could have drawn an elaborate 'friend-tree' of the people she knew.

When the Australia Council headquarters moved from Melbourne to Sydney in 1975, Michael Costigan followed, with an introduction to Elizabeth from their mutual friend Judah Waten. That friendship began after Costigan, a former priest, reviewed Waten's 1969 memoir, *Odessa to Odessa*, inspired by a trip back to the Soviet Union with Manning Clark. Waten had been educated at a Christian Brothers school in Perth and although an atheist, he remained interested in religion. He had suggested Costigan for the Literature Board directorship, which made him Harrower's correspondent for her 1973 fellowship. They met in person when Elizabeth held a dinner for Michael and his wife, Margaret, newly arrived in Sydney, with Vivian and Sybille Smith, Ron and Dorothy Geering, and Margaret Dick. So began a long friendship, unscarred by her meagre output on Literature Board funding and nourished by their shared love of the arts. When Michael had a spare ticket to see Joan Sutherland in *Norma* at the Opera House, Elizabeth joined his party, seated behind the Governor-General, Sir Zelman Cowen. The diva excited her ('She was like a priestess twice over') but she was less happy about sitting with Elwyn Lyn, chairman of the Visual Arts Board, and Bernard Hickey, an Australian literature professor visiting from Venice – a friend of Sir Zelman – whom she dismissed as 'very worldly and rather vain'.

Michael's twin brother, Frank Costigan, was a lawyer, Labor Party reformer and royal commissioner into union corruption. He was keen to meet Patrick White and Elizabeth passed on an invitation for dinner at Michael and Margaret's home at Kirribilli. Michael recalled:

> We told Frank about Patrick's punctuality and Frank said he would pick him up from where they lived ... When he got there Patrick and Manoly were coming down the steps and they met and they got on very well. Elizabeth was there, Margaret Dick, our daughters were young but they enjoyed meeting Patrick. We asked did he mind a photo. We took one with him and the children, but we didn't take one with Elizabeth and she gently chided us later. She said 'I've never had a photo with Patrick', and we hadn't had the initiative.

The Australia Council network also sparked a warm friendship with Antigone Kefala, a Greek-Romanian writer who was appointed to the Community Arts Board and later the Literature Board to encourage migrant applicants and multicultural projects. They often went together to arts events, and Kefala sent chatty, spirit-lifting postcards from Europe on her frequent travels. Behind her bright personality was a refugee's mournful backward look, expressed in postcard-spare poetry and prose, and fluency in Romanian, Greek, French and English. They were able to confide deep thoughts and emotions with a European seriousness that fed Elizabeth's soul. So many of her best friends were born, educated or much travelled abroad; in her novels European migrants gave the women an opening to the world.

David Malouf, when he was not in Italy, lived nearby in Cremorne and became 'very close' to Elizabeth through Patrick White and Sybille and Vivian Smith. He believed she had stopped writing 'because she decided at some point she had said what she had to say. I always thought that was a very noble position. She was a very good writer but I feel you publish only things that belong to your body of work and will not damage it.'

If Elizabeth were in any danger of becoming a lotus eater, or a North Shore lady who lunched, her intellectual engagement and challenging companions saved her. Within a few weeks in 1979, she enjoyed films as disparate as *Outrageous!* (featuring 'a drag queen and a schizophrenic'), Patrick White's *The Night the Prowler*, *Stevie* about the English writer Stevie Smith ('good but a bit claustrophobic'), *The Stud Farm* about Hungary in the 1950s ('very grim'), and 'two commercial and mildly boring Neil Simon films'. She surprised friends who thought her taste was highbrow by also being an avid fan of Elvis Presley and John Travolta.

*

Whether or not she was writing, Elizabeth Harrower was still being read. Through the 1970s and '80s, her stories reappeared in numerous anthologies, with 'The Cost of Things' a favourite of editors such as Beatrice Davis and Douglas Stewart, Judah Waten and Stephen Murray-Smith, Leonie Kramer and Adrian Mitchell, Barbara Ker Wilson, Murray Bail, and – in Japanese – Mikio Hiramatsu.

Japan's pre-eminent scholar of Australian literature from Henry Lawson to Patrick White, Hiramatsu had gone home from a trip to Australia in 1977 knowing many more writers. He enjoyed one of Nancy Phelan's garden parties in the Blue Mountains and morning tea under blue sky on Elizabeth's terrace with Margaret Dick, who gave him her critical study of Kylie Tennant's novels. Elizabeth kept up a friendly correspondence and in 1982 his translation of 'The Cost of Things' was included in his anthology, *Australian Literature – Short Story Masterpieces*. That year the professor returned to accept an honorary doctorate in Queensland and travel on to Sydney; with his grandsons he ate Sunday lunch on the terrace with Elizabeth, Kylie, Margaret and others.

There was a Czech translation of 'The Beautiful Climate', and Hungarian translations of 'English Lesson' and 'The Cost of Things' by Sára Karig, who had visited Sydney from Budapest and translated Patrick White's play *Big Toys*. This concentration of Harrower's stories was like a recycling of musical hits, not necessarily her best but her 'classics'. Whether she withheld others and pushed these forward, or the editors selected them, it might be that 'The Cost of Things' – written in the 1960s – appealed to contemporary readers for its cool critique of adultery. With more than a dozen strong stories written in the previous twenty years, Harrower seems never to have attempted a collection. After years of rejection, she had lost faith.

At the same time, she was maddeningly stubborn, and resistant to writing about herself unless she had a higher purpose. Among a few unpublished personal pieces she kept is one from the 1960s about becoming a blood donor, beginning with a wry intention on her to-do list: 'collect dry cleaning, toothpaste, finish novel … Blood Bank' and ending on a note of advocacy: 'If you like human beings, spilling a little blood … is pleasurable, almost a privilege. You are related to everybody.'

In the 1980s, Sylvia Hale, a partner in the small press Hale & Iremonger, engaged the poet Rosemary Dobson to commission a collection of essays by women about their writing lives. Elizabeth went to an initial lunch to discuss a six-thousand-word autobiographical piece I'm not going to write for inclusion in a book. All the other women are academic women. I'd be like an orange in a crate of apples, or vice versa. My writing, life and approach would be peculiarly different.

Two years later she told Hale she had intended to accept, but 'a certain amount of thought persuades me that I only like to write fiction and have nothing to say directly about writing or writers'. By then Kylie Tennant, Dorothy Green, Elizabeth Jolley, Dorothy Hewett, Fay Zwicky and others had sent contributions, but Hale abandoned the book as financially unfeasible.

*

Finally there were reasons beyond her own taste for Elizabeth to read the latest Australian books. In 1981 she was invited to be a paid judge of the two-year-old NSW Premier's Literary Awards, set up by Labor Premier Neville Wran. She gave the bureaucrat her practised refusal.

> I told him I was still writing and more interested in getting on with my own work than, at this time, taking days off to judge the work of others ... I didn't go into all the side-issues such as – my house being on show and myself in need of a new roof at any moment, and the ever present possibility that I'll (when the house is settled) rush out of Sydney or Australia for a needed change, or (in the new, small abode) settle strenuously to work.

That same evening she went to the city for a drinks party held by the National Book Council at the Hilton. She had a weakness for luxurious hotels. Nancy Keesing cornered her to ask if she would be a judge for their Banjo Awards, as if the decision had already been made. Elizabeth was about to say no but Margaret Dick, emboldened by free red wine, said, 'Why not? You always say no to everything.' And so she found herself reading ninety books of fiction, fact and poetry for no payment. Amused by her own flip-flop, she complained to Judah that 'as a person who has only ever won a coathanger, I can't see that I should be noble enough to give someone else $10 000 (or whatever) ...' Her fellow judges were the journalist Helen Frizell, a friend who had recently retired as literary editor of the *Sydney Morning Herald*, and Eric Rolls, who was about to publish his great environmental history of Australia, *A Million Wild Acres*. In an introductory letter to Rolls, Keesing gave a 'confidential' potted biography of Harrower, in part:

> She's a very good, imaginative novelist and, if she were a faster or more prolific writer would possibly be a major novelist. As it is she is such a perfectionist, and perhaps a bit too thin skinned, that she hasn't offered one or two books for publication – I think she withdrew one too ... Also over several years she has devoted most of her emotional energy to a friend and friend's family who have been in very dire trouble. She'll be a tough judge, though, and she's a very nice person indeed.

As Kylie Tennant's next-door neighbour in Hunters Hill, Keesing knew as much as anyone about her trials and Elizabeth's career.

The judges, who each knew 'exactly what they liked', gave the award to David Foster for his novel *Moonlite*, 'a difficult work' and 'a thoroughly irreverent look at immigration to Australia'. Foster was the rising author Elizabeth had *not* read when she mentioned him to Shirley in 1974 on the recommendation of Patrick and Kylie. They gave a second award to Albert Facey, who became a folk hero in his eighties with his autobiography, *A Fortunate Life*. Shortlisted books by women – Helen Garner's *Honour and Other People's Children* and Blanche d'Alpuget's *Turtle Beach* – came in for some praise and Jessica Anderson's *The Impersonators* 'caused the most discussion' but was put aside because the novel had weak characterisation and 'seemed to be written for the sake of writing'.

Elizabeth Harrower was indeed a tough judge but fair, and she developed a taste for judging. An extra incentive was that free books made generous gifts for her friends and relatives. In 1985 she read sixty-nine books for the *Age* Book of the Year, as a judge with academic Peter

Pierce and National Book Council chairman Michael Zifcak. They gave awards to Peter Carey's *Illywacker*, Chester Eagle's *Mapping the Paddocks* and Hugh Lunn's *Vietnam: A reporter's war*. At last she did judge (for a small payment) the NSW Premier's Literary Awards in 1987, when the fiction prize went to *Dancing on Coral*, Glenda Adams's satirical novel about an Australian expatriate's life among academics in New York. As an expat herself, Adams was denied the $10 000 prize money, and outrage in the literary community led to a rule change the following year. Christina Stead had been denied the Encyclopaedia Britannica Award in 1967 due to her long absence. By the time she won a NSW Premier's Literary Award for services to literature in 1982, Stead was so unwell that Elizabeth went in her place to receive the medal. This was the first time she had spoken from a platform. Poignantly, she noticed as she said 'my sentence' on behalf of Christina: 'People clapped loudly, hearing her name, because she's known to relatively few.'

Christina had only months to live, but there were still shared times while she stayed with her sister Kate at Cremorne. Elizabeth was contacted by Jonathan LaPook, a young American doctor who was coming to do a residency at Royal North Shore Hospital and bringing a gift from his friend Lillian Hellman, the American writer, for her friend and fellow communist Christina. Shirley Hazzard asked Elizabeth and Andrew Robertson to look after him and they 'surged about being hospitable'.

Christina took LaPook to lunch at a restaurant with Elizabeth, who noticed: 'She loved the young New York doctor. She had a marvellous time. She blew me kisses to thank me for my role in producing this congenial person.' His mission was to hand over a copy of Hellman's autobiographical book, *Pentimento,* inscribed to Christina from 'Perhaps her greatest and oldest admirer, Lillian Hellman'. With the book came a cheque for $10 000. When Christina died in March 1983, Elizabeth was one of seven people at her funeral, with the Geerings and family members. 'Christina was a great good friend,' she said at the end. 'Her life was a triumph, though the last two years were not good. We understood each other.'

*

With Kit Hazzard in professional care, the Steegmullers began to push Elizabeth to holiday with them, at their expense, in Italy and New York. They wanted to thank her for years of extraordinary kindness, which had allowed them to travel and write the books on which their reputations perched. Elizabeth had procrastinated about this, too, not wanting to spend her money, not wanting to accept theirs, her reluctance to travel hardening into aversion. Her focus was back on politics as former union boss Bob Hawke took leadership of the Labor Party from quiet-mannered Bill Hayden, whom she preferred to the cocky ladies' man. But after seven years of a Coalition Government under Malcolm Fraser, Hawke gave Labor a chance of winning the federal election in March 1983. Elizabeth nervously watched the results on television at Ferdi Nolte's place.

> At last, a simply wonderful little message started to run across the bottom of the screen: ALP WINS GOVERNMENT ... ALP WINS GOVERNMENT ... We waited and watched (ten of us at Hunter's Hill), afraid to believe it after all the suffering, and computers had been going mad all night, predicting a 300 per cent swing to the Liberals on one occasion. We waited then for Hawke or Fraser to appear. Fraser, I'm sure, was in his bunker, stamping feet with rage at not getting his own way for once. Since that happy night, like a villain in a pantomime or an opera, he has disappeared in a puff of smoke. He strode about like Frankenstein and now he's gone. There is a God. There is justice. Strangers talk to each other in the street. (Of course, it will never be 1975 again.)

Her spirits rose tentatively with Hawke's 'careful and reasonable approach, his calmness, the lessons all had learned from 1972/75', but were flattened by months of vague illness, with her old symptoms of high blood pressure, headaches and exhaustion.

Shirley Hazzard was invited to Sydney in 1984 to deliver the Boyer Lectures, an annual series broadcast by the ABC to stimulate discussion of ideas about culture, science and society. She had not been back since her 1976 visit and her talks were to be a counterpoint to her 'Letter from Australia' in the *New Yorker*, arguing that after the progressive optimism of the Whitlam years, the country under Malcolm Fraser had sunk back into complacent conservatism, materialism, nationalism, prejudice and misogyny. She drew again on reports from Elizabeth in letters, clippings and conversations. Some ABC listeners were offended by the condescension of an expatriate and Murray Bail told her she had been subject to 'malevolent jeers' at a dinner at Patrick White's place.

Nevertheless, Shirley enjoyed Sydney in the September spring weather, and was able to see her mother for a last time, although Kit thought she was someone else. Elizabeth held another party spilling onto the terrace and garden, which was remembered by Shirley as 'an evening of great quality ... Moonlight on North Head did no harm either.' More than thirty years later, Elizabeth recalled the eminent guest list:

> Gough Whitlam was being brought by Richard Hall, Shirley Hazzard was coming (with two very nasty ABC men), Murray came with the widow of Fred Williams, David Malouf, David Marr, Sybille and Vivian Smith, Col and Ruby Madigan, Salvatore Zofrea and partner Stephanie, the Souters [Gavin and Ngaire], Christina Stead, Antigone Kefala, Labor friend Ferdi Nolte, my cousin Margaret, Tom Carment, and many more.

Whitlam and Hall arrived late and 'Richard the Cool', as Elizabeth called him, spoke at length to his former boss about UNESCO, where Whitlam was about to become Australia's ambassador in Paris.

Shirley and Elizabeth had a pleasant time together and formed a plan to meet in Rome, Naples, Capri, and then New York, in October. When Francis joined in with enthusiasm and bookings, Elizabeth could not refuse. He boldly expressed their concern to get her away from her 'ingrown circle' of friends dominated by Patrick White's tyranny.

A year earlier Francis had suffered terrible injuries from an assault by bag snatchers on a motorcycle in Naples, but he was able to return to Italy in September 1984, a day after Shirley had sat next to Saul Bellow at an awards lunch for him on Capri, and ready to receive the visitor from Australia. They gave Elizabeth a splendid tour, starting in Rome, travelling by car to Naples, and by ferry to Capri. Shirley devoted herself to showing

Elizabeth the sights, taking her to museums and restaurants. On Capri they went up to Anacapri, where Graham Greene owned a house, and Sybille and Vivian Smith had an inherited house, where they met the housekeeper. Elizabeth had been there with her mother and stepfather in 1951, and Kempley had contemplated buying a house. Memories passed like clouds across the beauty of the ancient island. Shirley's friend Donald Keene reached Capri in early November and the four of them passed autumn days together. Donald and Elizabeth had got on like old friends in Sydney and before their trip Shirley had grasped at his idea that travel 'might bring forth her writing gift'.

Shirley's love and respect for Elizabeth were as real as her gratitude: 'She exists as something luminous in my mind; some suggestion of a great soul in my consciousness,' she told Donald. But the reality was disappointing for both women. In her diary Shirley expressed shock at Elizabeth's hostile, resentful, even deranged outbursts in Italy. They stayed at Rome's grand Hassler Hotel, where the Steegmullers had their usual suite and Elizabeth complained that her room had no view. When Shirley proposed a walk to Capri's Arco Naturale before lunch, she responded, 'There you go again; I don't accept orders.' At dinner she raised a toast 'To Francis, the kindest person at the table,' to which Shirley responded, 'It isn't a competition.'

Elizabeth abandoned Capri early and flew to Paris. Gough Whitlam was installed as Australia's ambassador to UNESCO and she stayed at the official residence, mostly in the company of Margaret Whitlam and Gough's sister, Freda. She caught up with her troublesome American friend, Leslie Schenk, who was living in Paris and, to her embarrassment, pressed on her his manifesto about the United Nations for Shirley. After two days in bed feeling unwell, Elizabeth went on to the safety of her Scottish relatives in Edinburgh and Cheshire, and then to London. From Auntie Minnie's kitchen in Edinburgh she wrote to Bill Cantwell that Rome had been 'beauteous' and 'Capri had its interest but I guess I don't like even beautiful islands as well as cities. Don't fence me in!' Shirley and Francis knew every inch of Italy, she said, and she had learnt and seen more than you would expect to do in months; had met their rich, charming friends and eaten out for every meal. Shirley 'seems keen to show me how wonderful the rest of the world is compared with Australia'. Elizabeth still had a ticket to fly from New York to Sydney on December 16 and was considering a group tour of the US, a stay with Jinx Nolan in Boston, and Christmas in New York. She needed quiet time for decisions.

Judah and Hyrell Waten were in London, too, so they all stayed at the President Hotel in Russell Square and went to the National Portrait Gallery together. Judah – 'another person who is apt to "take you over"' – led Elizabeth to a little church off Piccadilly where in the 1930s he'd known someone connected to Jean Cocteau, because he knew she had read Francis Steegmuller's biography of the French writer and filmmaker. Although the Steegmullers had paid for almost everything, she was feeling the cost of her trip and turned down the Watens' invitation to travel with them to Ireland.

In London she spoke about her escape from Italy to Alan Maclean, her former publisher at Macmillan. As Shirley's publisher and friend, he agreed she could be overbearing and had tested his usual politeness. Furious over an indiscretion she denied, he had shouted at her to admit she was wrong, just for once. Trapped on a plane by her relentless talk, he had said, 'Will you shut up?' and could only retreat to the toilet, wash his face, return to his seat and apologise. Alan encouraged Elizabeth to tell Shirley she was flying directly home to Sydney, which she did. Elizabeth recalled later: 'I was supposed to come back via New York but for all kinds of weird reasons I decided not to. [Judah] thought I should but I didn't.'

The tension between Shirley and Elizabeth was partly caused by misunderstanding. Elizabeth had proposed her itinerary a month before she left Sydney: to travel for six weeks, and after Italy spend a week in Paris or London, 'or flitting in a circle round the US, then perhaps a week in New York? ... Or perhaps that week could be a circle round Scotland.' The Steegmullers wanted her to stay longer, for months if she liked, but she explained her concerns to Shirley while she laid out poignant items for packing: suitcase bought in Edinburgh in 1972, Mastercard, passport (for which she had to prove she was 'Betty Harrower'), and a handkerchief with 'E' on it. The US visa was troublesome, and her accountant told her to work out a careful budget and not be away too long, 'because he and

I know that it's by staying in Sydney and putting first things first (seeing friends and fixing the roof) that the budget has just broken even'. She went on, in too much detail, as if pushing against a wall of pressure:

> Earlier on, before I moved into this house, before I sold the flats, before I went to the aid of a friend, if I had been more interested in my own affairs and applied more intelligence, I could have arranged for more prosperity. I might have gone away then and stayed for a while, but people had nervous breakdowns and died, and it didn't happen. Then a while ago there was talk of a film of *The Long Prospect*, but that fell through. At various times a holiday has seemed possible, but hasn't worked out. If I sold the house, too. But the bad experience of selling the flats at the wrong time has made me nervous of that. Almost all of the time I feel lucky and enjoy my life, apart from guilt about writing. Sometimes not having the freedom to go to Melbourne (Judah has asked me for years) and Canberra or Ayers Rock or the Barrier Reef is trying for about half an hour (perhaps more the idea, even, of not having the option), but then happiness, even-mindedness returns and remains. High spirits.

Barely hidden in this pitiful self-portrait was the needle that Shirley and Francis were living the 'lovely life' that Kit had used as a psychological weapon against them, while Elizabeth was imprisoned by self-imposed austerity. In fact, as Brigitta Olubas pointed out in her biography, the Steegmullers owned no property and lived on wealth inherited from Francis's first wife, sales of paintings, and their own constant work. In her last years Shirley needed the financial generosity of friends. Elizabeth had inherited property and Scottish frugality – she hated her stepfather's extravagance – and she knew that without husband or work, she only had her own thrift to rely on.

Elizabeth and Shirley don't seem to have discussed their clash in Italy. Their letters in the weeks afterwards were strained but polite. Safely home in December, Elizabeth declared herself 'a constant friend' who refused 'to be not cared for because all of a sudden I got worn down and ran out of energy'. Shirley reassured her, and their correspondence resumed with mutual care if less intensity, and a deepening layer of resentment on Elizabeth's part. When Kit Hazzard died in May 1985, Shirley flew to Capri rather than Sydney, leaving her sister, Valerie, and Elizabeth as the only mourners at the funeral.

In the world of life and death

Elizabeth had done all she could for Kit but her real grief was for dear Judah Waten, who died on his seventy-fourth birthday, July 29, 1985. She flew to Melbourne for his well-attended funeral. For his seventieth birthday she had sent a postcard of the Suez Canal with a small gift:

> Dear Judah, As this is going to be a fairly special birthday celebration, thought I should send you a red handkerchief to wear in court. If you should be in a court again. Happy times on 29th! Affectionately, Elizabeth.

She was not at the birthday celebration in Melbourne organised by Geoffrey Blainey, who read out a telegram from Manning Clark – historians from opposite ends of politics. In his speech Judah referred to the gift from 'a good friend of mine, Elizabeth Harrower ...' It was, he said, an allusion to 1928 when seventeen-year-old Waten and another young man had been charged with distributing communist pamphlets during Anzac Day commemorations. At their court appearance, sympathisers 'aggressively displayed' red handkerchiefs in their breast pockets. Elizabeth had not forgotten the old newspaper clipping, which Judah kept in his bulging coat pocket with other papers he wanted to show her. A few years earlier, Patrick White had told Elizabeth he would like to meet Judah, and she cooked dinner at Stanley Avenue for 'just the five of us' – Patrick and Manoly, Judah and Hyrell. 'It was a very successful, good evening, their only encounter.' She was 'extremely sad' when Patrick decided to give Judah the Patrick White Award in 1985 but would not announce his name before the traditional November date, despite her pleading that he was close to death. 'It would have meant so much to him,' she said. 'He cared a great deal about literature, and was very modest about his own work.'

As the years passed, Elizabeth was able to take an interest in her own family with greater detachment from the past. In 1981 she went up to Newcastle with Margaret Dick to visit her aunt Adell, the only one of her father's siblings still alive, and met Adell's daughters, her first cousins Verity Matzoll and Thurza Snelson, both teachers and mothers. This was an important day for Elizabeth, when she reunited the two sides of her divorced family. She and Auntie Dell kept up a warm correspondence until Adell's death in 2001. Meanwhile, Elizabeth and Thurza began to research the Harrower family's Scottish history and share their findings, which revealed the pleasing depth of her Scottish roots from all four great-grandparents. They exchanged letters, and Thurza visited Elizabeth whenever she went to Sydney for a theatre performance.

Elizabeth began a more private quest, too. On a visit to the War Memorial in Canberra she was shocked to see 'Uncle Rob', Robert Reid Hughes, on 'the tragic wall of names' of the dead in the Second World War and set out to learn about his fate. She searched her mother's papers, read about Japanese prisoner-of-war camps, and in January 1982 wrote gratefully to Peter Firkins, the author of *From Hell to Eternity*, about the Sandakan death marches. Australian Army Records and Australian War Graves gave her the stark facts of her uncle's service. As Staff Sergeant Hughes he had enlisted with the 2/10 Australian Field Ambulance in July 1940 and arrived in Singapore in August 1941. He was a member of B Force, taken prisoner by the Japanese and moved in July 1942 from the hellhole of Changi to the Sandakan prisoner of war camp in northern Borneo, where men were marched out every day to build an airfield for the Japanese. Robert died on March 20, 1945, from an unnamed 'illness' and possibly on the death march from Sandakan to Ranau.

As Elizabeth told Kylie Tennant, Uncle Rob had 'lived for a fairly long time in one of the worst camps and then died or was killed not long before the end of the war. At Sandakan, in Borneo, no-one was left – out of 2512 – when the allies got there'. In answer to a letter she placed in the newspaper for former POWs, letters and phone calls came from men who had been in the camps, two who remembered Robert as 'a bonzer chap'. She learnt that his grave was one of many marked 'Unknown Soldier' at the Labuan War Cemetery in Borneo, with his name on the Labuan

Memorial to the Missing. One veteran sent his sketch of the Sandakan camp, showing the hospital where Sergeant Hughes would have tried to save his men, and the huts where prisoners slept shoulder to shoulder on wooden ramps, surrounded by barbed wire, swamp and jungle. She briefly considered travelling to Borneo but in 1989 she made the less arduous trip to North Turramurra in Sydney for the dedication of the new Sandakan Memorial Park. War had marked her, and all her fictional characters, but these human stories helped her comprehend the horror of her uncle's death, her mother's loss and her grandmother's long bereavement. Honouring her renewed connection to family, in 1986 she made a quiet visit with Ferdi to her cousin Verity's daughter Maja just before she died in hospital from cystic fibrosis, on the eve of her fifteenth birthday. Elizabeth was moved that Maja

> was intelligent, lovely to look at, lived for ballet. She would leave the hospital to dance and then return within days to an oxygen tent. To the last she was lucid. Presents, cards, greetings from young friends were strewn about her hospital room. Her poor mother. She was an only child.

Elizabeth did not regret the husband and children she didn't have. Marriage was too much of a gamble – 'an ideal condition if it works out and the worst if it doesn't', she said in 1985. At that point, nearing sixty, she thought she would have been a good mother. She enjoyed the company of friends' children, got down on the floor to play, sent toys and books for birthdays, but she may not have been temperamentally suited to the daily drudgery and worries of motherhood. Whether she would have written more from the emotional and financial security of a happy marriage is questionable, too. Ignoring the demands of family, she once explained her lack of writing: 'I have allowed myself to be distracted [by] people. I tend to be friendly and I tend to be sociable. If you don't have obvious responsibilities – not having a family – people call on you.' In that interview, the title of her unpublished novel *In Certain Circles* was misheard as 'Slowly Spreading Circles', an apt description of the way her commitment to people had consumed everything else. In 1988, still living at Stanley Avenue, she wrote to Antigone Kefala:

> Today I feel that as long as I am in this house and in Sydney, I'm not likely to write. My phone goes too much, and people including nice but distant acquaintances suggest meetings. Too much. If I had a husband, I could say, 'George won't let me.'

There were always new excuses. If Elizabeth had been honest with herself she'd have seen that she had withdrawn from public life as an author. If she no longer cared about writing that was no problem. But she did. If she really had something urgent to share with the world she would have put her work before all else. But the urgency had left her. The demands of shaping a book, the anxieties of publishing, the intrusion of publicity, the negligible income from sales, meant that she might as well write for herself. Asked in 1985 if she had written any more novels since *In Certain Circles*, she said:

> I've written a lot of writing ... Well, thoughts. Things do get away from you, and they lose their freshness, if you don't put them down. On the one hand, I sometimes think I don't have to say everything I know ... Then there's the other aspect which says that unless you write it down in a novel, unless you work hard to refine it and sit at it day after day, you don't know yourself what you know. You find out by the writing. I have written a very, very long 'something'. It's never been a question of not having enough to say, it's always been a question of having too much to say.

*

For Elizabeth the season of loss stretched out as she entered her sixties and her closest friends expired. While Kylie Tennant battled on, she told Elizabeth she was writing an autobiography, 'Seventy-two years of mistakes'. Like many novelists, she did not much believe in the truths of straight autobiography. Kylie's final book, published in 1986, was titled *The Missing Heir* and told her crowded life story in a 'very funny book ... held together by its defiant, aggressive, sardonic tone rather than by its haphazard structure' and 'constant tension between the autobiographer and the novelist'. When her cancer returned a year later, Kylie wanted to end her life by throwing herself off a cliff in the Blue Mountains, but she was already too weak and instead became an advocate for voluntary euthanasia. Three weeks before she died in hospital in 1988, aged seventy-five, her 'last letter to a friend' ran on page one of the *Sydney Morning Herald*, urging readers to work at changing attitudes and laws. Elizabeth took up the slow cause, signed petitions and wrote letters, sharing Kylie's dread of prolonged suffering for herself and others.

At the age of sixty-one, Elizabeth faced her own mortality when she had a diagnosis of colon cancer and was rushed to hospital in November 1989. Young doctors with poor bedside manners gave her alarming information, and Margaret Brink, one of her South African friends, wept at her bedside after overhearing a dire prognosis. Ferdi Nolte visited every day and when she told him this might be the end he said, 'I'll go and have a cup of coffee.' Margaret Dick, on the other hand, brought her a book of the seventeenth-century metaphysical poets so she could read Andrew Marvell's poem 'The Garden', urging a retreat from society into nature and solitary reflection. As she awaited surgery, Elizabeth responded to the poem in a postcard to Shirley and Francis, writing that she liked solitude and had seldom had less. 'Tonight I'm alone for the first time for ages. I enjoy reflecting, thinking. It always feels interesting inside my head. This may be an illusion, but I like it.' She was fearful but calm, and she averted her attention by visiting a Hungarian woman she knew who was in the hospital and also facing a serious operation; she had survived 'wars & Nazis & experiences'. Despite the doctors' predictions, Elizabeth's surgery was successful and the cancer did not return.

Patrick White had been dying for years, with a catalogue of ailments. After a lifetime of asthma and bronchitis his lungs finally gave up in September 1990, when he was seventy-eight. Elizabeth went over to Centennial Park that day and sat quietly in the kitchen with Manoly. He gave her a stamp box that had sat on Patrick's desk and a pottery vase for Margaret. She would make the long commute to visit him for another thirteen years, until the last months of his life. Vrasidas Karalis, Professor of Modern Greek at Sydney University and translator of White's novels, went with them once to the restaurant in Centennial Park. 'Manoly was very fond of Elizabeth because she was always asking him about Byzantium,' he recalled. At lunch she 'questioned with irony and love Manoly's firm belief that his family came from the imperial family of Byzantium ... I told them most of these titles were fabricated and purchased during the eighteenth century. Elizabeth asked if he had any documents. Manoly replied that the reassurance of his father and aunties was enough. It was funny and tense at the same time.'

Neil Armfield had directed a successful revival of *The Ham Funeral* for the Sydney Theatre Company in 1989, and Patrick made his last public appearance on opening night. He worked until the end, mostly on plays. He left an intriguing fragment of a novel that he had begun in 1981 and put aside to write the play *Signal Driver*, launch People for Nuclear Disarmament, and take the heat from readers of his memoir, *Flaws in the Glass*. Long after his death, Barbara Mobbs, his literary agent, revealed papers he'd asked her to destroy – an instruction she ignored – and she gave permission for *The Hanging Garden* to be published as a novella in 2012. In the first third of his planned novel he brings together a boy and a girl, both only children, sent from war-torn Europe in 1942 to a boarding house on the tree-tangled rocky shore of Sydney Harbour. White was thinking back to his and Manoly's culturally complex childhoods, and he chose the northern suburb of Neutral Bay as their aptly named refuge. There's no proof that he intended a tribute to his friend Elizabeth Harrower, who was appalled by the publication. But it is bittersweet to imagine that on reading the book she saw a remembrance of the harbourside house at Neutral Bay that had imprisoned two sisters in *The Watch Tower*.

Elizabeth's friends demanded attention even after their deaths. Patrick had lived long enough to read the manuscript of David Marr's biography, which appeared the year after he died, and though he shed tears about the man portrayed, he was resigned to the telling. Marr went on to edit a volume of White's letters and included nine of the twenty-six letters Elizabeth had from him, mostly written when one of them was travelling. Her only objection was to a proposed biographical note that described her as one of Patrick's 'Lady Disciples'. This was a tag Manoly gave to Patrick's close women friends. She felt it 'credits me with a humility I've never possessed, indeed, with an alien – unAustralian! –

character that would startle people who know me'. Barbara Mobbs backed her with a note to Marr: 'Elizabeth couldn't have been a good friend for almost 30 years and been "a follower".' Although she claimed no interest in Harrower or her work, Mobbs particularly did not want to hurt Elizabeth because, in a unique concession, she had just written the introduction to a collection of Cynthia Nolan's travel memoirs for Angus & Robertson. Mobbs, Jinx Nolan and the publishers were 'thrilled with what Elizabeth has written'. Elizabeth had less contact with Sidney Nolan after Cynthia's death, but their daughter Jinx had become a next-generation friend who corresponded from her home in the US and visited when she came to Australia. She found Elizabeth in person a sensitive, perceptive friend, and thought her 'profile of mum' was 'brilliant'. The brief life story Elizabeth told was in lieu of the biography Cynthia had asked her to write in 1972. She saw that the travel books about Australia, Kenya, New Guinea and China, researched while she travelled with Nolan and so often seen as an adjunct to his career, were also 'Cynthia Nolan's expression of her own personality'.

After reading Marr's biography, in 1992 Elizabeth was prompted to write her own 10 000-word memoir about her friendship with Patrick, which remained as unfinished notes. Exasperated at her non-writing, she recalled, he had once thought of four books she could write, one of them about him. She was not interested and at times felt bullied; and she also refused an invitation to contribute to a posthumous book about White. But this was her private offering, more intimate than her tribute to Cynthia; twisting between empathy and conflict. Love had always been a battlefield for Elizabeth.

'It was certainly not a bland friendship, not calm and polite and dead,' she wrote. 'We sometimes shouted – he would start it, of course, but it reminded me of the way I behaved at fifteen, shouting at my mother in the spoilt and temperamental way of teenagers.' They bickered about Christina Stead and other friends: 'Patrick was Counsel for the Prosecution and I was Counsel for the Defence.' Elizabeth unloaded her own criticisms of mutual friends here, illustrating how she catastrophised and mythologised her life. Patrick had suggested dropping Kylie from their dinners together, she wrote, and so she did. Unaware that Kylie had extracted Patrick's strange pre-publication comment on *The Watch Tower* in 1966, hoping to help the book, Elizabeth raged about 'a literary couple who had leaned heavily on me, had no second thoughts about making use of me', and had reacted to Patrick's 'slighting and half-facetious comment' with 'the laughter of evil gnomes in an old fairy tale about good and evil'. She had observed 'their terror lest Patrick might have praised me unreservedly, and relief that he had not'. Could this fierce transformation have been the nucleus of a failed fiction she had begun to imagine? Patrick had detested 'warm' people and spoke of Shirley Hazzard's 'terrible American sweetness'; Elizabeth, too, found Shirley's excessive flattery hard to reciprocate. 'He was, somehow, thin, washed, clean, concentrated, even pure, though claiming past depravity. He wasn't "warm" and neither was I, but I left most meetings with him over twenty-six years smiling with affection, nourished, enlivened – occasionally inwardly rolling my eyes at his being totally hopeless, recalcitrant, irrational and irritating.'

In the late 1980s and '90s, David Carter, 'a clever and congenial academic' from Queensland, interviewed Elizabeth for his critical–biographical work on Judah Waten, and three prospective biographers visited her to talk about Christina Stead, but only two went ahead. She found it 'almost a pleasure to be cross-examined' but she had nothing negative to say about her friends so soon after their deaths, and was annoyed that Hazel Rowley pressed her to criticise Christina. No one asked her about Kylie, whose name and complicated role in her life she rarely mentioned. David Marr wrote that she had met Patrick through John Sumner, omitting Kylie's introduction altogether. With Shirley's biographer, much later, she would express her bitterness about Shirley's behaviour. Troubled by how much to expose Christina, she asked Shirley and Francis, as a revered biographer, what they thought of showing letters to biographers.

> When I look at those I've kept, they sometimes seem, appear, very
> personal, vulnerable and recent, and I wonder why any stranger
> should see them. C did speak about living people – people still living,
> relatives and others – very frankly … When I look back at the letters,
> I sometimes hear her say, 'Dear girl, what does it matter?', and at other
> times I feel a need to protect them, and private life from view.

They seem to have advised her to show them to those, if any, she felt she could trust. She got on best with Christine Williams, an ABC journalist with a young daughter and a Labor-activist husband. Williams had the first biography out in 1989 and Elizabeth felt she had done Christina justice with 'research worthy of Interpol'. Hazel Rowley's more scholarly biography was published four years later to international praise, but Elizabeth could not see her friend in the hard-edged, probing portrait.

Elizabeth Riddell told Rowley that Stead 'elicited affection and care' from women such as Elizabeth Harrower and Rosemary Dobson, and some thought 'she used Elizabeth ruthlessly. However, that is probably not Elizabeth's view.' Riddell had implied this kind of sapping friendship in her gossip about Elizabeth as a victim, which so upset her. She was right about some friends, but not Christina, with whom Elizabeth shared mutual kindness and understanding but took no responsibility. Rowley and Williams both reflected that tenderness in their books.

In 1992, Elizabeth honoured Christina by accepting a commission from *Overland* editor Barrett Reid to review two volumes of her letters compiled by Ron Geering. In Harrower style she praised her friend as 'A woman of almost genetic tolerance, rare in having immense strength without an accompanying urge to dominate others.'

Patrick White continued to care for Elizabeth after his death. He left her $10 000 in his will, which distributed most of his estate after Manoly's death to arts and charitable institutions. His last gift came in 1996 when Elizabeth Harrower was named winner of the Patrick White Literary Award. He had been adamant that he couldn't give the award to friends in his lifetime (but made exceptions for Thea Astley and Robert Gray). The judges – Rodney Wetherell, Michael Costigan and Joy Hooton – believed enough time had passed and Elizabeth was deserving in every way, as an older writer who had made a contribution to Australian literature but had not received due recognition; and as one White had admired, encouraged and badgered. This prize came with $25 000 and was her only prize for writing since the one she loved to mention, a coathanger for a primary school composition when she was six. She told the *Sydney Morning Herald*, 'I had thought I was going to hold the unique place of an Australian writer who had a lot of good reviews but never won an award.' Asked if she would ever write again, she replied, 'I think I would feel very fed up with myself if I didn't.'

After reviving *The Long Prospect*, *The Catherine Wheel* and *The Watch Tower* for Angus & Robertson, Richard Walsh had left the company. In 1989 A&R was absorbed by William Collins and became Collins/Angus & Robertson. Collins' publisher, Tom Thompson, took charge of the Angus & Robertson list, reprinting *The Catherine Wheel* in 1988. He kept Harrower's three novels alive for a while. She still had faint hope for a US publisher and made a last attempt in 1989 through the Sydney literary agent Rosemary Creswell, who organised a pleasant but fruitless drink with Andre Schiffrin from Pantheon Books. Creswell promised to send her books to other New York publishers and Harrower replied with calm resignation that she thought one or two of her books might flourish after she expired, 'but a bit of flourishing before that would be nice'.

Through those years at Collins/A&R, Tom Thompson maintained a flirtatious campaign urging Harrower to allow him to reissue *Down in the City*, or to write a memoir about her writer friends called 'Intimates', or gather her disparate notes into a book called 'Great Thoughts'. He offered her $2000 for a collection of her short stories and teased: 'Now that might mean you can escape again and NOT have to show me what else you've been writing!!' His ideas gave a glimpse into the amorphous 'something' she had been writing.

> It could hold little novels, stories and tales that beguile, inscriptions that you've been 'forced' to take down because they're so good. Anything in fact, it will have its own shape ... It must be possible because you seem to be driving your story-telling that way.

She resisted every suggestion with her familiar excuse: 'I feel an obligation to write might have the effect of halting the thoughts midway to the typewriter. Perhaps it's best to proceed in my own wilful way, and when something has been achieved to alert anyone likely to care.' She also made the tantalising aside that if she *were* to write her memoirs, she imagined they would be more like a volume of John Osborne's autobiography. She'd only read a review then of his 'incandescent prose' and when she later read the books, after Osborne's death in 1995, she found them 'extraordinarily sad' but recognised the London theatre scene in which he was a rare lower-middle-class boy made good. Her offhand remark was packed with implications. Osborne was the young playwright whose work she had followed in London in the 1950s, while she wrote *The Catherine Wheel*, from his landmark *Look Back in Anger* to his lambasted musical satire *The World of Paul Slickey*. His highly regarded two-volume autobiography, *A Better Class of Person* (1981) and *Almost a Gentleman* (1991), tells of the boy who loved his father and hated his mother, his start as an actor, his tumultuous success, and his five marriages. Harrower would have identified with his bleak childhood, creative excitement, and class consciousness. Her failed actor, Christian Roland in *The Catherine Wheel*, seems cut from the same fabric of theatre, adultery, anger and despair. What leaps out from Osborne's books is his juxtaposition of passages from his plays with details from his life that inspired them. Harrower raised the possibility that – had she written her memoirs – she, too, would have pulled back the curtain to show how she remade life as fiction. But, she reminded Thompson, she had no intention of doing so.

In the mid-1990s Thompson left Collins/Angus & Robertson, taking rights to some of the classics – including Elizabeth's novels – to his own small press, ETT Imprint. For all his enthusiasm and their good-natured dealings, Thompson let Harrower down as his company ran out of money. Soon after her Patrick White Award, she wrote to him that she had hoped this 'would have been a once in a lifetime opportunity for my books to reach a new audience', but she had learnt that her books were out of print again. 'So if it seems that the luck of winning has been somewhat reversed by a total absence of books and accurate information, you will understand why.' In a terse letter she asked that the rights all revert to her.

By now, not even Elizabeth believed the fiction she kept up about writing more books or even being read. She began to say she was confident that some future reader would discover her novels as buried treasure after she was dead.

Retirement

In the 1990s Elizabeth fully embraced a new phase of life, no longer a writer, her mind and body engaged in activities that soothed as well as stimulated. Cancer surgery left her wary, even less likely to travel, steering away from demanding people, and seeking calm influences. Long ago she had undergone hypnosis for migraines and anxiety, and now her interest in Buddhism from London days was revived by seeing a poster in a doctor's surgery. With a friend, Barry Willoughby, she travelled across town for classes at a Buddhism centre in Newtown, attracted by the focus on mindfulness, compassion and impermanence, her atheism unshaken. For a while she hung Tibetan flags and bells at home and always kept a small Buddha in her study.

Through the 1990s she and Margaret Dick took beginner's Italian lessons at the Workers Education Association (WEA) in the city. Elizabeth was devoted to her teacher, Roberto Pettini, an existentialist and adventurer from Bologna. She made a new circle of friends among the students, including a nun and, in particular, Nesli Karadeniz, a vivacious clinical psychologist who travelled often to Europe. After class they chatted in Italian and English over coffee in the arcades under Sydney Town Hall. Elizabeth had always been interested in Shirley Hazzard's reports from Italy, and a fan of the filmmaker Fellini, and now she watched Italian news, films and even soap operas on SBS, the multicultural television station. There was no practical purpose to her study – she certainly wouldn't return to Italy – but as she wrote to Shirley, 'Seeing Roberto weekly gives a strong feeling of being in touch with the place and the history. He is so generous, unsparing on himself.' When Roberto asked his students what work they would like to do if they were starting over, she said, 'That particular day it seemed nothing would have been more rewarding or enjoyable than a life given over to ancient history.' Elizabeth's strengths were grammar and reading, and with a later classmate, Max Henningham, she studied Dante's *Inferno* in English and Italian.

Politics was still her religion and with Labor back in government under Bob Hawke she remained a committed party member. When Paul Keating became prime minister in 1991 she had a new object of adoration who almost matched Whitlam. John Edwards, who was Keating's chief economics adviser, had met Elizabeth at Gavin and Ngaire Souter's place in the 1970s and occasionally saw her at Richard Hall's famous Friday lunches at the Mixing Pot, an Italian restaurant in Glebe. They became closer after Edwards left the prime minister's office in 1994 to write a book about Keating, and he was pleased to have the interest of 'an actual famous writer'. She made encouraging remarks: 'You have a first draft! I think it is so important to have a first draft.' In 2007 she finally met Paul Keating at Edwards' sixtieth birthday party. 'She was very pleased. She pretended to be agog with admiration, a little piece of theatre that was part of her considerable charm,' Edwards said. Her birthday gift to him was Christina Stead's 1936 novel *The Beauties and Furies*, with a dedication to Elizabeth in Christina's hand. Edwards couldn't remember ever discussing policies with her, and thought she was drawn to Labor circles for:

> her political sympathies but also the verve, gossip and fun of politics, perhaps. Her interest ... seemed to be in the personalities, and especially in personalities she admired, like Whitlam and Keating. Unlike many writers, she was not the least bit introverted – though never boisterous or loud. She was remarkable for her kindness. Also very sharp and observant, as you might expect.

Everyone knew about Elizabeth's political views, friends and strangers, and she would only see Labor-voting doctors. Ulrik Funch was her hairdresser in Cremorne from the mid-1970s onwards and they talked about 'politics, books, and flowers in the garden, everything and nothing'. Funch was presented with a business award in the early 2000s by the Liberal prime minister John Howard and hung a photograph of himself with Howard and Tony Abbott, the local Liberal member (and future prime minister), on the wall of his salon. Elizabeth would ask, 'Do you mind turning that around while I'm here?' He never did. 'We sometimes agreed to disagree. She was quite a strong personality.' But Elizabeth loved him too, invited him and his wife to dinner at Stanley Avenue, and all her friends heard about Ulrik. She was vain about her thick, strong hair and as it changed from sleek brown to steel grey and then white, he styled it more softly. He served her coffee and biscuits, she gave him her novels. When he was planning a trip to Spain, she passed on her mother's 1960s guide books to Cordoba, Granada and Toledo. If it rained he drove her home in his Porsche. Pampering and friendship were as important as the cut.

At last, in 1999, Elizabeth sold 5 Stanley Avenue. Climbing the 'mountain' of Awaba Street that rose steeply from Balmoral to the Mosman shops was too much in her seventies. She had injured herself when she slipped on the hill and then smashed a knee in her own mossy front courtyard. The suburb was changing: she saw 'merchant bankers & lawyers & "head-hunters" are everywhere. Fortunately, I don't know any. But they've moved in.' Property prices were rising quickly out of a long stagnation, not helped by Keating's 'recession we had to have', and she banked close to $2 million.

After twenty years of desultory searching, she bought a three-bedroom apartment on the fifth floor of a 1970s red-brick building at 26 Cranbrook Avenue, Cremorne. Her new home was more efficient than the old house, which infuriatingly sold again for six million after the renovations it desperately needed. But she was liberated from memories and repairs, and she had enough money for her old age. Her glamorous view of the harbour was higher and wider, stretching from her neighbour's tennis court to the horizon. Visitors gazed from their sofas at the white sails of yachts and the Opera House through balcony doors, while she sat in a chair to one side, avoiding headache-inducing glare and giving attention to her guests. One evening in 2009 while watching television, she failed to notice the murder of the tennis court's owner, Michael McGurk, shot dead on the street below by thugs hired by Ron Medich over their crooked business dealings. She laughed at herself for telling a detective the next day that the killer probably used a silencer – as if he wouldn't have thought of that.

The view she loved most was of the purple-flowering jacaranda and the camphor laurel trees whose branches were level with her kitchen window:

> Currawongs have built a nest, sat on the eggs patiently in all weather, and now have – as far as I can see – two eternally demanding young ones waiting for food. They're so close to me, swaying about in the wind, so high up. Every time I go to the kitchen sink I look to see what they're doing. And visitors follow, equally charmed by this domestic scene.

Andrew Robertson and his partner, Clem Yap, were among her closest friends, at first through care for Kit Hazzard and now as near-neighbours in Cremorne. Elizabeth loved their company, their kindness, their politics, and Andrew's acerbic humour. Always have some gay friends, she advised another woman, because they'll look after you. 'We just clicked,' said Andrew. 'She was chatty and warm and great company. She liked to talk about the same sort of things we did – films across the road, the opera, food, politics, people. She was very good at drawing you out and asking you things. This was her way of revealing herself: she'd get you to talk about yourself instead, very sophisticated.' Working in the field of psychiatry, he noticed that she knew a lot of psychologists and psychiatrists who shared her curiosity about human nature. Among them were Dorothy Rowe, a world-renowned expert in depression, and Valerie Newton-John, a clinical psychologist, stepmother to singer Olivia, and active Labor Party member.

Nesli Karadeniz, the Turkish-born psychologist from Italian classes, said: 'Elizabeth was like my psychologist, she was a natural at it; she could read people. From the books you can see it, too. She wanted to know everything with my love affairs, she followed them, and would give good advice. She had a great memory, whatever you were doing she was aware of it. I wondered, is she taking notes?' Nesli only had glimpses into her friend's past through mentions of her parents' divorce and her mother's death. When Nesli spoke of her partner drinking too much, Elizabeth said she knew how that felt, how sad it was to start counting somebody's drinks. 'Although she was closer to my mother in age, she was much more compassionate about my mother than I was. She said, "Just imagine how she's feeling, Nesli, if this is how frustrating it is for you".'

Friends were becoming younger, and as always Elizabeth was drawn to creative, energising thinkers. Her long-time friend Sally McInerney, a writer and artist who had been married to the poet Geoffrey Lehmann, visited with her children. She recognised that Elizabeth was both sociably outgoing and extremely private. 'It was her kindness and playful good humour, visible in her face, that particularly characterised her; her bright sparkly eyes observing the human scene, particularly including children if they were present.' Sally's daughter Lucy, who would become a writer, sent Elizabeth her drawings and, in thanks for a birthday card, 'a rather good poem' titled 'The Dragons' Minds'. On Elizabeth's wall hung a small etching drawn by Sally that Patrick White had given her in the 1970s: a drowning woman is waving her arms for help and someone has thrown her a line, but it's a fishing line that ends in a hook. A gift with a barbed message, no doubt intended by Patrick.

Sally's artist friend Tom Carment visited too, sometimes with his children, and sent postcards and letters as he travelled round Australia painting and writing. He was one of Elizabeth's most reliable correspondents in later years as others dropped away. She replied warmly, read his stories, and went to his exhibitions. 'I love those landscapes, skyscapes, seascapes and the rusty country gates with an eternity of space all round,' she wrote after one. To Shirley Hazzard she wrote: 'Tom's a lovely person, true artist, whose pictures are small gems. Critics sometimes advise him to "go bigger", but he doesn't want to. In the mornings I look out at the sky and see "Mandy's clouds" and in the afternoons in the other direction "Tom's clouds" and sometimes very early "Clarice Beckett's sky".' Artist Miranda (Mandy) Keeling, her next-door neighbour in Mosman, gave Elizabeth a luminous pastel painting of their view out to sea and another by her daughter, Anwyn, of a girl in a hallway that was said to be Elizabeth. But when Tom painted her portrait in 1989, she disliked the stern grey owl in glasses who stared back at her. Her bookseller friends Eve Abbey and Barry Willoughby approved, so she looked again 'calmly and quietly' and found herself 'interesting'. Margaret Dick bought the painting from Tom's well-reviewed exhibition, and later Elizabeth gave it to Barry Willoughby, a decorative arts collector who, she hoped, might pass it on to a gallery, as he would donate his glass and ceramics to the Powerhouse Museum. She'd met Barry through Salvatore Zofrea, and as well as studying Buddhism, they chatted every day on the phone. Charles Percy, an engineer she met with Barry, also became a friend through shared musical and political interests. Through Barry she met Max Henningham and his partner Brian Galway, and with Val Newton-John they started going to local ALP meetings again. She finally dropped out in 2010, angry at the way 'wicked' Julia Gillard replaced Kevin Rudd as prime minister. After Barry's death, Brian bought the portrait of Elizabeth from his estate and gave her a home on his wall in Neutral Bay.

Her circles of friends were still spreading, spiralling, overlapping, at the centre of her happiness, often a support and rarely a burden. When people disappointed her these days, she was quick to drop them. She was living in the present, where few people knew or cared who she once was. After she fell and broke her right wrist in 2001, friends rallied to keep her entertained:

> eating at the North China with Andrew and Clem, with the chef coming out to sing Chinese opera towards the end of the evening. Dinner at Japanese restaurants with Max and Brian. Italian (broken) conversation at the Art Gallery with Mirella Alessio. The Sydney Institute today with Barry to hear Kim Beazley. The National Maritime Museum yesterday with Jane to see the paintings of Jan Senbergs of the sinking of the Armidale in the Timor Sea in December, 1942. (Dear Col Madigan, architect of the National Gallery in Canberra, was a survivor, and there is now a book, too.) Lunch at Manly with Helene and Ferdi on Sunday, when we sat afterwards staring at the horizon, perfect sky and scene, feeling part of a painting. Invited yesterday to a rehearsal of <u>Peter Grimes</u> at the Opera House, but couldn't go. Tomorrow I'll meet Margaret in town for a coffee and a sandwich ...

Salvatore Zofrea, the Italian-born artist she knew through Geoffrey Lehmann, often joined Elizabeth for coffee and conversation about art, ideas, people.

'She was a genuine, sincere person who lived her art and maintained a very high standard,' he said. 'Art is contemplation, that's what I would get with Elizabeth Harrower, the honesty of the craft of her art. We both had standards which today have been watered down too much. I say, if you can't draw you can't paint, that's the fundamental.'

Elizabeth visited his studios and exhibitions, was curious about his art, but didn't buy paintings. All her art was made and given by friends. Salvatore remembered only one artwork on the bare walls at Stanley Avenue – a poster of Sidney Nolan's famous painting of Ned Kelly on horseback from behind. Ebullient Salvatore would do most of the talking, while Elizabeth was 'very gentle and very keen to hear what you have to say. She would never interrupt, she would let you unfold.' He and Stephanie Claire went to Elizabeth's 1984 party for Shirley Hazzard and a dinner with Patrick White, but each most remembered time alone with her.

Stephanie enjoyed her visits to Stanley Avenue on Sunday afternoons, when they would sit in the living room with a cup of tea. She noticed that the carpets and walls were pale grey and Elizabeth dressed in neutral tones, as if trying to disappear while she listened avidly to stories about Stephanie's large, colourful family.

'They were all ordinary people but she seemed to be looking at them with a telescope and taking note. She did not have any intuition about family and relationships, that was the funny thing, but she seemed to be very interested in how families worked and going at it in a forensic way. It made sense of things for my benefit when I had to make sense of something for Elizabeth. She asked good questions, like a psychiatrist. It was extremely pleasant.'

Elizabeth was listening as a friend and as a writer, still watching from her vantage point, and as Salvatore saw, 'extracting what she wanted of the human condition, and then she would construct an emotional image or thought'. Stephanie felt that in her own life Elizabeth wasn't always a good judge of character and would fall under the spell of people, whether politicians, real estate agents or friends, and she was vulnerable to infatuation and control.

Through these years Elizabeth still kept tiny diaries crammed with appointments, lists of friends she saw or spoke to by phone and 'gmail' (and those who failed to call). She swung like a boat at anchor from happy social days to exhaustion and retreat, boredom and loneliness. She hated public holidays. Every year she transferred to her new diary important birthdays and death days, her parents' marriage and divorce, her first dinner with Patrick. On days of too much reflection on the past she wrote notes: 'Felt in unusually bad mood last night thinking of my life & the people who have affected it. Humid. Hot. Storm.' 'Thinking of Shirley and what a rotten friend she was. Lovely day. Thinking of travel & OS.' 'Idle day. Library & reading. Thinking of travel & regretting for the millionth time misuse of inheritance.'

*

By the turn of the century Elizabeth's most trusted friend, Margaret Dick, was in her eighties and going blind from macular degeneration. Soon after moving herself to Cremorne, Elizabeth helped Margaret sell her flat and move to a retirement home in nearby North Sydney. Margaret stayed in good spirits, listening to audio books from the Royal Blind Society and doing crossword puzzles with a strong magnifying glass. Elizabeth visited, heavy-hearted but admiring of her cousin's dignity.

Too much of her energy was given to funerals, letters of condolence, and quiet sympathy. She had perfect pitch at these times. After Francis Steegmuller died in 1994, Elizabeth wrote to Shirley Hazzard:

> Shock freezes poor human heads and makes it impossible to accomplish much and give an impression of some reassuring kind to everyone around. But it's another world, even to the light in the sky ... I think of you going in to the apartment in New York, everything double-edged and unbelievable – Francis's presence and absence.

Antigone Kefala wrote a semi-fictional novella about her mother's death and described the empathy shown by a friend who was surely Elizabeth Harrower:

You know from Elizabeth's voice how you look, her voice begins full of apprehension that she wants to keep in check, not betray, but which propels her to more extravagant gestures, laughter, a sort of recklessness in attitude to counterbalance your obvious vulnerability.

And then that look of the concerned child appears in her eyes, she lowers her entire face to look at you with the tip of her eyes, as if to notice things better, take them in.

This was Elizabeth Harrower's late existence, full but fading, with a shortening prospect and no hint of the grand finale about to come.

Renaissance

In a fairytale telling of Elizabeth Harrower's life, this would be where the prince turns up and wakes her with a kiss. She had survived big bad wolves, wicked stepfathers and poisoned apples. As an author she had been asleep for forty years. She was eighty-three and living high in her tower above Sydney Harbour when a letter arrived to say another publisher wanted to reissue her books. Not quite trusting this astonishing news, Elizabeth wrote back with poise that she had always thought the books *should* be rediscovered one day. A month later, a few days before Christmas 2011, she caught a bus into the city to meet Michael Heyward and Penny Hueston, a married couple who ran the independent Text Publishing in Melbourne. Over afternoon tea at the Menzies Hotel they talked for hours about her books, their books, and books in general. As Elizabeth remembered, they became friends that day. Within months *The Watch Tower* reappeared as one of the first titles in the Text Classics paperback list. Its striking yellow cover had an image of the Harbour Bridge, which she had disliked as a cliché on the original UK design, but now she was enchanted. *The Watch Tower* became the bestseller of the growing list, and at last Elizabeth Harrower brushed off the ashes and went to the ball.

As a publisher, Michael Heyward had long wanted to revive important Australian books which had fallen out of print, and by the time he had found a hundred and forty such titles he realised 'what an impoverished ecosystem' Australian publishing had become for its literary history.

David Winter, an editor at Text Publishing, had recently worked on a new edition of Helen Hodgman's 1976 novel about 'stultifying suburbia', *Blue Skies*, and rights coordinator Alaina Gougoulis, also his wife, noticed a comparison by the ABC between Hodgman's book and *The Watch Tower*. Their curiosity was piqued. Winter read Harrower's novel in a day and 'I thought it was a really important book, shell-shocking, really.

I came in with very little context and made the assessment that it was one of the great novels of postwar Sydney.' He wrote a rave report insisting *The Watch Tower* must become a Text Classic. Meanwhile the writer Joan London told Penny Hueston that she had been passionate about the novel since making a random discovery in the library at the University of Perth in the 1960s; journalist Philippa Hawker also enthused. When Heyward read the book he thought, 'It's humbling that a book so powerful and so good has been allowed to go out of print.' No one was sure whether Elizabeth Harrower was alive when the letter went out to her.

Elizabeth said later that she hadn't taken the letter very seriously, because of all the letters she'd had from small companies that went nowhere and all the forgotten paperbacks in her cupboard. But this time felt different, and it was her last chance.

'We had coffee at the Menzies and we had a wonderful conversation about books, a real literary conversation that I hadn't really had in years. So then I did take it more seriously, because obviously something was going to happen.'

Joan London wrote an introduction for the Text Classics edition of *The Watch Tower*, looking back to her student encounter: 'The novel gripped me like a nightmare.' Its tension was undiminished forty years later, she said, with comparisons to the Russian masters and Elizabeth Bowen's novel of psychological cruelty, *The Death of a Heart*. Now she also saw the strength of the younger sister, Clare, as a 'gathering counter-force, the means of resistance to the malevolence of Felix Shaw'. By helping the young Dutch survivor of war at the end of the novel, Clare sees a way out of Shaw's control and saves herself. Joan London couldn't know that Elizabeth Harrower had found her purpose in saving people in life as well as literature. But she understood what Harrower wanted to show readers: 'Something runs clear and strong through this wonderful, painful novel, the dark and the light. The victim and the survivor. Suffering and joy. The knowledge of both. *Reality*.'

The Watch Tower came out in 2012 to a new round of journalists, critics and readers, fascinated by the author as well as her books. Reviewer Kerryn Goldsworthy saw 'an accomplished and sophisticated novel of great power and intensity', depicting the emotional and physical claustrophobia of pre-feminist Australia, where housing assumed a society made up of nuclear families. Helen Garner chose the novel as one of the year's best after 'decades of disgraceful neglect'. She had read *The Watch Tower* for the first time in the 1990s, a decade when she wrote 'Tower Diary' about the end of her own unhappy marriage from a flat high above Sydney.

'It bowled me over – a broken family, abandoned sisters, a bullying man – a tremendous piece of work, excruciating, muscular, frightening, yet "domestic" in scope – a combination of qualities I had been seeking all along, without being able to articulate them for myself.'

In the next two years all Harrower's novels were brought back to life in the order Heyward and his team ranked them – *The Long Prospect*, *Down in the City*, *The Catherine Wheel* – with introductions by younger women writers, Fiona McGregor, Delia Falconer and Ramona Koval. In his search, Heyward also learnt that a fifth novel sat unpublished in the National Library of Australia with the manuscripts and correspondence she had deposited in recent years. She had left *In Certain Circles* to be found when her papers became accessible after her death. But Heyward jumped the gun.

'I used to nag her and say, "Elizabeth, when are you going to let me read this novel in the National Library?" "Oh, you don't want to read that. I don't want to waste your time." This went on for quite a while and I sort of gave up. I didn't want to make a nuisance of myself. We spoke often on the phone and one day she said to me, "I don't know why it's taken so long, Michael, for you to ask if you can read that novel in the National Library".'

He found two cleanly typed versions of the novel she had sent to Alan Maclean at Macmillan, first in 1970 and then after working in stunned grief in the summer of 1971. Forty years later Heyward thought her revision of the manuscript was 'a masterclass in editing'. By closely comparing the two drafts he saw that she had not reconceived the novel but had expertly cut 10 per cent of her words, pruning sentences to give them shape, music and rhythm. Once or twice she had cut too severely, Heyward judged, compressing parts of the story rather than infusing life into the characters that she was too numb to feel. The process sounds like self-harm, as if by slashing words she could punish herself for failing.

'*In Certain Circles* is so polished, so finely honed, there's not a hair out of place. It was almost like the book needed a bit of the messiness of art to breathe and it felt as though it had been corseted by Elizabeth's desire to create a perfectly shaped and structured novel. There was nowhere to go after that.'

David Winter, who worked with Elizabeth as editor, also saw strengths and weaknesses in her final novel. 'The first four novels are all very dense and claustrophobic, and a couple of late stories and to a certain extent *In Certain Circles* show a maturity of voice. But there's also a degree of remoteness, because part of what works so well with *The Watch Tower* is the feeling that you're locked in a room in Neutral Bay with a predatory man who holds responsibility for your life.'

Heyward thought she had been badly served by Alan Maclean, who sought only one male reader's report, was 'phlegmatic' in his response and 'approached the whole thing in bad faith'. He saw, one publisher to another, that Maclean was reluctant to follow the commercial failure of her best book, *The Watch Tower*, with more risk. Heyward did not hesitate to publish the novel exactly as she'd left it in 1971, and Harrower decided he might as well not wait until she was dead. She expected some negative commentary but she was so far removed from the books and the person who wrote them that she wasn't concerned.

As an artefact from the vault, by a living writer who should have been famous, *In Certain Circles* was an extraordinary discovery. When this new-old novel appeared in 2014, the response was excitement, reviews mostly positive and sensitive to what Harrower had tried to convey. The young Australian novelist Jessica Au found the novel 'subtle yet wounding, and very much alive ... Less malignant than *The Watch Tower*, *In Certain Circles* is no less psychologically profound. Rather, its quietude and graceful turning of the screws bring it all the more closer to a kind of truth.' Feminist literary scholar Susan Sheridan wrote an essay observing that pity enslaved the pitiers in all Harrower's novels, but in manipulating a happy ending, she had sucked the intensity from this one. 'Celebrating change, in the end, rather than bare survival, takes *In Certain Circles* outside the destructive mode that distinguished Harrower's other novels.'

The Text Publishing editions of all Harrower's novels went on sale in the UK and – at last – the US and were taken seriously. In the *Times Literary Supplement*, Gwendoline Riley assessed the prose in each book as 'watchful, witty, unillusioned, exultant' and the voice of *In Certain Circles* as cooler and even sarcastic, but the novel 'doesn't feel coerced or artificial'. Perhaps the most gratifying tribute was a five-page review in the *New Yorker*, her long-unrequited love, in which James Wood wrote:

> Harrower was right about *In Certain Circles* being well written, but surely wrong to take its superb style for granted, as if mere literary muscle memory. Like the rest of her work, the novel is severely achieved: the coolly exact prose cannot be distinguished from the ashen exhaustion of its tragic fires.

He saw some structural flaws, a stifling atmosphere, but summed up her qualities: 'her wounded wisdom, the elegance and strictness and perilous poise of her sentences, the humane understanding, and ceaseless incisions, of her intelligence'.

At the end of the year, Wood claimed Harrower as his 'great discovery of 2014' and said more emphatically, 'I can't recommend this brilliant, austere writer strongly enough; reading her work was like discovering some long lost sister of Muriel Spark's ... funny and elegant and devastating.' Funny! A word not often used about Harrower's writing, but Wood recognised the mordant humour in sentences such as the description of Stella Vaizey, the 'vilely haughty mother' of Laura and Clare in *The Watch Tower*, 'She was like a park that had never once removed its *Don't Walk on the Grass* signs' or from *In Certain Circles*, 'Yet really, apart from the sense of irretrievable loss, there was nothing wrong at all.' He saw the influence of Henry James in Harrower's writing, and others found the connections with Elizabeth Bowen and Ivy Compton-Burnett, novelists she had read in full when she was a young writer in London. No one this time compared her with Patrick White, the giant who had loomed over her career.

Finally, in 2015 Text published *A Few Days in the Country and Other Stories*, a collection of twelve short stories. Their order followed the course of her life in an oblique way, opening with the first story she'd written, about a child, 'The Fun of the Fair', including her much-anthologised 'The Beautiful Climate' and 'The Cost of Things', as well as previously unknown stories, 'The North Sea' and 'The Cornucopia', and closing with 'It Is Margaret', about her mother's death, and 'A Few Days in the Country', the study of a suicidal woman. Two of her stories remain unpublished – 'Absent Friends' set in the city life of young working women, similar to stronger stories 'The City at Night' and 'Summertime'; and 'The Last Days', the anxious, haunting reprise of *The Catherine Wheel*'s Clemency James's effort to repel her former lover, Christian Roland, before she leaves London for Australia.

As Harrower's books rolled out across the English-speaking world, they built an international fan club. *The Watch Tower* and *In Certain Circles* were each translated into eight languages. The Irish novelist Eimear McBride couldn't remember a novel moving her more than *The Watch Tower*, and she said, 'Australians have their F. Scott Fitzgerald in Elizabeth Harrower.' The *Washington Post* critic Michael Dirda was reminded of Zola. The British actor Ben Whishaw named *The Watch Tower* as one of his cultural highlights of 2015 and went on to read more:

> I found her books incredibly moving and feel an affinity with her. She seems hyper-aware of currents under the surface of human relationships, the conflict between having to keep up a certain social normality and the burning emotions underneath.

After reading *The Long Prospect* he wanted to make a film about Emily Lawrence's adolescent love and suffering. 'Something in that book obsessed me,' he told a French journalist. Whishaw had starred in Jane Campion's film *Bright Star* about the poet John Keats, and his husband, Australian composer Mark Bradshaw, had written the score. On trips to Sydney he visited Elizabeth Harrower two or three times.

'They had long conversations that went all afternoon and they loved each other from the beginning,' Heyward said.

After a few years Whishaw had to admit the film was too hard. Even so, Elizabeth was delighted to meet the handsome, sensitive actor who had played Hamlet, Keith Richards, and the voice of Paddington Bear. 'She was one of the rare people I've met who made me feel like a little baby,' he said, '... the kindest artist in the world.'

Elizabeth gave interviews again, to a new generation of journalists, and spoke at public events for the first time in her career. She was worried Michael would lose money on her books, and she wanted to help sell them. In his safe company she talked to an audience at her local Mosman Library, and then to crowds and standing ovations at Melbourne and Sydney writers' festivals. She reminisced about her divorced childhood, her writing in London, the difficulty of being an Australian writer in the days when they were few, her wonderful friends Patrick, Christina and Judah – all that without telling secrets about her life or explaining her books. She said, half truthfully, she hadn't reread them and couldn't remember. Neither could she explain why she had stopped publishing so abruptly. She mentioned her disappointment at not winning the Miles Franklin Award, and that she had not wanted to be patronised by Alan Maclean: 'It surprises me that I could just end it like that, like a divorce. It's a great love affair over. Weird.' She could also put herself in a historical perspective.

'When people are studying the period, they will know I was here doing that. And then everything changed. All these things happened like the women's movement, Germaine Greer, the Pill, all of these things together and Australia began to be looked on as a possible market and a few more people would have been published in America. But there was this huge social change for women, burning the bra and Simone de Beauvoir. More people were published overseas or finding an agent and then the women set up in Melbourne with their publishing company [McPhee Gribble] and that made a difference. I missed it but by that time I'd done my dash; I'd written quite a lot.'

As Elizabeth realised she had readers and audiences hanging on her words, Heyward said:

> She became the grande dame. She adored it. For me as a book publisher, it was like a miracle. It was like a fairytale to be able to give back to Elizabeth after she'd given us these books and they were sort of lost. It transformed the last ten years of her life, and she really, really enjoyed it.

In Certain Circles brought Elizabeth her first prize since the Patrick White Award in 1996. Shortlisted for five awards, and on the longlist for the elusive Miles Franklin Award, it was chosen as winner of the Voss Literary Prize for best novel of the year by five judges from the Australian University Heads of English. They noted 'enormous interest from readers' for a novel 'fascinatingly in and out of its own time', which 'presents the fragility and tenuousness of human interconnection as a figure for the postwar world'; they were 'compelled by Harrower's incisive and stately prose and by the novel's subtle interweaving of perspectives in the drawing of its circles of sociability and seduction'.

Jane Novak, head of publicity at Text Publishing, helped persuade Elizabeth to do her public events and she was surprised to see her at ease with a microphone. 'I remember thinking, part of you has been waiting all of your life for this chance.' In the audience at the Melbourne Writers' Festival was Laura Kroetsch, then director of Adelaide Writers' Week, who decided she must have Elizabeth Harrower at her 2017 festival. The problem was that after flying nervously to Melbourne, Elizabeth decided she would never catch another plane. Meanwhile, Jane had moved to Sydney and taken over the literary agency of Barbara Mobbs, Patrick White's loyal representative. Jane was fond of Elizabeth, and took the hint when she pointedly wished she had a friend who could drive her to Adelaide, as Olaf Ruhen had done in 1962. In March 2017 Jane and her partner, David Pearson, shared the driving for two days, with Elizabeth in the back seat. They stayed a night at Hay in western New South Wales and crossed the endless Hay Plains, as flat as the Russian steppes, where they could see a car coming towards them for half an hour before it passed. Elizabeth started the singing with 'It Had to Be You', David sang another oldie, and she named as a favourite 'I Was Only Nineteen', a tragic hit song about a Vietnam veteran by the Australian band Redgum. They arrived triumphant and exhausted.

Laura Kroetsch dedicated Writers' Week to Elizabeth Harrower, honouring her return to Adelaide after fifty-five years as a 'titan of 20th century letters'. A crowd of almost two thousand spilled across the lawn in the Women's Memorial Gardens at midday on day one to hear Harrower and Heyward in conversation. Many queued to have books signed and receive wisdom from the author. To one man she said, 'Kindness is the greatest virtue.' Jane Novak remembered the scene: 'She was beaming, you couldn't have wiped the smile off her face. Michael barely got a word in at this point. She had the whole schtick down and she knew this was the biggest stage she was ever going to be on, and she loved every minute of it. I felt very emotional about it.' The drive home across the Hay Plains felt longer for everyone. Elizabeth remembered the singing ('I sang, let's face it, in tune') and having a fine old time with a certain defiance:

'I loved that trip, loved seeing the countryside, no cars, hardly a bird, an animal. The Hay Plain was like heaven. I'm sure they sometimes thought, why doesn't she disappear. Well, I'm not going to disappear. I should have reminded them I was the reason they were there.'

Reckoning

Other friends noticed a change in Elizabeth's demeanour, too, confidence verging on self-importance, vindicated belief in herself as a writer, and pleasure in the attention. Who could blame her? When a stranger helped her after a fall in the street, she said, 'You know I'm a writer' – or perhaps 'I'm a famous writer', as Stephanie Claire recalled. 'It showed me how she was losing it, she was very proud and not liking to see herself fallen down, an old woman on the pavement. I don't think she was amused or ironic. I think she felt it was a great indignity and wanted to salvage her self-respect. She was having to assert her place in society.'

No one except her closest friends understood how complicated the fairytale was for Elizabeth. On the one hand, she would say of her publishing experience, 'It's been wonderful, really going from wonderful to more wonderful, and they're lovely people.' On the other hand, she was tired and her renaissance had come too late. Margaret Dick had died aged ninety-eight on March 24, 2014 after two years in a nursing home, with a lovely room-mate called Mary. She had been too blind to read Elizabeth's crisp new paperbacks, and she was not there to hold the handsome hardcover edition of *In Certain Circles* published in May, and the short story collection a year later. Elizabeth had to give interviews while in mourning. She praised Margaret to journalists who had no idea how important this cousin had been to her for more than sixty years.

She organised a Scottish piper to play at Margaret's small funeral and gave a eulogy with quiet respect:

> She had the disposition of a scholar, words mattered, language mattered, thinking mattered. You might say she tolerated compliments with good grace, but was essentially not interested in herself, or the fine bone structure that stayed with her to the end. I think she marvelled that people could occupy themselves with such things.

Elizabeth finished: 'So goodbye, dear friend. You made a lasting impression.' She wrote to Margaret's niece, Lesley White: 'In the chapel there was no best friend left to sit next to me.' Stunned and sad, she and a friend of Margaret's scattered her ashes in Sydney's Royal Botanic Gardens, where they had often walked together.

Elizabeth thought of all the friends who had encouraged and pushed and appreciated her writing. None of them could share her pleasure. The last of her generation, Shirley Hazzard, died in December 2016, after being bedridden with dementia at her New York apartment, cared for by friends and nurses. Elizabeth had seen her in 1997 when she gave a dinner speech for the Sydney Institute, and in 2005 when she received the Miles Franklin Award – a kind of lifetime recognition – for her long-awaited final novel. *The Great Fire* drew its characters and story from her own travel and heartbreaking romance after the war. Elizabeth went to the dinner at the State Library of New South Wales to celebrate her friend and heard her give a learned but meandering speech. They met privately for meals and conversation, but Shirley was jet-lagged, tired and talked too much; Elizabeth had flashbacks to Capri. Andrew Robertson and Clem Yap were invited to a farewell dinner for Shirley at the Banana Blossom restaurant in Cremorne. They couldn't go, but Elizabeth told them afterwards, 'I won't be seeing her again.' Andrew remembered, 'They had a falling out over Thai food.' Perhaps Elizabeth just meant this was Shirley's last trip to Australia, but years later she told Michelle de Kretser that Shirley had said at dinner how upset she and Francis had been when she didn't travel to New York back in 1984. Elizabeth let her talk while silently eating her food. Andrew had the stark impression she had never really liked Shirley. 'She was very leant on by that family. One of the things I tried to do, not very successfully, was to hitch Kit up to services which would try and take the pressure off Elizabeth ... Then Elizabeth would say, "I've had a letter from the Americans. They have a very busy life." She talked about them in that sort of way: "Francis is doing this, he's had an award, we've met all these important people. We have to close up the flat because we have to be in Capri in June, and then we have to be back in October".'

Elizabeth's memories of the friendship were more nuanced. In 2017 her observations of fifty years poured out:

For a long time at the beginning Shirley and I were fond of each other. We had lots of lunches and dinners, we talked a lot. As she became more and more famous it affected her – the society and Francis's wealth and the way other rich people treated Francis and transferred that to her. It did change her and it's a pity. You know that sometimes when she would say things she would go on and on, and on and on and on. This was not a good sign, and also Francis saw some of these things. He did adore her and he was a lovely man, but there was something of a performance, which he noticed because he noticed everything. At the beginning though, when they read French classics, he would indicate there was no reason why she shouldn't be another Flaubert or something. Well, it's not good for people to hear that.

Elizabeth had been congratulating Shirley on her achievements for decades, and when her own celebration came, Shirley didn't know. Their forty-year correspondence stopped after that visit in 2005, except for Shirley's New Year's Eve calls and a poignant Christmas card from Elizabeth in 2008 after a muddled phone call. The short message ended with memory-laden affection (and a little joke about 'Your Mother'): 'I think of you and Francis, of YM (somewhat differently), the prodigious letters / thoughts exchanged, the girl in your story who often comes to mind, hoping to see things less clearly.' She was remembering the story 'A Place in the Country' in Shirley's collection *Cliffs of Fall*, which was published by Macmillan in 1963, when Elizabeth was a new employee. It follows the arc of an affair between a young woman, Nettie, and her cousin's husband. As they painfully break apart he says, 'Let's hope we can see things more clearly tomorrow' and she replies, 'I think I must hope to see them less clearly.' Shirley and Elizabeth shared the writer's sense of seeing other people with sometimes unbearably heightened sensitivity, and Elizabeth had also quoted this line in a 1973 letter about Kit. Nettie – or Net – was a nickname she used to sign letters to Margaret Dick from London in 1972, perhaps hinting at her close identification with the character during her hardest years.

Shirley had been knocked over in a Rome street in 2008, her injuries hastening her physical and mental frailty. She made her last public appearances in New York for a conversation with the American novelist Richard Ford in 2010 and in the audience of an event to honour her in 2012, organised by Brigitta Olubas, who would write her biography. 'Please speak up – I don't want to miss any compliments,' Shirley said from the front row. Olubas also co-edited a book of scholarly essays about Elizabeth Harrower's writing that was launched at the University of Sydney in 2017. Harrower sat in the front row and said later, 'Can't say I heard a word. It wouldn't have been appropriate anyway if they were saying good things; I didn't need to hear them.' In those spontaneous lines was a personality difference that marked their careers and their friendship.

Elizabeth went quite deaf one day while she was in the limelight. 'Luckily I still had my ears when I met Michael and Penny,' she said. 'I had them for about three years and then they disappeared. Isn't that a shame? They went quickly, walking down the street, and suddenly the traffic wasn't as loud as usual. I went to visit Margaret and Mary, I said, "Shout at me, girls".' Her hearing didn't improve and eventually she used hearing aids, but the days of long phone calls were over, and conversation became difficult unless her companion sat close to her chair. Visitors were still welcome, usually one or two at a time, met at the door by a straight-backed, white-haired, smiling host, who offered plunger coffee or tea, biscuits and pastries she bought locally. Fortunately she was already using an iPad and this became her main connection with the world, bringing her news and emails replacing letters to friends. She told Michelle de Kretser, 'We talk on the iPad now.' She still had clear vision for the screen and the many books that came from her publisher and friends. Emails kept her in touch with her few Scottish relatives, and Lesley White found she and Elizabeth had exchanged more than six hundred messages between 2014 and 2019, since sharing the deaths of Margaret Dick and of Lesley's mother, Stephanie Smith. 'Her emails were a source of interest, wisdom and humour and I greatly appreciated her support through several difficult experiences,' Lesley said. They had always got on well in spite of opposing political views and in 2016 Elizabeth began a robust exchange about Brexit:

> I've decided to vote Remain. Yes, I know I don't have a vote. Influenced by Stephen Hawking, John Oliver, Martin Vander Weyer (Spectator),

the thought of our banks collapsing ... Having been thoroughly irritating, I'll have a shower and start the day.

For important, private thoughts Elizabeth still went to the Olympia typewriter in her study. But the limelight, curiosity about her life, intrusive questions, dealings with biographers, had made her consider the snoops who might go digging in future. At the request of the National Library of Australia, she had dispatched two precious lots of her papers to the collections in 1990 and 1999, her manuscripts and letters from publishers and literary friends, following the lead of Patrick White and other friends. In 2006 she added the forty-year correspondence from Shirley Hazzard, with letters from Kit and Valerie, as if to declare that era closed. Everything she kept was vital to Australian literary history, but she destroyed her diaries and letters to her mother from London. In 2014 she tore up some early writing: 'Too clever.' Presumably she also discarded the last attempts at novels, the 'long something' she'd tinkered with for years, the Great Thoughts; unless someone reveals a hidden stash as Patrick White's disobedient agent, Barbara Mobbs, did years after his death.

New friends turned up, some of them younger women writers. When Irish novelist Eimear McBride went for tea, Elizabeth found her 'a friendly girl' and 'asked her life questions'. Joan London, who had championed *The Watch Tower*, made several visits and in 2015 their novels were shortlisted together for the Prime Minister's Literary Award. London's *The Golden Age* won the prize rather than *In Certain Circles* and, despite some disappointment, Elizabeth was already an admirer of the 'lovely book'. Fiona McFarlane, author of an acclaimed first novel, *The Night Guest*, was on a panel at Melbourne Writers' Festival in 2016 with Harrower and Heyward to talk about Text Classics. McFarlane had found a copy of a 1956 novel about workers in a Sydney factory, *The Dyehouse* by Mena Calthorpe, and wrote the introduction for the Classics edition. Elizabeth sent an email to say she had enjoyed reading *The Night Guest* and suggested, 'One day if you're free to come over to Cremorne for coffee, a biscuit, and some idle conversation, I'll ask you to sign my copy. I think we'll have things to talk about, not only books.' She wrote after Fiona's first visit, 'It's not so often that there's that sort of exchange from the inside, so to speak.' They were joint winners of the 2016 Steele Rudd Award for a short story collection – for *A Few Days in the Country* and *The High Places* – and Elizabeth wrote that she found the result 'totally satisfying'. Fiona became a regular visitor until she moved to California in 2019, and they spoke about 'writing, books, Sydney, Newcastle, the UK, Text, Michael, her friends (Patrick, Christina, Cynthia, and others less famous, like Andrew and Clem), and especially Margaret. We both liked a particular kind of weather in Sydney – a certain temperature and movement of the air, which she described as "a wind from paradise"'.

In December 2017 Fiona took with her Michelle de Kretser, a friend who had just published *The Life to Come*, her fifth novel and soon to be her second Miles Franklin Award winner. Michelle had read Elizabeth's novels and became another appreciative visitor, an audience to her tales of literary history and gossip. She was at the time writing an essay about the books of Shirley Hazzard, the first Australian writer she'd read who looked outwards to the world, and whose novels 'expanded my understanding of what it's possible for writing to achieve'. Elizabeth told Michelle she had liked Shirley's early stories and the first novels, *The Evening of the Holiday* and *The Bay of Noon*, but later her fiction became 'complicated'.

Andrew and Clem were the beloved stalwarts in Elizabeth's daily life, shopping and cooking, taking her to doctors and hospitals, celebrating Christmas Day together, chatting and chiding with the intimacy of old friends. Andrew realised she'd been his closest friend for almost fifty years. But after retiring, they travelled more to the Philippines to see Clem's family. Elizabeth felt insecure, even unfairly resentful, when they left and she had to turn to others for support.

Cynthia Kaye, a friend through Ken and Eve Levis, had calls from Elizabeth when she had 'episodes' and rang an ambulance one day when 'I knew she wasn't herself'. South African friend Jane Harris took her to David Jones to buy clothes, which were usually returned, and Jane's partner, James Mohr, cooked and carried meals to Elizabeth's apartment. Many people visited, took food and checked on her, but they all had busy lives and their own problems, and Elizabeth was stubbornly independent.

Michael Heyward hired a woman to shop and clean, and he and Penny dropped by when they were in Sydney. He was her new saviour and hero, and she told everyone, 'I love Michael.' The Text team were her Melbourne family, sending emails with family news and photos; she loved seeing David and Alaina's baby, and designer Chong's poodles. Chong Weng-Ho had designed all her books, emailed regularly and with his partner visited from Melbourne as genuine friends. For her ninetieth birthday in February 2018, they all flew up and with Jane Novak held a small party at Elizabeth's apartment. Lesley White and her husband, Jon, flew out from the UK. There were small gatherings over several days as she tried to manage her well-wishers. Many people noticed over the years that she had separate groups of friends that she kept apart, and she was used to being 'the manipulator of her certain circles'. She had always brought friends together if she thought they'd be compatible, and deliberately kept some apart. Now she had trouble hearing in a crowd.

By the time everyone saw the signs that Elizabeth was becoming forgetful, fretful, prickly, and in danger of falling, she was making plans. After a lifetime of feeling poor she had accumulated, through inheritance, saving and cautious investment, enough money to make substantial gifts. For a single woman with no immediate family, the question of heirs did not have a simple answer. She changed her will several times over the years as people died or disappointed her. At one stage Richard Hall was a beneficiary. As an investigative journalist, prolific author, and private secretary to Gough Whitlam, he had values she admired, and he had boosted Australian writers' welfare as a founder of the Literature Board and Public Lending Right payments. He had put a passage from *The Watch Tower* in *Sydney: An Oxford Anthology*, compiled for the Olympics in 2000. 'In the bitchy and jealous world of the arts and politics, Richard is so lacking in malice, worthy of trust. No wonder he's loved,' she had told Shirley. He was also down at heel, didn't care about money and died without any in 2003. His long-time partner, Kyrsty Macdonald, said, 'He had huge high regard for Elizabeth and she left money to him in her will. She was very cross when he died because it would have given him a lovely surprise.'

Elizabeth rewrote her will for the last time in May 2018. She made Linda Nolte, Ferdi's younger daughter, enduring guardian with Laurel Laurent, the daughter of another friend. As a judge's associate Laurel was also given power of attorney and made co-executor with a solicitor. Ferdi had died on Christmas Eve in 2012, five years after a stroke during a medical procedure, and Helene Nolte died in 2018.

Linda suddenly had to step up again when Elizabeth was taken to hospital dehydrated and confused in early 2019, and a doctor diagnosed dementia and recommended respite care. Linda and Laurel decided to keep her at Cremorne with full-time carers, but they took away her iPad on doctor's advice, and tried to control her friends' visits. A great tug of war began over Elizabeth's welfare. Friends were offended by their terse dismissal and worried that she was isolated and frightened. Linda and Laurel insisted they were protecting her from further distress. In her delirium Elizabeth may have thought of Ruth, the old woman in Fiona McFarlane's novel, *The Night Guest*, stalked by an imaginary tiger and a mysterious carer. She feared that a woman from Centrelink had stolen her mother's diamond ring until it was found in a drawer. But she also told a disbelieving carer that she had met Paddington Bear, a sweet memory of the actor Ben Whishaw. Unable to leave home, at the mercy of others, she might have imagined herself inside her own novels.

Linda and Laurel showed her some aged-care homes, including Lulworth, in Patrick White's childhood home at Elizabeth Bay, which had appalled her when she visited Gough Whitlam there. They drove her to the Blue Mountains, thinking she could be closer to where they both lived, but she was horrified. 'Too many trees!' Finally they moved her into Scalabrini at Drummoyne, a pleasant 'village' run by nuns and popular with Italian-Australian nonnas. If only Elizabeth could have called up some of Roberto's Italian lessons. Her large room was decorated with photos of family and friends, a painting by Jinx Nolan, first editions of her books, and the photo of Elizabeth from her last newspaper interview, with the headline 'Ninety ... and still dangerous'. She was pleased to see a stream of friends, her cousins Thurza and Verity, her hairdresser Ulrik with his scissors, but recognised them less and less. John Edwards last saw her shortly before her death. 'I went out there with Gavin Souter and a couple of others. I don't think she remembered me. She was forgetful, frail and anxious, but still arch and rather critical of the services provided at the facility. As an aside and out of his hearing, she told us that Gavin was becoming rather forgetful.'

Outside the Italian village, Sydney was being ravaged by drought and a heat wave at the end of 2019. Catastrophic bushfires turned the sky burnt orange, dropped ashes in suburban gardens, and consumed the countryside Elizabeth had loved from Blackheath to Diamond Head, where Kylie Tennant's old hut went up in flames. COVID-19 swept across the world the following year and emptied the streets of Sydney.

Unaware of fire or pandemic, Elizabeth saw only masked faces that winter. Linda sat with her as she sank and died. 'When she had the shot of morphine she looked at me, she held my hand and said, "That's wonderful, thank you." And then shortly after that she left.'

Elizabeth's friends and relatives were shocked to learn she had died on July 7, 2020, from a small death notice in the *Sydney Morning Herald*. Linda and Laurel had not told anyone. As word spread, there was outrage that the great Elizabeth Harrower, only recently rediscovered, could just vanish. Linda was adamant that Elizabeth had not wanted attention drawn to her death and her will stated there was to be no funeral. She had never liked funerals. But Linda, and Elizabeth, missed the point that many people needed to mourn and honour her. Obituaries appeared for the 'rock star writer' and 'acclaimed novelist' and 'the genius of Elizabeth Harrower', whose mysterious long life ended at the age of ninety-two. She was remembered at private gatherings, over afternoon teas and champagne toasts, where friends met for the first time and realised how much they had heard about each other.

Elizabeth's will held more surprises. For a start, she left an estate of more than $4 million once her apartment was sold. The careful distribution was a snapshot of those she held most important and deserving in 2018. First there was $250 000 each for the Scottish cousins, Lesley White and her brother, Robin Smith, which Elizabeth described as money Margaret Dick had inherited from family and left in her care. But Robin had died in a car accident shortly before Elizabeth's death, and his portion was absorbed into the estate. There was $60 000 for Laurel Laurent and $50 000 each for Linda and Karin Nolte, and Charles Percy, who had offered to be an executor. Gifts of $25 000 each went to Antigone Kefala, Nesli Karadeniz, Brian Galway, Cynthia Kaye, James Mohr, and to the Exodus Foundation, which cared for homeless people. The generous remainder was divided among Andrew Robertson, Clemente Yap, Chong Weng-Ho, and the largest share to Michael Heyward of Text Publishing. Mixed with personal gratitude, presumably, was her wish to support other Australian writers. She made Michael her literary executor and gave the rights to her books to him, and her jewellery, including her mother's famous diamonds, to Penny Hueston. The general contents of her home went to Laurel and a few items were for people who had given them to her or admired them. Fiona McFarlane received a Swedish wallhanging which she had recognised as a Dala folk art depiction of the adoration of the magi. Patrick White's Swedish translator had given it to him when he won the Nobel Prize, and Patrick gave it to Elizabeth.

Linda Nolte had read *The Watch Tower* when she came home from living in London to care for her dying father and her mother as she slipped into dementia. Her partner Barney had died a few years earlier and, unable to stay with her parents at Hunters Hill, she rented a house in the Blue Mountains. 'I was pulling out of the station going up to Blackheath when I read the end of the book when the girl is pulling out of the station, and that was very moving.' She reread *The Watch Tower* in the last years of Elizabeth's life and saw another layer of meaning in the domineering character of Felix Shaw. 'It struck me, when the mask was slipping, and you could get into who Elizabeth was ... she had so many facets and maybe that dark male character isn't somebody external it's something internal.'

Elizabeth's body was cremated but rather than place her ashes behind a plaque in a wall at the cemetery with her mother and stepfather, Linda kept them at her home for months. She had thrown Barney's ashes off a cliff at Blackheath in a wind that blew them into her face, and more carefully put her father's ashes into a nearby mountain stream. Thinking to keep her parents separate, she buried her mother's ashes in the back garden at Hunters Hill. One day in the mountains she went back to the same spot high on the escarpment at Govett's Leap. Elizabeth had known that dramatic view over the valley when she and Kylie had their cottage at Blackheath, the place where she had written *The Watch Tower* and struggled with *In Certain Circles*, where she had gazed at sky and clouds, a place of happiness and breakdown. Linda walked off the path to the stream and poured Elizabeth's ashes into the water that ran over the cliff edge through vertical forest to the bottom of the valley. She took the plaque from the urn and buried it under a rock in the stream, as she had done with Ferdi's. 'So my father and Elizabeth's ashes are mixed together down in the Grose Valley off Blackheath.'

Linda's decision was wild and creative, impetuous and selfish – and almost perfect. Elizabeth might have cried, 'Too many trees! Too many memories!' She was a city girl at heart, from Newcastle to London to Sydney. But the mountains had been home too, and she was also Clare Vaizey, running from Felix Shaw's house and catching a train to freedom:

> Abruptly the road by the train lines changed colour and character: it was a bush track – bright clay. And there were trees suddenly, swift-moving past – blossoming eucalyptus, pines. Alone in the compartment, Clare jerked the window up and leaned out into the day. The light was wonderful. Waves of air beat against her face, and it smelled of grass, or clover, or honey.
>
> Whatever it is, I remember it, she thought, breathing in. Her eyes paused here on a line of willows as they glided past, and the willows were familiar, too. She remembered it all.
>
> Yet it was funny that she should think so; for it did occur to her that she had only just arrived.

Acknowledgements

This biography would not exist without the gifts of Elizabeth Harrower. I am grateful for her extraordinary books, her intriguing life, and the time we spent together.

Michael Heyward of Text Publishing has done important work in reviving Harrower's books and many other Australian books in the Text Classics collection.

My great thanks to everyone at NewSouth Publishing for their enthusiasm, professionalism, support, and the pleasure of producing this book together. Special thanks to CEO Kathy Bail, executive publisher Elspeth Menzies, senior project editor Sophia Oravecz, internal book designer Josephine Pajor-Markus, copy editor Linda Funnell, cover designer Debra Billson, and marketing manager Rosina Di Marzo.

Brigitta Olubas is godmother to the biography, which was enriched by our shared passion for the work of Elizabeth Harrower and Shirley Hazzard and the book we co-edited, *Hazzard and Harrower: The letters*.

Enormous thanks to everyone who gave me interviews, listed in the Bibliography. Friends, relatives and acquaintances of Elizabeth Harrower provided many of the stories that bring her to life, as well as family history, publishing history, and photographs. Thanks for many kinds of help and guidance from a multitude of people, including (but not only) the following: Debra Adelaide, Dominic Amerena, Robyn Arrowsmith, Murray Bail, Angela Bowne, Bernadette Brennan, Tom Carment, Jude Conway and the Newcastle Family History Society, Julian Croft, Jim Davidson, Françoise Dussart, Michelle de Kretser, Catherine du Peloux Menagé, Helen Ennis, Suzanne Falkiner, Anna Funder, Sally Gibson, Giulia Giuffrè, Jane Grant, Margaret Harris, Carl Harrison-Ford, Harry Heseltine, Ivor Indyk, Gail Jones, Susan Lever, Elaine Lindsay, David Marr, Rosemarie Milsom, Newcastle Library staff, Marilla North, Voren O'Brien, Romy Oesterheld at Redlands archive, Ian Rankin, Della

Rowley, Robert Sessions, Dean Sewell, Garry Shead, Gavin Souter, State Library of NSW librarians, Hilary Wardaugh, Christine Williams.

Much of my archival research was done on a National Library of Australia Fellowship generously supported by the Stokes Family. I am grateful for use of the library's outstanding collections of Australian writers' papers, and for assistance from the librarians and other staff, especially Sharyn O'Brien and Simone Lark in the Fellowships Program. The digital collections on Trove, maintained by the National Library, were another valuable resource.

Warm thanks to my family and friends for understanding why I was absent and silent for long periods, and for their interest in my work. Endless thanks to my husband, Paul Sheehan, for his thoughtful care and some cracker ideas, and to Leo the cat for making me take frequent breaks from work.

Picture section photo credits

Harrower as a nurse and as a Spanish dancer, courtesy of the Harrower family; with her mother, used with permission of the Estate of Elizabeth Harrower; Frank Harrower, courtesy of the Harrower family; Margaret and Richard Kempley with Barbara Ward, courtesy of Barbara Ward; at Newcastle Baths, on the beach and in 1951, courtesy of the Harrower family; with Margaret Dick in Greece, courtesy of Barbara Ward; with Margaret Dick in 1959, used with permission of the *Sydney Morning Herald*; 1961 portrait, photograph by Jill Crossley/State Library of NSW collections, used with permission of Jill Crossley; with dachshunds, photograph by Ferdinand Nolte, courtesy of Linda Nolte; on the cruise, used with permission of the Estate of Kylie Tennant; with Shirley Hazzard, photograph by Martin Webby, courtesy of ABC Library Sales; in Capri, photograph by Shirley Hazzard, used with permission of the New York Society Library; with Ferdi Nolte, courtesy of Jane Harris and James Mohr; in Cremorne, photograph by Lidia Nikonova, used with permission of the *Sydney Morning Herald*.

Select bibliography

Books

Arnott, Georgina ed., *Judith Wright: Selected writings*, La Trobe University Press, Melbourne, 2022

Bennett, Bruce and Pender, Anne eds., *From a Distant Shore: Australian writers in Britain 1820–2012*, Monash University Publishing, Melbourne, 2013

Bennie, Angela, *Crème de la Phlegm: Unforgettable Australian reviews*, The Miegunyah Press, Melbourne, 2006

Carter, David ed., *Judah Waten: Fiction, memoir, criticism*, University of Queensland Press, Brisbane, 1998

Chegwidden, Cath, *Mighty Mayfield Then and Now: Book 1: The early years*, Newey Printing Company, Newcastle, 2022

Chegwidden, Cath, *Mighty Mayfield Then and Now: Book 2: Industry and change*, Newey Printing Company, Newcastle, 2023

De Kretser, Michelle, *On Shirley Hazzard*, Black Inc., Melbourne, 2019

Deacon, Vera, *Singing Back the River: A miscellany of selected writings by and for Vera Deacon*, Yarnspinners Press Collective, Leura, 2019

Dick, Margaret, *Point of Return*, William Heinemann, London, 1958

Dick, Margaret, *Rhyme or Reason*, William Heinemann, London, 1959

Dick, Margaret, *The Novels of Kylie Tennant*, Rigby, Adelaide, 1966

Dutton, Geoffrey, *Snow on the Saltbush: The Australian literary experience*, Penguin Books Australia, Melbourne, 1984

Dutton, Geoffrey, *Out in the Open: An autobiography*, University of Queensland Press, Brisbane, 1994

Falkiner, Suzanne, *Mick: A life of Randolph Stow*, UWA Publishing, Perth, 2016

Geering, RG, *Christina Stead: A critical study*, Angus & Robertson, Sydney, 1979 (1st pub. 1969)

Geering, RG, *Recent Fiction: Australian writers and their work*, Oxford University Press, Melbourne, 1974

Giuffrè, Giulia, *A Writing Life: Interviews with Australian women writers*, Allen & Unwin, Sydney, 1991

Grant, Jane, *Kylie Tennant: A life*, National Library of Australia, Canberra, 2005

Hazzard, Shirley, 'Letter from Australia' (article), *The New Yorker*, January 3, 1977, pp. 33–59

Hazzard, Shirley, *Collected Stories*, Brigitta Olubas ed., Virago Press, London, 2020

Hetherington, John, *Forty-Two Faces: Profiles of living Australian writers*, FW Cheshire, Melbourne, 1962

Heyward, Michael, *The Ern Malley Affair*, University of Queensland Press, Brisbane, 1993

Joyce, Clayton ed., *Patrick White: A tribute*, Angus & Robertson, Sydney, 1991

Kefala, Antigone, *Summer Visit: Three novellas*, Giramondo Publishing Company, Newcastle, 2002

Kent, Jacqueline, *A Certain Style: Beatrice Davis, a literary life*, Penguin Books Australia, Melbourne, 2001

Lamb, Karen, *Thea Astley: Inventing her own weather*, University of Queensland Press, Brisbane, 2015

Macintyre, Stuart, *The Party: The Communist Party of Australia from heyday to reckoning*, Allen & Unwin, Sydney, 2022

McMahon, Elizabeth and Olubas, Brigitta eds., *Elizabeth Harrower: Critical essays*, Sydney University Press, Sydney, 2017

Marr, David, *Patrick White: A life*, Jonathan Cape, London, 1991

Marr, David ed., *Patrick White Letters*, Random House Australia, Sydney, 1994

Olubas, Brigitta, *Shirley Hazzard: A writing life*, Virago Press, London, 2022

Olubas, Brigitta and Wyndham, Susan eds., *Hazzard and Harrower: The letters*, NewSouth Publishing, Sydney, 2024

Olubas, Brigitta ed., *Expatriates of No Country: The letters of Shirley Hazzard and Donald Keene*, Columbia University Press, New York, 2024

Phelan, Nancy, *Writing Round the Edges: A selective memoir*, University of Queensland Press, Brisbane, 2003

Rowley, Hazel, *Christina Stead: A biography*, Henry Holt and Company, New York, 1994

Sheridan, Susan, *Nine Lives: Postwar women writers making their mark*, University of Queensland Press, Brisbane, 2011

Spurling, Hilary, *Ivy: The life of I. Compton-Burnett*, Richard Cohen Books, London, 1995

Stead, Christina, *Ocean of Story: The uncollected stories of Christina Stead*, Penguin Books Australia, Melbourne, 1985

Summers, Anne, *Damned Whores and God's Police: The colonisation of women in Australia*, NewSouth Publishing, Sydney, 2016 (1st pub. 1975)

Tennant, Kylie, *The Man on the Headland*, William Heinemann, London, 1971

Tennant, Kylie, *Tantavallon*, Macmillan, Melbourne, 1983

Tennant, Kylie, *The Missing Heir: The autobiography of Kylie Tennant*, Macmillan, Melbourne, 1986

White, Patrick, *Flaws in the Glass: A self-portrait*, Jonathan Cape, London, 1981

White, Patrick, *The Hanging Garden*, Random House Australia, Sydney, 2012

Wilding, Michael, *Living Together*, University of Queensland Press, Brisbane, 1974

Williams, Chris, *Christina Stead: A life of letters*, McPhee Gribble Publishers, Melbourne, 1989

Williamson, Geordie, *The Burning Library: Our great novelists lost and found*, The Text Publishing Company, Melbourne, 2012

Library collections

Papers of Elizabeth Harrower, 1937–2005, National Library of Australia, MS 8237, Acc06.016, Acc.06.142, used with permission of the Estate of Elizabeth Harrower

Papers of Bill Cantwell, 1934–1989, NLA, MS 8238

Papers of David Carter, c. 1800–1980, NLA, MSAcc13.114, quoted with permission of David Carter

Shirley Hazzard correspondence and other papers, 1966–c. 2005, MLMSS#10249, State Library of NSW, used with permission of the New York Society Library

Papers of Antigone Kefala, collection 3: 1961–2013, SLNSW, MLMSS 11109

Papers of David Marr, 1920s–1996, NLA, MS 9356, used with permission of David Marr

Papers of Benison Rodd, 2008, NLA, MS Acc08.178, NLA, quoted with permission of Benison Rodd

Papers of Eric C. Rolls, 1821–2009, NLA, MS 7027

Papers of Hazel Rowley, 1923–2021, NLA, MS 9244, quoted with permission of the Estate of Hazel Rowley

Papers of Christina Stead, 1937–1988, NLA, MS 8645, used with permission of the Estate of CE Blake aka Stead

Papers of Kylie Tennant, 1891–1989, NLA, MS 10043, used with permission of the Estate of Kylie Tennant

Papers of Judah Waten, 1912–1985, NLA, MS 4536, used with permission of the Estate of Judah Waten

Papers of Patrick White, 1930–2002, NLA, MS 9982, used with permission of the Estate of Patrick White

Papers of Christine Williams, 1876–2006, NLA, MS 8065, used with permission of Christine Williams

The Macmillan Archive, quoted with permission of Macmillan Publishers International Ltd

Hazel de Berg interview with Elizabeth Harrower for the Hazel de Berg collection, 1967, NLA, ORAL TRC 1/299

Hazel de Berg interview with Margaret Dick for the Hazel de Berg collection, August 22, 1969, NLA, ORAL TRC 1/391, quoted with permission of the Estate of Elizabeth Harrower

Hazel de Berg interview with Kylie Tennant for the Hazel de Berg collection, December 8, 1967, NLA, ORAL TRC 1/341-342, quoted with permission of the Estate of Kylie Tennant

David Carter interview with Elizabeth Harrower, early 1990s, NLA, MS-SAV002403 Series. Cassette Recordings, Box 144, quoted with permission of David Carter

Select bibliography

Jim Davidson interview with Elizabeth Harrower in the Meanjin collection, 1980, NLA, ORAL TRC 5217/14, quoted with permission of Jim Davidson

Giulia Giuffrè interview with Elizabeth Harrower, 1985, ORAL TRC 2525/4, quoted with permission of Giulia Giuffrè

Ken Henderson interview with Kylie Tennant, July 27, 1980, NLA, ORAL TRC 801, quoted with permission of the Estate of Kylie Tennant

Christine Williams interview with Elizabeth Harrower 1986, Christine Williams MS 8065 collection [sound recording], NLA, ORAL TRC 2625/1-3/Recording, NLA, quoted with permission of Christine Williams

Susan Wyndham interviews

Elizabeth Harrower, phone, November 8, 1996, and Sydney, in person, April 11, 2014, April 26, 2017, December 21, 2017
Ellen Ash, phone, March 28, 2023
Judy Brady, email, May 25, 2023
David Carter, phone, August 19, 2024
Stephanie Claire, Sydney, in person, August 6, 2024
Margie Clarke, phone, June 22, 2024
Michael Costigan, Sydney, in person, June 9, 2024
Jill Crossley, phone, April 15, 2025
Barbara Darvall, email, February 18, 2024
John Edwards, email, March 11, 2024
Toni Eyles, email, May 1, 2024
Ulrik Funch, Sydney, in person, June 4, 2024
Brian Galway, phone, March 27, 2023
Helen Garner, email, April 13, 2025
Jane Harris, Sydney, in person, March 27, 2023
Yvonne Harrower, phone, November 20, 2023 and Newcastle, in person, January 4, 2024
Michael Heyward, phone, February 3, 2025
Nesli Karadeniz, Sydney, in person, July 1, 2023
Vrasidas Karalis, email, September 11–12, 2024

Cynthia Kaye, phone, February 14, 2023
Kyrsty Macdonald, phone, April 11, 2024
Fiona McFarlane, email, March 28, 2024
Sally McInerney, Sydney, in person, January 21, 2025
David Malouf, phone, February 24, 2023
Verity Matzoll, Newcastle, in person, January 4, 2024
James Mohr, Sydney, in person, March 27, 2023
Linda Nolte, Hobart, in person, September 6, 2023
Kasavere Nolte-Wilson, phone, May 10, 2024
Jane Novak, Sydney, in person, July 30, 2024
Mary Quinion, phone, March 23, 2023
Andrew Robertson, Sydney, in person, August 24, 2023
Benison Rodd, phone, May 19, 2024
Gabrielle Smith, email, April 9, 2024
Morgan Smith, phone, April 7, 2025
Vivian Smith, phone, June 6, 2023
Thurza Snelson, Newcastle, in person, January 4, 2024
Richard Walsh, email, January 23, 2023
Rodney Wetherell, phone, January 1, 2025
Lesley White, email, March 6, 2024
Michael Wilding, phone, April 4, 2024
Geordie Williamson, phone, June 17, 2024
David Winter, phone, June 11, 2024
Clem Yap, Sydney, in person, August 24, 2023
Salvatore Zofrea, Sydney, in person, August 6, 2024

Editions of Elizabeth Harrower's works

Books
Down in the City:
Cassell, London, 1957
Text Classics, The Text Publishing Company, Melbourne, 2013

The Long Prospect:
Cassell, London, 1958
Sun Books, Melbourne, 1966
Sirius Quality Paperbacks, Angus & Robertson, Sydney, 1979
Text Classics, The Text Publishing Company, Melbourne, 2012

The Catherine Wheel:
Cassell, London, 1960
Sirius Quality Paperbacks, Angus & Robertson, Sydney, 1979
Text Classics, The Text Publishing Company, Melbourne, 2014

The Watch Tower:
Macmillan, London and Melbourne, 1966
Angus & Robertson Classics, Sydney, 1977
Text Classics, The Text Publishing Company, Melbourne, 2012

In Certain Circles:
The Text Publishing Company, Melbourne, 2014

A Few Days in the Country and Other Stories:
The Text Publishing Company, Melbourne, 2015

Short stories

'Lance Harper, His Story':
Australian Letters, Adelaide, vol. 4, no. 2, December 1961
The Vital Decade: Ten Years of Australian Art and Letters, ed. Geoffrey Dutton and Max Harris, Sun Books, Melbourne, 1968

'The Cost of Things':
Summer's Tales 1, ed. Kylie Tennant, Macmillan, Sydney, 1964
Short Stories of Australia: The Moderns, ed. Beatrice Davis, Angus & Robertson, Sydney, 1967
Classic Australian Stories, ed. Judah Waten and Stephen Murray-Smith, Wren, Melbourne, 1974
The Oxford Anthology of Australian Literature, ed. Leonie Kramer and Adrian Mitchell, Oxford University Press, Melbourne, 1985
The Faber Book of Contemporary Australian Short Stories, ed. Murray Bail, Faber, London, 1988

'English Lesson':
Summer's Tales 2, ed. Kylie Tennant, Macmillan, Melbourne, 1965
Australian Writing Today, Penguin, London and Melbourne, 1968
The Penguin Book of Australian Short Stories, ed. Harry Heseltine, Penguin, Melbourne, 1976

'The Beautiful Climate':
Modern Australian Writing, ed. Geoffrey Dutton, Fontana, London, 1966
The Oxford Book of Short Stories, ed. Michael Wilding, Oxford University Press, Melbourne, 1994

'The Retrospective Grandmother':
The Herald, Melbourne, January 3, 1976

'A Few Days in the Country':
Overland, no. 67, 1977

'Another Heartless Band', excerpt from *The Watch Tower*:
Sydney: An Oxford Anthology, ed. Richard Hall, Oxford University Press,
    Melbourne, 2000

'Alice':
The New Yorker, February 2, 2015

'Summertime':
Literary Hub, June 19, 2015

'The City at Night':
The Guardian, October 21, 2015

'The Cornucopia':
Harper's Magazine, October 2015

'It Is Margaret':
Australian Book Review, no. 375, October 2015

'The North Sea':
The Canary Press, issue 8, winter 2015

'The Last Days':
HEAT, series 3, no. 21, September 2025

Essays

'The Short Story: Australia', 'The International Symposium on the Short
    Story', part 3, *Kenyon Review*, vol. 32, no. 4, 1969

'Introduction', *Outback and Beyond: The travels of Cynthia and Sidney
    Nolan*, Angus & Robertson, Sydney, 1994

Notes

Abbreviations
   EH: Elizabeth Harrower
   NLA: National Library of Australia
   SLNSW: State Library of NSW
   SW: Susan Wyndham

All usage, spelling and punctuation are as in the original texts.

Introduction

1 **ST Barnard**: '27,000 adjectives from Outer Mongolia', *Australian Book Review*, December, 1963, quoted in Angela Bennie, *Crème de la Phlegm*, MUP, Melbourne 2006, p. 116
2 **'The only person'**: Elizabeth Harrower to Shirley Hazzard, January 9, 1976, Papers of EH, NLA
3 **'I didn't know'**: Joan London, 'The Only Russian in Sydney', Introduction to Elizabeth Harrower, *The Watch Tower*, The Text Publishing Company, Melbourne, 2012, p. viii
3 **'rescue me from myself'**: SW, 'Ahead of her time but rewards flow 30 years after last novel', *Sydney Morning Herald*, November 9, 1996, p. 16
4 **'Someone asked me'**: SW, 'Elizabeth Harrower doesn't want spoilers to her own novel', *Sydney Morning Herald*, May 3, 2014, online edition
5 **'I always took'**: SW interview with EH, December 21, 2017. She quotes Fiona Wright, 'Stories and True Stories review: The joys of heartbreak and hope with Helen Garner', *Sydney Morning Herald*, December 7, 2017, online edition
5 **'in one of her stories'**: Helen Garner, 'The Art of the Dumb Question', in *True Stories*, The Text Publishing Company, Melbourne, 1996, p. 6
5 **'powers of observation'**: Nadine Gordimer, 'Introduction' to *No Place Like: Selected stories*, Penguin Books, 1978, p. 12

Betty

11 **'hundreds of corrugated iron rooftops'**: EH, *The Long Prospect*, Text Publishing, Melbourne, 2012, p. 7
11 **'I think the emotional truth'**: Jim Davidson interview with EH, May 5, 1980, in *Meanjin* Vol. 39, No. 2, July 1980
12 **'because I don't like Newcastle'**: Hazel de Berg interview with EH, October 18, 1967, transcript, Hazel de Berg collection, NLA
12 **creamy skin**: EH email to Lesley White, March 14, 2017
15 **Vera Deacon**: *Singing Back the River: A Miscellany of Selected Writings by and for Vera Deacon*, Yarnspinners Press Collective, 2019, p. 48
15 **Mayfield East Public School**: some details of the suburb from Cath Chegwidden, *Mighty Mayfield Then and Now: Book 1: The early years*, 2022, and *Book 2: Industry and Change*, 2023, Newey Printing Co & Cath Chegwidden

Notes

15	**'When I was small'**: SW interview with EH, December 21, 2017
15	**'tragic, dirty, patched'**: Giulia Giuffrè interview with EH, recorded 1985, transcript, p. 25, NLA
16	**'three wee witches'**: SW interview with EH, December 21, 2017
16	**Looking back**: Giulia Giuffrè interview, 1985, NLA
17	**'irrational, raucous, bony'**: EH, 'Alice', in *A Few Days in the Country and Other Stories*, The Text Publishing Company, Melbourne, 2025, p. 15
17	**'woke up married'**: *A Few Days in the Country and Other Stories*, p. 22
17	**'demanding, critical, sarcastic'**: *A Few Days in the Country and Other Stories*, p. 29
17	**'two who could never'**: *A Few Days in the Country and Other Stories*, p. 29
17	**'no more pleasing'**: *A Few Days in the Country and Other Stories*, p. 30
17	**'But *I* know'**: *A Few Days in the Country and Other Stories*, p. 31
18	**'She could out-shout'**: EH, 'The Retrospective Grandmother – A Weekend Story', *The Herald*, Melbourne, January 3, 1976, pp. 26–27. All following quotes from this publication.
19	**she lay down on the road**: SW interview with Andrew Robertson, August 24, 2023
19	**'Youth, hard times'**: EH to Frances McInherney, March 9, 1981, Papers of EH, NLA
20	**a legal notice**: *The Sun*, Sydney, March 29, 1937, p. 4
20	**'For my part'**: Divorce papers Francis Sharp Hastings Harrower – Margaret Burns Harrower, 06-11-1936 to 31-08-1937, NSW State Archives Collection
20	**'I know that you'**: Divorce papers Francis Sharp Hastings Harrower – Margaret Burns Harrower, 05-05-1939 to 30-11-1939, NSW State Archives Collection
20	**'I thought we could go'**: SW interview with EH, December 21, 2017
21	**Helen Hughes also filed**: Divorce papers: Helen Hughes – Robert Hughes 23-01-1940 to 23-04-1941, NSW State Archives Collection
21	**'armed neutrality'**: 'Divorce Court', *Newcastle Sun*, October 3, 1940, p. 2
21	**Margaret Harrower**: 'Mayfield woman seeks divorce', *Newcastle Morning Herald and Miners' Advocate*, October 4, 1940, p. 18
22	**an anonymous letter**: 'Suit for divorce dismissed', *Newcastle Sun*, October 4, 1940, p. 2
22	**'halfway mad'**: 'Committed for trial on perjury charge', *Newcastle Sun*, December 9, 1940, p. 2
22	**fined ten pounds**: *Newcastle Herald and Miners Advocate*, February 4, 1941, p. 3
22	**sought her divorce**: Divorce papers, Helen Hughes – Robert Hughes 09-10-1940 to 15-11-1943, NSW State Archives Collection
23	**'I just always kept writing'**: SW interview with EH, December 21, 2017
23	**One of her few friends**: SW interview with Toni Eyles, daughter of Barbara Ward (Johnson), May 1, 2024
23	**her mother's two brothers**: SW interview with EH, December 21, 2017
23	**He would get down**: EH to Peter Firkin, January 11, 1982, Papers of EH, NLA
24	**'These thoughts were always'**: SW interview with EH, December 21, 2017

A shady character

25	**Their divorce was finalised**: Divorce papers Francis Sharp Hastings Harrower – Margaret Burns Harrower 05-04-1940 to 04-09-1941, NSW State Archives Collection
25	**'best in English'**: SW interview with EH, December 21, 2017
26	**gave her address**: Register of Nurses, as at 31st December, 1940, *Government Gazette of the State of New South Wales*, Sydney NSW: 1901–2001, September 16, 1941
27	**He was short**: Royal Navy Registers of Seamen's Services 1848–1939
27	**At eighteen he was**: 1911 England Census

27	**In 1919 he**: Register of firms index, 1903–1922, RH Kempley & Company, public accountant, place 'various', November 25, 1919, and Kempley Martin & Company with Albert Irving Martin
27	**'bright, keen, dark-eyed'**: 'Bitter Pill for Ex-Manager of Sweets College', *Truth*, September 20, 1925, p. 12
28	**Mrs Cohen accused**: 'Confectionery Colleges', *Daily Telegraph*, October 7, 1925, p. 4
28	**'of shady character'**: 'Liberty Sweets Memories Become Bitter: Richard Kempley Appeals and Crashes Heavily', *Truth*, October 18, 1925, p. 5
28	**A country newspaper**: 'Richard's Luck', *Southern Record and Advertiser*, Candelo, NSW, August 11, 1923, p. 2
29	**He swore he hadn't**: 'Scone Police Court', *Scone Advocate*, July 15, 1932, p. 2
29	**He and his brother**: 'Two illicit stills', *Muswellbrook Chronicle*, January 5, 1932, p. 2
29	**Kempley's name was linked**: 'Open Verdict Wickham Fire Inquiry', *Newcastle Morning Herald and Miners' Advocate*, June 30, 1922, p. 14
29	**Olive Beatrice Kempley**: 'House destroyed at lake, Coroner holds inquiry', *Newcastle Sun*, May 31, 1933, p. 7
29	**He was briefly**: *Newcastle Sun*, September 4, 1934, p. 9
30	**'a graceful lace cape'**: 'Artists' Ball, merry throng at Palais Royale', *Newcastle Morning Herald and Miners' Advocate*, July 15, 1936, p. 11
31	**'When Mum talked'**: SW interview with Toni Eyles, May 1, 2024
31	**'I was always good'**: SW interview with EH, December 21, 2017
31	**Throwing snowballs**: EH to David Winter, August 31, 2018
32	**'They would probably'**: 'Black Liquor Prices to USA Servicemen', *The Telegraph*, Brisbane, February 23, 1944, p. 2
33	**They boldly, but unsuccessfully**: 'Minister to show cause', *Courier-Mail*, Brisbane, December 18, 1943, p. 3
33	**'The High Court'**: 'Black Market Liquor', *Australian Worker*, Sydney, June 28, 1944
33	**'dearly loved father'**: Family Notices, *Sydney Morning Herald*, December 1, 1945, p. 29
34	**'everybody was going'**: SW interview with EH, December 21, 2017
34	**She considered following**: all details of her early jobs, SW interview with EH, December 21, 2017
34	**McGinley and Carpenter**: SW interview with Margie Clarke, June 22, 2024
35	**'harried women'**: SW interview with EH, December 21, 2017
35	**'Auntie Betty'**: SW interview with Margie Clarke, June 22, 2024
35	**'like a mother'**: SW interview with Margie Clarke, June 22, 2024
35	**'mad as a hatter'**: EH diary, January 4, 1951, Estate of EH
36	**'The strange silent world'**: EH, 'The City at Night', in *A Few Days in the Country and Other Stories*, p. 39
36	**'felt slighted by'**: EH, 'Summertime', in *A Few Days in the Country and Other Stories*, p. 45
36	**'a dull, tedious'**: SW interview with EH, December 21, 2017
37	**'I spent all my life'**: SW interview with EH, December 21, 2017
37	**'the smell of the downstairs'**: Jessica Anderson, *Tirra Lirra by the River*, Penguin Books Australia, 1990, p. 41
37	**'I was so full'**: SW interview with EH, December 21, 2017
37	**'talked and talked'**: EH diary, January 14, 1951, Estate of EH
37	**'I was so miserable'**: EH diary, January 9, 1951, Estate of EH

Notes

37	**'Mum got through'**: EH diary, January 10, 1951, Estate of EH
38	**In the winter of 1948**: 'Social Chat', *Morning Bulletin*, June 2, 1948, p. 3
38	**'Had it'**: EH diary, January 4, 1951, Estate of EH
38	**'supra-casual'**: EH, 'The Beautiful Climate', in *A Few Days in the Country and Other Stories*, p. 116
39	**'Let me *die*'**: *A Few Days in the Country and Other Stories*, p. 114
39	**'the Old Country'**: *A Few Days in the Country and Other Stories*, p. 117
39	**'Out in the world'**: *A Few Days in the Country and Other Stories*, p. 120
39	**The *New Yorker* editors**: CM Newman letter to Miss Irma Weitzman at Willis Kingsley Wing, with *Redbook* comment attached, December 18, 1961, Papers of EH, NLA.
39	**Harrower herself described**: EH to Shirley Hazzard, August 8, 1984, Papers of Shirley Hazzard, State Library of NSW
39	**'ideal introduction'**: John Colmer, 'Elizabeth Harrower', *Contemporary Novelists*, ed. James Vinson, St James Press, London, 1972, p. 607
39	**'Last news of Kempley'**: *Government Gazette of the State of NSW*, No. 44, March 16, 1951, p. 751

The Old Country

41	**'When you don't'**: EH diary, March 29, 1951, Estate of EH
41	**'I couldn't forget'**: EH diary, March 21, 1951, Estate of EH
41	**'The bottom seemed'**: EH diary, March 31, 1951, Estate of EH
41	**'Mum & UD'**: EH diary, April 16, 1951, Estate of EH
42	**'We asked for bread'**: SW interview with EH, December 21, 2017
42	**'about Russia & Communism'**: EH diary, April 28, 1951, Estate of EH
42	**'Since I've met her'**: EH diary, April 30, 1951, Estate of EH
42	**'tremendously touching'**: EH diary, May 12, 1951, Estate of EH
42	**'I went everywhere'**: SW interview with Andrew Robertson, August 24, 2023
42	**'beautiful Capri'**: EH to Shirley Hazzard, May 4, 1973, Papers of Shirley Hazzard, SLNSW
43	**Cammeray**: 15 Cowdroy Ave, Cammeray was the Kempleys' address in the shipping records, January 25, 1952, p. 6, National Archives of Australia NAA K269
43	**'I was so completely'**: EH diary, July 25, 1951, Estate of EH
44	**'There was a beautiful'**: EH email to Lesley White, undated, courtesy of Lesley White
44	**a book of Scottish ballads**: EH to Shirley Hazzard, November 21, 1984, Papers of Shirley Hazzard, SLNSW
44	**The youngest, Anne**: Lesley White email to SW, March 6, 2024. Many family details courtesy of Lesley White.
45	**'a terrible person'**: Hazel de Berg interview with Margaret Dick, August 22, 1969, Hazel de Berg Collection, DeB 391, transcript, p. 2, NLA
45	**'tremendously conservative'**: Hazel de Berg interview with Margaret Dick, p. 1
45	**Instead she studied**: EH eulogy for Margaret Dick, March 2014, courtesy Lesley White
45	**James Dick's father**: Lesley White email to SW, March 6, 2024
46	**'I had never'**: SW interview with EH, December 21, 2017
46	**'The Church of Scotland'**: SW interview with EH, December 21, 2017
46	**The first story**: EH to Elizabeth McMahon, June 6, 2016, cited in *Elizabeth Harrower*, ed. Elizabeth McMahon and Brigitta Olubas, Sydney University Press, 2017, p. 136

46	**'was ghastly'**: 'Local setting for new novel', *Sunday Telegraph*, September 11, 1966, p. 75	
48	**it ran in the issue**: Margaret Dick, 'The Gift of Knowledge', *New Statesman and Nation, The Week-end Review*, October 10, 1953, pp. 414–416	
48	**'confounded thing'**: SW interview with EH, December 21, 2017	

Elizabeth Harrower

49	**She wrote at night**: Jim Davidson interview with EH, *Meanjin* 1980
50	**'a little love song'**: 'Ahead of her time but rewards flow 30 years after last novel', SW, *Sydney Morning Herald*, November 9, 1996, p. 16
50	**To another she said**: Pat Rolfe, 'Harrowing work', *The Bulletin*, November 1, 1988, p. 120
51	**'Antonia Reid had'**: Juliet O'Hea to EH, April 9, 1957, Papers of EH, NLA
51	**'desolately aware'**: EH, undated travel article, unpublished, Papers of EH, NLA
51	**'Her neighbours'**: Kensington and Chelsea Electoral Register 1958
52	**'Sleeping Beauty'**: Delia Falconer, 'Oblivion at the Edges', Introduction to *Down in the City* by EH, The Text Publishing Company, Melbourne, 2013
53	**'Sunlight exploded'**: EH, *Down in the City*, The Text Publishing Company, Melbourne, 2013, p. 280
53	**'The author has'**: 'Three Small Worlds', *Times Literary Supplement*, August 2, 1957, Papers of EH, NLA
53	**'Shy Est married'**: John Metcalf, 'Change for the Better', unidentified UK newspaper clipping, Papers of EH, NLA
53	**'vague and sketchy'**: 'Novels in Brief', *The Bulletin*, undated clipping, p. 59, Papers of EH, NLA
54	**'Having stated that'**: Ray Mathew, 'City Charms', *Sydney Morning Herald*, October 19, 1957, p. 13
55	**'Emily turned'**: EH, *The Long Prospect*, The Text Publishing Company, Melbourne, 2012, p. 224
55	**'a stinker'**: Paul Scott to EH, July 11, 1957, Papers of EH, NLA
56	**Fortunately that was**: EH to Paul Scott, July 15, 1957, Papers of EH, NLA
56	**'I was really astonished'**: EH to Barbara Ward (Johnson), July 8, 1958, courtesy of Toni Eyles
56	**'prominent place'**: Sidney J Baker, 'Tender Australian Tale of a Lonely Child', *Sydney Morning Herald*, June 28, 1958, p. 12
57	**the second Miles Franklin**: 'Author wins £500 award', *Sydney Morning Herald*, April 23, 1959
58	**'I like comparatively'**: EH to Barbara Ward (Johnson), July 8, 1958, courtesy of Toni Eyles
58	**'have to trail on'**: EH to Barbara Ward (Johnson), July 8, 1958
59	**'self-contained village'**: EH, *The Catherine Wheel*, The Text Publishing Company, Melbourne, 2014, p. 83. All quotations from this edition.
61	**'London was paradise'**: SW interview with EH, December 21, 2017
61	**'She read all'**: Jim Davidson interview with EH, *Meanjin* 1980
61	**'all the people'**: EH to Shirley Hazzard, December 10, 1972, Papers of Shirley Hazzard, SLNSW
61	**'To as much as dispute'**: EH to Shirley Hazzard, March 6, 1975, Papers of Shirley Hazzard, SLNSW
61	**'Years ago I stopped'**: EH to Shirley Hazzard, December 29, 1974, Papers of Shirley Hazzard, SLNSW

61	**'the forbidding'**: Geordie Williamson, *The Burning Library*, The Text Publishing Company, 2012, p. 160
63	**'just seemed to make'**: SW interview with EH, December 21, 2017
64	**'began to feel'**: Patricia Rolfe, 'Harrowing work', *The Bulletin*, November 1, 1988, p. 120
65	**She told the writer**: EH to Shirley Hazzard, September 25, 1973, Papers of Shirley Hazzard, SLNSW
65	**'The charisma'**: quoted in Ramona Koval, 'Playing with Fire', Introduction to Elizabeth Harrower, *The Catherine Wheel*, The Text Publishing Company, Melbourne, 2014, p. xii
65	**'the gambling losses'**: EH, *The Catherine Wheel*, p. 268
66	**'as though it were'**: Hazel de Berg interview with Margaret Dick, August 1969, recording tape 391 (1), transcript, p. 4, NLA
66	**'should have overthrown'**: EH, letter to the editor, 'Suez: For and Against', *Sunday Times*, November 11, 1956
67	**'real talent for'**: reviews by JB Priestley and others quoted on the back cover of Margaret Dick, *Rhyme or Reason*, William Heinemann, London, 1958
67	**'mature in form'**: review of Margaret Dick, *Point of Return*, 'Books', *The Bulletin*, August 6, 1958, p. 59
68	**'But he and Mum'**: EH to Barbara Ward (Johnson), July 8, 1958, courtesy of Toni Eyles
68	**sales of 2576 copies**: David Bolt to EH, August 11, 1959, Papers of EH, NLA
69	**'The Last Days'**: EH, 'The Last Days', unpublished short story, undated, Papers of EH, NLA

Homecoming

70	**'Women's Letters'**, *The Bulletin*, Vol. 80, No. 4142, July 1, 1959, p. 56
70	**'I like the life'**: 'Cousins have success with novels', newspaper clipping with no details, Papers of EH, NLA
70	**'You'd soon run out'**: 'Cousins write novels', newspaper clipping with no details, Papers of EH, NLA
71	**'We couldn't stay'**: EH to Michelle de Kretser, March 12, 2019, courtesy of Michelle de Kretser
72	**'the stock response'**: EH, 'Young Rebels in Britain and The U.S.', review of Gene Feldman and Max Gartenberg eds., *Protest*, Souvenir Press, London, 1959, *Sydney Morning Herald*, September 19, 1959
72	**'Writing about books'**: EH to David Marr, June 22, 1994, Papers of David Marr, NLA
72	**They were among**: 'Women's Letters, *The Bulletin*, December 30, 1959, p. 56
73	**'familiar and well-tried'**: 'Censorship', *The Bulletin*, November 2, 1963, p. 39
73	**'Deletions are always'**: John Hetherington, 'Elizabeth Harrower: The Student Suddenly Began Writing Novels, *Age Literary Supplement*, April 29, 1961, p. 18
74	**'emerge with abrupt'**: 'Spoiled Beauties', *Times Literary Supplement*, October 28, 1960
74	**'really excellent'**: 'Salt in Your Eyes', Olga Stringfellow, *John O'London's*, December 29, 1960, p. 817
74	**'A strange one'**: book review, *Belfast Telegraph*, November 3, 1960
74	**'A fine study'**: book review, *Evening Express*, Aberdeen, October 28, 1960
74	**'Life in London'**: EH to JM Douglas Pringle, December 5, 1960, Papers of EH, NLA

74	**Pringle wrote**: JM Douglas Pringle to EH, December 15, 1960, Papers of EH, NLA
74	**'clumsy and irritatingly'**: Nancy Keesing, 'Australians in London', *The Bulletin*, December 14, 1960
75	**'no secondhand emotions'**: Barbara Jefferis, 'Wisdom from the Well of Anguish', *Sydney Morning Herald*, December 31, 1960
75	**'one of the most'**: 'Australiana', *The Sun*, February 8, 1961, p. 32
75	**'gift for sensitive'**: 'Good Books Lately', *Australian Women's Mirror*, March 15, 1961
75	**Harrower was the youngest**: Sidney J Baker, 'Outstanding Part in Our Literature', Australia Unlimited special feature, *Sydney Morning Herald*, 1961
75	**This came about**: EH to Max Harris, August 30, 1961, Papers of EH, NLA
75	**'many authors whose work'**: John Hetherington, 'Elizabeth Harrower: The Student Suddenly Began Writing Novels', *Age Literary Supplement*, April 29, 1961, p. 18
77	**'The North Sea'**: this story was first published in 2015 in *Canary Press* magazine and in *A Few Days in the Country and Other Stories*
77	**'sensitive, gentle'**: SW interview with Jill Crossley, April 15, 2025
77	**he reported rejections**: Willis Kingsley Wing to EH, December 11, 1961, Papers of EH, NLA
77	**The *New Yorker* passed**: CM Newman, *The New Yorker*, to Miss Irma Weitzman, Willis Kingsley Wing, February 8, 1962, Papers of EH, NLA
77	**Wing advised**: Willis Kingsley Wing to EH, June 16, 1961, Papers of EH, NLA
78	**she told Wing**: EH to Willis Kingsley Wing, June 27, 1963, Papers of EH, NLA
78	**Eventually he wrote back**: David Bolt to EH, May 9, 1960, Papers of EH, NLA
79	**Harrower entered**: EH to Willis Kingsley Wing, June 1, 1962, Papers of EH, NLA
79	**'the least original'**: EH to Willis Kingsley Wing, June 27, 1962, Papers of EH, NLA
79	**'Is there a paying market?'**: EH, 'The Short Story: Australia', in 'The International Symposium on the Short Story, Part 3' *Kenyon Review*, Vol. 31, No. 4, 1969, pp. 479–485
80	**via Geoffrey Dutton**: George Lunning to Geoffrey Dutton, December 21, 1967, Papers of EH, NLA
80	**she refused**: EH to Laurie Hergenhan, July 22, 1981, Papers of EH, NLA

New connections

81	**'reputation of fractiousness'**: Sidney John Baker by WS Ransom, *Australian Dictionary of Biography*, Vol. 13, 1993, John Ritchie and Diane Langmore eds, Melbourne University Press, Carlton
81	**a deflating note**: Sidney J Baker to EH, January 9, 1961 (he wrongly wrote 1960), Papers of EH, NLA
82	**Harrower dared to write**: EH to Sir Allen Lane, July 5, 1961, Papers of EH, NLA
82	**'*The Long Prospect* represents'**: Max Harris to EH, July 4, 1961, Papers of EH, NLA
82	**'of singularly intellectual'**: Max Harris to EH, September 6, 1961, Papers of EH, NLA
82	**She replied**: EH to Max Harris, July 26, 1961, Papers of EH, NLA
82	**she had dreamt of him**: EH to Max Harris, October 26, 1961, Papers of EH, NLA
83	**'perfunctory critical attention'**: Max Harris, 'The Novels of Elizabeth Harrower', *Australian Letters*, Vol. 4, No. 2, December 1961, p. 16
83	**'Olaf Ruhen sang'**: SW interview with EH, December 21, 2017

Notes

84	**The week-long program**: The Adelaide Festival of Arts, Writers Week program, March 19–25, 1962, <wakefieldpress.com.au>
84	**newspaper journalist**: SW interview with Ted Smith's daughter, Sydney bookseller Morgan Smith, April 7, 2025
84	**Harrower wrote to Harris**: EH to Max Harris, May 15, 1962, Papers of EH, NLA
85	**'At his best Mungo MacCallum'**: ST Barnard, '27,000 adjectives from Outer Mongolia', *Australian Book Review*, December, 1963, quoted in Angela Bennie, *Creme de la Phlegm*, MUP, 2006, pp. 115–116. Mungo MacCallum was father of the political journalist Mungo MacCallum.
85	**'abortive attempts'**: EH to Max Harris, August 8, 1962, Papers of EH, NLA
86	**'both very charming people'**: Ken Henderson interview with Kylie Tennant, July 27, 1980, transcript, 801/2/9, NLA
87	**she dusted the display**: EH to Margaret Dick, January 12, 1964, Papers of EH, NLA
87	**She impressed them**: SW interview with Mary Quinion, March 23, 2023
87	**'like living on'**: SW interview with Ellen Ash (née Nixon), March 28, 2023
87	**'I would not have taken'**: Ellen Nixon and Mary Quinion, 'An Interview with Elizabeth Harrower', *Outlook Literary Magazine of the Writers' Group of Alexander Mackie College* 1963, pp. 22–24
88	**'the only person'**: Tony Rudkin to Kylie Tennant, April 8, 1963, Papers of Kylie Tennant, NLA
88	**'lying on her bed'**: Nancy Phelan, *Writing Round the Edges: A selective memoir*, University of Queensland Press, Brisbane, 2003, p. 121
88	**'We were friends'**: EH to David Carter, March 7, 1989, Papers of EH, NLA
88	**'the first Australian writer'**: David Carter ed., *Introduction to Judah Waten: Fiction, Memoir, Criticism*, University of Queensland Press, Brisbane, 1998, p. ix
89	**'I am a clumsy writer'**: Judah Waten to EH, September 7, 1963, Papers of EH, NLA
89	**'new and surprising'**: EH to Judah Waten, November 5, 1963, Papers of Judah Waten, NLA
90	**'I haven't any doubt'**: 'Rache' Lovat Dickson to Kylie Tennant, November 6, 1963, Papers of Kylie Tennant, NLA
90	**'devoid of any'**: Judah Waten to Kylie Tennant, November 26, 1964, Papers of Kylie Tennant, NLA
90	**'she wants to strike'**: Lewis Rodd to Judah Waten, April 24, 1964, Papers of Kylie Tennant, NLA
91	**'The plots may not'**: Kylie Tennant to Mrs MED Moore, April 26, 1966, Papers of Kylie Tennant, 1966, NLA
91	**Harrower liked to say**: David Marr, ed. *Patrick White Letters*, Random House Australia, Sydney, 1996, paperback, p. 637
92	**'down by the cowbails'**: Kylie Tennant, 'Writes in "Stained Glass"', *Sydney Morning Herald*, September 26, 1956
93	**'pretty appalling'**: quoted from EH memoir of friendship with Patrick White, written 1992, unpublished, Estate of EH
93	**'that warren where'**: Patrick White to EH, May 1, 1972, Papers of EH, NLA
94	**'Silly things'**: Margaret Kempley to EH, July 18, 1965, Estate of EH
94	**'I know exactly'**: Margaret Kempley to EH, November 30, 1964, Estate of EH
95	**'Privet Hedge Rodd'**: Kylie Tennant, *The Missing Heir*, Macmillan, Melbourne, 1986, p. 144
95	**Bimble Box**: *The Missing Heir*, p. 158. Some other family details also taken from this autobiography.

96	**'I can't think'**: Ken Henderson interview with Kylie Tennant, July 27, 1980, transcript, 801/2/9, NLA
96	**'Elizabeth is typing'**: Kylie Tennant to Mavis Cribb, September 27, 1968, quoted in Jane Grant, *Kylie Tennant: A life*, NLA, Canberra, 2005, p. 100

The Watch Tower

97	**'Now that your father's gone–'**: EH, *The Watch Tower*, The Text Publishing Company, Melbourne, 2012, p. 5
98	**'an almost defunct'**: *The Watch Tower*, p. 46
98	**55 Shellcove Road**: Honda in Neutral Bay identified in Brigid Rooney, 'White, fierce, shocked, tearless: *The Watch Tower* and the Electric Interior', in Elizabeth McMahon and Brigitta Olubas eds, *Elizabeth Harrower*, p. 88
98	**'"Bluebeard!" Felix cried'**: EH, *The Watch Tower*, p. 72
99	**'to be in the presence'**: *The Watch Tower*, p. 210
100	**'the only Russian'**: *The Watch Tower*, p. 108
100	**'up into the watch-tower'**: John Donne, from 'The Second Anniversary', *Songs and Sonets*, 1601, <bartleby.com>
101	**at least one friend**: SW interview with Andrew Robertson, August 24, 2023
101	**'a monster'**: EH to Michelle de Kretser, March 12, 2019, courtesy of Michelle de Kretser
101	**'their best with a situation'**: Kylie Tennant, '*The Watchtower* by Elizabeth Harrower', undated report, Papers of Kylie Tennant, NLA
102	**'Her work has reached'**: Kylie Tennant to Alan Maclean, June 14, 1964, Papers of Kylie Tennant, NLA
102	**'Whatever my books'**: EH to Michael Horniman, March 2, 1965, Papers of EH, NLA
102	**'having a hack'**: EH to Robert Cross, May 13, 1968, Papers of EH, NLA
103	**'book of the week'**: Julian Croft, review of *The Long Prospect*, *Newcastle Morning Herald and Miners' Advocate*, April 16, 1966
103	**'a diluted Lolita'**: Richard Murphett, '*The Long Prospect*', in *Lot's Wife*, March 15, 1966
104	**'I was totally blind'**: EH to Alan Maclean, May 13, 1966, Papers of EH, NLA
104	**'Elizabeth is of course'**: Nicholas Byam Shaw to Kylie Tennant, January 13, 1966, Papers of Kylie Tennant, NLA
104	**'very subtle'**: Kylie Tennant to Robert Cross, August 2, 1966, Papers of Kylie Tennant, NLA
105	**'very jolly' quote**: Nicholas Byam Shaw to Kylie Tennant, August 23, 1966, Papers of Kylie Tennant, NLA
105	**Gavin Souter reported**: Gavin Souter, 'Data', *Sydney Morning Herald*, October 24, 1966
105	**'a patient, sensitive'**: AR Chisholm, 'Two Sisters', *The Age*, December 10, 1966
106	**she moaned to Margaret**: EH to Margaret Dick, 'Monday', undated note, Papers of EH, NLA
106	**'It's necessary to have'**: 'Commas caused full stop', *Australian Women's Weekly*, August 3, 1966
106	**'Because I am interested'**: *Australian Women's Weekly*, August 3, 1966
106	**'flippant off the typewriter'**: Gavin Souter, 'Data', *Sydney Morning Herald*, July 1, 1966
107	**'My ideas for a novel'**: Stuart Sayers, *The Age*, December 10, 1966
107	**'If you had rung'**: Judah Waten to EH, undated note on *Age* clipping, Papers of EH, NLA

107	**'powerful, intelligent and very well'**: Ronan Farren, 'Best of the year at home', *Irish Independent*, January 14, 1967
107	**'This excellent novel'**: Com Brogan, 'Recent Fiction', *Yorkshire Post*, September 29, 1966
107	**'extraordinarily compelling'**: LJ Clancy, 'A lively Australian first', *The Australian*, March 18, 1967
108	**'To create a monster'**: HG Kippax, 'Of good and evil – in Neutral Bay', *Sydney Morning Herald*, November 19, 1966, p. 15
108	**'I admire both writers'**: 'Local setting for new novel', *Sunday Telegraph*, September 1, 1966
108	**'Elizabeth Harrower's prose'**: Geoffrey Lehmann, 'Portrait in Black', *The Bulletin*, November 12, 1966
109	**'I can't help hoping'**: 'Morning Call', ABC Radio, national broadcast, April 18, 1967
109	**'the first Australian'**: Max Harris, 'In the land of mad words', *The Australian*, July 2, 1966
109	**'no more memorable'**: HG Kippax, best books of the year, *Sydney Morning Herald*, December 17, 1966
109	**an impressive list**: Alec Chisholm and Neil Jillett, 'Best novels of the year', *The Age*, December 9, 1966
109	**'a simple little plot'**: Stephen Murray-Smith, 'Books for comment', No. 85, ABC-2FC, December 23, 1966
109	**Max Harris named**: Max Harris, 'Backing the locals', *The Australian*, December 10, 1966
109	**'The Watch Tower is'**: Nancy Keesing, 'Writer and Reader', *Southerly*, No. 2, 1967, pp. 139–41
110	**'writers in Australia'**: Geoffrey Dutton, 'The Struggle for Prose', *The Bulletin*, December 31, 1966
111	**'always felt a little sad'**: EH to Alan Maclean, March 11, 1971
111	**'wrote in his diary'**: David Marr, *Patrick White: A life*, Alfred A. Knopf, New York, 1992, p. 464
112	**'one of the few creative'**: Patrick White to Juliet O'Hea, May 7, 1967, quoted in David Marr, *Patrick White: A life*, p. 464
112	**after a tip-off**: Kylie Tennant to Alan Maclean, April 27, 1967, Papers of Kylie Tennant, NLA
112	**'if he had to choose'**: Tom Maschler to Juliet O'Hea, January 5, 1968, quoted in David Marr, *Patrick White: A life*, p. 489
112	**'highly praised worst-seller'**: Richard Cameron, 'The Art of Being a Writer', *The Bulletin*, July 6, 1968

Allies and impediments

113	**an outraged letter**: Margaret Dick, Letter to the Editors, *Australian Book Review*, April 22, 1967
114	**'the shock of Scotland'**: EH to Shirley Hazzard, November 4, 1972, Papers of Shirley Hazzard, SLNSW
114	**'in the eye of'**: Margaret Dick, 'Southern Latitude', unpublished manuscript, p. 1, Papers of EH, NLA
115	**'didn't come off'**: Elizabeth Harrower to Shirley Hazzard, October 31, 2000, Papers of Shirley Hazzard, SLNSW
115	**'beautifully constructed'**: Joyce Burnard, 'Desires and Scruples', *The Bulletin*, January 30, 1965, p. 40

116	**'quite a revealing experience'**:	Hazel de Berg interview with Margaret Dick, recording 390, side 2, transcript, p. 2, NLA
116	**Information on Margaret Dick at SCEGGS Redlands**:	Redlands Archives, Cremorne, NSW
117	**'five feet 10 inches'**:	John Hetherington, 'Elizabeth Harrower: The Student Who Suddenly Began Writing Novels', *Age Literary Supplement*, April 29, 1961, p. 18
117	**'the disposition of'**:	EH, eulogy for Margaret Dick, March 2014, courtesy of Lesley White
117	**'lovely people'**:	Lesley White email to SW, February 17, 2024
118	**'visitor from overseas'**:	Dorothy Green, 'Dubious compliments', *The Australian*, October 15, 1966, p. 10
118	**'We are extremely different'**:	Hazel de Berg interview with Margaret Dick, August 22, 1969, recording 391, side 1, transcript, p. 5, NLA
118	**'a political journalist'**:	Hazel De Berg interview with Kylie Tennant, December 8, 1967, tape 342, side 1, NLA
118	**she recruited Harrower**:	April Hersey, 'Back to the Battling', *The Bulletin*, April 29, 1967, p. 32
118	**'full of penicillin'**:	Kylie Tennant to Robert Cross, November 4, 1966, Papers of Kylie Tennant, NLA
119	**'I was v. pleased'**:	EH to Shirley Hazzard, November 4, 1972, Papers of Shirley Hazzard, SLNSW
120	***The Watch Tower* was reviewed**:	Professor John Colmer, 'Feminine Achievements', *Australian Book Review*, September, 1966, pp. 218–219
121	**'Max's professor'**:	EH to Nicholas Byam Shaw, October 5, 1966, Papers of EH, NLA
121	**'extremely congenial'**:	EH to Shirley Hazzard, November 16, 1966, Papers of Shirley Hazzard, SLNSW
121	**'told in your'**:	Shirley Hazzard to EH, June 24, 1967, Papers of EH, NLA
122	**'I have a gentle'**:	EH to Shirley Hazzard', December 13, 1967, Papers of Shirley Hazzard, SLNSW
122	**'My friends were ready'**:	EH to Shirley Hazzard', December 13, 1967
123	**The eight fellowships**:	'Woman writer gets $6,000', *Courier-Mail*, Brisbane, October 28, 1967
123	**'the future seems dark'**:	EH to Shirley Hazzard, December 13, 1967, Papers of Shirley Hazzard, SLNSW
123	**social visit by Macmillan**:	Robert Cross to David Marr, June 16, 1989, Papers of David Marr, NLA, described in Marr, *Patrick White: A life*, p. 488
123	**In a personal letter**:	Harold Macmillan to EH, February 22, 1968, Papers of EH, NLA
123	**'marvellously difficult'**:	EH to Robert Cross, May 13, 1968, Papers of EH, NLA
124	**Roddy sent daily letters**:	Lewis Rodd to Kylie Tennant, 'Ash Wednesday, 1970', Papers of Kylie Tennant, NLA
125	**'an eternal place'**:	EH to Kylie Tennant, after Ernie Metcalfe's death, undated, Papers of Kylie Tennant, NLA
125	**'too moody and descriptive'**:	EH to Helen Frizell, September 24, 1968, courtesy of Frizell's niece, Sally Gibson
125	**'Frizell quoted at length'**:	Helen Frizell, 'Goodbye to the rent and Diamond Head', *Sydney Morning Herald*, October 31, 1968
126	**'so hot and dry'**:	EH article, 'Diamond Head', manuscript courtesy of Sally Gibson
126	**As a schoolgirl**:	Benison Rodd, 'The Curse of Cliff View', unpublished manuscript, Papers of Benison Rodd, NLA

Notes

Orphan Betty

127	**'But Frank Harrower was alive'**: details of Frank's second marriage and family from SW interviews with his daughter, Yvonne Harrower, November 20, 2023 and January 4, 2024	
128	**'He called me'**: EH to Margaret Dick, January 19, 1965, Papers of EH, NLA	
129	**'very plotty and extraverted'**: EH to Michael Horniman, July 11, 1970, Papers of EH, NLA	
129	**'Everyone was heartily sick'**: EH to Shirley Hazzard, August 16, 1971, Papers of Shirley Hazzard, SLNSW	
129	a **'genius' specialist**: EH to Judah Waten, April 15, 1970, Papers of Judah Waten, NLA	
129	**In her final report**: EH to Mr WR Cumming, secretary, Commonwealth Literary Fund, Prime Minister's Department, June 9, 1970, Papers of EH, NLA	
130	**'a practically flawless book'**: EH to Margaret Dick, March 9, 1970, Papers of EH, NLA	
130	**'not by temperament'**: CH Derrick, Reader Report, January 20, 1963, The Macmillan Archive, Macmillan Publishers International Ltd	
130	**'an interesting and perhaps'**: CH Derrick, Reader Report, June 25, 1965, The Macmillan Archive, Macmillan Publishers International Ltd	
131	**'It doesn't help'**: EH to Judah Waten, September 29, 1970, Papers of Judah Waten, NLA	
132	**'I took your advice'**: EH to Judah Waten, September 29, 1970	
132	**unpublished until 2015**: EH, 'It Is Margaret', in *A Few Days in the Country and Other Stories*, pp. 165–181	
133	**'I only feel I knocked myself out'**: SW interview with EH, December 21, 2017	
133	**give it the organic 'something'**: EH to Michael Horniman, September 28, 1970, Papers of EH, NLA	
134	**'Whether it will be'**: EH to Shirley Hazzard, January 10, 1971, Papers of Shirley Hazzard, SLNSW	
134	**he had collapsed**: EH to Judah Waten, March 17, 1971, Papers of Judah Waten, NLA	
134	**ruptured abdominal aortic aneurysm**: Richard Herbert Kempley death certificate, London, January 22, 1971, Probate Papers, NSW State Archives Collection	
135	**'I did my best'**: EH to Shirley Hazzard, March 19, 1971, Papers of Shirley Hazzard, SLNSW	
135	**'the exciting news'**: Shirley Hazzard and Francis Steegmuller to EH, December 7, 1970, Papers of EH, NLA	
135	**'a more distilled'**: Report on *In Certain Circles* for Macmillan by CH Derrick, March 19, 1971, The Macmillan Archive, Macmillan Publishers International Ltd	
136	**'Your assessment is'**: EH to Alan Maclean, April 2, 1971, Papers of EH, NLA	
136	**'Next time, I must'**: EH to Michael Horniman, April 5, 1971, Papers of EH, NLA	
136	**Maclean admitted**: Alan Maclean to EH, April 14, 1971, Papers of EH, NLA	
137	**'so kindly, such considerate'**: EH to Shirley Hazzard, April 21, 1971, Papers of Shirley Hazzard, SLNSW	
137	**'That's when I decided'**: SW interview with EH, April 26, 2017	
137	**She wasn't sure why**: EH to Shirley Hazzard, March 24, 1971, Papers of Shirley Hazzard, SLNSW	
139	**'It was often suggested'**: EH, *In Certain Circles*, The Text Publishing Company, Melbourne, 2014, p. 248	
139	**'What I do understand'**: *In Certain Circles*, pp. 192–193	

140	**'sitting at death-beds'**: EH to Judah Waten, November 5, 1963, Papers of Judah Waten, NLA
140	**Kit Hazzard was 'pre-suicide'**: EH to Margaret Dick, March 10, 1970, Papers of EH, NLA
141	**'one morning I woke up'**: EH, *In Certain Circles*, p. 239
141	**'The universe was hostile'**: EH, 'A Few Days in the Country', in *A Few Days in the Country and Other Stories*, p. 185
141	**'suicide thought of her'**: *A Few Days in the Country and Other Stories*, p. 189
141	**'Caroline's small valley'**: *A Few Days in the Country and Other Stories*, p. 196
142	**In Australia he left**: Richard Herbert Kempley, date of death 19-01-1971, probate granted 01-03-1972, NRS-13660-63-189-Series 4_726547, NSW State Archives Collection
142	**Margaret Kempley left everything**: Margaret Burns Kempley, date of death 13-09-1970, probate granted 15-01-1971, NRS-13660-60-231-Series 4_703367, NSW State Archives Collection
143	**'this is my house'**: Margaret Dick, 'Southern Latitude', unpublished manuscript, p. 89, Papers of EH, NLA
144	**'an enormous amount'**: Patrick White to Geoffrey Dutton, July 9, 1972, Papers of David Marr, NLA
144	**'I am rather wishing myself'**: EH to Judah Waten, April 19, 1971, Papers of Judah Watern, NLA
144	**'Elizabeth was standing'**: SW interview with Yvonne Harrower, November 20, 2023

La vie bohème

149	**'immensely likeable'**: EH to Shirley Hazzard, December 13, 1967, Papers of Shirley Hazzard, SLNSW
149	**'forthright and intelligent'**: Patrick White to David Moore, September 15, 1958, quoted in David Marr, *Patrick White: A life*, pp. 343–344
150	**'Harrower is loved'**: Shirley Hazzard to EH, June 26, 1971, Papers of EH, NLA
150	**'alarmed to hear'**: Patrick White to EH, August 20, 1971, Papers of EH, NLA
150	**'written two poems'**: EH to Shirley Hazzard, December 13, 1971, Papers of Shirley Hazzard, SLNSW
151	**'Heavens! I'll be silent'**: EH to Margaret Dick, 'Fairstar – Tuesday', undated, January 1972, Papers of EH, NLA
151	**'clammy pervasiveness'**: EH to Margaret Dick, February 19, 1972, Papers of EH, NLA
151	**'being a trial to you'**: EH to Margaret Dick, 'Fairstar – Monday', undated, Jan-February 1972, Papers of EH, NLA
151	**'I'm not at the moment'**: EH to Margaret Dick, 'Fairstar – Monday'
152	**Conrad's *Nostromo***: in 1970 Harrower gave Patrick White a copy of *Nostromo*, which left him 'breathless at times with admiration and delight' and led him to read more Conrad. Patrick White to EH, February 24, 1971, Papers of EH, NLA
152	**'Leslie's accomplishments'**: EH to Margaret Dick, Fairstar, January 11, 1972, Papers of EH, NLA
152	**'Omar's bowl'**: refers to 'And that inverted Bowl they call the Sky' from *The Rubaiyat of Omar Khayyam*, Macmillan & Co., London, 1903, p. 51
152	**'It's strange and exciting'**: EH to Margaret Dick, February 2, 1972, Papers of EH, NLA
153	**'Heaven knows if'**: EH to Margaret Dick, January 29, 1972, Papers of EH, NLA

154	**'I saw the famous'**: EH to Margaret Dick, February 24, 1972, Papers of EH, NLA
154	**'She is a tall lady'**: EH to Margaret Dick, March 22, 1972, Papers of EH, NLA
154	**'Anyway, they are'**: EH to Margaret Dick, March 18, 1972, Papers of EH, NLA
155	**'I wouldn't like you'**: EH to Margaret Dick, March 18, 1972, Papers of EH, NLA
155	**'white wine, hilarity'**: EH to Shirley Hazzard, July 26, 1972, Papers of Shirley Hazzard, SLNSW
155	**Shirley's friend Patricia Clarke**: Brigitta Olubas, *Shirley Hazzard: A writing life*, Virago, London, 2022, p. 176
156	**'We got on well'**: Christine Williams interview with EH 1980, Christine Williams MS 8065 collection [sound recording], ORAL TRC 2625/1-3/Recording, NLA
156	**'You have a remarkable'**: Christina Stead to EH, November 6, 1969, in RG Geering ed., *Christina Stead, A Web of Friendship: Selected Letters (1928–1973)*, Angus & Robertson, 1992, p. 36
156	**'rather forbidding'**: Patrick White to EH, March 19, 1972, in David Marr, ed., *Patrick White Letters*, Random House Australia, Sydney, 1994, p. 396
156	**'Higher Junta of'**: Patrick White, Letters to the Editor, *Sydney Morning Herald*, July 13, 1967, p. 2
157	**'She really loves men'**: EH to Margaret Dick, March 30, 1972, Papers of EH, NLA
157	**'Pretty horrific they are'**: EH to Margaret Dick, March 30, 1972
157	**'I had a letter from one'**: EH to Christina Stead, Wednesday, undated, 1972, Papers of Christina Stead, NLA
158	**'the eclipse, the decay'**: David Cleaver to EH, February 28, 1972, Papers of EH, NLA
158	**'The long-sustained'**: EH to Christina Stead, Wednesday, undated, 1972, Papers of Christina Stead, NLA
159	**'Alan is an angel'**: EH to Margaret Dick, March 18, 1972, Papers of EH, NLA
159	**'vast gulfs'**: EH to Margaret Dick, March 18, 1972
159	**'faintly' like Richard Kempley**: EH to Margaret Dick, March 22, 1972, Papers of EH, NLA
159	**'poor old thing'**: EH to Margaret Dick, June 6, 1972, Papers of EH, NLA
160	**'Awfully good'**: EH to Margaret Dick, March 22, 1972, Papers of EH, NLA
161	**'was extremely beautiful'**: EH to Margaret Dick, March 30, 1972, Papers of EH, NLA
161	**'Said it was a chef d'oeuvre'**: EH to Margaret Dick, March 18, 1972, Papers of EH, NLA
161	**'What of the Nolans?'**: Patrick White to EH, June 1, 1972, Papers of EH, NLA
161	**'was amazed and irritated'**: EH to Margaret Dick, May 8, 1972, Papers of EH, NLA
162	**'I've been insulted!'**: EH to Margaret Dick, May 8, 1972
162	**'She had been insulted'**: EH, 'English Lesson', in *A Few Days in the Country and Other Stories*, p. 158
162	**'exactly the same'**: EH to Margaret Dick, May 11, 1972, Papers of EH, NLA
162	**'I thought I was having'**: EH to Margaret Dick, May 11, 1972
162	**'I feel bound'**: EH to Margaret Dick, May 31, 1972, Papers of EH, NLA
163	**'the prettiest, most packed'**: EH to Margaret Dick, June 11, 1972, Papers of EH, NLA
164	**'enormous light eyes'**: EH to Margaret Dick, May 18, 1972, Papers of EH, NLA
164	**'wanted to know'**: EH to Margaret Dick, June 11, 1972, Papers of EH, NLA
164	**'you just had to make'**: EH to Margaret Dick, July 12, 1972, Papers of EH, NLA
164	**'it would be better'**: Patrick White to EH, July 16, 1972, Papers of EH, NLA

165	**He asked to read**:	Richard Scott Simon to EH, July 13, 1972, Papers of EH, NLA
165	**the Australian setting**:	Brigitta Olubas, *Shirley Hazzard: A writing life*, p. 313
165	**sent a cheque**:	EH to Margaret Dick, March 22, 1972, Papers of EH, NLA
165	**'the reluctance'**:	EH to Judah Waten, April 19, 1971, Papers of Judah Waten, NLA
165	**Ron Ferguson**:	EH to Margaret Dick, March 18, 1972, Papers of EH, NLA
166	**'Cynthia said'**:	EH to Margaret Dick, February 13, 1972, Papers of EH, NLA
166	**'Above all, what sort'**:	EH to Margaret Dick, March 18, 1972, Papers of EH, NLA
166	**'I am relieved'**:	EH to Margaret Dick, March 18, 1972
166	**'I had another shot'**:	EH to Margaret Dick, July 12, 1972, Papers of EH, NLA
167	**Elizabeth had told Kylie**:	SW interview with Benison Rodd, May 19, 2024
168	**'Where will I go'**:	EH to Margaret Dick, August 5, 1972, Papers of EH, NLA

Whitlamania

170	**'But it does look out'**:	EH to Shirley Hazzard, October 8, 1972, Papers of Shirley Hazzard, SLNSW
170	**'also radiant, smelling'**:	EH to Shirley Hazzard, September 20, 1972, Papers of Shirley Hazzard, SLNSW
170	**'with little mop trees'**:	EH to Shirley Hazzard, October 8, 1972, Papers of Shirley Hazzard, SLNSW
171	**'Even now I can't'**:	EH to Shirley Hazzard, October 10, 1972, Papers of Shirley Hazzard, SLNSW
171	**'It is the only'**:	EH to Shirley Hazzard, October 10, 1972
171	**'I, and my Mob'**:	EH to Shirley Harrower, December 5, 1972, Papers of Shirley Hazzard, SLNSW. Elizabeth used the expression 'My Mob' to describe her closest friends, playing on the title of John O'Grady's novel *They're a Weird Mob*.
172	**'They were very close'**:	SW interview with Linda Nolte, September 26, 2023
172	**'what moral legs'**:	EH to Shirley Hazzard, August 13, 1973, Papers of Shirley Hazzard, SLNSW
173	**'Thanks for your letter'**:	Patrick White to EH, March 19, 1972, Papers of EH, NLA
173	**'he reads Greek'**:	EH to Shirley Hazzard, March 20, 1973, Papers of Shirley Hazzard, SLNSW
174	**'I haven't been swayed'**:	EH to Shirley Hazzard, August 11, 1975, Papers of Shirley Hazzard, SLNSW
174	**'anything I said'**:	Stephen Murray-Smith to Judah and Hyrell Waten, September 15, 1980, Papers of Judah Waten, NLA
176	**'A week of Blackheath'**:	EH to Shirley Hazzard, November 3, 1972, Papers of Shirley Hazzard, SLNSW
176	**'like going through'**:	EH to Shirley Hazzard, March 5, 1973, Papers of Shirley Hazzard, SLNSW
176	**'such a brilliant'**:	EH to Shirley Hazzard, January 17, 1973, Papers of Shirley Hazzard, SLNSW
177	**'the devoted'**:	Kylie Tennant to Nancy Phelan, January 17, 1973, Papers of Kylie Tennant, NLA
178	**'I'm sad about it'**:	EH to Shirley Hazzard, March 18, 1973, Papers of Shirley Hazzard, SLNSW
178	**'I hoped someone'**:	EH to Shirley Hazzard, April 10, 1973, Papers of Shirley Hazzard, SLNSW
179	**'there is a disorder'**:	Shirley Hazzard to EH, April 22, 1973, Papers of EH, NLA
180	**a light-hearted book**:	Lewis Rodd to Nancy Phelan, August 16, 1973, Papers of Kylie Tennant, NLA

Notes

180	**'I wouldn't be too sorry'**: Kylie Tennant to Mavis Cribb, July 11, 1973, Papers of Kylie Tennant, NLA
180	**'It was written'**: EH to Richard Scott Simon, draft, undated, 1972, Papers of EH, NLA
180	**'Actually I agree'**: Richard Simon to EH, November 22, 1972, Papers of EH, NLA
180	**'He thinks that'**: EH to Shirley Hazzard, January 19, 1973, Papers of Shirley Hazzard, SLNSW
181	**'with the hope'**: EH to Shirley Hazzard, January 5, 1973, Papers of Shirley Hazzard, SLNSW
181	**'She is living'**: EH to Shirley Hazzard, July 25, 1973, Papers of Shirley Hazzard, SLNSW
181	**'at least some macabre'**: Shirley Hazzard to EH, August 1, 1973, Papers of EH, NLA
181	**'a climate of'**: Margaret Jones, 'For our authors, million-dollar tranquilliser', *Sydney Morning Herald*, June 25, 1973
181	**'Writers were thin'**: Valerie Miner, 'Australia – A Literature of Their Own', *The Guardian*, September 11, 1988
181	**'part of the thinking'**: SW interview with Michael Costigan, June 9, 2024
182	**'While I would not'**: EH to Michael Costigan, September 10, 1973, Papers of EH, NLA
182	**'In an effort'**: EH to Shirley Hazzard, September 25, 1973, Papers of Shirley Hazzard, SLNSW
183	**'I said to Patrick'**: EH to Shirley Hazzard, September 2, 1973, Papers of Shirley Hazzard, SLNSW
184	**'I said I was thanking'**: EH to Judah Waten, October 11, 1973, Papers of Judah Waten, NLA
184	**'Explain to us'**: Patrick White to Geoffrey Dutton, March 5, 1970, in David Marr, ed., *Patrick White Letters*, p. 362
184	**'resistible there too'**: EH to Shirley Hazzard & Francis Steegmuller, November 3, 1972, Papers of Shirley Hazzard, SLNSW
184	**'Australia – impossible'**: Artur Lundkvist, 'Australien – omöjligt att skriva om!', undated Swedish newspaper clipping, Papers of EH, NLA
184	**'but it was not my kind'**: Stuart Sayers, 'Patrick White in Sweden', *The Age*, March 28, 1970
184	**'very subtle nuances'**: Ken Henderson interview with Kylie Tennant, July 27, 1980, transcript, 801/2/9, NLA
185	**'a universally valid'**: Artur Lundkvist, *Dagens Nyheter*, September 6, 1973, trans. David Harry, *The Australian*, October 17, 1973, p. 14, quoted in David Marr, *Patrick White: A life*, p. 534
185	**'the new land'**: David Marr, *Patrick White: A life*, p. 535
185	**'Next day there was'**: EH to Shirley Hazzard, October 24, 1973, Papers of Shirley Hazzard, SLNSW
185	**'with doves, balloons'**: EH to Shirley Hazzard, October 24, 1973
186	**'We drank champagne'**: EH to Shirley Hazzard, October 2, 1973, Papers of Shirley Hazzard, SLNSW
186	**'probably for the first'**: EH to Shirley Hazzard, October 24, 1973
186	**Elizabeth felt 'listless'**: EH to Shirley Hazzard, March 15, 1974, Papers of Shirley Hazzard, SLNSW
187	**'YM doesn't ever'**: EH to Shirley Hazzard, September 25, 1973, Papers of Shirley Hazzard, SLNSW

187	**'They say that every'**: EH to Shirley Hazzard, September 25, 1973
187	**'You know I understand'**: EH to Shirley Hazzard, September 25, 1973
188	**Judah Waten, jumping**: Judah Waten to EH, August 20, 1973, Papers of EH, NLA
188	**'I hope to lead'**: EH to Judah Waten, October 11, 1973, Papers of Judah Waten, NLA
189	**'When I start'**: EH to Shirley Hazzard, September 25, 1973, Papers of Shirley Hazzard, SLNSW
189	**'To Patrick White'**: David Marr, *Patrick White: A life*, p. 535
189	**'dismal' market for him**: David Marr, *Patrick White: A life*, p. 537
189	**'White's magnanimity'**: Shirley Hazzard, 'The new novel by the new Nobel Prize winner', *New York Times Book Review*, January 6, 1974, pp. 1, 12, 14
189	**'one of those'**: Rodney Wetherell interview with Patrick White, ABC Sunday Night Radio 2, December 9, 1973, quoted in David Marr, *Patrick White: A life*, p. 496
190	**'is full of interesting things'**: Patrick White to Clem Semmler, May 10, 1970, quoted in *Patrick White Letters*, David Marr, ed., pp. 362–363
190	**'with my typewriter'**: EH to Christina Stead, 1982, undated, Papers of Christina Stead, NLA
190	**'in the hope'**: EH to Shirley Hazzard, November 25, 1973, Papers of Shirley Hazzard, SLNSW
190	**'VERY GOOD NEWS'**: Shirley Hazzard to EH, December 1, 1973, Papers of EH, NLA
190	**'Yes, some writing'**: EH to Shirley Hazzard, September 21, 1975, Papers of Shirley Hazzard, SLNSW
190	**'I have enough'**: EH to Christina Stead, April 22, 1975, Papers of Christina Stead, NLA
191	**'that Penelope's web'**: Kylie Tennant to Mavis Cribb, June 4, 1975, Papers of Kylie Tennant, NLA
191	**she might also**: EH to Keith Connolly, June 25, 1975, Papers of EH, NLA
191	**'published the story'**: EH, 'The Retrospective Grandmother – A Weekend Story', *The Herald*, Melbourne, January 3, 1976, pp. 26–27
191	**'No, she didn't marry'**: EH to Shirley Hazzard, February 23, 1975, Papers of Shirley Hazzard, SLNSW
192	**'I think they help'**: EH to Margaret Dick, September 15, 1975, Papers of EH, NLA
192	**Elizabeth learnt**: EH to Margaret Dick, September 18, 1975, Papers of EH, NLA
192	**'Let us hear'**: EH, 'Effrontery', Letters to the Editor, *The Australian*, May 13, 1974
193	**'the gesture of friendliness'**: Christine Williams interview with EH, 1980, for the Christine Williams MS 8065 Collection [sound recording], ORAL TRC 2625/1-3/ Recording, NLA
193	**'Why does all'**: Christina Stead to Ettore Rella, October, 1974, undated, quoted in Christine Williams, *Christina Stead: A life of letters*, McPhee Gribble, 1989, p. 282
193	**'K and C and I'**: EH to Shirley Hazzard, September 21, 1975, Papers of Shirley Hazzard, SLNSW
194	**Canberra 'sweet-smelling'**: EH to Shirley Hazzard, November 17, 1975, Papers of Shirley Hazzard, SLNSW
194	**'But that's terrible'**: EH to Shirley Hazzard, November 17, 1975
194	**'I stepped back'**: Christine Williams interview with EH, 1980, Christine Williams Collection, NLA
194	**'Switched on radio'**: EH to Shirley Hazzard, November 17, 1975, Papers of Shirley Hazzard, SLNSW

Notes

195	**'Had a delightful'**: Christina Stead to Dorothy Green, November 19, 1975, Papers of Dorothy Green, NLA, MS54678, quoted in Hazel Rowley, *Christina Stead: A biography*, p. 523
196	**'a throughly enchanted'**: EH to Shirley Hazzard, November 30, 1975, Papers of Shirley Hazzard, SLNSW
196	**'to grieve for'**: EH to Shirley Hazzard, January 9, 1976, Papers of Shirley Hazzard, SLNSW

Stanley Avenue

197	**'In fact, there is'**: EH to Shirley Hazzard, January 13, 1974, Papers of Shirley Hazzard, SLNSW
197	**'resented anybody's having'**: Patrick White to Laurie Collison, November 27, 1964, quoted in David Marr, ed., *Patrick White Letters*, pp. 273–274
198	**'a bit miserable'**: Astley quoted in email from Robert Sessions to SW, January 28, 2023
198	**'a huge fuss'**: EH to Shirley Hazzard, January 13, 1974, Papers of Shirley Hazzard, SLNSW
198	**'There is a sort'**: EH to Shirley Hazzard, January 13, 1974
199	**'free to enjoy'**: Shirley Hazzard to Patricia Clarke, May 2, 1976, quoted in Brigitta Olubas, *Shirley Hazzard: A writing life*, p. 331
199	**'little white cubes'**: EH to Shirley Hazzard, October 4, 1995, Papers of Shirley Hazzard, SLNSW
199	**'unforgettable' pleasure**: Shirley Hazzard to EH, April 2, 1976, Papers of EH, NLA
199	**'to Elizabeth'**: Shirley Hazzard to EH, June 26, 1976, Papers of EH, NLA
200	**'the most poignant'**: Shirley Hazzard to EH, April 2, 1976, Papers of EH, NLA
200	**'an unassembled kaleidoscope'** and **'I must go'**: EH to Christina Stead, April 15, 1976, Papers of Christina Stead, NLA
200	**'We'll ask people'**: EH to Shirley Hazzard, March 25, 1976, Papers of Shirley Hazzard, SLNSW
200	**'and every day'**: EH to Shirley Hazzard, June 10, 1976, Papers of Shirley Hazzard, SLNSW
201	**'I know I've been'**: EH to Judah Waten, July 17, 1976, Papers of Judah Waten, NLA
202	**'took into account'**: Judah Waten to EH, July 22, 1976, Papers of EH, NLA
202–203	**'That was kind'**: EH to Christina Stead, November 30, 1976, Papers of Christina Stead, NLA
203	**'We are grieving away'**: EH to Christina Stead, November 30, 1976
203	**'or we'll turn you'**: EH, 'A Few Days in the Country', in *A Few Days in the Country and Other Stories*, pp. 195–196
204	**'Thank you for saying'**: EH to Christina Stead, October 27, 1977, Papers of Christina Stead, NLA
205	**'it dawned on me'**: Giulia Giuffrè interview with EH, 1985, ORAL TRC 2656, transcript, NLA
206	**'Where were you'**: EH to Judah Waten, March 21, 1980, Papers of Judah Waten, NLA
206	**'I don't vote'**: SW interview with Vivian Smith, June 6, 2023
206	**'I suspect she'**: EH to Christina Stead, May 29, 1978, Papers of Christina Stead, NLA
206	**'Like many plays'**: EH to Judah Waten, June 14, 1977, Papers of Judah Waten, NLA
207	**'neurotic and trendy'**: EH to Shirley Hazzard, April 29, 1984, Papers of Shirley Hazzard, SLNSW

207	**'the irrational and sentimental'**: EH to Shirley Hazzard, January 17, 1988, Papers of Shirley Hazzard, SLNSW	
207	**'surely there is'**: Shirley Hazzard to EH, March 11, 1988, Papers of EH, NLA	
208	**'Your pin-up'**: Christina Stead to EH, June 24, 1975, Papers of EH, NLA	
208	**'Don't tell anyone'**: EH to Christina Stead, June 10, 1975, Papers of Christina Stead, NLA	
208	**'Not sure what'**: EH to Shirley Hazzard, November 8, 1976, Papers of Shirley Hazzard, SLNSW	
208	**'he tried to read'**: SW interview with Michael Wilding, April 4, 2024	
209	**'In an unpublished memoir'**: Benison Rodd, 'The Curse of Cliff View', transcribed by her friend Janette Newman, NLA Acc 08/178 No: 1 of 1, November 5, 2008	
209	**'If you can persuade'**: Kylie Tennant to Mavis Cribb, February 9, 1977, Papers of Kylie Tennant, NLA	
210	**'K and R make it easy'**: EH to Shirley Hazzard, April 16, 1978, Papers of Shirley Hazzard, SLNSW	
210	**'all black'**: EH to Shirley Hazzard, July 11, 1978, Papers of Shirley Hazzard, SLNSW	
211	**'a disturbed person'**: EH to Shirley Hazzard, January 9, 1979, Papers of Shirley Hazzard, SLNSW	
211	**'No doubt, if'**: EH to Judah Waten, June 28, 1978, Papers of Judah Waten, NLA	
211	**'like visitors from'**: EH to Shirley Hazzard, January 9, 1979, Papers of Shirley Hazzard, SLNSW	
211	**'I think they did'**: Benison Rodd, 'The Curse of Cliff View'	
211	**'an unremitting'**: EH to Christina Stead, May 29, 1978, Papers of Christina Stead, NLA	
211	**'*Bad* was good'**: EH to Judah Waten, May 10, 1978, Papers of Judah Waten, NLA	
211	**'It was fun'**: EH to Judah Waten, June 28, 1978, Papers of Judah Waten, NLA	
212	**'idle conversation'** and **'I said you had'**: EH to Christina Stead, October 31, 1979, Papers of Christina Stead, NLA	
212	**'all the death'**: EH to Shirley Hazzard, May 30, 1978, Papers of Shirley Hazzard, SLNSW	
212	**'an imitation academic'**: EH to Shirley Hazzard, July 11, 1978, Papers of Shirley Hazzard, SLNSW	
213	**'In spite of numerous'**: EH to Christina Stead, August 20, 1978, Papers of Christina Stead, NLA	
213	**'the one who understands'**: EH, undated notes with *The Catherine Wheel* MS, Papers of EH, NLA	
213	**'used every opportunity'**: EH, report to Michael Costigan, Literature Board, on her term as writer in residence, January 1, 1979, p. 3, Papers of EH, NLA	
214	**'In the rather rare'**: EH to Judah Waten, October 25, 1979, Papers of Judah Waten, NLA	
214	**'I say, friends'**: EH to Shirley Hazzard, January 9, 1979, Papers of Shirley Hazzard, SLNSW	

Slowly spreading circles

215	**'Elizabeth Harrower must'**: Anne Summers, *Damned Whores and God's Police*, NewSouth Publishing, Sydney, 2016 (1st pub. 1975), p. 140
215	**'the pain and intellectual'**: Summers, p. 139
216	**'the ownership and'**: Judith Wright, 'Women Writers in Society', first published in *Australian Author*, Vol. 2, No. 2, 1976, reproduced in Georgina Arnott ed., *Judith Wright: Selected Writings*, La Trobe University Press, 2022, p. 300

Notes

216	**'was very reclusive'**: Richard Walsh email to SW, January 23, 2023
216–217	**'such an intelligent writer'**: Jean Bedford, 'Australian Classics', *National Times*, April 14, 1979, p. 33
217	**'an under-estimated'**: 'New Australian Series', *24 Hours*, June 1979, p. 65
217	**a readable piece**: Interview with EH, Jim Davidson, *Meanjin* 1980
217	**'I told him we had'**: EH to Judah Waten, September 7, 1980, Papers of Judah Waten, NLA
217	**'Your call and all the lovely'**: EH to Shirley Hazzard, October 22, 1982, Papers of Shirley Hazzard, SLNSW
218	**'I didn't want to'**: EH to Shirley Hazzard, April 28, 1982, Papers of Shirley Hazzard, SLNSW
218	**'awaits the critical assessment'**: Nancy Keesing, *Australian Postwar Novelists: Selected critical essays*, Jacaranda Press, 1975, quoted in Nola Adams, 'Review of Harrower's novels', *Westerly*, No. 3, September 1980, p. 109
219	**Adams wrote**: Nola Adams, 'A Dark Realism: The Fiction of Elizabeth Harrower', MA thesis, 1982, Papers of EH, NLA
219	**'Nola was thrilled'**: Gail Jones email to SW, January 30, 2015
219	**'Desperately lonely'**: EH, undated note among correspondence with the Michael Karolyi Memorial Foundation, 1979, Papers of EH, NLA
220	**'a sudden responsibility'**: EH to Madame Caroline Karolyi, March 11, 1979, Papers of EH, NLA
220	**'having got all that'**: EH to Judah Waten, August 4, 1979, Papers of Judah Waten, NLA
221	**'We've been through'**: EH to Judah Waten, December 15, 1979, Papers of Judah Waten, NLA
221	**'some *Who's Who*'**: Christina Stead to EH, March 29, 1979, Papers of EH, NLA
221	**'If Christina had only'**: EH to Judah Waten, October 25, 1979, Papers of Judah Waten, NLA
222	**'an undeserved reputation'**: Bill Pearson to Hazel Rowley, November 27, 1993, 'Reminiscences of Christina Stead prompted by Hazel Rowley's biography' in Papers of Hazel Rowley, MS9224. He did not name Harrower but her identity is obvious.
222	**'I liked your great'**: EH to Christina Stead, undated, 1982, Papers of Christina Stead, NLA
222	**To her annoyance**: SW interview with Linda Nolte, September 6, 2023
222	**'I certainly knew'**: SW interview with EH, December 21, 2017
223	**'an emotional affair'**: SW interview with Kasavere Nolte-Wilson, May 10, 2024
223	**'He thought I was'**: SW interview with EH, December 21, 2017
224	**'He was a lovely man'**: SW interview with Linda Nolte, September 6, 2023
224	**'Nancy is a great'**: EH to Judah Waten, December 15, 1979, Papers of Judah Waten, NLA
225	**'I'm sorry, but'**: Patrick White to Geoffrey Dutton, June 1, 1982, in David Marr, ed., *Patrick White Letters*, p. 562
225	**'impressive insights'**: Patrick White to Shirley Hazzard, July 9, 1979, in David Marr, ed., *Patrick White Letters*, pp. 524–525
226	**'We certainly didn't'**: SW interview with EH, December 21, 2017
226	**'where friends write'**: EH to Shirley Hazzard, October 22, 1982, Papers of Shirley Hazzard, SLNSW
227	**'Elizabeth keeps her principles'**: Patrick White to Shirley Hazzard, June 22, 1980, in David Marr, ed., *Patrick White Letters*, p. 533

227	**'found her exceedingly'**: EH to Shirley Hazzard, July 16, 1980, Papers of Shirley Hazzard, SLNSW
227	**'Shirley's mother still runs'**: EH to Judah Waten, March 21, 1980, Papers of Judah Waten, NLA
227	a **'monstrous task'**: Shirley Hazzard to EH, September 4, 1980, Papers of EH, NLA
228	**'send S. necklace'**: undated list among Hazzard letters, Papers of EH, NLA
228	**'regular spring lunch'**: EH to Judah Waten, September 7, 1980, Papers of Judah Waten, NLA
228	**After a dinner there**: EH to Kylie Tennant, April 22, 1977, Papers of Kylie Tennant, NLA
229	**'She was like a priestess'**: EH to Christina Stead, August 20, 1978, Papers of Christina Stead, NLA
229	**'We told Frank'**: SW interview with Michael Costigan, June 9, 2024
230	**'because she decided'**: SW interview with David Malouf, February 24, 2023
230	**she enjoyed films**: EH to Judah Waten, June 28, 1979, Papers of Judah Waten, NLA
231	**'collect dry cleaning'**: EH, 'Pleasures of Blood-Banking', undated, unpublished, Papers of EH, NLA
232	**'a six-thousand-word'**: EH to Shirley Hazzard, February 23, 1984, Papers of Shirley Hazzard, SLNSW
232	**'a certain amount'**: EH to Sylvia Hale, April 21, 1986, Papers of EH, NLA
232	**'I told him I was'**: EH to Judah Waten, May 11, 1981, Papers of Judah Waten, NLA
233	**'as a person who has only'**: EH to Judah Waten, May 11, 1981
233	**'She's a very good'**: Nancy Keesing to Eric Rolls, May 21, 1981, Papers of Eric Rolls, NLA
233	**'caused the most discussion'**: Andrew McKay, 'NBC awards: Moonlite shines on a fortunate life', *Weekend Australian Magazine*, undated clipping, October, 1981
234	**'People clapped loudly'**: EH to Shirley Hazzard, October 22, 1982, Papers of Shirley Hazzard, SLNSW
234	**'She loved the young'**: EH to Shirley Hazzard, October 22, 1982
234	**a cheque for $10,000**: Hazel Rowley, *Christina Stead: A life*, p. 555
234	**'Christina was a great'**: EH to Shirley Hazzard, April 12, 1983, Papers of Shirley Hazzard, SLNSW
235	**'At last, a simply wonderful'**: EH to Shirley Hazzard, March 15, 1983, Papers of Shirley Hazzard, SLNSW
235	**'careful and reasonable'**: EH to Shirley Hazzard, May 31, 1983, Papers of Shirley Hazzard, SLNSW
236	**'malevolent jeers'**: Brigitta Olubas, *Shirley Hazzard: A writing life*, p. 375
236	**'an evening of great quality'**: *Shirley Hazzard: A writing life*, p. 377
236	**'Gough Whitlam was being'**: EH email to Jane Novak, June 21, 2017, courtesy Jane Novak
236	**'ingrown circle'**: Francis Steegmuller to EH, September 19, 1984, Papers of EH, NLA
237	**'She exists as something luminous'**: Shirley Hazzard to Donald Keene, October 28, 1982, in Brigitta Olubas ed., *Expatriates of No Country: The letters of Shirley Hazzard and Donald Keene*, Columbia University Press, New York, 2024, p. 34
237	**'There you go again'**: Shirley Hazzard diary, November 4, 1984, quoted in Brigitta Olubas, *Shirley Hazzard: A writing life*, p. 380
237	**'Capri had its interest'**: EH to Bill Cantwell, November 26, 1984, Papers of Bill Cantwell, NLA

238	**'another person who'**: EH to Bill Cantwell, November 26, 1984
238	**Trapped on a plane**: SW interview with EH, December 21, 2017
238	**'I was supposed to come'**: David Carter interview with EH, early 1990s, NLA MS-SAV002403 Series, Cassette Recordings, Box 144 (1 micro cassette). Transcribed February 20, 2024.
238	**'or flitting in a circle'**: EH to Shirley Hazzard, September 12, 1984, Papers of Shirley Hazzard, SLNSW
239	**'Earlier on, before I moved'**: EH to Shirley Hazzard, September 12, 1984
239	**'a constant friend'**: EH to Shirley Hazzard, postcard, December 10–11, 1984, Papers of Shirley Hazzard, SLNSW

In the world of life and death

241	**'a fairly special birthday'**: EH to Judah Waten, postcard, July 21, 1981, Papers of Judah Waten, NLA
241	**'a good friend of mine'**: Judah Waten, 'Seventy Years', *Overland*, Vol. 88, 1981, p. 16
241	**'very successful, good evening'**: EH to David Carter, March 7, 1989, Papers of David Carter, NLA
241	**'It would have meant'**: EH to David Carter, March 7, 1989
242	**'the tragic wall'**: EH to Peter Firkins, January 11, 1982, Papers of EH, NLA
242	**Uncle Rob had 'lived'**: EH to Kylie Tennant, December 7, 1981, Papers of Kylie Tennant, NLA
243	**One veteran sent**: Bill Young to EH, June 25, 1980, Papers of EH, NLA
243	**Maja 'was intelligent'**: EH to Shirley Hazzard, April 30, 1986, Papers of Shirley Hazzard, SLNSW
243	**'an ideal condition'**: Giulia Giuffrè interview with EH, 1985, ORAL TRC 2525/4, transcript, NLA
243	**'I have allowed'**: Giulia Giuffrè interview with EH, 1985, NLA
244	**'Today I feel'**: EH to Antigone Kefala, October 8, 1988, Papers of Antigone Kefala, SLNSW
244	**'I've written a lot'**: Giulia Giuffrè interview with EH, 1985, NLA
244	**'Seventy-two years of mistakes'**: EH to Shirley Hazzard, April 29, 1984, Papers of Shirley Hazzard, SLNSW
244	**'very funny book'**: Maurice Dunlevy, 'Tennant's inconsistent but delightful memoir', *Canberra Times*, March 29, 1986, p. 17
245	**'last letter to a friend'**: 'Kylie Tennant's choice: death with dignity', *Sydney Morning Herald*, February 6, 1988, p. 1
245	**Ferdi Nolte visited**: SW interview with EH, December 21, 2017
245	**'Tonight I'm alone'**: EH to Shirley Hazzard, November 4, 1989, Papers of Shirley Hazzard, SLNSW
245–246	**'Manoly was very fond'**: Vrasidas Karalis emails to SW, September 11–12, 2024
246	**'credits me with'**: EH to David Marr, November 8, 1993, Papers of EH, NLA
247	**'Elizabeth couldn't have been'**: Barbara Mobbs to David Marr, fax, January 12, 1994, Papers of David Marr, NLA
247	**'thrilled with what'**: Barbara Mobbs to David Marr, January 12, 1994
247	**'profile of mum'**: Jinx Nolan to Barbara Mobbs, February 3, 1994, Papers of EH, NLA
247	**'Cynthia Nolan's expression'**: EH, Introduction to *Outback and Beyond: The travels of Cynthia and Sidney Nolan,* Angus & Robertson, Sydney, 1994, MS in EH papers, p. 6, NLA
247	**'It was certainly not'**: all quotations from EH memoir of friendship with Patrick White, written 1992, unpublished, Estate of EH

248	**'almost a pleasure'**: EH to Shirley Hazzard, January 7, 1987, Papers of Shirley Hazzard, SLNSW
248	**'When I look at'**: EH to Shirley Hazzard, February 12, 1987, Papers of Shirley Hazzard, SLNSW
249	**'elicited affection and care'**: Elizabeth Riddell to Hazel Rowley, March 18, 1987, comment not used, Papers of Hazel Rowley, NLA
249	**'A woman of almost'**: EH, review of Christina Stead, *A Web of Friendship: Selected Letters (1928–1973), Talking into the Typewriter: Selected Letters (1973–1983),* RG Geering, ed, Angus & Robertosn, in *Overland* 128, 1992, pp. 77–79
249	**'I had thought I was going'**: SW, 'Ahead of her time but rewards flow 30 years after last novel', *Sydney Morning Herald*, November 9, 1996, p. 16
250	**'but a bit of flourishing'**: EH to Rosemary Creswell, February 20, 1989, Papers of EH, NLA
250	**'Now that might mean'**: Tom Thompson to EH, November 20, 1996, Papers of EH, NLA, quoted with permission of HarperCollins Publishers Australia
250	**'It could hold'**: Tom Thompson to EH, December 11, 1990, Papers of EH, NLA
250	**'I feel an obligation'**: EH to Tom Thompson, June 11, 1992, Papers of EH, NLA
251	**'extraordinarily sad'**: EH to Tom Carment, March 13, 1995, courtesy of Tom Carment
251	**'would have been a once'**: EH to Tom Thompson, November 20, 1996, Papers of EH, NLA

Retirement

252	**'Seeing Roberto weekly'**: EH to Shirley Hazzard, October 18, 1992, Papers of Shirley Hazzard, SLNSW
252	**'That particular day'**: EH to Shirley Hazzard, October 18, 1992
253	**'an actual famous writer'**: John Edwards email to SW, March 11, 2024. All quotes from this correspondence.
253	**'politics, books, and flowers'**: SW interview with Ulrik Funch, June 4, 2024
254	**'merchant bankers & lawyers'**: EH to Shirley Hazzard, June 17, 1989, Papers of Shirley Hazzard, SLNSW
255	**'Currawongs have built'**: EH to Shirley Hazzard, October 1, 2000, Papers of Shirley Hazzard, SLNSW
255	**'We just clicked'**: SW interview with Andrew Robertson, August 24, 2023
255	**'Elizabeth was like my psychologist'**: SW interview with Nesli Karadeniz, July 1, 2023
256	**'It was her kindness'**: SW interview with Sally McInerney, January 21, 2025
256	**'I love those landscapes'**: EH to Tom Carment, May 5, 1993, courtesy of Tom Carment
256	**'Tom's a lovely person'**: EH to Shirley Hazzard, July 23, 2000, Papers of Shirley Hazzard, SLNSW
256	**'calmly and quietly'**: EH to Tom Carment, October 9, 1989, courtesy of Tom Carment
257	**Brian bought the portrait**: SW interview with Brian Galway, March 27, 2023
257	**'eating at the North China'**: EH to Shirley Hazzard, June 14, 2001, Papers of Shirley Hazzard, SLNSW
258	**'She was a genuine, sincere'**: SW interview with Salvatore Zofrea, August 6, 2024
258	**'They were all ordinary'**: SW interview with Stephanie Claire, August 6, 2024
259	**'Felt in unusually'**: EH diary, March 9, 1989, Estate of EH
259	**'Thinking of Shirley'**: EH diary, July 8, 1989, Estate of EH

Notes

259 **'Idle day'**: EH diary, February 19, 1996, Estate of EH
259 **'Shock freezes poor human'**: EH to Shirley Hazzard, November 15, 1994, Papers of Shirley Hazzard, SLNSW
260 **'You know from Elizabeth's voice'**: Antigone Kefala, 'Conversations with Mother', in *Summer Visit: Three Novellas*, Giramondo, 2002, p. 110

Renaissance

261 **'I thought it was'**: SW interview with David Winter, June 11, 2024
262 **'It's humbling that'**: SW interview with Michael Heyward, February 3, 2025
262 **'We had coffee'**: SW interview with EH, December 21, 2017
262 **'The novel gripped me'**: Joan London, Introduction to *The Watch Tower*, p. viii
262 **'gathering counter-force'**: Joan London, Introduction to *The Watch Tower*, p. xii
262 **'Something runs clear'**: Joan London, Introduction to *The Watch Tower*, p. xiii
262 **'an accomplished'**: Kerryn Goldsworthy, '*The Watch Tower* by Elizabeth Harrower', *Australian Book Review*, October 2012, no. 345, online edition
263 **'It bowled me over'**: Helen Garner email to SW, April 13, 2025
263 **'I used to nag'**: SW interview with Michael Heyward, February 3, 2025
264 ***In Certain Circles* is so polished'**: SW interview with Michael Heyward, February 3, 2025
264 **'The first four novels'**: SW interview with David Winter, June 11, 2024
264 **'subtle yet wounding'**: Jessica Au, '*In Certain Circles* by Elizabeth Harrower – book review', *The Guardian*, April 28, 2014, online edition
264 **'Celebrating change'**: Susan Sheridan, 'Pity's cost', *Sydney Review of Books*, August 12, 2014, online edition
265 **'watchful, witty, unillusioned'**: Gwendoline Riley, 'Elizabeth Harrower's watchful brilliance', *Times Literary Supplement*, undated, online edition
265 **'Harrower was right'**: James Wood, 'No Time for Lies', *New Yorker*, October 20, 2014, pp. 90–94
265 **'I can't recommend'**: James Wood, 'Favourite Books of 2014', *New Yorker*, December 22, 2014, online edition
265 **Wood recognised**: James Wood, 'No Time for Lies', *New Yorker*, October 20, 2014, pp. 90–94
266 **'Australians have their F. Scott Fitzgerald'**: Eimear McBride, quoted in Gay Alcorn, 'Elizabeth Harrower: Australia's buried literary treasure is unearthed', *The Guardian*, July 7, 2014, online edition
266 **'I found her books'**: On my radar: Ben Whishaw's cultural highlights, *The Guardian*, November 8, 2015, online edition
266 **'Something in that book'**: Ben Whishaw, 'je suis conscient que je n'ai pas les attributs d'une masculinité classique', *Trois Couleurs*, July 27, 2023, online edition
266 **'They had long conversations'**: SW interview with Michael Heyward, February 3, 2025
267 **'one of the rare people'**: Ben Whishaw, *Trois Couleurs*, July 27, 2023, online edition
267 **'It surprises me'**: SW interview with EH, December 21, 2017
267 **'She became the grande dame'**: SW interview with Michael Heyward, February 3, 2025
268 **'I remember thinking'**: SW interview with Jane Novak, July 30, 2024
269 **'Kindness is the greatest'**: SW interview with EH, December 21, 2017
269 **'She was beaming'**: SW interview with Jane Novak, July 30, 2024
269 **'I loved that trip'**: SW interview with EH, December 21, 2017

Reckoning

270	**'It showed me how'**: SW interview with Stephanie Claire, August 6, 2024
270	**'It's been wonderful'**: SW interview with EH, December 21, 2017
270	**'She had the disposition'**: EH, eulogy for Margaret Burns Dick, undated, March 2014, courtesy of Lesley White
271	**'In the chapel'**: EH to Lesley White, undated, 2014, courtesy of Lesley White
271	**Shirley had said at dinner**: Michelle de Kretser notes of conversation with EH, March 12, 2019, courtesy of Michelle de Kretser
271	**'She was very leant on'**: SW interview with Andrew Robertson, August 24, 2023
272	**'For a long time'**: SW interview with EH, December 21, 2017
272	**'I think of you'**: EH to Shirley Hazzard, Christmas card, undated, 2008, Papers of Shirley Hazzard, SLNSW
272	**'Let's hope we can'**: Shirley Hazzard, 'A Place in the Country', in *Cliffs of Fall*, Playboy Paperbacks, New York, 1981 (1st pub. 1963), p. 60
273	**'Please speak up'**: Brigitta Olubas, *Shirley Hazzard: A writing life*, p. 463
273	**'Olubas also co-edited'**: Elizabeth McMahon and Brigitta Olubas, eds, *Elizabeth Harrower*, Sydney University Press, Sydney, 2017
273	**'Can't say I heard'**: SW interview with EH, December 21, 2017
273	**'Luckily I still had my ears'**: SW interview with EH, December 21, 2017
273	**'We talk on the iPad'**: Michelle de Kretser notes of conversation with EH, December 16, 2018, courtesy of Michelle de Kretser
273	**'Her emails were a source'**: Lesley White email to SW, March 6, 2024
273	**'I've decided to vote'**: EH to Lesley White, June 22, 2016, courtesy of Lesley White
274	**'Too clever'**: EH diary, July 29, 2014, Estate of EH
274	**'a friendly girl'**: EH diary, May 24, 2014, Estate of EH
274	**'lovely book'**: EH diary, August 17, 2014, Estate of EH
274	**'One day if you're free'**: All details of Fiona McFarlane and EH exchange in Fiona McFarlane email to SW, March 28, 2024
275	**'expanded my understanding'**: Michelle de Kretser, *On Shirley Hazzard*, Black Inc., Melbourne, 2019, p. 3
275	**her fiction became 'complicated'**: Michelle de Kretser notes of conversation with EH, July 12, 2018, courtesy of Michelle de Kretser
275	**'I knew she wasn't herself'**: SW interview with Cynthia Kaye, February 14, 2023
276	**'the manipulator'**: SW interview with Linda Nolte, August 24, 2023
276	**'In the bitchy'**: EH to Shirley Hazzard, November 3, 1997, Papers of Shirley Hazzard, SLNSW
276	**'He had huge high regard'**: SW interview with Kyrsty Macdonald, April 11, 2024
277	**'Ninety … and still dangerous'**: SW, 'Ninety … and still dangerous', *Weekend Australian*, February 3–4, 2018, p. 18
277	**'I went out there'**: John Edwards email to SW, March 11, 2024
278	**'When she had the shot'**: SW interview with Linda Nolte, August 24, 2023
279	**admired them**: in the will SW received a print by artist Helen Eager, a gift from Patrick White to Margaret Dick
279	**'Swedish wallhanging'**: Fiona McFarlane email to SW, March 28, 2024
279	**'I was pulling out'** and **'It struck me'**: SW interview with Linda Nolte, August 24, 2023
280	**'So my father'**: SW interview with Linda Nolte, August 24, 2023
280	**'Abruptly the road'**: EH, *The Watch Tower*, p. 335

Index

Please note: *ps* refers to photographs

Abbey, Eve 256
Abbott, Tony 253–54
Abels, Cyrilly 165
Adam-Smith, Patsy 84, 90
Adams, Glenda 234
    Dancing on Coral 234
Adams, Nola 218–19
    'A Dark Realism' 218–19
    'The Gothic Sensibility in Fiction by Australian Women' 219
Adelaide Advertiser Literary Competition 115
Adelaide Festival of the Arts 84
Adelaide Writers' Week 83–85, 130, 188, 197, 268–69
Age Book of the Year 233–34
Albee, Edward 163
    All Over 163
Alessio, Mirella 257
Alexander Mackie Teachers' College 87, 172, 212
Allan, Robert 66
Allison, James 193, 226
Ambrosine, Joseph 68
Amis, Kingsley 152
    Girl, 20 152
Anchor Bookshop 172
Anderson, Ethel 75
Anderson, Jessica 37, 130, 224–25
    The Impersonators 130, 233
    Tirra Lirra by the River 37, 130, 224
Anderson, Jim 157
Andreas-Salome, Lou 161
Anger, Per 186
Angus & Robertson 84, 118, 216, 247, 250
    A&R Classic 216–17
Anthony, Doug 192
Archibald Prize 32
Armfield, Neil 246
Armstrong, Gillian 218
Arts for Labor 196
Ashbolt, Alan 73
Ashcroft, Peggy 160, 163
Asquith, Cynthia 160
    Married to Tolstoy 160
Astley, Thea 197–98, 219, 249
    The Well-Dressed Explorer 197
Attlee, Clement 4, 46, 171
Au, Jessica 264
Australasian Book Society 88
Australia Council for the Arts 181, 201–202, 215, 229, 230
Australian Book Review 82, 85, 113, 120

Australian Book Society 88
Australian Broadcasting Commission (ABC) 116, 235
    Four Corners 73
    Poet's Tongue 116
    Quality Street 116
    24 Hours 217
Australian Labor Party (ALP) 171, 172, 173, 195, 206, 235, 253, 257
Australian Letters 82, 83
Australian Literary Studies 80
Australian Society of Authors 110

Bail, Margaret 226
Bail, Murray 226, 230, 236
Baker, Barbara 81
Baker, Sidney J 56, 72, 75, 81–82, 86, 92, 125
    The Australian Language 82
Baldwin, James 73, 152
Banjo Awards 232
Barnes, Valerie 137, 175, 186, 240
Barrie, JM 16, 49
Barwick, Garfield 32
Bavin, Sir Thomas Rainsford 21
Beaver, Bruce 198, 199, 228–29
Bedford, Jean 216–17
Bell, John 196, 206
Bellow, Saul 185, 236
Bergman, Ingmar 211
BHP Steelworks, Newcastle 12, 13, 15
Bicentenary celebrations 207
Blainey, Geoffrey 103, 181, 193, 241
    The Tyranny of Distance 103
Blair, Ron 206
    Mad, Bad and Dangerous to Know 206
Blake, Audrey 174
Blake, (Blech) Bill 155, 156, 222
Blake, Jack 174
Blank, David 33
Blond & Briggs 102
Boireau, Louis 68
Bolt, David 68–69
Bompuy, Jeannie 68
Bowen, Elizabeth 61, 262, 265
Boyd, Martin 57
Boyd, Robin 114
    The Australian Ugliness 114
Braddon, Russell 57
Bradshaw, Mark 266
Briggs, Desmond 102
Brink, John 172
Brink, Margaret 172, 245
Brookes, Dame Mabel 118

Riders of Time 118
Brophy, Brigid 160–61
   Black Ship to Hell 160–61
Brown, Kay 90
Browning, Robert 50
bushfires 2019–2020 278
Buzo, Alex 198
Byam Shaw, Nicholas 104–105, 121, 129

Callil, Carmen 217
Cantwell, Ida 'Bill' 149, 151, 167, 178, 179, 203, 224, 237
Capote, Truman 76, 109
   In Cold Blood 109
Carey, Peter 208
   Illywhacker 234
Carment, Tom 236, 256–57
Carter, David 248
Cassell & Company 50–51, 55, 68, 73, 75, 89, 102
Cato, Nancy 84, 123
censorship 72–73
Chaloner, Reg and Phoebe 69, 153–54, 158
Chapman, Norma 120
Charles, Gerda 155
Chekhov 37, 61, 100, 121
Chisholm, Alec 105
Claire, Stephanie 228, 236, 258, 270
Clark, Kenneth 163
   Civilisation 163
Clark, Manning 181, 206, 229, 241
Clarke, Margie 35
Clarke, Patricia 155
Clancy, Laurie 107–108
Classic Australian Short Stories 208
Clay's Bookshop 120
Cleaver, David 151, 157–58, 168
Clift, Charmian 57, 140
Clint, Alf 220
Cohen, Victoria Flora 27–28
Colette 74
Colmer, Professor John 39–40, 119, 120–21
Commonwealth Literary Fund 81, 110, 122, 129, 181, 183 *see also* Literature Board
Community Arts Board 230
Compton-Burnett, Ivy 3, 61, 139, 265
Connolly, Keith 191
Conrad, Joseph 152
Coombs, Herbert Cole 'Nugget' 221, 222
Cooper, Christine 89, 140, 141, 153
Costigan, Frank 229
Costigan, Margaret 229
Costigan, Michael 181, 182, 201, 214, 229, 249
Cowen, Sir Zelman 229
Cox, Hilary 73
Crapper, Edith 154
Creswell, Rosemary 250
Cribb, Mavis 96, 180, 209

Croft, Julian 103
Cross, Robert 87, 104, 111, 112, 120, 123–24, 133–34, 149, 168
Crossley, Jill 77
Curtis Brown 51, 165
Cusack, Dymphna 25
   Morning Sacrifice 25

d'Alpuget, Blanche 233
   Turtle Beach 233
Dark, Eleanor 75
David Higham Associates 68–69, 81 *see also* Pearn, Pollinger & Higham
Davidson, Jim 217
Davies, Bryn 82
Davies, Yolande 199
Davis, Beatrice 84, 111, 113, 230
Davison, Frank Dalby 84
de Beauvoir, Simone 74, 216, 267
de Kretser, Michelle 271, 273, 275
   The Life to Come 275
de Maistre, Roy 92
Deacon, Vera 15
Derrick, CH (Christopher) 130, 134, 135–36, 139
Devanny, Jean 95
Dick, Anne 44, 46, 156, 162
Dick, James 42, 43–44, 192
Dick, Margaret Burns (cousin)
   ABC, association with 116
   book reviews by 73, 115, 116, 119, 165
   'Choosing' 115–16
   death 270–71, 273
   employment in Sydney 73, 165, 191
   first trip back to Britain 191–92
   France, connections with 68
   'The Gift of Knowledge' 48
   Harrower and 44–46, 57, 58, 66, 69, 70–73, 76, 81–86, 94, 106, 110, 113–14, 116–17, 127–28, 130, 142, 151, 152–53, 165–67, 169–70, 184, 199, 200, 220, 222, 224, 229, 232, 242, 245, 252, 256–57, 259, *ps*
   Kit Hazzard and 227
   The Novels of Kylie Tennant 113, 117–18, 119
   PEN Committee on Censorship 72–73
   Point of Return 66–67, 115
   retirement 220, 224
   Rhyme or Reason 67, 68
   short stories 90, 115–16, 191
   'Southern Latitude' 114–15, 138, 143
   'Summer Sunday' 115
   talks and lectures 118–19
   Tennant and 117
   writing 48, 66–67, 90, 113, 114–16, 117–18
Dick, Mary Reid 'Minnie' (great-aunt) 42, 43–44, 58, 117, 159, 162, 191, 192
Dick, Stephanie (Smith) 42, 44, 159, 162, 192, 273

Index

Dickson, 'Rache' Lovat 89–90
Digby, Desmond 226
Dirda, Michael 266
Dobell, William 32
Dobson, Rosemary 231, 249
Dunstan, Don 194
Durack, Mary 75, 84, 90
   Kings in Grass Castles 84
Dutton, Geoffrey 80, 93, 111, 184, 198
   Adelaide Writers' Week 84, 188, 197
   family 163
   Harrower advocacy 102–103, 110, 183
   Harrower, friendship with 163
   Literary Board 181
   literary entrepreneurship 82, 111
   reviews by 76, 225
Dylan, Bob 100
   'All Along the Watchtower' 100

Eagle, Chester 234
   Mapping the Paddocks 234
Edwards, John 253, 277
Encyclopaedia Britannica Award 111, 156, 234
Ern Malley hoax 82
ETT Imprint 251
Evatt, HV 'Doc' 124
Exodus Foundation 278
Eyre & Spottiswoode 102, 111

Faber and Faber 85, 102
Facey, Albert 233
   A Fortunate Life 233
Falconer, Delia 263
Fallon, Judy 57
Fellowship of Australian Writers 110
Ferguson, Ron 165, 191
Ferrier, Carole 218
Fink, Margaret 218
Firkins, Peter 242
   From Hell to Eternity 242
Fitzgerald, RD 198
Forbes, Sandra 201
Ford, Richard 273
Forster, EM 119
   Maurice 119
Foster, David 198, 233
   Moonlite 233
Fox, Winifred 153, 161
Frame, Janet 219
Fraser, Malcolm 194, 196, 235, 236
Friedan, Betty 216
   The Feminine Mystique 216
Frizell, Helen 125–26, 233
Fugard, Athol 205
Funch, Ulrik 253–54

Galway, Brian 257, 278

Gare, Nene 84
Garner, Helen 3, 5, 219, 263
   Honour and Other People's Children 233
   Monkey Grip 219
   True Stories 5
Geering, Dorothy 155, 199, 228, 229
Geering, Ron 155, 199, 228, 229, 249
Gentry, Bryen 50
Gielgud, Sir John 58, 153
Gillard, Julia 257
Goldsworthy, Kerryn 262–63
Gollancz 102
Golson, Clare 194
Gordimer, Nadine 5, 76, 80, 119, 172
   The Conservationists 119
Gougoulis, Alaina 261, 276
Gray, Robert 228, 249
Great Depression 14–15, 17, 29, 45
Green, Dorothy 118, 193–94, 195, 232
Greene, Graham 43, 109, 112, 237
   The Comedians 109
Greer, Germaine 57, 157, 267
Gribble, Diana 219
Grose, Peter 165
Gunew, Sneja 218

Hale & Iremonger 231–32
Hale, Sylvia 231–32
Hall, Richard 181, 183, 236, 253, 276
Harris, Jane 172, 275
Harris, Max 82–85, 102–103, 109, 115, 120, 215
   The Land That Waited 85
Harrower, Adell (aunt) *see* McIntosh, Adell (aunt) (née Harrower)
Harrower, Catherine (paternal grandmother) 12, 13, 191
Harrower, David (half-brother) 128
Harrower, David (paternal grandfather) 12
Harrower, Elizabeth (Betty)
   Aboriginal rights movement, views on 206–207
   'Absent Friends' 51, 266
   aged-care home 277–78
   'Alice' 16–17, 18, 26, 141, 191
   anti-nuclear activism 62–63
   beach, on *ps*
   'The Beautiful Climate' 38–40, 47, 79, 208, 231, 266
   Beginners' Class 78–79
   book reviews by 72
   The Bosom of the Family 78
   Buddhism 63, 252, 257
   bush, love for *ps*
   business school 34
   The Catherine Wheel 3, 59–65, 68, 69, 73, 74, 77, 78, 81, 109, 120, 213, 216, 250, 251, 263, 266

'The City at Night' 36, 51, 266
City of Sydney Public Library 37
Commonwealth Literary Fund fellowship 122–23, 129
comparisons with White 56–57, 82, 83, 108–109, 120–21
'The Cornucopia' 77–78
correspondence 2, 6, 42–43, 56, 57, 61, 63, 68, 84–85, 87, 89, 104, 111, 119, 120, 121–22, 123, 128, 130, 131, 134–35, 137, 144, 151, 152–54, 157, 158, 162–63, 166–68, 176, 178, 204, 207, 208, 212–13, 214, 217–18, 221, 227, 232, 235, 239, 241, 243, 246, 274
'The Cost of Things' 91, 230, 231, 266
Cremorne, move to 254–55, *ps*
death 278–80
declined invitations 219–21, 228, 232
diaries and notes 258–59
Down in the City 3, 50–54, 89, 97, 225, 250
early life 11–32, *ps*
'English Lesson' 91, 162, 208
eulogy for Margaret Dick 270–71
'The Expatriate' 77
family history research 242–43
father and, post-divorce 127–28
feminism and 139, 216, 218
'A Few Days in the Country' 140–42, 202–204, 275
A Few Days in the Country and Other Stories 265, 266
film-going 37, 72, 211, 230
friendships 1, 2, 4, 23, 44, 46, 81–88, 142, 149, 150, 171–72, 204–206, 211, 219, 222–26, 228–30, 244–48, 252–58, 266–67, 270–71, 274–75, 276
'The Fun of the Fair' 47–48, 266
grandparents 12–14, 17–19, 21–22
Hazzard and *see* Hazzard, Kit; Hazzard, Shirley; Steegmuller, Francis
health 38–39, 188–89, 200–201, 202, 235, 245, 257, 273, 275, 276–77
Hillside Farm, Blackheath 94, 97, 124–25, 166–67, 169–70, 175–76, 179, 183, 188, 200
Hunters Hill 169–73, 200–201, *ps*
In Certain Circles 3–4, 96, 129–30, 133–40, 141, 177, 180, 182, 190, 202, 243, 244, 263–65, 268
influences 265
inheritance from mother 142–43, 200, 204–205, 228, 254
interviews with 3–5, 70, 75–76, 106–107, 205, 217, 244, 249–50, 267, 270
'It is Margaret' 131–32, 266
Italian lessons 252–53
judging literary awards 232–33
Kit Hazzard and *see* Hazzard, Kit

'Lance Harper, His Story' 82–83
'The Last Days' 69, 77, 266
Literature Board fellowship 181–83, 201–204, 214
London life 43, 48, 49–69, 251
London visit 149, 150–68
The Long Prospect 3, 11, 18, 52, 54–57, 68, 77, 81, 82, 89, 103, 109, 120, 156, 191, 216, 217, 250, 263, 266
Macmillan employment 86–88, 91, 102, 122, 123, 149
Manly Grammar School for Girls 25, 26
Margaret Dick and *see* Dick, Margaret
marriage, thoughts on 243
material for writing 16–18, 26, 38–40, 47, 50, 54–55, 63–65, 97–98, 100–101, 129–31, 138, 142, 213
Michael Karolyi Memorial Foundation residency 219–20
Miles Franklin Award 111–13
mother's death 131–33, 142–44
mother's second 'marriage' *see* Kempley, Richard Herbert
neglect as writer 1–2, 215–17
Nolans and *see* Nolan, Cynthia; Nolan, Sidney
'The North Sea 77, 266
obituaries 278
office work 34–37, 41, 49–50, 73
pacificism 63, 66
parents' divorce 19–21, 22–23, 25, 30, 127
Patrick White and *see* White, Patrick
Patrick White Award 1996 249, 251, 268
political beliefs/involvement 46, 63, 66, 118, 170–74, 188, 192, 194–96, 206, 235, 253, 257, 273–74
pseudonym Antonia Reid 50–51
publication of first novel 50–51
radio broadcasts 160
reclusiveness, perception of 2, 216
recognition in later life 218, 261–69, 270
reissues of novels 3, 216–17, 250, 261–64
resistance to writing 183, 190–92, 214, 231, 243–44, 250–51
'The Retrospective Grandmother' 18, 30, 47, 191, 201
return to Australia 70–80
reviews of 1–2, 53–54, 56, 73–75, 77, 103, 105, 107–110, 120–21, 130, 134, 135–37, 139, 215–19, 262–66
romantic relationships 222–23
royalties 110
schools 25, 34
Scotland 43–48
Scottish heritage 4, 12, 13, 14, 42, 43
short stories 36, 38, 46–47, 50–51, 77, 82, 90–91, 191, 192, 230–31, 250, 265–66
'The Short Story: Australia' 79–80
Steele Rudd Award 275

Index

'Summertime' 36, 51, 266
Sydney, move to 25–26, 31, 34–37
Tennant and *see* Tennant, Kylie
theatre, love of 37, 58, 61, 91–92, 153, 159, 163, 206, 211
translations of short stories by 231, 266
travel with mother/stepfather 41–43
US market 77, 81, 84, 85, 250, 265
The Watch Tower 1, 2, 3, 18, 39–40, 97–112, 120–21, 122, 150, 165, 180, 184, 215–16, 250, 261–63, 266, *ps*
'The Wicked Stepfather' 132
will 276–77, 278–79
writer in residence 212–14
writer's block 183, 190–92, 214
Harrower, Elma (née King) 127–29, 144–45
Harrower, Francis Sharp Hastings (Frank) (father) 12, 19–20, 25–26, 30, 127–28, 204, *ps*
   death 128–29
   second marriage and family 127–29, 144–45
Harrower, Margaret Burns (Daisy) (née Hughes) (mother) 12, 26, 33
   death 131, 142
   divorce 19–21, 25, 30
   Elizabeth and 16, 85–86, 175, *ps*
   family conflicts 14
   Kempley and 26, 30–32, 38, 68, 70–71, 121–22, 130
   will 142–43
Harrower, Yvonne Adell (half-sister) 127–28, 144–45
Hawke, Bob 235, 253
Hawker, Philippa 262
Hayden, Bill 235
Hazzard, Kit 224, 235, 236
   Harrower and 119–22, 130, 135, 137–38, 140, 150–51, 154–55, 165, 168, 175–76, 181, 182, 186–88, 194–95, 199, 214, 224, 227–28, 240, 245
   mental health 135, 137, 140
Hazzard, Reg 119–20
Hazzard, Shirley 1, 6, 130, 271–73 *see also* Hazzard, Kit; Steegmuller, Francis
   Adelaide Writers' Week 197–200
   The Bay of Noon 119, 130, 135, 275
   Boyer Lectures 235–36
   Cliffs of Fall and Other Stories 119, 272
   death 271
   Defeat of an Ideal 155, 175
   The Evening of the Holiday 109, 119, 121, 130, 275
   The Great Fire 271
   Harrower and 2, 42–43, 61, 65, 115, 119–22, 134–35, 137, 150, 154–55, 170–71, 174, 175, 178–79, 182, 185–87, 189, 190, 197–200, 207, 217–18, 226–28, 235–40, 248–49, 259, 271–72, *ps*
   'Letter from Australia' 199, 235
   People in Glass Houses 66, 121
   Transit of Venus 218, 225–26
   White and 227, 248
Heller, Joseph 81
   Catch-22 81, 113
Hellman, Lillian 234
   Pentimento 234
Hellyer, Jill 110
Helpmann, Robert 88
Henderson, Darryl 151–52
Henderson, Judy 151–52
Heney, Helen 75
Henningham, Max 253, 257
Henry, Margaret 75
   Unlucky Dip 75
Herbert, Xavier 84
   Capricornia 84
Hergenhan, Laurie 80
Hertzberg, Mark 199
Hetherington, John 75–76
Hewett, Dorothy 232
Heyward, Michael 261, 263–64, 266, 267, 269, 274, 275–76, 270
Hickey, Bernard 229
Hill, Ernestine 75
Hiramatsu, Mikio 230–31
   Australian Literature – Short Story Masterpieces 231
Hodgman, Helen 261
   Blue Skies 261
Hooton, Joy 249
Hope, AD 74, 92, 115, 181, 197
Hope, John 125, 167
Horne, Donald 114
   The Lucky Country 114
Horniman, Michael 102, 133, 134, 137, 141, 165
Houghton, Douglas 45
Howard, John 253–54
Hueston, Penny 261, 275, 279
Hughes, Helen (maternal grandmother) 13, 14, 18, 21–22, 23, 24, 26, 30, 43, 117, 151, 191
   divorce 21–22
Hughes, James (uncle) 21, 23, 191
Hughes, Margaret Burns *see* Harrower, Margaret Burns (Daisy) (née Hughes)
Hughes, Robert (maternal grandfather) 13, 21–22, 65
Hughes, Robert Reid 'Uncle Rob' 21, 23–24, 33, 242
   war service 23–24, 242–43
Hugo, François 164
Humphery, Miss Isobel 116
Humphreys, Christopher 63
   Buddhism 63
Humphries, Barry 57
Hungerford, TAG 84

International PEN *see* PEN Australia
International Women's Year 215

James, Clive 57
James, Henry 61, 121
Jefferis, Barbara 74–75
Jensen, Gertrude 51, 93
Johnson, Barbara (Ward) 23, 30–31, 34, 37, 56, 94, 58, 68 , *ps*
    children 94
Johnston, George 57, 123, 140
    My Brother Jack 123
Jolley, Elizabeth 219, 232
Jonathan Cape 112
Jones, Margaret 181

Karadeniz, Nesli 252, 255–56, 278
Karalis, Professor Vrasidas 245–46
Karig, Sára 231
Kaye, Cynthia 275, 278
Keating, Paul 253
Keeling, Miranda (Mandy) 256
Keene, Donald 218, 237, *ps*
Keesing, Nancy 74, 109–110, 181, 183, 184, 199, 218, 232–33
Kefala, Antigone 230, 243–44, 259–60, 278
Kelly, Carmel 208
Kelly's Bush campaign 173
Kempley, Ellen 26, 42
Kempley, Jack 27, 42
Kempley, Jessie (née Hawkins) *see* Kempley, Richard Herbert
Kempley, John (Richard's brother) 27, 30, 33, 159–60
Kempley, John (Richard's father) 26, 27, 33
Kempley, Margaret *see* Harrower, Margaret Burns (Daisy) (née Hughes) (mother)
Kempley, Richard 27, 142
Kempley, Richard Herbert 'Uncle Dick' 40, 42, 65, 68, 70–71, 94, 131–32, 159–60, *ps*
    business dealings 27–30, 32–33, 143, 201
    death 134, 142–43
    Felix Shaw, comparison 39–40, 98–99, 101, 160
    first wife Jessie (née Hawkins) 27
    Harrower and 31, 38–39, 70–71, 132
    Harrower's mother and 26, 30–33, 71, 131
    Olive Beatrice Kempley 29
    will 142
Keneally, Thomas 184, 198, 212
    The Chant of Jimmy Blacksmith 198
Kerr, Sir John 194, 208
Kippax, Harry 108, 109
Koch, Christopher 83
Koston, Paul 157, 158
Koval, Ramona 263
Kramer, Leonie 2, 90, 230

Coast to Coast 90
    Harrower opinion on 2
Kroetsch, Laura 268
Kurosawa 206

Lane, Sir Allen 82
Langley, Eve 75
Lansbury, Angela 163
LaPook, Jonathan 234
Lascaris, Manoly 92, 93, 149, 150, 185, 186, 199, 226, 245–46, 249
Laurent, Laurel 276–77, 278, 279
Lawler, Ray 77, 91–92
    The Summer of the Seventeenth Doll 77, 91–92
Lawrence, DH 56, 61, 72, 75
Lee, Harper 100
    Go Set a Watchman 100
Lehmann, Geoffrey 108–109, 198, 199, 228, 257
Lehmann, Rosamund 61, 74
Leigh, Vivien 37, 88
Leighton, Margaret 58, 61
Lessing, Doris 217
Levis, Eve 224, 275
Levis, Ken 212, 224, 275
Literature Board 181–83, 190, 199, 202, 204, 212, 214, 229, 230, 276 *see also* Australia Council for the Arts
London, Joan 262, 274
    The Golden Age 274
Lord, Mary 221, 228
Lundkvist, Arnold 1, 184–85
Lunn, Hugh 234
    Vietnam: A reporter's war 234
Lyn, Elwyn 229

McAuley, James 82
McBride, Eimear 266, 274
MacCallum, Mungo 85
    Son of Mars 85
Macdonald, Kyrsty 276
McFarlane, Fiona 274–75, 277, 279
    The High Places 275
    The Night Guest 274, 277
McGregor, Craig 195
McGregor, Fiona 263
McGurk, Michael 254
McInerney, Sally 228, 256
McInherney, Frances 218
McIntosh, Adell (aunt) (née Harrower) 13, 14, 24, 39, 242, *ps*
McIntosh, Charles 24
Maclean, Alan 111, 112, 267
    Harrower advocacy 88, 102
    Harrower visit UK 158–59
    Hazzard/Steegmuller friendship 130, 150, 154, 238

Index

In Certain Circles and 129–30, 134, 136–37, 180, 263, 264
   Macmillan director in London 87–88, 101–104
   visit to Sydney 120
Maclean, Donald 87–88
Maclean, Robin 154, 159
McMahon, Billy 206
Macmillan & Co 79, 86, 89–90, 102, 104, 123, 130, 133–34, 110–11, 117, 133–34
   Summer's Tales 90–91, 115
Macmillan, Harold 88, 123
McPhee, Hilary 219
Madigan, Col 206, 236, 257
Madigan, Ruby 206, 236
Malouf, David 181, 199, 226, 230, 236
Mandela, Nelson 171–72
Mann, Thomas 64, 213
   Tonio Kroger 64, 213
Marcel, Gabriel 190
   Being and Having 190
Marr, David 72, 236, 246–47, 248
Marshall, Alan 95
Martin, Albert Irving 27
Martin, David 198
Marvell, Andrew 245
   'The Garden' 245
Mary Martin's Bookshop 82
Maschler, Tom 112
Masters, Olga 219
Mathers, Peter 110, 111–12
   Trap 111–12, 113
Mathew, Ray 54
Matthiessen, Peter 109
   At Play in the Fields of the Lord 109
Matzoll, Verity (cousin) (née McIntosh) 24, 242, 277
   daughter Maja 243
Meanjin 217
Medich, Ron 254
Melbourne Writers' Festival 268, 274
Menzies, Prime Minister Robert 46, 122, 170
Meredith, Gwen 72
   Blue Hills 72
Merritt, Robert 206
   The Cakeman 206
Metcalf, John 53
Metcalfe, Ernie 125
Miles Franklin Literary Award 57, 92, 111–13, 197, 219, 267, 268, 271
Mitchell, Adrian 230
Mobbs, Barbara 246, 247, 268, 274
Mohr, James 172, 275, 278
Monsieur Hulot's Holiday 72, 152
Moorhouse, Frank 198, 208
Mudie, Ian 84
Mundey, Jack 173

Murdoch, Iris 109, 136, 217
Murphet, Richard 103
Murphy, Joseph 152
   The Power of Your Subconscious Mind 152
Murray, Les 198
Murray-Smith, Stephen 109, 174, 202, 208, 230

National Book Council 232, 234
National Book Critics Circle Award 218
National Library of Australia 5–6, 115, 140, 263, 274
Neruda, Pablo 184
Neville, Jill 57
Neville, Richard 57, 157
Newton-John, Valerie 255, 257
Nixon, Ellen 87
Nixon, President 171, 186
Nolan, Cynthia 1, 153
   death 203, 225, 247
   Harrower and 1, 149–50, 158, 161–65, 178, 179, 186, 203
   Open Negative: An American Memoir 149
   writing 149, 163–64, 247
Nolan, Jinx 164, 178, 226, 238, 247, 277
Nolan, Sidney 1, 149–50, 153, 158, 163–64, 170, 178, 186, 203, 225, 247
   Snake 163
Nolte, Ferdinand 'Ferdi' 171–73, 188, 196, 204, 206, 211, 223, 235, 236, 245, 257, 276–77, *ps*
Nolte, Helene 171–73, 196, 206, 211, 223, 257, 277
Nolte, Karin 223, 278
Nolte, Linda 172, 223–24
   daughter Kasavere 223–24
   Harrower and, relationship 276–80
Novak, Jane 268, 269, 276
NSW Builders Labourers' Federation 173
NSW Premier's Literary Awards 232, 234

Oakley, Barry 198
Oatley, Claire 35
O'Brien, Edna 155
   A Pagan Place 155
O'Conner, Elizabeth 75
O'Connor, Frank 91
O'Grady, John 84, 114
   They're a Weird Mob 84, 114
O'Hea, Juliet 51
Olivier, Laurence 37, 60, 61, 88
   The Entertainer 61
Olubas, Professor Brigitta 6, 239, 273
Osborne, Charles 163
Osborne, John 60, 72, 250–51
   autobiography 250–51
   The Entertainer 60
   Look Back in Anger 60, 72, 92, 251
   The World of Paul Slickey 76, 251

Overland 109, 141, 174, 202, 249
The Oxford Book of Australian Short Stories 208
Oz 157

Palmer, Nettie 95
Pantheon Books 250
Park, Ruth 75
Partridge, Mary (Miss Maclean) 35, 41
Patchett, Mary Elwyn 57
Patrick White Award 3, 186, 193, 198, 241, 249, 251, 268
Pearn, Pollinger & Higham 55
Pearson, David 268
PEN Australia 72–73, 75, 83, 110
Penguin Books 82
Penton, Brian 119
   Landtakers 119
People for Nuclear Disarmament 246
Percy, Charles 257, 278
Perrault, Charles 98–99
   'La barbe bleu' 98
Pettini, Roberto 252
Phelan, Nancy 88, 90, 175, 199, 204, 224
Phelan, Peter 175
Pierce, Peter 233–34
Plackett, Marion 35
Porter, Hal 85, 90, 102, 115, 184, 198, 221
Porter, Peter 228
Powell, Anthony 109
   The Soldier's Art 109
Prichard, Katharine Susannah 75, 95
Priestley, JB 67
Prime Minister's Literary Awards 274
Pringle, John Douglas 74
Private Eye 157
Prokofiev 186
   War and Peace 186
Proust 61
Public Lending Right program 183

Queen Elizabeth 49, 185
Quinion, Mary 87

Rattigan, Terence 58, 60
   Variations on a Theme 58–59
Rees, Lloyd 196
Reid, Barrett 249
Reid, Elizabeth 188
Richardson, Henry Handel 75, 89, 197
   Maurice Guest 89
Richardson, Ralph 61
Richler, Mordecai 80
Riddell, Elizabeth 181, 226, 249
Rigby 118
Riley, Gwendoline 265
Roberts, David E 189
   Existentialism and Religious Belief 189

Robertson, Andrew 135, 187, 199, 234, 255, 257, 271, 275, 279
Rodd, Benison 'Benno' 94, 95, 124, 126, 167–68, 176, 177, 179, 188, 200, 209, 211
Rodd, John 'Bim' 94, 95, 124, 126, 166–67, 175–77, 180, 188, 209–11
Rodd, Lewis 'Roddy' 90, 94–95, 124–25, 140, 151, 167–68, 169, 176–77, 184, 220
Rolfe, Patricia 90
Rolls, Eric 233
   A Million Wild Acres 233
Ross, Gordon 134
Rowbotham, David 84
Rowe, Dorothy 255
Rowley, Hazel 222, 248–49
Rudd, Kevin 257
Rudkin, Tony 87
Ruhen, Olaf 72, 83–84

Sagan, Françoise 121
Saroyan, William 80
Saxby, Maurice 87
Schenk, Leslie 152, 162, 237
Schiffrin, Andre 250
Scott, Paul 55
Scott, Paul 109
   The Jewel in the Crown 109
Second World War 20–21, 22, 23–24, 33, 242–43
   Sandakan Memorial Park 243
Seidler, Harry 196
Semmler, Clem 111, 189–90
Serkin, Rudolf 163
Seton, Hilary 67
Shadbolt, Maurice 80
Shapcott, Tom 181
Sharp, Martin 157
Shaw, Elvy 19–20
Sheppard, Alex 72–73
Sheridan, Susan 264
Simon, Richard Scott 165, 180
Simpson, Helen 75
Sirius Quality Paperbacks 216
Sitwell, Dame Edith 88
Slessor, Kenneth 84, 198
Smith, Alec 44, 159, 162
Smith, Joshua 32
Smith, Maurice Temple 155
Smith, Nancy 84
Smith, Robin 278
Smith, Stevie 230
Smith, Sybille 228 29, 230, 236
Smith, Ted 84
Smith, Vivian 228–29, 230, 236
Snedden, Billy 192
Snelson, Thurza (cousin) (née McIntosh) 24, 242, 277

Index

Snow, CP 87
Society of Australian Authors 57, 74
   The Sunburnt Country: Profile of Australia 57
Society of Women Writers of New South Wales 119
Solzhenitsyn, Aleksandr 61
Souter, Gavin 105, 106, 222, 236, 253, 277
Souter, Ngaire 236, 253
South Africa Defence and Aid Fund (Australia) 172
Southerly 109
Spark, Muriel 87, 265
Stead, Christina 1, 2, 75, 103, 165, 197, 199, 206, 225, 236
   The Beauties and the Furies 253
   biographies 248–49
   brother Gilbert 193
   For Love Alone 155, 216, 218
   Harrower and 101, 155–57, 190–91, 193–95, 199, 202–203, 206, 207–208, 213, 221–22, 228, 234, 248–49, 253
   The Little Hotel 193, 216
   The Man Who Loved Children 155, 207, 212
   'Ocean of Story' 80
   Seven Poor Men of Sydney 118–19, 216
Stead, David 207
Steegmuller, Francis 135, 217, 245 *see also* Hazzard, Shirley
   Adelaide Writers' Week 188, 197
   assault in Naples 236
   Cocteau: A biography 119, 130, 135, 158, 238
   death 259
   Harrower and 150, 154–55, 165, 184, 235, 236–39, ps
   Stories and Short Stories 119
Stendhal 61, 189
Stephenson, PR 'Inky' 110
Stewart, Douglas 122, 230
Stewart, Harold 82
Stivens, Dal 57, 110
Stone, Walter 72
Stonier, Brian 103
Stow, Randolph 57, 83, 184, 198
   To the Islands 57
Strachan, Miss Stella 25
Strachey, Lytton 49
Strindberg 160
   The Father 160
Summers, Anne 215, 218
   Damned Whores and God's Police 215, 218
Sumner, John 91–92, 248
Sun Books 102–103
Sutherland, Joan 229
Sydney Opera House 185–86
Sydney: An Oxford Anthology 276
Syron, Bryan 206

Tabloid Story 208
Tasker, John 92
Tennant, Kylie 75, 84, 232, 244–45
   cancer 209, 245
   death 245
   Diamond Head 125–26, 278
   Evatt: Politics and justice 177
   family problems 94–95, 166–68, 176–77, 200–201, 209–11
   Foveaux 86, 119
   Harrower and 1, 86, 88, 89–96, 101–102, 104–105, 112, 118, 122–26, 138, 142, 150–51, 166–69, 175, 177–80, 191, 193, 199, 200–201, 209–11, 220–21, 244–45, 248, ps
   The Honey Flow 122, 177
   Lost Haven 117
   Macmillan, reader for 86, 89–91, 101–102, 104–105, 112
   The Man on the Headland 125, 177
   Margaret Dick and 117–19
   The Missing Heir 176, 244–45
   Ride on Stranger 86, 215, 220
   sister 'Doff' 169, 179, 220
   Tantavallon 177
   Tell Morning This 117–18
   Vietnam War protests 118
   The Watch Tower review 101
   White and 92–93, 173
Tennant, Thomas 177, 179
Text Publishing 3, 261–65, 268, 274, 276
Thiele, Colin 84
Thomas Nelson 134, 168
Thompson, Tom 250, 251
Tognetti, Richard 223
Travolta, John 230
Trist, Margaret 72
Trollope, Anthony 61
Turner, George 85
Tynan, Kenneth 58

Ullmann, Professor Stephen 45

Vietnam War 118, 170
Virago Press 217
Visual Arts Board 229

Walker, Patricia 194
Wallace-Crabbe, Chris 84
Walsh, Richard 181, 216–17, 250
   Ward, Barbara *see* Johnson, Barbara
Warhol, Andy 211
Waten, Alice 155, 185, 223
Waten, Hyrell 174, 223, 238, 241
Waten, Judah 1, 88–89, 90, 109, 181, 198, 204, 248
   Alien Son 89
   death 241

Distant Land 90
Harrower and 88–89, 107, 122, 129, 131, 132, 142, 144, 155, 174, 183, 188–89, 191, 201–202, 206, 208, 211, 214, 217, 220–21, 223, 229, 230, 238, 241
Odessa to Odessa 229
Season of Youth 109
Shares in Murder 89
The Unbending 9, 122
Watergate scandal 186
Watson, Keith 102
The Roo Shooter 102
Weaver, Jacki 196
Webb, Elizabeth 57
Into the Morning 57
Webb, Francis 198
Weng-Ho, Chong 276, 279
West, Morris 83, 106, 110
The Shoes of the Fisherman 106
West, Rebecca 87
Westwood, Bryan 207, 208
Wetherell, Rodney 249
WH Smith Literary Award 111
Whishaw, Ben 266–67, 277
White Australia policy 170
White, Harold 122
White, Lesley (née Smith) 44, 117, 162, 271, 273–74, 276, 278
White, Patrick 51, 92–93, 172, 196, 197, 198, 206
The Aunt's Story 92, 149
Big Toys 231
death 245–46
death duties and 143–44
dropped friendships 225
The Eye of the Storm 168, 175, 181, 185, 189–90, 197
Flaws in the Glass 1, 225, 226, 246
A Fringe of Leaves 192
The Ham Funeral 92, 246
The Hanging Garden 246
Happy Valley 111
Harrower and 1, 57, 91–93, 104–106, 142, 150, 155, 156, 161, 164–65, 168, 169, 173, 180–81, 184–86, 189–90, 192, 199, 219–20, 226–27, 229, 230, 236, 241, 246–48, 249
health 225, 245
Memoirs of Many in One 225, 227
The Night the Prowler 230

Nobel Prize 1, 184–86, 189
Nolans and, friendship 1, 149–50, 161, 178, 203, 225
prizes for novels 111
Riders in the Chariot 111
Signal Driver 246
The Solid Mandala 105–106, 109, 110, 111
The Tree of Man 57, 74, 77, 92, 111
The Twyborn Affair 225
The Vivisector 112, 185
Voss 57, 92, 111, 149
White, Ruth 189
Whitlam, Gough 172, 173–74, 176, 183, 186, 188, 192–93, 194, 199, 206, 236, 237, 276, 277
dismissal 194–96
sister Freda 237
Whitlam, Margaret 196, 237
Wighton, Rosemary 82
Wilde, Aston 32
Wilding, Michael 207–209
The Short Story Embassy 208
William Collins 72, 250
William Heinemann 66–68, 115
Williams, Christine 156, 249
Williams, Margery 155, 225
Williamson, David 198
Don's Party 198
Jugglers Three 198
The Removalists 198
Williamson, Geordie 61
Willoughby, Barry 252, 256–57
Wilmot, Chester 57
Wilson, Barbara Ker 230
Wine, Maria 184
Wing, Willis Kingsley 77–79
Winter, David 261–62, 264
Wood, James 265
Workers Education Association (WEA) 212, 252
Wran, Premier Neville 232
Wright, Judith 109, 172, 198, 215–16
'Images of Women in English Literature' 215–16
The Nature of Love 109

Yap, Clemente 'Clem' 255, 257, 271, 275, 279

Zifcak, Michael 234
Zofrea, Salvatore 228, 236, 257–58
Zwicky, Fay 232

www.ingramcontent.com/pod-product-compliance
Lightning Source LLC
Chambersburg PA
CBHW021342300426
44114CB00012B/1046